Understanding Futures Markets

ROBERT W. KOLB
University of Miami

ROBERT S. HAMADA
Series in Finance

SCOTT, FORESMAN AND COMPANY
Glenview, Illinois   London, England

To Debbie

Acknowledgments

Acknowledgments continue on p. 288, which constitutes a legal extension of the copyright page.

Table 4.2, Figure 5.3. From *International Monetary Market Yearbook,* 1981, published by the Chicago Mercantile Exchange. Reprinted by permission.   **Table 4.3.** From "Gold: A conservative, prudent, diversifier" by Eugene J. Sherman, *The Journal of Portfolio Management,* Spring 1982, p. 24. Copyright © 1982 Institutional Investor, Inc. Reprinted by persmission.   **Table 4.4.** From "Does gold have a role in investment portfolios?" by Anthony and Edward Renshaw, *The Journal of Portfolio Management,* Spring 1982, p. 29. Copyright © 1982 Institutional Investor, Inc. Reprinted by permission.   **Table 6.1.** From *Understanding Futures in Foreign Exchange,* prepared by International Monetary Market, Division of Chicago Mercantile Exchange. Reprinted by permission.   **Tables 6.2, 6.3.** Data based on the Federal Reserve Bank of New York's Foreign Exchange Turnover Survey (March 1980). Reprinted by permission.   **Table 6.6.** From "The Efficiency of Markets for Foreign Exchange: A Review and Extension" by Richard M. Levich in *International Financial Management, Theory and Application,* edited by Donald R. Lessard. Copyright © 1979 by Warren, Gorham & Lamont. Reprinted by permission.   **Tables 7.1, 7.2, 7.3, 7.4, 7.6.** From *Inside S&P 500 Stock Index Futures,* prepared by Index and Option Market, Division of Chicago Mercantile Exchange. Reprinted by permission.   **Tables 7.9, 7.10.** From *Commodities* (now *Futures)* Magazine, February 1983, pp. 50, 52. Copyright © 1983 Commodities Magazine, Inc. Reprinted by permission.   **Table 8.1.** Source: *Managed Account Reports,* 200 Joseph Square, Columbia, MD 21044, 301–730–5365. **Table 8.2.** From "The rush to commodity funds" by Edward J. Doherty, *Financial World,* December 1–15, 1982, p. 33. Copyright © 1982 by Financial World Partners. Reprinted by

Library of Congress Cataloging in Publication Data.

Kolb, Robert W.
  Understanding futures markets.

  Includes bibliographies and index.
  1. Commodity exchanges—United States.   2. Financial futures—United States.   I. Title.
HG6049.K65   1985   332.64 ′4   84–22192
ISBN 0–673–15976–0 (soft)

  3 4 5 6–KPF–89 88 87 86 85

Preface

Understanding Futures Markets surveys the broad sweep of futures markets as they exist in the United States. In the last decade, futures markets in the U.S. have exploded in a renaissance that promises to continue through the 1980s. New contracts have been introduced, and entirely new possibilities are being explored.

Almost all of this activity began as recently as 1973, with the introduction of futures contracts on foreign exchange. It was followed by the inception of interest rate futures contracts in 1975, stock index futures contracts in 1982, and options on futures contracts shortly thereafter. In many respects, these innovations in futures markets have had an influence on the entire market for financial claims. Stock market practice and the operation of many types of financial institutions have been changed in fundamental ways as a result of the new activity in futures markets. Even the older futures contracts, those on agricultural and metallurgical commodities, have been revitalized in the process. Today, for example, the market for energy futures is emerging as a strong market.

This book attempts to cover all of these developments in a way that will be accessible to a wide range of readers. The mathematical demands placed on the reader are minimal, but the text also includes several mathematical appendices and numerous references to scholarly articles for those readers wishing more mathematical detail and justification for the claims made in the book.

Realizing that not every reader will be interested in every aspect of the futures markets, I have organized the chapters to facilitate access to a treatment of special areas. The first three chapters of the book are general in treatment but cover virtually every phase of futures trading. After reading the first three chapters, the reader is prepared to go immediately to the chapter covering the kind of futures that holds particular interest. Chapters 4–8 focus on specific groups of futures contracts. For example, Chapter 4 covers agricultural and metallurgical futures, while Chapter 6 takes foreign exchange futures as its topic. While the book is intended to be read straight through, this feature of its organization is designed to make it useful as a reference work as well.

While the first three chapters touch on virtually every question of importance in understanding futures markets, it is impossible to include sufficient detail on the entire futures market in these first three chapters. Accordingly, specific themes are developed in more detail in the subsequent chapters. Two examples will help clarify this strategy.

Many cash prices exhibit strong seasonal fluctuation; prices for grain, for example, vary with the harvest. A central issue in understanding futures markets is the question of the relationship between futures prices and the cash price of a seasonal good. While this topic is addressed briefly in the first three chapters, it is explored in detail in Chapter 4, which focuses on the agricultural and metallurgical commodities.

Another key issue in understanding futures markets is the forecasting ability of futures prices. Do futures prices really tell us anything about the likely course of spot prices? The foreign exchange market has received the most attention in this context, so the forecasting reliability of futures prices is addressed most specifically within the context of Chapter 6, *Foreign Currency Futures*.

This means that not every issue is treated in detail for every market. Doing so would have resulted in a multi-volume work. Instead, I pursued detail about particular issues when discussing the markets where those issues emerge most clearly. This organization allows the important issues to be analyzed in the clearest way.

ACKNOWLEDGMENTS

In writing a book of this type, one must rely on a large set of one's colleagues. This book was read by a number of scholars who made very useful comments. I would like to thank the following people, who reviewed the project either in part or in its entirety:

- Lloyd Besant, Chicago Board of Trade
- Brad Cornell, UCLA
- Gerald Gay, Georgia State University
- Theoharry Grammatikos, University of Wisconsin
- Shantaram Hegde, University of Notre Dame
- James Hoag, University of California, Berkeley
- Jonathan Ingersoll, Yale University
- Albert Kagan, University of Northern Iowa
- Robert Lindsay, New York University
- John Merrick, New York University
- Anne Peck, Stanford University
- A. J. Senchack, University of Texas
- Hans Stoll, Vanderbilt University
- Howard Zitsman, Ohio State University

Special thanks are due to Gerry Gay who used the entire manuscript for his class on futures. I also would like to thank my students, both here and abroad, who allowed me to experiment upon them with different versions of the manuscript. I believe the book is stronger for the comments it has received and from its class testing.

Finally, I would like to thank Andrea Coens for an excellent editing job. I would also like to give a special word of thanks to George Lobell of Scott, Foresman, who encouraged me to write this book and who has been supportive and helpful throughout the entire process of bringing this book to life.

Robert W. Kolb

Contents

3   USING FUTURES MARKETS   54

4   AGRICULTURAL AND METALLURGICAL FUTURES CONTRACTS   85

1 Futures Markets in the United States

INTRODUCTION

This chapter discusses a number of topics that are essential to understanding futures markets in the United States. First, the chapter explores the origins of futures markets and focuses on their current existence in the United States, where futures markets are currently the most complete and provide the widest range of trading opportunities. Futures markets, as they now exist in the United States, are a fairly recent development, but understanding their origins helps in comprehending the usefulness of these markets and the subsequent likely stages in their development.

Futures contracts have emerged as a highly institutionalized form of *forward contracting*. Forward contracting, however, has existed for many centuries. The ways in which futures markets differ from forward markets, the chapter's second topic, is important for understanding the techniques that can be applied in futures trading today.

Without question, the current organization of active futures markets is more important for the potential user than any historical account. Accordingly, the discussion soon focuses on organized futures exchanges as they exist in the United States. Before entering the arena of the futures market, it is vital to understand the organizational form of the futures exchanges, the types of contracts that are traded, and the ways in which different futures exchanges compete with each other for business.

The purposes that futures markets serve and the participants in the markets are then briefly characterized in this chapter. These themes are further developed in Chapter 3. Because regulation is important in determining whether futures markets can serve their social function and the interests of the trading parties, the chapter next discusses the regulatory framework, closing with a description of the taxation of futures markets.

ORIGINS OF FORWARD CONTRACTING

Forward contracting, as it occurs in both forward and futures markets, always involves a contract initiated at one time and performance in accordance with the terms of the contract occurring at a subsequent time. Further, the type of forward contracting to be considered here is always an exchange. The price at which the exchange will take place is determined at the initial contracting, with the actual payment and delivery of the good occurring subsequently. So defined, almost everyone has engaged in some kind of forward contract.

A very simple, yet frequently occurring, type of forward contract can be illustrated by the following example. Having heard that a highly prized St. Bernard has just given birth to a litter of pups, a dog fancier rushes to the kennel to see the pups and to try to buy one from the breeder. After seeing the pups and inspecting the pedigree of the parents, the dog fancier offers to buy a pup from the breeder, and they agree upon a price of $400. The exchange, however, cannot be completed at this time, since the pup is too young to be weaned. The fancier and breeder thus agree that the dog will be ready to go in six weeks and that the fancier may pay the $400 in six weeks and pick up the pup at that time. This contract is not a conditional contract; both parties are obligated to go through with it as agreed.[1]

The puppy example represents a very basic type of forward contract. The example could have been made more complicated by the breeder requiring a deposit, but that would not change the essential character of the transaction.

From the simplicity of the contract and its obvious usefulness in resolving uncertainty about the future, it is not surprising that such contracts have had a very long history. The origin of forward contracting is not clear. Some authors trace the practice to Roman and even classical Greek times. Strong evidence suggests that Roman emperors entered forward contracts to provide the masses with their supply of Egyptian grain. Others have traced the origin of forward contracting to India.[2]

While there may not be much agreement about the geographical origins of forward contracting, it is clear that trading originated with contracts similar in form to that of the puppy example. In fact, such contracts continue to be important today, not only among dog lovers, but in markets for credit and foreign exchange. Billions of dollars of foreign currencies change hands daily in a very sophisticated market that trades contracts for German marks and English pounds that are very similar in structure to the puppy contract. While these kinds of forward markets are very large and important, and while they have numerous points of contact with futures markets, the primary concern of this book is to develop an understanding of futures contracts and the organized exchanges where they are traded. A comparison of the structure of forward and futures contracts helps to illuminate the essential similarities and differences between these two kinds of contracts. This comparison is discussed in the following section.

FORWARD VERSUS FUTURES MARKETS

While the historical origins of forward contracts are obscure, the emergence of organized futures markets can be traced with great accuracy to nineteenth-century Chicago and the opening of the Chicago Board of Trade in 1842.[3] Despite the loss of records in the great Chicago fire in 1871, it appears clear that futures contracts, as opposed to forward contracts, were being traded on the Board of Trade by the 1860s. Since that time the basic structure of futures contracts has been adopted by a number of other exchanges. It is important to understand how the futures contracts differ from other forms of forward contracts exemplified by the puppy example.

Forward contracts and futures contracts can be distinguished on four principal grounds: (1) The organized exchange; (2) the contract terms; (3) the clearinghouse; and (4) the requirement for daily resettlement.

The Organized Exchange

Futures contracts are always traded on an organized exchange. The organization of the Chicago Board of Trade, the oldest and largest futures exchange in the United States, is typical and will be used to illustrate the institutional characteristics of the other exchanges. The exchange is a voluntary, nonprofit association of its members. Memberships may be held only by individuals, and these memberships are traded in an active market like other assets. Members in an exchange have a right to trade on the exchange and to have a voice in the exchange's operation. Members also serve on committees to regulate such phases of the exchange's operations as rules, business conduct, audit, and public relations. Often administrative officers of the exchange manage the ordinary operation of the exchange and report to the membership.

According to the rules of the exchange, trading may take place only during the official hours for the exchange in the designated trading areas called "pits." In contrast to the specialist system used on stock exchanges, futures contracts are traded by a system of "open outcry." In this system, any offer to buy or sell must be made to all traders present in the pit. An unofficial, but highly developed, system of hand signals is also used by traders to express their wishes to buy or sell. The official means of communication remains, however, the technique of open outcry.

The individuals trading in the pits fall into two categories. They are either members of the exchange, who are trading for their own account, or representatives of trading firms acting as brokers and trading on behalf of themselves or clients outside the exchange. The members who are trading are typically *speculators* who hope to make a profit by exercising their trading acumen. By executing orders for others, the brokers earn commissions. The individuals beyond the trading floor who act through a broker may be other speculators seeking profit or they may be *hedgers* trying to use the futures markets to reduce some risk.

Some of the parties trading for their own account may not be full members in their own right. It is possible to lease a seat on the exchange from a full member and to secure the right to trade in return for a monthly fee. Also, some exchanges have created special licenses that allow nonmembers to trade in certain contracts in which the exchanges are anxious to build volume. While only individuals may be members of the exchange, brokers are also afforded the opportunity to trade for their clients or for their own accounts. The brokers trading on the exchange are often representatives of the large brokerage houses such as Merrill Lynch or Prudential Bache.

This organized structure for the trading of futures contracts differs from the organization of forward markets. Forward markets are loosely organized and have no physical location devoted to the trading. From the puppy example, this difference is clear. Perhaps the best-developed forward market is the forward market for foreign exchange. It is a worldwide network of participants, largely banks and brokers, who communicate with each other electronically. There is no organized exchange and no central trading point.[4]

Standardized Contracts

Other differences between forward and futures markets abound. One of the most important differences is the fact that futures exchanges trade only standardized contracts. The puppy example is typical of forward contracts in its lack of standardization. The good to be traded was not a standardized item; the time of delivery was merely agreed to by the trading parties; and there was no mechanism external to the traders to guarantee that the contract would be fulfilled. Such is not the case in a futures market. Futures contracts are highly uniform and well-specified commitments for a carefully described good to be delivered at a certain time and in a certain manner.

As an example, consider a Chicago Board of Trade wheat contract. This contract calls for the delivery of 5000 bushels of wheat, with delivery taking place in one of the designated delivery months, July, September, December, March, or May. Further, only certain kinds of wheat will be accepted for delivery: No. 2 Soft Red, No. 2 Hard Red Winter, No. 2 Dark Northern Spring, or No. 1 Northern Spring. The Chicago Board of Trade also controls the permitted price fluctuations and the way in which the prices on the contract are reported. Quotations are given in dollars, cents, and quarter-cents per bushel, with the minimum price fluctuation being one-quarter cent per bushel. This means that the minimum price fluctuation on a contract is $12.50 (.0025¢

× 5000 bushels). The Board of Trade also sets maximum daily price movement limits, but these are changed fairly frequently. In addition to these terms, the delivery mechanism for completing the contract is also stipulated. Delivery is accomplished by registered receipts issued by warehouses approved by the Board of Trade. These warehouses must be in the Chicago Switching District or the Toledo, Ohio, Switching District. If delivery is to be made in Toledo, however, the delivery price must be two cents per bushel under the contract price.

While appearing highly restrictive, these rules actually serve to promote trading. Since the item to be traded is so highly standardized, all the participants in the market know exactly what is being offered for sale and the terms of the transactions. This helps to promote liquidity. All futures contracts have such a highly developed framework, which specifies all phases of the transaction, from the amounts the prices can move to the appropriate ways of making delivery. The prospective trader should consult a given contract for these exact details before initiating any trading. Each exchange makes these contracts available to the public.

The Clearinghouse

To ensure the smooth functioning of trading in these futures contracts, each futures exchange operates a clearinghouse, which plays a crucial role in the functioning of the futures market. The essential purpose of the clearinghouse is to guarantee performance to all of the participants in the market.[5] It serves this role by adopting the position of buyer to every seller and seller to every buyer. This means that every trading party in the futures markets has obligations only to the clearinghouse and has expectations that the clearinghouse will maintain its side of the bargain as well.

The clearinghouse takes no active position in the market, but interposes itself between all parties to every transaction. In the futures market, the number of contracts bought must always equal the number of contracts sold. So, for every party expecting to receive delivery of a commodity, the opposite trading partner must be prepared to make delivery. If we were to add up all of the outstanding long and short futures market positions, the total would always equal zero.[6]

The typical trading situation is shown in Table 1.1. On May 1, Party 1 trades on the futures exchange to buy one oats contract of 5000 bushels for delivery in September. In order for Party 1 to be able to buy the contract, some other participant must sell to Party 1. In panel (a) of the table it is apparent that Party 1 and Party 2 have exactly complementary positions in the futures market. Notice that the time of delivery, the amount of oats to be delivered, and the price all match. Otherwise, there could have been no transaction.

In all probability the two trading parties will not even know each other. It is perfectly possible that each will have traded through a broker

TABLE 1.1

Futures Market Obligations. The oat contract is traded by the Chicago Board of Trade. Each contract is for 5000 bushels, and prices are quoted in cents per bushel.

(a) Party 1	Party 2
May 1	
Buys 1 September contract for oats at 171 cents per bushel	Sells 1 September contract for oats at 171 cents per bushel

(b) Party 1	Clearinghouse
Buys 1 September contract for oats at 171 cents per bushel	Agrees to deliver to Party 1 a September 1 contract for oats at a price of 171 cents per bushel
Party 2	**Clearinghouse**
Sells 1 September contract for oats at 171 cents per bushel	Agrees to receive from Party 2 a September 1 contract for oats and to pay 171 cents per bushel

from different parts of the country. In such a situation, problems of trust may arise. How can either party be sure that the other will fulfill the agreement? The clearinghouse exists to solve that problem. As panel (b) indicates, the clearinghouse guarantees fulfillment of the contract to each of the trading parties. After the initial sale is made, the clearinghouse steps in and acts as the seller to the buyer and as the buyer to the seller. The buyer of the futures contract, Party 1, is guaranteed by the clearinghouse that it will make delivery at the initially agreed time and price. To the seller, Party 2, the clearinghouse agrees that it will receive delivery at the agreed time and price.

Because of this action by the clearinghouse, it is clear that the two trading parties do not need to trust each other any longer. Instead, they only have to be concerned about the reliability of the clearinghouse. But the clearinghouse is, in effect, a large, well-capitalized financial institution. Its failure to perform on its guarantee to the two trading parties would bring the futures market to ruin. In the history of futures trading the clearinghouse has always performed as promised, so the risk of a future default by the clearinghouse is very small.

A more careful examination of panel (b) gives further reason to rest assured that the clearinghouse will perform. In total, the clearinghouse has no independent position in oats. It is obligated to receive oats and pay 171 cents per bushel, but it is also obligated to deliver oats and receive 171 cents per bushel. These two obligations net out to zero, so the clearinghouse really has no independent position in the futures market. Since it maintains no futures market position of its own, the riskiness of the clearinghouse is less than it may appear.[7]

Other safeguards for the marketplace exist. Chief among these is the requirement for "margin." To be allowed to trade a futures contract, an individual must post a specified amount of money with a broker. The amount of this margin varies from contract to contract and may vary with the broker as well. The margin amount may be posted in cash, a bank letter of credit, or in short-term U.S. Treasury instruments. The trader who posts this margin retains title to it. However, since the broker holds the cash or security, it acts as a good-faith deposit, or *surety bond,* on the part of the trader. This "initial margin" is approximately equal in value to the maximum daily price fluctuation permitted for the contract in question. Upon proper completion of all obligations associated with a trader's futures position, the initial margin is returned to the trader. If one has deposited a security as the margin, then the trader earns the interest that has accrued while the security has served as the margin.

Daily Resettlement

For most futures contracts, the initial margin may be 5 percent or less of the underlying commodity's value.[8] It may seem strange that the initial margin is so small relative to the value of the commodity underlying the futures contract. The smallness of this amount is reasonable, however, because there is another safeguard built into the system in the form of "daily resettlement." In the futures market, traders are required to realize any losses in cash on the day they occur.

To see how this works, consult Table 1.1 again and consider Party 1, who bought one contract for 171 cents per bushel. Assume that the contract closes on May 2 at 168 cents per bushel. This means that Party 1 has sustained a loss of 3 cents per bushel. Since there are 5000 bushels in the contract, this represents a loss of $150. This amount is deducted from the margin deposited with the broker. When the value of the funds on deposit with the broker reaches a certain level, called the "maintenance" or "variation margin," the trader is required to replenish the margin, bringing it back to its initial level. The maintenance margin is generally about 75 percent of the amount of the initial margin. For example, assume that the initial margin was $1400, that Party 1 had deposited only this minimum initial margin, and that the maintenance margin is $1100. Party 1 has already sustained a loss of $150, so the value of his margin account is $1250. The next day, assume that the price of oats drops 4 cents per bushel, generating an additional loss for Party 1 of $200. This brings the value of his margin account down to $1050, which is below the level of the required maintenance margin. This means that the broker will require Party 1 to replenish his margin account, bringing it back up to $1400, the level of the initial margin. This additional maintenance margin must be paid in cash.

Futures contracts will typically involve a cash flow every day. If a trader really had to communicate with the broker every day to issue or receive checks resulting from futures price fluctuations, it would be a serious nuisance. The easiest way to avoid this problem is for the trader to provide the broker with an extra liquidity pool of cash from which the maintenance margin can be drawn as needed. The pool of cash that is not needed can be invested by the broker on behalf of the trader.

This practice of posting maintenance or variation margin and daily resettlement helps to make the futures market safer. Assume that Party 1 posted only the initial margin, the bare minimum to have his trade executed, and then suffered the loss mentioned in the example. Assume further that he was unable or refused to post the required additional margin. The broker in such a situation is empowered to close out the futures position by deducting the $350 loss from the trader's initial margin and returning the balance, less commission costs, to the trader. The broker would also close the trader's entire brokerage account as well. Failure to post the required maintenance margin is a violation of a trader's agreement with the broker. Now it becomes apparent why the initial margin is so small. The initial margin needs to cover only one day's price fluctuation, since any losses will be covered by the posting of additional variation margin or the futures position will be closed out.

In the discussion of variation margin it was asserted that the broker might close out the position after trading on May 2. The careful reader might remember that the initial trade shown in Table 1.1 called for a September delivery. In view of that fact, it may not seem that the futures position could be closed out in May. There are, however, two ways of fulfilling the commitment that one undertakes in trading a futures contract. You may either make or take delivery of the prescribed commodity as stipulated in the rules of the exchange for the commodity in question, or you may enter a "reversing trade."

A *reversing trade* is a trade that brings a trader's net position in some futures contract back to zero. Consider again the situation depicted in Table 1.1. The first party has an obligation to the clearinghouse to accept 5000 bushels of oats in September and to pay 171 cents per bushel for them at that time. Perhaps the trader does not wish to actually receive the oats. Perhaps he no longer has any wish to be in the futures market as of, say, May 10. He may fulfill his commitment by entering the futures market again and making the reversing trade depicted in Table 1.2.

The first line of Table 1.2 merely repeats the initial trade that was made on May 1. On May 10, Party 1 simply takes exactly the opposite position by selling a 1 September contract for oats at the current futures price of 180 cents per bushel. This time he transacts with a new entrant to the market, Party 3. After this reversing trade, Party 1's net position is zero. The clearinghouse recognizes this, and Party 1 is absolved from any further obligation. In this example, the price of September oats rose 9 cents per bushel during this period, happily yielding Party 1 a profit of $450. Party 2, the original seller, is not affected by Party 1's reversing trade. Party 2 still has the same commitment, since the clearinghouse continues to stand ready to complete this transaction described in panel

TABLE 1.2
The Reversing Trade.

Party 1's Initial Position	Party 2
May 1	
Bought 1 September contract for oats at 171 cents per bushel	Sold 1 September contract for oats at 171 cents per bushel

Party 1's Reversing Trade	Party 3
May 10	
Sells 1 September contract for oats at 180 cents per bushel	Buys 1 September oats contract at 180 cents per bushel

(b) of Table 1.1. Now the clearinghouse also assumes a complementary obligation to the new market entrant, Party 3. Note that the position of the clearinghouse has not really changed due to the transactions that took place on May 10. Also, Party 2 and Party 3 have complementary obligations after the new trades, just as Party 1 and Party 2 had complementary obligations after the initial transactions on May 1.

In entering the reversing trade, it is crucial that Party 1 sell exactly the same contract that was originally bought. Note in Table 1.2 that the reversing trade matches the original trade in the good traded, the number of contracts, and the maturity. If it does not, then the trader undertakes a new obligation instead of cancelling the old. If Party 1 had sold a 1 December contract on May 10 instead of the September contract, he would be obligated to receive oats in September and to deliver oats in December. Such a transaction would result in a "spread," a position in two or more related contracts, instead of a reversing trade.

While futures and forward contracts are clearly similar in many respects, they certainly differ in important ways as well. By considering the differences between the contracts on these four parameters (the existence of an exchange, the presence of a clearinghouse, the daily resettlement, and the highly structured form of contracting), it is also apparent that futures markets represent a highly developed and strongly specialized type of financial institution. What is perhaps also surprising is the tremendous range of goods traded on futures exchanges.

THE TYPES AND VARIETIES
OF FUTURES CONTRACTS

Since the founding of the Chicago Board of Trade in 1842, futures markets have flourished. The past decade has been a period of extraordinary growth for futures markets, due largely to the development of entirely new types of contracts in foreign exchange, interest rates, and stock

TABLE 1.3
Futures Exchanges in the United States.

Chicago Board of Trade

Chicago Mercantile Exchange

Coffee, Sugar, and Cocoa Exchange (New York)

Commodity Exchange, Inc. (New York)

Kansas City Board of Trade

Mid-America Commodity Exchange (Chicago)

Minneapolis Grain Exchange

New York Cotton Exchange, Inc.

Citrus Associates of the New York Cotton Exchange, Inc.

Petroleum Associates of the New York Cotton Exchange, Inc.

New York Futures Exchange

New York Mercantile Exchange

---

indices. Within the last few years, several new types of contracts have been developed, including futures on stock indices and options on futures contracts. The future promises to be a period of continued explosive growth for the industry.

Currently, there are twelve futures exchanges in the United States, as listed in Table 1.3. The oldest of these is more than 140 years old, while the youngest, the New York Futures Exchange, just began trading in 1981. Differences in size among these exchanges are striking, ranging from the New York Cotton Exchange, which by state law can trade only cotton futures, to the very large exchanges, such as the Chicago Board of Trade and the Chicago Mercantile Exchange, which have more than 1000 members each and trade a wide variety of futures. The futures markets of Chicago alone directly employ 40,000 people (as of 1984).

The types of futures contracts that are traded fall into five categories. The underlying good traded may be an agricultural or metallurgical commodity, an interest-earning asset, a foreign currency, or a stock index. Contracts for more than forty different goods are currently available. While Chapters 4 through 7 deal specifically with each of the different groups of commodities, it is useful to have some appreciation for the range of goods that are traded on the futures market.

In the agricultural area, contracts are traded in grains (corn, oats, and wheat), oil and meal (soybeans, soymeal, and soyoil, and sunflower seed and oil), livestock (live hogs and cattle and pork bellies), poultry (eggs and live broilers), forest products (lumber and plywood), textiles (cotton), and foodstuffs (cocoa, coffee, orange juice, potatoes, and sugar). For many of these commodities, several different contracts are available for different grades or types of the commodity in question. For most of the goods, there are also a number of months for delivery. The months chosen for delivery of the seasonal crops generally fit their harvest patterns. The number of contract months available for each commodity also depends on the level of trading activity. For some relatively inactive futures contracts, there may be trading in only one or two delivery months in the year.[9] By contrast, an active commodity, such as soybean meal, may have trading in eight delivery months.

The metallurgical category includes the genuine metals, as well as petroleum contracts. These two kinds of goods are really more similar than appears. As will become clear in Chapter 4, they can be treated in a similar way, since both petroleum and metals share an important common characteristic: they can be stored indefinitely. Among the metals, contracts are traded on gold, silver, silver coins, platinum, palladium, and copper. Of the petroleum products, only heating oil, crude oil, gasoline, and propane are traded on futures markets.

Futures trading on interest-bearing assets started only in 1975, but the growth of this market has been tremendous. Contracts are traded now on Treasury bills, notes, and bonds, on bank Certificates of Deposit, Eurodollar deposits, and GNMAs, which are government-backed, single-family mortages. Other contracts have been introduced, such as those on commercial paper and short-term Treasury notes, but both of these have failed. With the existing contracts, almost the entire yield curve is spanned, so that it is possible to trade for instruments with virtually every maturity. A number of contracts are traded on instruments with three-month maturities (the T-bill, Eurodollar, and CD contracts). This makes possible trading based on anticipated interest rate differentials for the same maturity.

Active futures trading of foreign currencies dates back to the inception of freely floating exchange rates in the early 1970s. Contracts are traded on the British pound, the Canadian dollar, the Japanese yen, the Swiss franc, and the West German mark. Contracts are also listed on French francs, Dutch guilders, and the Mexican peso, but these have met with only limited success. The foreign exchange futures market represents the one case of a futures market existing in the face of a truly active forward market, which is many times larger than the futures market. Many people believe that the presence of the forward market deterred the introduction of futures trading in foreign exchange.

The last major group of futures contracts is for stock indices. Beginning only in 1982, these contracts have been quite successful, with trading on four broad market indices in full swing. Four different exchanges trade contracts on three different indices: the Standard and Poor's 500, a Major Market Index, the New York Stock Exchange Index, and the Value Line Index. In addition, numerous contracts on industry indices are now trading as well. Many new entries into this market are planned. One of the most striking things about these stock index contracts is that they do not admit the possibility of actual delivery. A trader's obligation must be fulfilled by a reversing trade or a cash settlement at the end of trading.

EXCHANGE SPECIALIZATION AND COMPETITION

With such a diversity of goods being traded, it is not surprising that we find both *specialization* among exchanges and *contract duplication* from exchange to exchange. Often being the first exchange to introduce a contract is a key element of success. For example, only the International Monetary Market (IMM) of the Chicago Mercantile Exchange (CME) trades contracts in foreign exchange. Because the IMM was the first to start foreign exchange futures trading, it was able to erect a barrier to entry for the other exchanges. If one exchange is established in trading a certain contract, then traders will tend to remain with the first exchange since that contract has the needed trading volume to provide liquidity. The second exchange that wishes to offer the same contract has a very difficult battle.

In addition to being first with a contract, an exchange may also achieve a certain degree of control by trading contracts in a group of related contracts. The Chicago Board of Trade (CBT) trades contracts in the soybean complex, offering contracts on soybeans, soymeal, and soyoil. Trading contracts on all three gives traders the opportunity to trade one contract against the other. With all three contracts trading, there is little opportunity for another exchange to enter the field. If the CBT were to trade only the soybean contract, then other exchanges might try to enter the market by offering contracts on soymeal or soyoil in an effort to draw away the business from the CBT. To date, the CBT has been successful in maintaining its position in the soybean complex. No other exchange has been successful in this area, although the Mid-America Commodity Exchange is trying to compete in soybeans by offering smaller (1000 versus 5000 bushel) contracts.

Another example of the grouping phenomenon can be drawn from the interest-rate futures market. Successful contracts are traded on interest-rate futures at the CBT and the IMM. The IMM trades contracts on only very short maturity instruments. The CBT trades the contracts on instruments of long maturities, but has recently been introducing contracts on instruments with shorter maturities.

For some commodities, there are contracts on a number of exchanges, which gives the appearance of a very heated competition among the exchanges. In such cases, some product differentiation usually makes the competition less direct. A good example of this occurs in the case of wheat. Wheat contracts are traded on the CBT, the Kansas City Board of Trade, the Mid-America Commodity Exchange, and the Minneapolis Grain Exchange. These futures contracts are, however, differentiated in a number of ways. The standard trading unit is 5000 bushels for most exchanges, but the Mid-America Exchange trades a contract for 1000 bushels, thereby appealing to the smaller trader. For all four of the contracts, there are differences in the kinds of wheat that are being traded, although a different kind of wheat may be substituted for the one actually written into all of the wheat futures contracts. Such substitutions result in a price differential established by the exchange.

By specifying different deliverable grades of wheat, the exchanges may carve out their own market niches. For example, the Kansas City contract is written for No. 2 Hard Winter wheat with a maximum moisture content of 13.50%. The Minneapolis Grain Exchange contract is for U.S. No. 2 Northern Spring wheat, with 13.50% protein or higher. The CBT contract calls for delivery of one of the following types of wheat: No. 2 Soft Red, No. 2 Hard Red Winter, No. 2 Dark Northern Spring, or No. 1 Northern Spring. Since the kind of wheat called for is slightly different in each case, direct competition is avoided.

In the case of wheat, another very important factor in keeping contracts alive on four exchanges is geographical distance. Each contract must specify how and where delivery is to be made. The CBT, Kansas City, and Minneapolis contracts all call for delivery at different places. If we actually consider the cost of taking delivery, then the difference between a Kansas City and a Minneapolis delivery is very important, since wheat's bulk makes its transportation quite expensive.

Another way of blunting the competition is to offer contracts on different delivery cycles. Gold futures are traded by a number of exchanges, with the IMM and the Commodity Exchange (COMEX) having the most successful contracts. The contracts are both written for 100 troy ounces, and the quality conditions are almost identical. The IMM, however, trades gold futures for delivery in March, June, September, and December. By contrast, COMEX contracts mature in January, February, April, June, August, October, and December.

In still other cases, exchanges succeed even though they compete head on. Silver appears to be such a case, with the most active contracts being traded by the CBT and the COMEX. Although the two exchanges are based in Chicago and New York, respectively, geographical distance does not seem sufficient to account for their sustained success. Both offer contracts of 1000 and 5000 troy ounces of silver of .999% fineness or higher. The peculiar thing about this market is the apparent dominance by the COMEX in the 5000-ounce contract, and by the CBT in the 1000-ounce contract. The COMEX 5000-ounce contract has a market almost ten times as large as that for the CBT 5000-ounce contract. Yet both markets appear to be well established.

This is just one of the many puzzling developments regarding competition and contract success in the futures markets. Certainly, absence of competition, product differentiation, geographical dispersion of markets, trading of related commodities, and early market entry all contribute to the success of a futures contract. Other factors are also required, such as the ability to deliver a sufficiently large supply of the underlying commodity, active trading interest among the public, and a certain degree of price volatility on the underlying commodity. In spite of these apparent determinants of futures market success, much is still

unknown. Among the exchanges themselves, there is considerable con-
sternation about what makes a futures contract successful.

For the exchanges, this is an important question, since introducing a
new futures contract requires a substantial expense. The contract must
first be designed and then approved by the regulators. Trading must be
organized, and the contract must be promoted through advertising. To
commit all of these resources and still fail is very frustrating. Yet, by recent estimates, only 70% of the futures contracts that are introduced
become profitable. This low success rate for new contracts indicates how
much remains to be learned in the areas of contract design and competition.

PURPOSES OF FUTURES MARKETS

Any industry as old and as large as the futures market must serve some
social purpose. If it did not, it would most likely have passed from existence some time ago. Traditionally, futures markets have been
recognized as meeting the needs of three groups of futures market users:
those who wish to discover information about future prices of commodities; those who wish to speculate; and those who wish to transfer
unwanted risk to some other party. While the uses that these three groups
make of futures markets are discussed in detail in Chapter 3, some idea
of the social role of futures markets will be introduced here.

As has been discussed above, in buying or selling a futures contract
a trader agrees to receive or deliver a given commodity at a certain time
in the future for a price that is determined now. In such a circumstance,
it is not surprising that there is some relationship between the futures
price and the price that people expect to prevail for the commodity at the
delivery date specified in the futures contract. While the exact nature of
that relationship is unclear and will be considered in detail in Chapter 2,
the relationship is predictable to a high degree. By using the information
contained in futures prices today, it is possible to form estimates of what
the price of a given commodity will be at a certain time in the future. The
forecasts of future prices that can be drawn from the futures market
compare in accuracy quite favorably with other types of forecasts.
Futures markets serve a social purpose by helping people to form a better
idea of what future prices will be, so that they can make their consumption and investment decisions more wisely.

It may be strange to count the provision of a speculative opportunity
as a benefit to society. Without question, however, futures markets do
provide the opportunity for speculation. From the potential speculator's
point of view, that produces a benefit to society. Even if one regards
speculative activity as evil or immoral, there seems to be strong evidence
that the presence of speculators benefits the other users of futures

markets by helping to provide liquidity. The way in which this result is achieved is also described in Chapter 3.

Many futures market participants trade futures in order to avoid some unwanted risk. The classic example concerns the farmer who trades in the futures market to avoid the risk associated with the uncertain price at harvest of the crop he or she is producing. This activity of *hedging* is the prime social rationale for futures trading. It is a concern that will occupy a great deal of attention throughout the book. Chapter 3 explains the use that the hedger makes of the futures markets, while the techniques and applications of hedging are elaborated for specific markets in Chapters 4 through 7.

The participants in the futures markets are either speculators or hedgers, or the agents of one of these two groups. Yet the benefits provided by the futures market extend to many other sectors of society. The individual interested in forecasts of future prices need not enter the market to benefit. The forecasts are available for the price of the daily newspaper. The chance for hedgers to avoid unacceptable risks by entering the futures market also has wide implications for social welfare. Some individuals would not engage in certain clearly beneficial forms of economic activity if they were forced to bear all of the risk of the activity themselves. By being able to transfer risk to other parties via the futures market, economic activity in general is enhanced. Of course, a general stimulation of economic activity benefits society as a whole.

REGULATION OF FUTURES MARKETS

Like most financial markets in the United States, the futures market falls within the jurisdiction of a federal regulatory agency called the Commodity Futures Trading Commission (CFTC). The CFTC operates under a form of "sunset regulation" and its term was extended for another four years in 1982. One important area of CFTC jurisdiction concerns the approval of new contracts. Before trading, an exchange must submit the newly designed contract to the CFTC for approval. The CFTC is charged with the responsibility of determining whether trading in such a contract is contrary to the public interest. To receive approval, the contract must show promise of serving an economic purpose, such as making for fairer pricing of the commodity in some way or in making hedging possible. Providing an arena for speculation is not enough justification to show that a futures contract would serve an economic function.

The CFTC also regulates the trading rules for futures contracts, including the daily permitted maximum price fluctuation, certain features of the delivery process, and minimum price fluctuation limits. Generally, the CFTC is not involved in determining membership in the exchanges, but it is empowered to review complaints of membership exclusion or other unfair treatment by the exchanges. Perhaps the most striking power of the CFTC is the emergency power to intervene in the conduct of the market itself when the commission believes manipulation is present. Also the CFTC has the power to require competency tests of brokers and commodity representatives.

Many of the permitted powers of the CFTC are not being exercised. Long hampered by a lack of funding, the CFTC is now acknowledging that the industry itself will largely be responsible for its own regulation. The CFTC recently approved the formation of the National Futures Association (NFA), which is similar in design to the National Asociation of Security Dealers. The NFA will play an important role in regulating the futures market, with the exact division of effective responsibility between the CFTC and the NFA still to emerge.

In taking up its role of self-regulation, the NFA will largely be following a long tradition of self-regulation in the futures markets. The exchanges have long regulated the types of orders that are permitted on the exchange and have conducted the price-reporting process. The exchanges typically restrict trading to well-defined hours and permit it only in the appropriate pit on the floor of the exchange.

Certain unfair and unethical activities are also prohibited by the exchanges. These include violation of exchange rules, fraudulent activity, such as fictitious trading, disseminating false or misleading information, lying to the exchange, refusing to submit trading books to the exchange for inspection, withholding orders from the market for the convenience of oneself or another trader, or violating the responsibility of trust that one holds from another, such as an off-the-floor market participant. The implementation of these rules differs from exchange to exchange. They are enforced by committees of members that regulate trading and business practices. In sum, the rules are developed to provide a safe market where firms and individuals may trade without fear of being cheated. The maintenance of such discipline is clearly in the interest of the exchanges, as their financial well-being depends upon the flow of orders from the public at large.

THE TAXATION OF FUTURES CONTRACTS

In 1982 Congress passed a new law regarding the taxation of gains and losses in futures trading that had dramatic effects on the ways in which futures contracts could be used. The new law stipulated that all paper gains and losses on futures positions must be treated as though they were realized at the end of the tax year. For tax purposes, this new law meant that the futures positions must be marked to market at the end of the year. Forty percent of any gains or losses are to be treated as short-term gains; sixty percent are to be treated as long-term capital gains or losses.

The motivation for the new law was to eliminate "tax straddles."

Before the new law was passed, a trader could take a position in the futures market that was likely to give no overall gain or loss, although one contract might show a paper loss. For example, a trader might buy one contract of corn and sell one contract of wheat. Since corn and wheat prices move together, the combined corn-wheat position might have neither a gain nor a loss. However, if futures prices rose by year end, the short position in the wheat contract would show a loss. The trader engaging in this tax straddle could close the wheat position prior to the end of the year and show a loss for tax purposes. There would be no economic loss, however, since there would be an offsetting gain on the corn contract. The profit on the corn contract could then be recognized in the next tax year, or better yet, held until it qualified for the more favorable tax treatment of a long-term capital gain. (Trading futures contracts merely to generate tax benefits was always illegal, but identifying tax straddles as such was very difficult.) With the new law, such straddles are effectively eliminated since traders must realize, at least for tax purposes, all gains and losses in effect at the end of the year.

CONCLUSION

As the story of this first chapter indicates, forward trading has grown out of a need that has been felt for centuries. With the passage of time and the development of a more complex society, futures markets have emerged as a special kind of forward contracting. With their special characteristics of organized exchanges, clearinghouses, financial safeguards, and standardized contracts, futures markets represent a kind of highly developed forward trading developed in the middle of the nineteenth century and brought into fruition over the last quarter century.

Futures markets depend on well-developed financial markets and on the existence of widely available homogeneous commodities. The availability of standard commodities depends, in turn, on a sophisticated economic infrastructure, with the key element being an integrated transportation system. Futures markets, almost by their very nature, serve a geographically disperse group of participants. This means that futures markets also depend on the existence of an elaborate communications system.

With these facts in mind, it is clear to see that futures markets could not really have developed before they did, when telegraphic communication and a suitable financial environment were coming into existence. Their growth, which has recently accelerated, makes futures markets an important economic phenomenon, and one well worth studying. As is the case with many economic phenomena, one of the most important issues is the pricing of the goods traded in the market, the subject of the next chapter.

NOTES

1. The mutual obligation of both buyer and seller of a futures contract is an important feature of the futures market that helps to distinguish futures contracts from options. If you buy a call option, then you buy the right to obtain a good at a certain price, but the buyer of a call has no obligation. Instead, as the term implies, he has an *option* to buy something but *no obligation* to do anything. The buyer of a futures contract, by contrast, undertakes an obligation to make a payment at a subsequent time and to take delivery of the good that is contracted. The initiation of any futures contract implies a set of future obligations.

2. For a discussion of the historical origins of futures contracting, see A. Loosigan. *Interest Rate Futures,* Princton, NJ: Dow Jones Books, Inc., 1980, or L. Venkataramanan. *The Theory of Futures Trading,* New York: Asia Publishing House, 1965.

3. For an account of the early days of the Chicago Board of Trade, see *The Commodity Trading Manual,* Chicago: Chicago Board of Trade, 1982.

4. Chapter 6 discusses the foreign exchange forward market in some detail as a preliminary to the discussion of the foreign exchange futures market.

5. In his article "Market Incompleteness and Divergences Between Forward and Futures Interest Rates," *Journal of Finance,* May 1980, 221–234, Edward J. Kane argues that the costliness of the performance guarantees provided by the clearinghouse is sufficient to cause a divergence between the prices of forward and futures contracts. Other justifications for such divergences have emerged, and this topic is considered in greater detail in Chapter 2.

6. Notice that this is different from the stock market. Stocks represent title to the real assets of the firms, and these are owned by someone at every point in time. The long and short positions in the stock market, when "netted out," always equal the number of shares actually in existence, not zero, as in the futures market.

7. We might say that the clearinghouse is "perfectly hedged." No matter whether futures prices rise or fall, the wealth of the clearinghouse will not be affected. This is the case since the clearinghouse holds both long and short positions that perfectly balance each other. The concept of hedging is introduced in Chapter 3 and is pursued through all subsequent chapters.

8. One startling example is for the Treasury Bill futures contract. An initial margin deposit of $1,500–2,500 serves as the security for a contract on $1,000,000 face value of Treasury Bills.

9. Often there may be a number of delivery months on which trading is permitted, but contracts with little trading volume will actually have an active market in only one or two delivery months at a time.

2 *Futures Prices*

INTRODUCTION

Having explored the basic institutional features of the futures market in Chapter 1, this chapter considers futures prices. In an important sense, the study of the prices in a market is the essential key to everything else, since understanding the prices and the factors that determine those prices will ultimately influence every use of the market.

The tremendous current excitement about the futures market, and the new types of futures that are now being traded, means that the futures prices are studied with great diligence. In spite of such concentrated attention, there are many issues on which people disagree. These differences of opinion are reflected in the mode of analysis that is employed and the kinds of opportunities that different market participants seek in the futures market.

This chapter examines the factors that affect futures prices in general. There is little doubt that the determinants of foreign exchange futures prices and orange juice futures prices, for example, are very different. However, it must also be recognized that a common thread of understanding links futures contracts of all types. This chapter follows that common thread, while subsequent chapters will explore the individual factors that affect prices for particular kinds of commodities. Perhaps the most basic and most common factor about futures prices is the way in which their prices are quoted. Our discussion of futures prices begins with reading the price quotations that are available every day in the *Wall Street Journal*.

Futures market prices, which are so readily observable, bear economically important relationships to other observable prices as well. An important goal of this chapter is to develop an understanding of those relationships. The futures price for delivery of coffee in three months, for example, must be related to the *spot* (or current) *price* of coffee.[1] So important is such a relationship that it even has a name: the difference between the futures price and the spot price is called *the basis*. Likewise, the futures price for delivery of coffee in three months must be related in some fashion to the futures price for delivery of coffee in six months. This difference in price for two futures contracts, identical except for date of delivery, is called *the spread.* As we will see, the spread can also be an economically important variable.

Since futures contracts call for the delivery of some good at some particular time in the future, there can be no doubt that futures prices are determined to a large extent by the expectations of people who participate in the futures market. If people believed that gold would sell for $50 per ounce in three months, then the price of the futures contract for the delivery of gold in three months could not very easily be $100. So strong is the connection between futures prices and expected future spot prices that some people believe that the two are equal.

By the same token, the price for storing the good underlying the futures contract turns out to be very important as well in the determination of the relationships (1) among futures prices and (2) between the futures price and the spot price. By storing goods, it is possible, in effect, to convert corn received in March into corn that can be delivered in June. The difference in price between the March corn futures and the June corn futures must, therefore, be related to the price for the storage of corn.

With so many price relationships, it should not be surprising that there is considerable disagreement on what those relationships are or what they mean. Further, there is also considerable disagreement about the appropriate way in which we should study futures prices. One school of thought, called *technical analysis,* believes that the past history of prices gives useful information about the future direction of prices. If that is correct, then the diligent application of the techniques of technical analysis can lead to profitable trading.

Another technique for the study of futures prices is called *fundamental analysis.* Adherents of this view believe that the economic fundamentals can be studied to reveal the future direction of prices. For example, in analyzing platinum prices and trying to determine whether a platinum futures price is too high or low, fundamental analysts would stress the economic factors of supply and demand. If the analyst believed that the need for platinum was going to increase unexpectedly so that the price of platinum would rise, this would be a reason to believe that the platinum futures contract might be underpriced, thereby constituting a profit opportunity.

All of these issues about futures prices are interconnected. The basis, the spreads, the expected future spot price, the cost of storage, all form a system of related concepts. These in turn tie into the appropriate mode of analysis, whether it be technical or fundamental analysis, or yet some other way of thinking about futures prices. The purpose of this chapter is to describe those linkages among these concepts that cut across all futures contracts. The discussion begins with the futures prices themselves.

READING FUTURES PRICES

One of the most complete and widely available sources for futures prices is the *Wall Street Journal,* which publishes futures prices and other information on a daily basis. The futures prices reported in the *Journal* fall into three categories. First, the *Journal* publishes each day the complete price and volume information for a wide variety of active contracts in its regular section. These prices are reported in a standardized format, as shown in Figure 2.1. Figure 2.1 also shows the second kind of price quotation in the *Journal,* those for "Less Active Markets." For these futures contracts, not all delivery months are shown and the information is not as complete.

The third type of price listing found in the *Wall Street Journal* consists of advertisements placed by the futures exchanges themselves. When contracts are first introduced, they typically go through a period with very little active trading. During this time, the exchanges advertise those contracts by reporting their prices on the futures page of the *Journal.* As the contracts advertised are frequently changing, they are not shown in Figure 2.1 and are not discussed further. The formats for these advertisements are not fixed, but a familiarity with the regular listings of prices gives you everything necessary to understand the advertisements for the new contracts. Most contracts that are shown in the regular listing of Figure 2.1 started out being advertised. Listing in the regular section is a mark of some success for a futures contract, in that it means that there is enough activity in the contract to warrant regular listing by the *Journal.* It also relieves the exchange of the cost of running the advertisement.

One advantage of focusing on the *Wall Street Journal* quotations is the fact that they appear in the same format in about the same part of the paper each day. The date for the futures prices in Figure 2.1, March 1, 1984, is the date for the actual prices shown, and these prices appeared in the paper for Tuesday, March 2, 1984. As the heading states, the open interest, to be discussed below, pertains to the preceding trading day. The contracts are always separated into the categories as shown in Figure 2.1. For each contract, there appears in boldface just above the prices themselves the following: the good being traded, the exchange where it is traded, the amount of the good for one contract, and the units in which the price is stated are shown. For example, the very first contract is for the corn contract traded by the CBT. One contract is for 5,000 bushels and the prices are quoted in cents-per-bushel.

At this point a word of warning is appropriate. The information about the contracts shown with the prices is very useful, but it is also incomplete. In the case of corn, the type of corn that is traded is not mentioned, nor is the delivery procedure. Further, the useful information about daily price limits is not presented and it does not say what the

FIGURE 2.1
Futures Price Quotations.

Futures Prices

Thursday March 1, 1984

Open Interest Reflects Previous Trading Day.

	Open	High	Low	Settle	Change	Lifetime High	Lifetime Low	Open Interest
–GRAINS AND OILSEEDS–								
CORN (CBT) 5,000 bu.; cents per bu.								
Mar	331	333	329¾	331¼	+½	386¼	278½	22,591
May	331	334½	331	333	+¾	390	285	75,589
July	332	333¾	331	332¼	+¾	388	288¼	63,270
Sept	303	304½	302¾	304	+¼	356½	295½	8,317
Dec	286	287½	285½	286¾	+¼	330	279¾	20,065
Mar85	296	297	295¾	296¾	+¼	314	289¾	2,602
May	300	301½	300	301¼	+¼	312¾	295½	375
Est vol 41,600 vol Wed 68,178; open int 192,809, +5,139.								
CORN (MCE) 1,000 bu.; cents per bu.								
Mar	331½	333¼	329⅞	331¼	+½	386¼	278½	3,400
May	332	334⅞	331½	333	+¾	390	285½	6,729
July	332¼	334	331¼	332¼	+¾	388⅛	288½	3,844
Sept	303¾	304	303¾	304	+¼	355	298½	270
Dec	286	287½	285⅝	286¾	+¼	330	281¼	3,264
Mar85	296¾	296¾	296¾	296¾	+¼	314	292¼	72
May	....	....	....	301¼	+¼	311	292	13
Est vol 6,700; vol Wed 6,266; open int 17,592, +687.								
OATS (CBT) 5,000 bu.; cents per bu.								
Mar	169¼	170¾	168½	170¼	+1¾	219	161½	543
May	170	171¾	169	171	+2¼	226	163	2,713
July	171¾	173½	171½	173	+1½	226	166¼	906
Sept	172½	174½	172½	173¾	+¾	219	164¾	441
Dec	179½	179½	178¼	179	+1	190	168½	248
Est vol 1,200 vol Wed 1,624; open int 4,851, –202.								
SOYBEANS (CBT) 5,000 bu.; cents per bu.								
Mar	751	755	746	750½	+½	993½	616	9,641
May	768	772	762	768	+3	996	630	43,338
July	775	781½	771¾	778½	+5	992½	634½	23,209
Aug	765	772½	763	772	+4¾	956¾	640	6,695
Sept	737	744½	737	742½	+5¼	860	705½	6,594
Nov	722	729	721	725½	+4¼	772¼	661	17,385
Jan85	731½	740	731½	737¾	+4¼	745	676	2,311
Mar	744	751	744	750	+5½	758	692	529
May	755	758	754	757	+5	771	729½	71
Est vol 51,900; vol Wed 79,254; open int 109,773, +2,415.								
SOYBEANS (MCE) 1,000 bu.; cents per bu.								
Mar	746	769	746	750½	+½	993½	620½	1,854
May	760	778½	760	768	+3	996	636	4,908
July	776	782	772	778½	+5	992½	645	2,624
Aug	765	773	765	772	+4¾	955	646	375
Sept	740	742½	740	742½	+5¼	853	708	151
Nov	721	728⅞	721	725½	+4¼	772¼	661	2,005
Jan85	730½	740	730½	737¾	+4¼	744	678	128
Mar	744	752	744	750	+5½	757	722	121
May	754	754	754	757	+5	759	733	9
Est vol 9,450; vol Wed 7,615; open int 12,175, +404.								
SOYBEAN MEAL (CBT) 100 tons; $ per ton.								
Mar	194.50	199.00	194.50	198.80	+4.10	268.50	179.50	5,053
May	201.00	204.50	200.50	204.30	+3.60	267.50	185.00	22,979
July	205.50	209.50	205.50	208.90	+4.10	267.50	188.00	10,266
Aug	207.00	210.00	206.50	209.70	+4.00	251.00	192.50	3,361
Sept	204.00	205.50	204.00	205.50	+1.70	243.00	193.00	4,012
Oct	199.50	202.00	199.50	202.00	+2.00	240.00	182.00	3,654
Dec	202.00	204.00	200.50	203.80	+3.00	227.00	182.50	4,224
Jan85	203.00	205.00	203.00	204.50	+2.80	205.00	184.00	1,271
Mar	....	....	....	205.50	+.40	202.50	195.00	55
Est vol 27,800; vol Wed 28,262; open int 54,875, –1,352.								
SOYBEAN OIL (CBT) 60,000 lbs.; cents per lb.								
Mar	27.75	27.95	27.50	27.78	–.20	36.65	18.33	4,916
May	28.10	28.27	27.76	28.10	–.15	35.85	19.75	23,979
July	28.00	28.10	27.65	28.10	–.05	35.25	20.00	10,226
Aug	27.15	27.40	27.00	27.32	–.08	33.25	20.30	3,606
Sept	26.36	26.60	26.25	26.38	–.27	31.00	23.45	3,383
Oct	25.01	25.45	25.00	25.25	–.20	29.25	23.50	3,500
Dec	25.00	25.15	24.85	24.87	–.13	28.75	23.45	4,083
Jan85	25.05	25.05	24.80	24.85	–.15	27.60	24.05	842
Mar	....	....	....	25.00	–.08	25.60	25.25	1
Est vol 22,800; vol Wed 23,851; open int 54,536, –1,807.								
WHEAT (CBT) 5,000 bu.; cents per bu.								
Mar	325½	334	325½	334	+7¾	437	319½	5,392
May	330½	336½	330	336½	+5¼	441	324½	15,062
July	327½	330	325½	329½	+1¾	427	322	21,716
Sept	329½	333½	329½	332½	+¾	432	325	4,816
Dec	343½	346¼	342½	345¼	+¾	418	337½	7,429
Mar85	350½	353	350	352¼	+¼	379	344	1,849
Est vol 11,200; vol Wed 19,702; open int 56,264, –1,585.								
WHEAT (KC) 5,000 bu.; cents per bu.								
Mar	365	367¾	363½	367¾	+2¾	433	356¾	3,485
May	355¼	358¾	355	358½	+2½	436	352¾	7,178
July	343¼	346½	343	346¼	+3	419	339¾	3,395
Sept	346	350½	346	350½	+5	417	343½	1,213
Dec	358	362	357½	362	+4¾	373¼	355	249
Est vol 4,036; vol Wed 4,411; open int 15,520, –906.								
WHEAT (MPLS) 5,000 bu.; cents per bu.								
Mar	390½	393½	390½	393	+1½	449	377½	1,347
May	385	388¾	385	388¼	+2¼	450	377	2,026
July	378	378½	378	378¼	+1½	430	372½	536
Sept	367	369	367	369	+2	404½	364½	518
Dec	....	....	....	370	+½	399¾	366½	263
Est vol 1,320; vol Wed 1,469; open int 4,690, –196.								
WHEAT (MCE) 1,000 bu.; cents per bu.								
Mar	326	335	326	334	+7¾	437	319¾	3,218
May	331	337	333⅝	336½	+5¼	441	324¼	1,603
July	327½	329⅝	325¾	329½	+1¾	428	322⅜	3,449
Sept	332¼	332¼	331½	332½	+¾	430	327	65
Dec	343½	346½	344	345¼	+¾	408¾	340	1,524
Mar	352	352	352	352¼	+¼	379	348	141
Est vol 2,980; vol Wed 7,729; open int 10,000, –155.								
BARLEY (WPG) 20 metric tons; Can. $ per ton								
Mar	126.80	129.70	126.70	129.30	+2.80	141.00	103.50	2,850
May	128.90	130.80	128.60	130.30	+1.40	142.10	120.70	5,131
July	129.70	131.50	129.70	131.00	+1.30	141.20	126.00	1,267
Oct	121.00	122.50	121.00	122.50	+1.50	130.00	118.90	1,450
Est vol 1,600; vol Wed 1,899; open int 10,698, –66.								
FLAXSEED (WPG) 20 metric tons; Can. $ per ton								
Mar	....	....	....	353.00	+3.90	444.00	317.50	1,625
May	353.00	358.00	353.00	356.70	+3.70	454.00	350.00	3,540
July	362.00	363.00	362.00	362.50	+4.00	415.00	355.00	890
Oct	355.00	358.00	355.00	358.00	+6.00	406.80	347.00	574
Dec	356.00	358.00	356.00	356.50	+8.00	392.00	351.30	335
Est vol 750; vol Wed 1,479; open int 6,964, +143.								
RAPESEED (WPG) 20 metric tons; Can. $ per ton								
Mar	406.50	412.00	406.50	412.00	+4.50	463.00	314.50	2,345
June	403.00	407.00	403.00	405.00	+1.50	467.40	330.00	9,563
Sept	386.00	388.90	383.50	383.50	–3.00	428.50	367.00	3,056
Nov	365.30	369.00	363.50	363.90	–.90	425.00	347.50	1,767
Jan85	....	....	....	373.50	–.50	394.00	359.00	76
Est vol 2,800; vol Wed 3,991; open int 16,807, –506.								
RYE (WPG) 20 metric tons; Can. $ per ton								
Mar	....	....	....	127.00	+1.70	173.00	124.20	1,512
May	129.00	131.00	129.20	131.00	+1.70	170.00	128.00	2,852
July	....	....	....	133.50	+1.00	147.40	132.00	103
Oct	....	....	....	130.30	+3.40	131.50	125.00	99
Est vol 203; vol Wed 424; open int 4,566, +94.								

SOURCE: Reprinted by permission from *The Wall Street Journal*, March 2, 1984.

minimum price change permitted is. Another example indicates the dangers that lurk in activity based on such incomplete information. The quotation for Treasury bills shows that they are traded on the IMM of the Chicago Mercantile Exchange. The amount is shown as $1 million and the price is quoted as "points of 100%." The information that is omitted is equally important. The information about the contract does not reveal that the contract is for Treasury bills having 90 days to maturity when the futures contract expires or that the amount of bills to be delivered is a "face value amount," not an actual cash amount. Also omitted is the way in which the interest rate is computed to get those "points of 100%" and the fact that each movement of one-hundredth of a point of 100% represents a profit or loss of $25 on each Treasury bill contract. With so much information left out, it is very clear that you should not trade based just on what is shown in the *Wall Street Journal.* To have a good insight into the price behavior and the price fluctuations of a contract requires additional information.

For each of the delivery months, the price listings have a row of data, with the first line going to the contract that matures next, also called the *nearby contract.* Each succeeding line pertains to another maturity month. Contracts that mature later are called *distant or deferred contracts.* The first three columns of data give the opening, high, and low prices for each contract for the day of trading being reported.

Next comes the *settlement price,* which is the price at which contracts are settled at the close of trading for the day. Yet it is not exactly the last trade price of the day, as it would be with stocks. In Chapter 1, the feature of daily resettlement was examined, and the settlement price determines what has to be paid to settle a contract for the day's trading. The change in variation margin from one day to the next is the change in the settlement price from one day to the next.

The settlement price, typically, will be the last trading price for the day, but it is not universally so. Most exchanges have a settlement committee, composed of members of the exchange, which meets immediately at the close of trading to establish the settlement price. Their job is to establish a settlement price that fairly indicates the value of the futures contract at the close of trading. When trading is active at the end of the day, the settlement committee has an easy job. The prices recorded from trades will be continuous, fluctuating little from trade to trade. In such cases the committee may simply allow the final trading price to be the settlement price.

Difficulties arise, however, when a contract has little trading activity. Imagine that the last trade for a particular maturity of a given commodity was three hours before the close of trading and that significant information pertaining to that commodity was discovered in the interim. The last actual price at which the contract was traded might not represent what the price should be at the close of trading. In such a case, the settlement committee performs an important function by establishing a settlement price that differs from the price on the last recorded trade.

To do so, the members use information on other maturity months for the same commodity. The difference between prices of contracts for different delivery months is very stable, at least relative to the futures prices themselves. So the settlement committee will use that price difference, or *spread,* to establish the settlement price on the contract that was not recently traded. Even more drastic situations might arise from time to time, but the settlement committee must establish a settlement price even when there is very little information to go on. Having this function performed by a committee helps to rule out the possibility that an inaccurate settlement price might be chosen to generate a windfall gain for the person choosing the settlement price.

The next column, after the settlement price, is denoted as "Change." This value represents the change in the settlement price from the preceding day to the current one. The next two columns show the lifetime high and low prices for each contract. A perusal of Figure 2.1 indicates how radically prices may differ for some contracts over their life. For the contracts about to mature, the difference between the lifetime highs and lows can truly be enormous. For the contracts that have just been listed, there has been little time for the lifetime high and low prices to diverge radically.

The final column is headed by the title of "Open Interest," which shows the total number of contracts outstanding for each maturity month. The Open Interest shows the number of futures contracts for which delivery is obligated. To understand the meaning of this more clearly, assume that the December 1985 corn contract has just been listed for trading, but that no trading has taken place yet. At this point, the open interest in the contract is zero. Trading begins and the first contract is bought, and necessarily sold to the buyer by some other party. This transaction creates one contract of open interest, since there is one contract now in existence for which delivery is obligated.

Subsequent trading can increase or decrease the open interest. If the two parties who originated trading in the December 1985 corn contract reversed their positions by trading with each other, the open interest would fall to zero. Of course, this is not the typical pattern that the level of open interest follows. Instead, the open interest is typically very low for contracts when they just begin trading. From Figure 2.1 it is apparent that the distant maturity contracts have little open interest. As the contracts approach maturity, the open interest will typically build. Most often the contract closest to delivery, the nearby contract, will have the highest level of open interest. As the nearby contract comes very close to maturity, however, the open interest will fall. This is due to the fact that traders will be closing out their positions to avoid the obligation to deliver. *In fact, more than 99% of all futures contracts are closed out by a reversing trade, rather than through the delivery process.* Upon maturity of the futures contract, all parties with remaining open interest must fulfill their obligations by making or taking delivery, and the open interest goes to zero. Recall, also, that the open interest figures reported in the *Wall Street Journal* are for *the day preceding* the day on which prices are reported.

Beneath the lines for each of the contract maturities, more trading information is reported. The estimated volume for all maturities for a given commodity is reported, followed by the actual volume for the preceding day. Next the open interest for all contract maturities is shown. (This figure should equal the sum of the open interest figures shown for the individual contracts.) Finally, the last number reports the change in the open interest since the preceding day. We may also note that it is not unusual for the volume of trading to exceed the number of contracts of open interest. This will occur when trading activity is particularly heavy for a given commodity on a certain day. In the next chapter, the different trading parties who give rise to the trading volume and open interest are considered.

THE BASIS

Basis is a term that receives a great deal of attention in the world of commodity futures trading. The *basis* is the current cash price of a particular commodity at a specified location minus the price of a particular futures contract for the same commodity:

Basis = Current Cash Price − Futures Price.

There are several points in this definition that require elaboration. First, basis is built upon a cash price of a commodity at a specific location. The cash price of corn, for example, might differ between Kansas City and Chicago, so the basis for those two locations will also differ. Normally, one good cannot sell for different prices in two markets. If such a good had two prices, you could buy the commodity in the cheaper market and sell it in the market with the higher price, thereby reaping an *arbitrage profit*—a sure profit with no investment. Prices for corn in Chicago and Kansas City can differ, of course, because of the expense of transporting corn from one location to another. If corn is grown near Chicago, then we might reasonably expect the price of corn in Chicago to be lower than the price of corn in Kansas City. So the basis that is calculated in considering futures prices may differ, depending upon the geographic location of the spot price that is used.

Usually people speaking of the basis are referring to the difference between the cash price and the nearby futures contract. There is, however, a basis for each outstanding futures contract, and this basis will often differ in systematic ways, depending upon the maturities of the individual futures contracts. This phenomenon is illustrated in Figure 2.2,

FIGURE 2.2
Gold Prices and the Basis, December 16, 1982.

CASH (London A. M.)	$441.50
DEC (Futures)	441.00
MAR 83	449.20
JUN	459.40
SEP	469.90
DEC	480.70
MAR 84	491.80

The Basis

DEC $.50

0—————————————————————————————————————

        MAR − $7.70

            JUN − $17.90

                SEP − $28.40

                    DEC − $39.20

                        MAR − $50.30

which shows gold prices, both spot and futures, for December 16, 1982. The cash, or spot, price that is used is the London A.M.fix, or morning quotation, so the basis is for London. The futures prices are from the IMM. The graph at the bottom of the exhibit, which is not to scale, shows the stair step of the basis. The basis is positive for the nearby (December) contract, but is negative for all other maturity months.

The chart of the basis shows that it is possible to contract for the future sale or purchase of gold at a price that is higher than its current cash price. The difference between the current cash price of $441.50 per ounce and the price of the more distant futures contracts is striking, as much as $50.30 per ounce for the most distant March 1984 contract. It appears that the futures market anticipated a rather large increase in the price of gold over the period from December 1982 to March 1984.[2]

The interpretation of the basis can be very important, particularly for agricultural commodities. For many commodities, the fact that the harvest comes at a certain time each year introduces seasonal components into the series of futures prices.[3] Many traders believe that understanding these seasonal factors can be extremely important for successful speculation. Also, as will become clear, the basis, such as that shown in the chart of Figure 2.2, can be used as a valuable information source in predicting future spot prices of the commodities that underlie the futures contract.

FIGURE 2.3
Convergence of Cash and Futures.

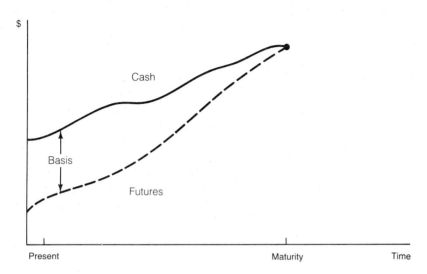

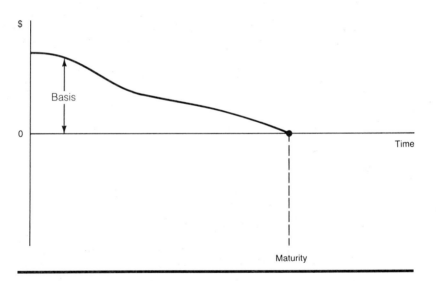

A further point about basis emerges from a consideration of Figure 2.2. Notice that the basis for the nearby contract is only $.50, and there is good reason that it should be so small. The December 1982 contract is extremely close to delivery on the date in question, December 16, 1982. At delivery the futures price and the cash price must be equal, except for minor discrepancies due to transportation and other transportation costs. If someone were to trade the December contract on the day in

FIGURE 2.4
T-Bonds, T-Bond Futures, and the Basis.

U.S. Treasury Bond 14
With September 82 basis
January 1981–July 1982

32nd of 100 PCT.

U.S. Treasury Bond 14

September 1982
U.S. Treasury Bond
Futures Contract

$$14 \text{ of } 2006 - 11 - \frac{US}{\text{Sep. 82}} \times 1.6359$$

21 28 4 11 18 25 1 8 15 22 1 8 15 22 29 12 5 19 26 3 10 17 24 31 7 14 21 28 5 12 19 26 2
Jan.   Feb.   Mar.   Apr.   May   Jun.   Jul.

Reprinted courtesy Data Lab Corp., Chicago, Illinois.

question, the trade would be for the delivery of gold within a very short time span, less than two weeks. The price of gold for delivery within two weeks must be very close to the current spot price of gold.

At the moment of delivery, the futures price and the spot price of gold must be the same. The basis must be zero, again subject to the discrepancy due to transaction costs. This behavior of the basis over time is known as *convergence,* as Figure 2.3 illustrates. In Figure 2.3 the futures price is shown lying below the cash price. As time progresses, and the futures contract is approaching maturity, the basis narrows. At the time of the maturity of the futures contract, the basis is zero, consistent with the nonarbitrage requirement that the futures price and cash price are equal at the maturity of the futures contract. In the bottom panel of the Figure, the basis is shown by itself. The basis is positive, initially, but it declines to zero as the futures contract approaches maturity.

One other feature of the basis is very important for futures trading, which Figure 2.4 illustrates. Data on the Treasury bond futures contract is shown for the period from January 1981 to July 1982. The graph in the figure also plots the spot price of the U.S. Treasury bond with a coupon rate of 14%. Over this period, the prices of both the spot bond and the futures contract were falling sharply. In spite of the rather extreme volatility of the bond prices and the associated futures contract, the difference between the two remained relatively stable.

The basis over the period was rather constant, as is reflected in two ways. First, the vertical distance between the two contracts shows little variance. When the spot bond's price rose or fell, the futures price tended to follow. This tendency is illustrated in a second way, by the bottom line in the graph, which illustrates the behavior of the basis over the same time span. The basis, as shown in the graph, is adjusted for the value of the particular bond (the 14s of 2006–2011) in its delivery against the futures contract. (This adjustment is accomplished by the adjustment term of 1.6359. The delivery process for Treasury bond futures is discussed in some detail in Chapter 5.) When the adjusted basis is plotted, as it is in the figure, it is extremely constant and near zero. This is another important point about the basis: the variability of the basis is usually much less than the variability of the spot price or the futures price considered alone. While spot and futures prices may be extremely volatile when considered alone, the difference between them is relatively constant. The relatively low variability of the basis is very important for hedging and for certain types of speculation, as will be discussed in Chapter 3.

SPREADS

Just as there is an important relationship between each futures contract and the cash price of the commodity, the relationships among futures prices on the same good (same type of contract) are themselves important. The difference between two futures prices is known as a *spread*. Spreads are important because they indicate the relative price differentials for a commodity to be delivered at two points in time. As we will see, there are strong economic relationships that govern the permissible spreads that may exist between any two futures contracts.

Spread relationships are important for speculators. Much speculation involves some kind of spread position—the holding of two or more related futures contracts. If a trader hopes to use futures markets to earn speculative profits, an understanding of spread relationships is essential. Since most speculation uses spreads, the search for a profit turns on an ability to identify spread relationships that are economically unjustified. While the understanding of the spread relationships in a particular commodity requires considerable knowledge about the commodity itself, certain general concepts and principles apply to spreads in general.

The spreads that might typically exist for a commodity are shown in Figures 2.5 and 2.6. In Figure 2.5, the broken line shows the futures prices for the No. 2 Heating Oil contract that is traded on the New York Mercantile Exchange (NYME), and covers the period ending in early April 1982. The continuous line in the upper portion of Figure 2.5 represents the cash price of heating oil over the same period. The difference, of course, is the basis. The number of contracts outstanding (the open interest) and the trading volume are shown in the bottom portion of the figure. The high variability in both the futures and the cash price is clearly revealed by the graphs.

Figure 2.6 shows the spread relationships that have existed over the eight months prior to mid-April 1982. At the time the graphs were made, the nearby contract was the June 1982 contract, and the graphs of the various spreads all relate to that nearby contract. At the very bottom of Figure 2.6 the basis is shown. Notice in this graph that the spot price of heating oil in New York is subtracted from the price of the nearby futures contract. So what is shown is not actually the basis itself, but its negative value. From Figure 2.5, it is clear that the basis was initially negative, since the futures price is above the cash price. Later, about November 25, 1981, the basis became positive, and remained so through the period under examination, except for the last four trading days. The bottom graph in Figure 2.6 merely reverses that relationship and shows the negative of the basis.

The top three graphs all depict the spreads between the nearby June contract and other more distant contracts. Overall, the spread between the June and July contracts is slightly negative, but near zero. As other contracts are compared with June contract, the spreads are increasingly negative. The spread between the June and October contracts was almost as large as − $.06 per gallon in early March. From the graphs it is clear that the spot price exceeded the nearby futures price ever since late November 1981, again with the exception of the last days shown. Further, the June futures price exceeded that of the July contract. In fact, the more distant the futures maturity, the cheaper was the price. (This is certainly an example of an inverted market.)

It is usually difficult to say exactly why the observed spread relationships prevail. If we knew exactly what the spreads meant, we could soon make a fortune in the futures market. In the case of the heating oil contracts, and with the advantage of hindsight, the answer seems rather clear, however. Often the negative spread relationships, such as those

FIGURE 2.5

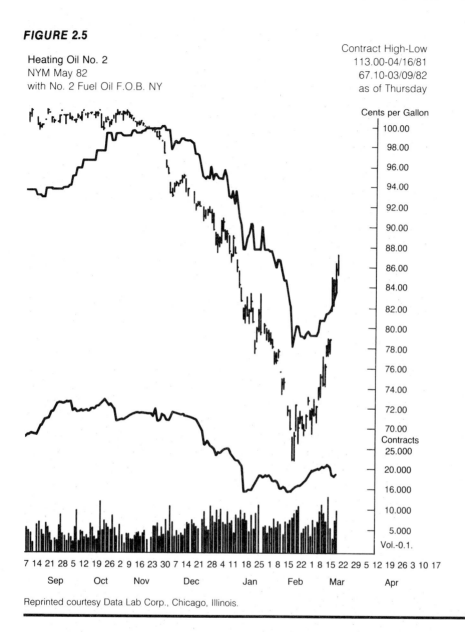

Heating Oil No. 2
NYM May 82
with No. 2 Fuel Oil F.O.B. NY

Contract High-Low
113.00-04/16/81
67.10-03/09/82
as of Thursday

Cents per Gallon
100.00
98.00
96.00
94.00
92.00
90.00
88.00
86.00
84.00
82.00
80.00
78.00
76.00
74.00
72.00
70.00
Contracts
25.000
20.000
16.000
10.000
5.000
Vol.-0.1.

7 14 21 28 5 12 19 26 2 9 16 23 30 7 14 21 28 4 11 18 25 1 8 15 22 1 8 15 22 29 5 12 19 26 3 10 17
Sep   Oct   Nov   Dec   Jan   Feb   Mar   Apr

Reprinted courtesy Data Lab Corp., Chicago, Illinois.

shown for heating oil, indicate that the market expects a drop in the price of the good. Since the more distant the futures contract, the lower the price, the market is expressing its unwillingness to contract for the distant future delivery of heating oil at the current spot price.

A perusal of Figure 2.5 shows that both cash prices and the price of the nearby futures contract were generally trending downward over the period shown. The fact that the spreads of Figure 2.6 were all negative at

FIGURE 2.6

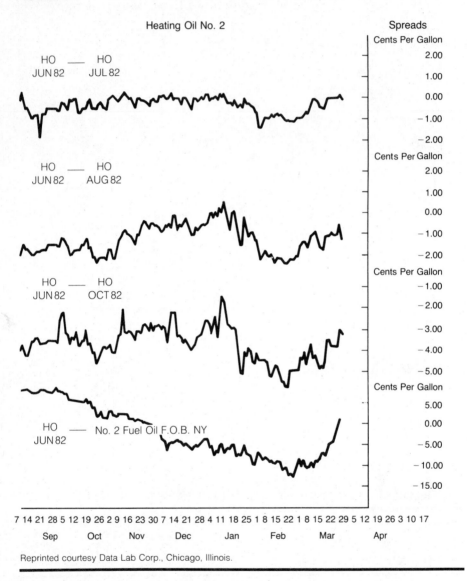

Heating Oil No. 2

Reprinted courtesy Data Lab Corp., Chicago, Illinois.

the end of the period can reasonably be interpreted to mean that the market expected further decreases in prices. Now, looking back on 1982, it appears that the market was exactly correct. The year 1982 was the year of the oil glut, with petroleum prices in general falling substantially. The futures market for heating oil seems to have anticipated this fall in the cash price of petroleum products, since it reflected this belief by the negative spreads.

Had prices of heating oil generally been expected to rise over the period, we would have reasonably expected the spreads to be positive. In a period of high inflation, such as that experienced before 1982, the more distant prices of commodities would be expected to be higher than current prices.[4] In such a case, spreads would be positive. Without question, futures prices, and the spreads between them, give information about expected prices for the commodities in the future. When more distant futures prices are higher than nearby prices, and when spreads are accordingly positive, the market is expressing its belief that prices will be rising. By the same token, when more distant futures prices are lower than nearby prices, spreads are negative, and the market is expressing the view that prices will be falling.

FUTURES PRICES AND EXPECTED FUTURE SPOT PRICES

Every serious student of the futures markets would agree that there is an important relationship between futures prices and expected future spot prices. Within this broad framework of agreement, there is considerable room for differences of opinion about what that relationship is. The simplest and most straightforward view is easily stated: Futures prices are equal to expected future spot prices.

For example, if the futures price for wheat that will be delivered in six months is $5.54 per bushel, then, according to this view, the market expects the price of wheat to be $5.54 six months from now. The expectation is the product of all of the participants in the market, who vote on the correct future spot price by their trading on the value of the commodity at the delivery date in the future. If a trader foresees correctly that the prevailing futures price for delivery of a good in six months exceeds what he expects that good to be worth, then he can profit by selling a futures contract on that good.

If all other participants in the market view the problem in the same light, then the resulting futures price will be the outcome of market participants trading to capture profits when the futures price differs from their expectations. The process is an ongoing one, with new information reaching the market on a continuous basis, requiring adjustments of expectations and shifts in futures positions. However, since the market is an active one with low transaction costs and readily available information, the futures prices may reasonably be thought to equal the market's expectation of future spot prices.

Even the most vociferous advocates of the view that futures prices equal expected future spot prices do not neglect the economic realities of the marketplace. Not everyone has an equal vote in determining what the futures prices will be. The influence that one trader exerts on futures prices is directly proportional to the number of contracts traded. So those traders who take larger positions in support of their beliefs have a greater impact on futures prices. In effect, traders vote with their money about the proper level of futures prices.

In spite of the initial plausibility of the view that futures prices equal expected future spot prices, there are three reasons to think that the equality might not hold. First, some theorists maintain that the risk-bearing services of speculators will be forthcoming only if the futures price differs from the expected future spot price. Second, the feature of daily resettlement prevalent in the futures market could cause futures prices and expected future spot prices to diverge under certain circumstances. Third, there is an alternative concept of futures pricing that relies on *carrying charges* to determine futures pricing relationships. The carrying charges are the costs associated with storing commodities from one point in time to another. These three grounds for believing that the futures prices need not equal expected future spot prices will be discussed in turn, with the carrying charges framework being the topic of the next section.

Prices and Risk Aversion

The traders in futures markets can be classified, at least roughly, into hedgers and speculators. Hedgers enter the futures market to decrease a pre-existing risk, while speculators trade in the hope of profit. Entering the futures market as a speculator is a risky venture. However, if people are risk averse, they will incur risk willingly only if the expected profit from bearing the risk is enough to compensate them for the risk exposure. Without doubt, most participants in financial markets are risk averse, so they are looking for the compensation to justify their taking a risky position.[5] In the futures markets, the only way to profit as a speculator is to have a favorable movement in the price of a futures contract.

Assume for the moment that speculators are rational, that is, they make assessments of expected future prices based on the wealth of information that is readily available. In assessing this information, the speculators make mistakes from time to time, but since their assessment is rational, they process the information efficiently on the whole, so that their expectations, on average, are realized. This is not to say that they are mistake free. Instead, they make errors of assessment that are not biased.[6] The errors that they make are randomly distributed around the true price that the commodity will have in the future. Assume also that speculators have "homogeneous expectations," that is, they agree about what to expect.

Such a group of speculators might confront the prices that are prevailing in a futures market and find those prices in accordance with their expectations. If the futures price matches what you expect the price of the commodity to be at the time the futures contract matures, then there is no reason to speculate in futures. If the futures price matches a speculator's expectation of subsequent cash prices for the commodity, then the speculator must expect neither a profit nor a loss by entering the futures market. Yet, by entering the market under such conditions, the speculator would certainly take on additional risk. After all, his expectations might be incorrect. Faced with such a situation, speculators would not enter the market, since they face additional risk with no compensating return.

Putting the speculators aside for the moment, let us consider the hedgers. The hedgers, taken as a group, will need to be either long or short in the futures market to reduce the risk they face in their businesses. A trader who buys a contract has a long position. The seller of a contract has a short position. If the hedgers are net short, for example, the speculators must be net long. For the sake of simplicity, consider a single speculator who is considering whether to take a long position. As just noted above, it will be rational for the speculator to take a long position in the futures market only if the future spot price of the commodity is expected to be greater than the current futures price. Otherwise, the speculator must expect not to make any profit.

The hedger, in turn, needs to be short to avoid unwanted risk. The hedger, according to this line of reasoning, must be willing to sell the futures contract at a price that is less than the expected future spot price of the commodity. Otherwise, the hedger cannot induce the speculator to accept the long side of the contract. From this point of view, the hedger is, in effect, buying insurance from the speculator. The hedger transfers his unwanted risk to the speculator, and pays the speculator for bearing the risk. The payment to the speculator is the difference between the futures price and the expected future spot price. Even so, the speculator does not receive any sure payment. The speculator must still wait for the expected future spot price to materialize to capture the profit expected for bearing the risk.

Thus far, the discussion has focused on a single hedger and a single speculator. It is necessary, however, to try to do justice to the fact that the marketplace is peopled by many individuals with different needs, different levels of risk aversion, and different expectations *(heterogeneous expectations)* about future spot prices. Figure 2.7 graphically depicts the situation that might prevail in the futures market for some commodity, by showing the relevant positions of hedgers and speculators as two groups.

Figure 2.7 summarizes the *net* positions desired by hedgers and speculators taken as two groups. As the futures price varies, the number of contracts desired by the two groups will naturally vary as well. In the example, the hedgers are assumed to be net short. At no futures price will hedgers, taken as a group, desire a long position in the futures.[7] This is reasonable given the definition of a hedger as one who enters the futures market to reduce a pre-existing risk. The hedgers' desired position in the futures market is shown on line *WX*. At higher prices, hedgers are willing to sell more futures contracts, as the downward slope for line *WX* indicates.[8]

Speculators, by contrast, are willing to hold either long or short net positions as the situation demands. Assuming that the speculators, as a group, correctly assess the appropriate expected future spot price, they will be neither long nor short when the futures price equals the expected future spot price. At point *E,* the futures price equals the expected future spot price, and speculators hold a zero net position in the futures market. (In such a situation, some speculators would be long, others short, reflecting their divergent opinions. But, in the aggregate, they would hold a net zero position.) The speculators' alternative positions are shown on the line *YZ.* If the futures price lies above the expected future spot price, then the speculators will desire to be net short as well as the hedgers. If the futures price lies below the expected future spot price, then speculators will wish to be net long, holding some position between *E* and *Z* on line *YZ.*

Not all positions shown on the graph are feasible. If the futures price lies above point *E,* then both the hedgers and speculators desire to be short. Yet, the number of short contracts held must, at all times, equal the number of long contracts. As it is drawn, there is only one price at which all of the demand of the hedgers and speculators can be satisfied, and that is at the price shown as point *B.* With a price of *B,* the net short position desired by the hedgers is exactly offset by the net long position desired by the speculators. This is reflected graphically by the fact that the distance *AB* is equal to the distance *BC.* Through the typical process by which markets reach equilibrium, the futures market may reach an equilibrium price at *B,* with the futures price lying below the expected future spot price.[9]

This account explains how it is possible for the futures price not to equal the expected future spot price. Likewise, if the demand of the hedgers were to be net long, then the speculators must be net short. If the speculators are net short, then they can earn a return for their risk-bearing services only if the futures price lies above the expected future spot price. Again the futures price need not equal the expected future spot price. Instead, the relationship between the futures price and the expected future spot price depends on whether the hedgers need to be net short or net long.

This way of thinking about the determination of futures prices goes back to the work of John Maynard Keynes and John Hicks. The view that hedgers are net short, as shown in Figure 2.7, is associated with Keynes and Hicks. Over the life of the futures contract, the futures price must move toward the cash price. (This is already clear, since the basis must be equal to zero at the maturity of the futures contract, as was discussed earlier.) If the expectation about the future spot price is correct, and hedgers are net short, then the futures price must lie below the expected future spot price. In such a case, futures prices can be expected

FIGURE 2.7

Hypothetical Net Positions for Hedgers and Speculators.

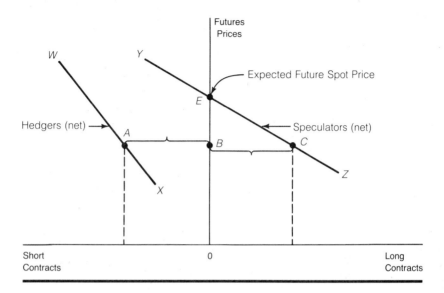

to rise over the life of a contract, and this process is known as one of *normal backwardation*. Conversely, if hedgers are net long, then the futures price would lie above the expected future spot price, and the price of the futures contract would fall over its life. This pattern of falling prices is known as a *contango*. These price patterns are depicted in Figure 2.8.[10]

Figure 2.8 illustrates the price patterns for futures that we might expect under different scenarios. In considering the Figure, assume that market participants correctly assess the future spot price, so that the expected future spot price of the Figure turns out to be the actual spot price at the maturity of the futures contract. If the futures price equals the expected future spot price, then the futures price will lie on the dotted line, which is set equal to the expected future spot price. With initially correct expectations, and no information causing a revision of expectations, the futures price should remain constant over its life.

Alternative conceptions certainly exist, two of which were discussed above. If speculators are net long, as suggested by Keynes and Hicks, then futures prices must rise over the life of the contract if the speculators are to receive their compensation for bearing risk. Prices then follow the path that is labeled "Normal Backwardation" in Figure 2.8. With the futures price rising over its life, the speculator earns a return for bearing risk. Notice that the line for normal backwardation terminates at the expected future spot price. This is necessary since the futures price and the spot price must be equal at the maturity of the futures contract and it was assumed for purposes of making the figure

FIGURE 2.8
Patterns of Futures Prices.

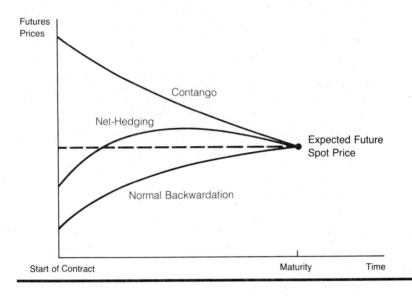

that the expected future spot price turned out to be the subsequently observed spot price.

If speculators are net short, and are to receive pay for bearing risk, then futures prices must follow a contango, as is also illustrated in Figure 2.8. The fall in futures prices, as the contract approaches maturity, gives the short speculators the needed compensation that induced them to enter the market.

One final traditional possibility is also shown in Figure 2.8, and it is known as the *net hedging hypothesis*. According to this view, the net position of the hedgers might change over the life of the futures contract. At the outset of the contract, the hedgers are net short and the speculators, accordingly, net long. In such a situation, the futures price lies below the expected future spot price. Over time, the hedgers gradually change their net position. Eventually, the hedgers are net long, requiring that the speculators be net short. For the speculators to receive their compensation in this case, the futures price must lie above the expected future spot price, as was the case with the contango.[11]

Perhaps this account of hedgers changing from being net short to net long over the life of the contract appears dubious, but it is certainly conceivable. Consider grain farmers who wish to hedge the crop that they will be producing. To hedge the price risk associated with harvest, they will need to be short. Cereal producers have a need for the grain, and hedge their price risk by being long. To see how the price could follow the pattern suggested by the net hedging hypothesis, imagine that the farmers hedge first, making the hedgers net short. Later, the cereal producers begin to hedge their future need for the grain, and the net hedging position of the farmers and cereal producers taken together tends to move toward zero, being neither short nor long. Time passes, and still more cereal producers hedge by going long. Eventually, the long hedgers come to predominate and all hedgers taken together are net long. Under such a condition, the futures price must lie above the expected future spot price if the speculators are to receive compensation for risk bearing.[12]

Prices and Daily Resettlement

If any of the hypotheses of normal backwardation, contango, or net hedging were sustained, then there would be ample reason to believe that the futures price would not equal the expected future spot price. The equality of futures prices and expected future spot prices has also been attacked from another quarter that relies on the distinction between forward and futures contracts. The argument becomes quite mathematical, but it basically turns on the fact that the interest rates that will prevail between a given point in time and the maturity of a futures contract are unknown. The fact that interest rates are *stochastic,* that is, that they follow some probability distribution, means that futures and forward contracts need not sell for the same price.[13] Since futures contracts are resettled daily, there will be cash flows associated with the futures contract prior to the contract's maturity.

Depending upon what traders believed about the pattern that interest rates were going to follow during the time before the futures contract matured, there could be a reason to favor the futures over the forward contract, or the forward over the futures contract. In other words, the feature of daily resettlement on the futures contract provides a rational ground for the divergence of the futures and forward prices. However, since it appears that the forward price should equal the expected future spot price, if the futures price does not equal the forward price, it cannot equal the expected future spot price. Whether this divergence is of an important magnitude remains a question that is not yet fully resolved. In fact, the entire question of the relationship between futures prices and expected future spot prices remains an open question. This question is addressed in more detail later, after a discussion of the relationship between carrying charges and futures prices.

FUTURES PRICES AND CARRYING CHARGES

Without question, expectations regarding future spot prices play an important role in determining futures prices. But another extremely important factor in futures price determination is the carrying charge. The *carrying charge* is the total cost to carry a good forward in time. For example, wheat on hand in June could be carried forward to December. Carrying charges fall into three basic categories: storage costs, transportation costs, and financing costs. (Speculators hardly want the commodity delivered to their door, but remember, hedgers are concerned with delivery of a good at some point in the future at their agreed upon price.)

Storage costs include the cost of warehousing the commodity in the appropriate facilty. For many commodities, the futures exchanges will specify approved warehouses. For anyone contemplating making delivery on a futures contract, storage in an approved warehouse can be important, since the exchange will accept the warehouse receipts only from approved warehouses. (The warehouse receipt would state that a certain amount of a particular commodity is stored in the warehouse.) For many commodities, delivery against a futures contract is accomplished by transferring ownership of the goods in an approved warehouse. This is done by signing over to the receiving party the appropriate warehouse receipt.

In addition to the actual cost of warehousing the commodity, the storage costs include insurance costs. Many physical commodities should be insured for the time that they are under storage. The idea of warehousing seems most appropriate to physical commodities, such as wheat or gold. But the same concept applies to financial instruments as well. Financial instruments are warehoused with depository banks approved by the exchanges.

The carrying charges also include, in some cases, transportation costs. Wheat in a railroad siding in Kansas must be carried to delivery in two senses. It must be stored until the appropriate delivery time for a given futures contract, but it must also be physically carried to the appropriate place for delivery. As will become obvious, transportation costs between different locations determine price differentials between those locations. Without question, transportation charges play different roles for different commodities. Transporting wheat from Kansas to Chicago could be an important expense. By contrast, delivery of Treasury bills against a futures contract is accomplished by a wire transfer, which costs only a few dollars.

One of the most significant carrying charges in the futures market is the financing cost. In the idea of the carrying charge, only the charges involved in carrying a commodity from one time or one place to another are considered. The carrying charges do not include the value of the commodity itself. So, if gold costs $400 per ounce and the financing rate is 1% per month, the financing charge for carrying the gold forward is $4 per month (1% × $400).

Most participants in the futures markets face a financing charge on a short-term basis that is equal to the "repo rate." The *repo rate* is the rate on repurchase agreements. In a *repurchase agreement* a person sells securities at one point in time, with the understanding that they will be repurchased at a certain price at a later time. Most repurchase agreements are for one day only and are known, accordingly, as overnight repos. The repo rate is relatively low, exceeding the rate on Treasury bills by only a small amount.[14] The financing cost for such goods is so low because anyone wishing to finance a commodity may offer the commodity itself as collateral for the loan. Further, most of the participants in the market tend to be financial institutions of one type or another who have low financing costs anyway, at least for very short-term obligations.

The carrying charges just described are important because they play a crucial role in determining pricing relationships between spot and futures prices and the relationships among prices of futures contracts of different maturities. The carrying charge relationship gives rise to a set of pricing rules:

The futures price must be less than or equal to the spot price of the commodity plus the carrying charges necessary to carry that spot commodity forward to delivery:

$$F \leq S(1 + c),$$

where F = **the futures price,**
       S = **the spot price,**
       c = **the cost of carry, expressed as some percentage of the spot price, necessary to carry the good forward from the present to the delivery date on the futures.**

If this condition did not hold, then you could borrow funds, buy the spot commodity with the borrowed funds, sell the futures contract, and carry the commodity forward to deliver against the futures contract. This would constitute a certain profit without investment, or an arbitrage opportunity. There would be a certain profit, because it is guaranteed by the sale of the futures contract. Also, there would be no investment, since the funds needed to carry out the strategy were borrowed and the cost of using those funds was included in the calculation of the carrying charge. Such opportunities cannot exist in a rational market.

So far, it is established that $F \leq S(1 + c)$. What if a situation arises where $F < S(1 + c)$? This gives rise to another kind of opportunity. In this situation, you could engage in "reverse arbitrage." Here the strategy would work as follows. Buy the futures contract and sell the spot commodity short. Selling the spot commodity short involves borrowing the good, selling it, using the proceeds, S, to earn a rate of return equal to the cost of carry, c, and buying it back later to return to the original owner. In this case, the trader arranges at the outset to acquire the good later, by buying a futures contract, and paying F. Clearly, this arrangement also leads to an arbitrage profit, which is an impossibility in a rational market. The existence of these two arbitrage strategies implies:

With unrestricted short selling it must be the case that the futures price equals the spot price plus the cost of carrying the spot commodity forward to the delivery date of the futures contract:

$$F = S(1 + c).$$

It must be acknowledged that this argument explicitly does not include transaction costs. Transactions costs exist on both sides of the market, whether it be the purchase or sale of the futures. However, in many markets, the transactions costs for short selling are considerably more expensive, which limits the applicability of the second side of the strategy.

These same cost-of-carry relationships also determine the price relationships that can exist between futures contracts on the same good that differ in maturity. The spread between two futures contracts cannot exceed the cost of carry to carry the good from one delivery date forward to the next. That is:

The distant futures price must be less than or equal to the nearby futures price plus the cost of carrying the spot commodity from the nearby delivery date to the distant delivery date:

$$F(d) \leq [F(n)](1 + c),$$

where $F(d)$ = **the futures price for the distant delivery contract**
$\quad\quad\;\; F(n)$ = **the futures price for the nearby delivery contract**
$\quad\quad\;\; c$ = **the cost of carrying the good from time** = n **to time** = d.

If this relationship did not hold, you could buy the nearby futures contract and sell the distant contract. Then you would accept delivery on the nearby contract, and carry the good until the delivery of the distant contract, thereby making a profit.

With unrestricted short selling, it must also be the case that:

The distant futures price must equal the nearby futures price plus the cost of carrying the delivery commodity from the nearby to the distant delivery date:

$$F(d) = F(s) (1 + c).$$

If these relationships were ever violated, profit-hungry traders would immediately recognize the chance and trade until prices adjusted to eliminate all of the arbitrage opportunities.[15]

FUTURES PRICES, EXPECTED FUTURE SPOT PRICES, AND CARRYING CHARGES

Futures prices are clearly related to the market's expectation of future spot prices. Also, the carrying charges that prevail for different commodities put restrictions on futures prices. It remains to examine the relationships between expected future spot prices and the carrying charge framework developed in the preceding section. Only by reconciling the expected future spot prices with the prices implied by the carrying charges that exist can a consistent theory of futures prices emerge.

In beginning to explore the relationship between expected future spot prices and carrying charges, it is important to note that the carrying charge relationship limits the amount by which futures prices can differ from spot prices or the amount by which distant futures prices can deviate from nearby futures prices. Sometimes futures markets are inverted, with the distant futures price lying below that of the nearby contract. Such was the case with the example of the Heating Oil contract that was discussed in Figures 2.5 and 2.6. Obviously, an inverted market cannot possibly violate one of the carrying charge price relationships discussed in the preceding section, that $F \leq S(1 + c)$.

If gold sells for $400 per ounce, and the total carrying charge for gold is 1% per month, then the futures price for the delivery of gold one month later cannot be more than $404. However, this means that the expected future spot price for gold cannot be much more than $404 either. To see why this is so, imagine that no gold futures market exists, and that the expected price for gold one month later is $410. In such a circumstance, you could buy an ounce of gold and store it for one month. The total cost of acquiring and carrying that ounce of gold forward one month would then by $404. If you expected to be able to sell the gold for $410 at the end of that month, the situation represents an attractive speculative opportunity. It is a risky opportunity, and therefore not an arbitrage opportunity, since you face the risk that the price of gold in one month might not be $410. It might, instead, be only $403, a price which would generate a loss of $1 per ounce.

It is clear, however, that we could not expect the price of gold in one month to be much in excess of $404 per ounce. If it were, people would find it very advantageous to buy gold and hold it for sale in one month. This would generate excess demand for gold at the current price of $400 and would drive the cash price of gold up. The cash price of gold would have to increase until the attractive opportunity no longer existed. When the difference between the cash price and the expected cash price one month later differed by only 1% (the carrying charge for one month), it is certain that the attractive opportunity would no longer exist.

However, it is possible that the differential between the spot price of gold and the expected future spot price in one month might not close to equal the 1% carrying charge. Assume that the spot price of gold is $400 per ounce, and the expected future spot price for one month later is $404.25. There is still the expected profit of $.25 per ounce to be made by buying the gold now and carrying it forward. However, there is risk involved. Whether market participants would try to capture the expected profit of $.25 would depend on how risk averse they were. Perhaps the expectation of a $.25 profit per ounce is not enough to induce the traders to bear the price risk of holding gold for one month. If so, then the expected future spot price could exceed the sum of the current spot price plus the carrying charges. In such a case the expected profit would have to be small, relative to the risk involved. Otherwise, traders would try to take advantage of the opportunity to capture the profit. If there are risk-neutral market participants, they will try to take advantage of all expected profit opportunities and ignore the risk.[16] While it may not be correct to think that there are sufficient numbers of risk-neutral traders available to try to exploit all profit opportunities whatsoever, it is reasonable to believe that there are large numbers of futures market traders who are very risk tolerant. These traders demand some compensation for bearing risk, but the price they charge for bearing risk is not very high.

Any gold market participant has the opportunity to ignore the futures market, and trade in the way suggested in the preceding paragraph. This opportunity means that the difference between the current cash price and the expected future cash price cannot deviate from the carrying charge, except by an amount too small to attract trading interest. The carrying charge analysis of futures prices means that the price differential between the spot and futures price cannot differ from the carrying charge at all, again assuming unrestricted short selling. Putting these two ways of thinking together gives an interesting result. Ignoring the risk premium that might be demanded by traders to store commodities against a risky expected future spot price, the maximum difference between the current spot price, on the one hand, and the futures price or the expected future spot price, on the other, equals the carrying charge. This means that futures prices cannot exceed the expected future spot price. Even if we allow that some storers of commodities might demand a risk premium for taking the risk of holding the commodity, the result still holds.

It must be acknowledged that, on occasion, the futures price may lie below the spot price. This is the case in any inverted market. In markets where reverse arbitrage is possible, due to low barriers on short selling and the storability of the commodity, the deviation from the relationship, $F = S(1 + c)$, is constrained by the pricing relationships just examined. The possession of any physical good has a *convenience yield*. For example, it is customary to speak of the convenience yield of cash. Cash, as opposed to a security, offers convenience at crucial times—such as when dealing with traffic courts. One way of explaining an inverted market is to say that the convenience yield of holding the actual good exceeds the cost of carry.

It must be noted that all of the development of the carrying charge framework depends on two assumptions that have only been implicit to this point. *First, it has been implicitly assumed that the commodity in question is storable.* Not all futures contracts, however, are for storable commodities. Fresh eggs, for example, are not storable for very long.

Certain kinds of financial instruments are not really storable either, since they are eligible for delivery against the futures contract for only a day or two.

A second assumption that is implicitly being used here is that the commodity for which the futures contract is being written is deliverable. With the advent of the stock index futures contracts (discussed in Chapter 7), the opportunity to deliver can no longer be assumed. The fact that stock index futures are settled only with cash, and not the delivery of securities, turns out to be important in the pricing of these futures contracts.

DO FUTURES PRICES EQUAL EXPECTED FUTURE SPOT PRICES?

As mentioned previously, the debate continues over the relationship between futures prices and expected future spot prices. If the question of whether they are equal is intended as a commentary on the state of scientific knowledge, the answer must be that no one knows. If the question is intended to develop a useful rule of thumb, then it is safe to answer, "Yes, but with reservations."

Most observers agree that futures prices must be close to the expected future spot prices. Otherwise profit seekers would trade until the opportunities were gone, leaving the futures price close to the expected future spot price. Perhaps the Hicks-Keynesian hypothesis of normal backwardation is correct, but it has never been fully sustained by scientific inquiry. Rather, the case seems to be that we never really know whether the hedgers and speculators are net long or net short, so we usually have no real ground for believing that the futures price lies above or below the expected future spot price. If that is an accurate depiction of our state of knowledge, then taking the futures price as the best estimate of the subsequent spot price is a reasonable stance.

Although futures prices may not equal forward prices and expected future spot prices at certain times due to the stochastic character of daily resettlement cash flows, we cannot really know when that circumstance prevails. Further, the best empirical evidence available on the subject indicates that the differences between futures and forward prices are too small to be even statistically significant, much less economically significant.[17]

It appears that the best estimate that we can make of future spot prices is to take the futures price as the estimate of the future spot price. Considerable evidence exists to support the thesis of futures prices as estimators of subsequent spot prices.[18] The fact that the futures prices are market consensus estimates, estimates that emerge from the trading activity of many parties, must also be remembered. It is, of course, possible for an individual's expectations to differ from those of the market's.

Thus far, the discussion of futures prices has focused on interpreting the prices from the point of view of the market itself. Yet futures prices may be analyzed in other ways in an attempt to identify those occasions when the market makes mistakes in pricing and misgauges expected future spot prices.

Technical Analysis

One approach to forecasting the direction of futures prices is known as technical analysis. This approach is defined by reference to the restricted information set it uses in its analytical procedures. *Technical analysis makes uses of only historical market-related data in its attempts to forecast futures prices.* These data include past price and volume information as a key element. But technical analysis also makes use of such information as the amount of open interest, volume figures, and other traders' positions, such as reports of market commitments.

Technical analysis is used in virtually every financial market, yet it seems to be strongest in futures markets. The technical analyst, or technician, or chartist, uses as a main tool charts that record market prices over a period of time. The belief is that certain formations of price movements occur with regularity in advance of other price movements. The technician's main job, then, is to find the tell-tale price patterns and use the information revealed in them to guide a profitable trading strategy.

Three basic kinds of charts guide the technical analyst: bar charts, moving average charts, and point and figure charts. As entire books have been devoted to the practice of technical analysis in futures markets, only an example of the analysis will be given here.[19] One of the most famous kinds of formations is known as the "head and shoulders" formation, illustrated in Figure 2.9. This type of chart is known as a bar chart. Each of the bold vertical lines pertains to a single trading period, usually a day. The hash mark on each line indicates the closing price for that trading period. The formation earns its name from the fact that the price pattern resembles a drawing of a head and shoulders. In the bottom panel of the figure, the inverted head and shoulders formation is shown. The occurrence of a head and shoulder price pattern indicates, according to the theory of technical analysis, a major change in the direction of the market.

There are numerous other formations that the technical analysts interpret to mean different things, and most have colorful names: inverted saucer, rounded bottom, ascending triangle, bull flags, and bear pennants. So popular is technical analysis among traders that a number of firms exist whose main line of business is selling prepared charts of price movements.[20]

Does technical analysis work? Perhaps the strongest argument that can be made for the benefits of technical analysis rests on the fact that

FIGURE 2.9
Head and Shoulders Formations.

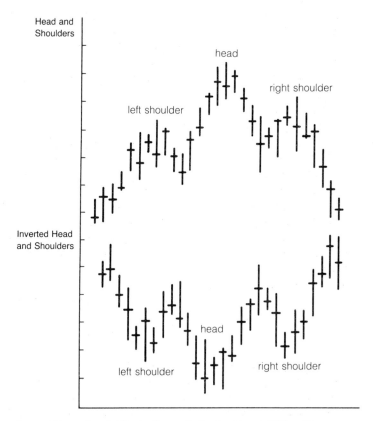

Source: Chicago Board of Trade: *Commodity Trading Manual,* 1982, p. 96.

there are large numbers of technical analysts happily trading in the pits of Chicago, Kansas City, New York, and the sites of other futures markets. If technical analysis were totally useless, we would expect these practitioners to have found other lines of work some time ago. Further, many of the largest and most respected brokerage firms in the United States continue to employ technical analysts. The analysts prepare a blizzard of recommendations for their brokerage clients. Figure 2.10 shows a page of the Merrill Lynch Guide to technical analytical methods. Brokerage firms are largely motivated by profits, so if the technical analysts did not earn their keep, they would certainly not be retained by the brokerage firm. Earning their keep, in this context, is defined as providing useful analysis of the markets, or at least analyses of the market that are perceived to be useful by the brokerage clients.

Opposed to the view that technical analysis is useful stands a

FIGURE 2.10
Falling Wedge.

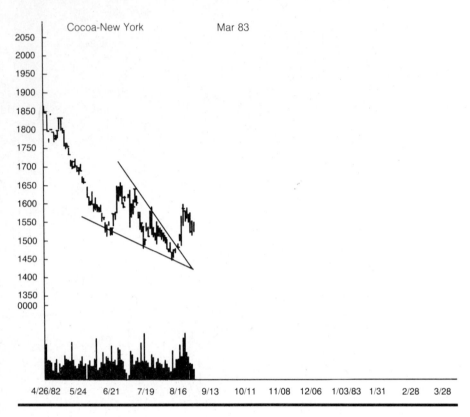

tremendous number of academic studies.[21] The overwhelming conclusion of these studies is that technical analysis is not useful for directing profitable trading strategies. These studies focus on the equity markets, as well as the futures markets. Almost without exception, the academic studies fail to find any way in which technical analysis could be used profitably. Some of these studies do find trends in market prices, but these trends are, almost without exception, very weak and cannot be exploited to generate profits that would exceed the transaction costs involved. Seldom in economic analyses is it possible to find such widespread agreement as that which exists in opposition to the usefulness of technical analysis.[22]

It would be presumptuous to think that the conflict between the results of academic research and the continued flourishing of technical analysts could be resolved here. One possible answer, that would please neither side, is that the technical trader makes a living from trading, but that the accounting profits that might be realized do not represent economic profits.[23] In other words, the technically minded trader may just earn a fair return on the capital invested in the seat on the exchange and on the commitment of time and energies. This idea is developed in more detail in Chapter 3. The best advice to a new entrant to the futures market is not to rely on technical analysis to guide a trading strategy. The weight of evidence seems to be against technical analysis, in spite of the fact that so many technical analysts continue in employment.

Fundamental Analysis

The other dominant mode of price analysis in futures markets, as in most other financial markets, is known as fundamental analysis. *The fundamental analyst pays attention to the economic fundamentals in attempting to forecast prices and in attempting to develop a profitable trading strategy.*

The economic fundamentals differ, of course, depending on the commodity in question. However, they essentially revolve around the determinants of supply and demand for the commodity in question. As an example, consider the fundamental analyst focusing on wheat. Without question, wheat is a difficult commodity to analyze since it has become so important politically. Governments may take unexpected actions that drastically affect the price of wheat in the open market. Governments may even take action, as they have done in the past, to close the wheat market and bring everything under government control. In the United States, the government may restrict or encourage the sale of wheat to the USSR. It may change the structure of subsidies that help to determine the extent of wheat production in this country. The USSR, for its part, typically strives to keep its crop yield secret, so that other countries will not know the extent of its demand for wheat. Such was certainly the case in the great "grain robbery" of 1972.[24] Other important wheat exporting countries, notably Canada and Argentina, may also exert their political influence in the wheat market.

The wheat analyst needs to be knowledgeable about meteorology and agronomy as well as international politics. The amount of rain that falls during the growing season is, of course, critical in determining the supply of wheat. More subtly, the weather conditions have a drastic influence on the protein content of the different kinds of wheat. Bakers need the right protein content to make their bread, so weather factors that influence wheat protein can have a very strong effect on the prices of one kind of wheat relative to others. European wheat, for example, typically has a lower protein content than some American wheat. If the European growing season is hot and dry, however, the protein content of the wheat will be increased. This means that European bakeries will not need to import as much of the American durum wheat, which is especially high in protein.

Even after the wheat is harvested, weather continues to play an important role. If you knew with certainty when the Great Lakes were to become impassable in winter, this information could easily be parlayed into a fortune. Fortunes have been made and lost by being right or wrong about the freezing date of the Lakes. The good fundamental analysts for wheat will be well acquainted with all of these factors, as well as many others. The information collected will be used to try to predict the future direction of prices. If the analyst is successful, this information could be used to guide a successful trading strategy.

Fundamental analysts are even more firmly entrenched in the futures markets than are the technical analysts. Few traders restrict themselves solely to technical analysis, so those traders who use both methods must also be reckoned among the fundamental analysts as well. Every major brokerage house has a staff of fundamental analysts that prepares advisory letters for its clients. Further, fundamental analysis seems so reasonable, concentrating, as it does, on factors that must affect prices of commodities. Yet, the academic evidence from numerous studies also strongly rejects the benefits of fundamental analysis.[25] The conclusion against fundamental analysis is not quite as strong as the rejection of technical analysis, but it is nonetheless clear. According to the weight of research results, fundamental analysis cannot be used to guide a successful speculative strategy. (As will be explained more fully in Chapter 3, a successful speculative strategy is one that earns more return than would be economically justified on grounds of the risk borne and the resources employed.)

From the point of view of the best research, technical analysis and fundamental analysis are in the same boat. Neither works. Since these are the two major analytical strategies open to the speculator, it appears that the speculator's life cannot be an easy one of regular fat profits and little worry. When we reflect that futures prices are reasonably interpreted as the price expected by the market, this conclusion begins to make sense. If futures prices represent the collective wisdom of all market participants trying to estimate future spot prices, then it seems unlikely that many speculators by themselves will be able to outperform the joint effort that has gone into creating the estimate of future spot prices.

CONCLUSION

While futures markets have a reputation for high risk and wild price swings, this chapter has stressed the underlying rationality of futures prices. We cannot deny that prices vary suddenly and sharply in the futures market, but it is quite possible that these price movements accurately reflect the arrival of new information at the market. Further, it is also apparent that futures prices observe the economic laws elaborated above. Both the expected future price framework and the carrying charges framework provide rational procedures for thinking about the behavior of futures prices. It must also be admitted that futures prices, on the whole, conform to these theories.

If the conclusions reached about futures pricing above are correct, then a picture of the usefulness of the market begins to emerge. If prices are rational, in that they reflect available information, and if spread relationships are strongly interlinked, and if futures prices are good estimates of expected future spot prices, it is possible to understand the uses that can be made of the market by different elements of society. These different groups in society were identified above as those who wish to discover price information by observing futures markets, as speculators and as hedgers. If futures prices are close to expected future spot prices, then the price discovery function is well served. Speculators, on the other hand, will have a difficult life. Hedgers, for their part, have an apparent opportunity to reduce their risk exposure with relatively little cost.

The uses that these different groups can make of the futures market are explored in detail in the next chapter. The difficulties facing speculators are examined more closely, along with the benefits that the futures markets provide to hedgers and to society as a whole.

NOTES

1. The *spot price* is simply the price at which you can purchase a good for immediate delivery. In a restaurant, for example, you buy a cup of coffee at the spot price. The spot price is also called the "cash price" or the "current price."

2. Futures markets can either exhibit a pattern of *normal* or *inverted* prices. When the prices go up, the more distant the maturity, the prices are normal. When the distant futures contracts are priced lower than the nearby contract, the market is said to be inverted.

3. As is explained in some detail in Chapter 4, we would expect the price of seasonal goods to be relatively high just before harvest and relatively low just after harvest. It is this kind of consideration that leads futures market observers to expect systematically fluctuating differences in basis over the year.

4. As will become clear in Chapter 5, this relationship will not hold for prices of interest-bearing assets. Expectations of high inflation will typically have a very strong negative impact on the prices of bonds. Often, it seems, it does not hold for other financial assets either.

5. In his book, *Risk and Risk Bearing,* Chicago: University of Chicago Press, 1940, Charles O. Hardy gives a different interpretation of the behavior of speculators. He likens the futures market to a gambling casino. In Hardy's view, if we ignore transaction costs in the futures market, the expected outcome of any trade is no gain and no loss. If transactions costs are considered, then the expected outcome is slightly negative. This, Hardy suggests, makes the futures market like a gambling casino, since people play, even when they should expect to lose money.

6. An estimator is *unbiased* if and only if the expected value of the

estimator equals the actual value of the parameter being estimated. Rational expectations theory has been applied to the commodities markets in this context. See Thomas J. Sargent. "Commodity Price Expectations and the Interest Rate," *Quarterly Journal of Economics, 83,* February 1969, 126–140 and J. F. Muth. "Rational Expectations and the Theory of Price Movements," *Econometrica, 29,* July 1961, 315–335.

7.   By assuming that hedgers will be net short no matter what the futures price, we are merely assuming that their pre-existing risk requires a short position. Some potential hedgers would, of course, abandon their risk-reducing short position if the futures price were low enough. However, in so doing, the potential hedger would have abandoned the intention of hedging and would be speculating. This is clear if we recall that the risk-reducing futures trade is to go short.

8.   Lines *WX* and *YZ* are drawn as straight lines, but that is only for convenience. Also, note that the hedgers hedge different amounts depending on the futures price. With low prices, they sell fewer contracts, thereby hedging less of their pre-existing risk than they would if futures prices were high.

9.   Notice that the slope of *WX* (the hedgers' line) is steeper than that of *YZ* (the speculators' line). The more gentle slope of *YZ* expresses the greater tolerance of the speculators toward risk. For any drop in the futures price below the expected future spot price, *E,* the increase in the speculators' demand for long contracts exceeds the drop in the hedgers' desire to hold the short contracts. Indeed, this must be the case. Graphically, we can show that there will be some equilibrium price, *B,* if the slopes of the two lines are as depicted. Economically, the speculators must be more risk tolerant than the hedgers. After all, the speculators, in this model, accept the risk that the hedgers are unwilling to bear. Therefore, the speculators must be more risk tolerant. The idea for Figure 2.7 was suggested by a presentation by Hans Stoll.

10.   A normal market gives rise to "normal backwardation" and an inverted market is consistent with prices following a "contango." (In the French futures market you may sometimes encounter the "Last Contango in Paris." Sorry.)

11.   Figure 2.8 is drawn from William Sharpe's book, *Investments,* Englewood Cliffs, NJ: Prentice Hall, Inc., 1981.

12.   Perhaps such an account is plausible, but there remains one very disconcerting element in Figure 2.8. Apparently, any observed movement of futures prices can be rendered consistent with a contango, normal backwardation, or with the net-hedging hypothesis. The view that futures prices equal expected future spot prices can also be rendered consistent with any observed pattern of futures prices. By using the fact that expectations might be wrong, each theory is consistent with any observed movement, at least in the short run. This fact makes it very difficult to determine which view is correct. The hope, in testing these competing views, is to gather enough data so that mistakes in expectations are averaged out. For one attempt to deal with the problem, see Kolb, Jordan, and Gay. "Futures Prices and Expected Future Spot Prices," *Review of Research in Futures Markets, 2,* 1983, 110–123. This paper contains references to many other such attempts.

13.   Several papers have appeared to argue against the necessary equality of forward and futures prices. See, for example, George E. Morgan. "Forward and Futures Pricing of Treasury Bills," *Journal of Banking and*

Finance, December 1981, 483–496; R. Jarrow and G. Oldfield. "Forward Contracts and Futures Contracts," *Journal of Financial Economics,* December 1981, 373–382; J. Cox, J. Ingersoll, and S. Ross. "The Relation Between Forward Prices and Futures Prices," *Journal of Financial Economics,* December 1981, 321–346; and S. Richard and M. Sundaresan. "A Continuous Time Equilibrium Model of Forward Prices and Futures Prices in a Multigood Economy," *Journal of Financial Economics,* December 1981, 347–371. In B. Cornell and M. Reinganum. "Forward and Futures Prices: Evidence from the Forward Exchange Markets," *Journal of Finance,* December 1981, 1035–1045, which is the only published empirical test of the difference between forward and futures prices, the authors find no statistically significant difference between forward and futures prices.

14. For a very informative and readable account of repurchase agreements, see Bowsher. "Repurchase Agreements," *Instruments of the Money Market,* Richmond: Federal Reserve Bank of Richmond, 1981.

15. See Figures 3.5 and 3.6 and the accompanying text for an example of how to conduct such arbitrage. Anne Peck and Shantaram Hegde made very useful comments on an earlier draft of this section.

16. A risk-neutral trader is indifferent to risk. By definition, he simply undertakes every venture with a positive expected return, no matter what the risk.

17. See B. Cornell and M. Reinganum. "Forward and Futures Prices: Evidence from the Forward Exchange Market," *Journal of Finance,* December, 1981, 1035–1046. This question has not been fully tested in most markets.

18. Chapter 6 examines the performance of market-based forecasts of future spot prices and compares these results with those of professional forecasting firms.

19. *Futures* is a monthly periodical that tends to emphasize the technical approach to trading. For the latest thinking on technical analysis, see the books advertised there. Chapter 4 considers an example of technical analysis in the gold futures market in some detail.

20. To become acquainted with these firms, you may simply consult *Futures.*

21. Two classic articles are: S. Smidt. "A test of the Serial Independence of Price Changes in Soybean Futures," *Food Research Institute Studies, 5,* 1965, 41–49; and R. Stevenson and R. Bear. "Commodity Futures: Trends or Random Walks?" *Journal of Finance,* March 1970, 65–81.

22. The virtues of technical analysis have been explored even more fully for the stock market. For a survey of some of these results, see E. Fama. "Efficient Capital Markets: A Review of Theory and Empirical Work," *Journal of Finance,* May 1970, 383–417.

23. "Accounting profits" do not reflect the opportunity cost of employing capital in an alternative usage. "Economic profits" are gained only when earnings are greater by employing capital in one manner instead of the next best alternative manner.

24. For a very interesting account of the "grain robbery" and the world wheat market in general, see D. Morgan. *Merchants of Grain,* New York: Penguin Books, 1981.

25. Fama also surveys the evidence on fundamental analysis in his classic article, "Efficient Capital Markets: A Review of Theory and Empirical Work," op. cit.

3 Using Futures Markets

INTRODUCTION

The two preceding chapters discussed the institutional setting of futures markets and the ways in which prices in these markets are determined. In order for any market to exist, however, there must be activity in the market. This chapter explores the uses that different people make of the futures markets. As a point of special interest, one may note that futures markets may serve the needs of some people even if they are not active traders in the market. Some people may simply use futures prices as a source of information without actually transacting themselves. Also, as explained below, some individuals and firms enter the futures market hoping to make profits, while others hope to lessen their own level of risk.

If the futures markets are to serve the interests of society, then the markets must serve the needs of certain individuals or groups in society. This chapter analyzes each of the ways that individuals and firms may use the futures markets. First, the futures market provides a means of *price discovery*. Since the prices in the futures markets provide information that is not readily available elsewhere, the markets serve people's needs. Note particularly that one need not trade in the market to receive this benefit; it is available to anyone for the price of a newspaper.

A second major group of users to benefit from the existence of the futures markets are the *speculators*. It may seem strange to list an opportunity for speculation as a service to society, but consider the following examples. Gambling houses provide speculative opportunities for citizens, and that might be reckoned as a public service. Professional and college sports teams also provide a way for people to speculate by betting.

Clearly, sports teams do not exist so that people can bet on them, but the chance to bet is a side effect, and perhaps a side benefit, of the existence of sports. The situation is similar in the futures markets. The chance to speculate may not be the reason that futures markets should exist from the point of view of society. However, the existence of speculative opportunities is certainly a consequence of the fact that there are futures markets. Whether one regards the provision of speculative opportunities as a service to the public is a question for political and moral philosophy. Futures markets do provide opportunities for speculation, and some members of society, who wish to speculate, will regard this as a benefit.

A third major group of futures market users, the *hedgers,* employ the futures markets to avoid unwanted risks. This use of the futures market is probably the most important from the point of view of society. Some agents in society find themselves exposed to certain risks as a consequence of their line of business or in the ordinary conduct of life. Often these risks are undesired, and the futures market provides a way in which risk may be transferred to some other individual who is willing to bear it. If people know that unwanted risks may be avoided by transacting in the futures market at a reasonable cost, then they will not be afraid to make decisions that will expose them initially to certain risks. They know that they can "hedge" that risk.

From the point of view of society as a whole, this has important advantages. Enterprises that are profitable, but that involve more risk than certain individuals wish to take, can still be pursued. The unwanted risk can then be transferred in the futures market. If these profitable but risky opportunities are pursued, then society as a whole will be better off. This is the strongest argument for the existence of futures markets. By providing a way of efficiently transferring risk to those individuals in society who are willing to bear it cheaply they contribute to the economy.[1]

Each of these three functions of futures markets, price discovery, speculation, and hedging, will be considered in turn in this chapter. Speculators and hedgers come in different varieties, and a full understanding of futures markets requires that the different types of market participants be recognized and distinguished. In subsequent chapters, examples of each of the different functions of futures markets will be considered and illustrated with specific futures market transactions.

PRICE DISCOVERY

In Chapter 2, the connection between futures prices and future expected spot prices was discussed in some detail. Although we considered the possibility of a bias in the futures prices, we concluded that the bias must be small or non-existent. Following this line of argument, futures prices might be treated as a consensus forecast by the market regarding future prices for certain commodities. This line of argument makes clear the idea that futures markets help market watchers "discover" prices for the future.

Students of futures markets admit a close connection between futures prices and expected future spot prices. Our question is how the futures market can be used to reveal information about subsequent commodity prices. The usefulness of price forecasts based on futures prices depends on three factors:

1. The need for information about future spot prices;
2. The accuracy of the futures market forecasts of those prices;
3. The performance of futures market forecasts relative to alternative forecasting techniques.

Information

Many individuals and groups in society need information about the future price of various commodities. If anyone had information about the price of gold one year from now, it would be relatively simple to make a fortune. Certainly, speculation would be much more rewarding if one had a private and infallible source of information about future spot prices. Aside from such dreams of wealth, information about future spot prices is also needed for more mundane purposes, such as the planning of future investment and consumption. Futures markets can be used to provide such information for the planning processes of individuals, corporations, and governmental bodies.

Consider an underpaid college professor who wants to buy a house. Interest rates are high, so taking a long-term mortgage in such times would commit him to a lifetime of large payments. On the other hand, if he does not buy a house, then he cannot take advantage of the tax deduction that the interest portion of the house payments would provide. If interest rates were to drop soon, then it would be reasonable to wait to buy the house. By consulting the financial pages of the newspaper, the professor could find out what the market believed about the future level of interest rates.[2] A futures contract on long-term mortgage rates called the GNMA contract is traded on the Chicago Board of Trade. If the interest rate for a mortgage to be delivered in six months is three percentage points lower than current interest rates, then there is good reason to expect interest rates will fall over the next six months. In such a situation, the college professor might well wait a few months to buy his house.

Another example concerns a furniture manufacturer who makes plywood furniture. Assume that she is printing her catalog now for the next year and must include the prices of the different items of furniture. Setting prices in advance is always a very tricky affair. In addition to other problems, the price she charges will depend upon the expected future price of plywood. The cost of plywood varies greatly, depending largely on the health of the construction industry, so it is difficult for her to know how to include that cost factor in her calculations. One way in which she might deal with this is to use the prices from the plywood futures market as a way to estimate the costs of the plywood that she will have to purchase later on. In doing so, she uses the futures markets for their *price discovery* benefit.[3]

In both of these examples, individuals used futures prices to gauge the expected spot price at some future date. The advisability of such a technique depends on the accuracy of the forecasts that are drawn from the futures market. Futures prices may, of course, differ from subsequently observed spot prices. If there is a large discrepancy, the futures forecasts may not be very useful. Errors could result from two sources: inaccurate but unbiased forecasts and bias in the forecast itself.

Accuracy

An estimator is unbiased if the average value of the forecast equals the value of the variable to be forecasted.[4] Thus, futures prices might provide unbiased forecasts with very large errors. The situation is reminiscent of the joke about the two economists who predicted the unemployment rate for the next year. The first predicted that 12% of the work force would be unemployed, while the second put the figure at full employment, or 0% unemployed. The actual rate turned out to be 6%, from which the economists cheerfully concluded that, on average, they were exactly right. In forecasting the unemployment rate, one could say that the economists had provided an unbiased forecast, but one that had large errors.

As is typical for many commodities, the forecasts from the futures market have large errors. Futures prices fluctuate radically, which means that most of the time they provide an inaccurate forecast of the spot price of the underlying commodity at the time of delivery. Without question, the large size of the forecast errors from the futures markets limits the reliance that one should place in the forecasts themselves.[5] In Chapter 6 we consider an actual example of the sizes of forecast errors that are typical in forecasting foreign exchange prices.

One might reasonably wonder why there should be such large errors. According to the theory of finance, prices in well-developed markets reflect all available information. As new information becomes available, futures prices adjust themselves very swiftly. As a consequence, futures prices tend to exhibit radical fluctuations, which means that the prices will be inaccurate as estimates of subsequent spot prices.

In addition to the large errors that one can observe in futures market forecasts, there is also the possibility that futures prices may be biased. One possible reason for this was considered in Chapter 2. Futures prices may embody a risk premium that keeps the futures price from equaling the expected future spot price. In general, the possibility of bias is not too great a concern, at least for practical matters. While there is still no real agreement about the existence of biases, there is agreement that, if they do exist, they are small. For practical purposes, the errors in futures forecasts are so large that they tend to drown out any biases that may also be present.

Performance

Since forecasts based on futures prices seem to be so poor, why would anyone care about them? Before discarding the forecasts, consider the alternatives. What other forecast might be more accurate? A considerable amount of study on this topic has failed to lead to any final answer. Nonetheless, evidence suggests that forecasts based on futures prices are not excelled by other forecasting techniques. Futures forecasts have been compared to other techniques and have not been found to be inferior, and the current situation in forecasts of the foreign exchange rate is typical. Compared to professional forecasting firms, some of which charge large fees, the futures price does very well. As detailed in Chapter 6, many professional firms have recently turned in forecasting records that were worse than chance. The title of a recent article, "Currency Forecasters Lose Their Way," tells the story of the professional forecasts.[6]

In spite of the large errors in forecasts based on futures market prices, the futures market seems to do better than the alternatives. The situation may be summarized as follows: the accuracy of futures forecasts is none too good, but it is certainly better than the alternatives. One might also note that the futures market forecasts are free. Someone needing a forecast of future spot prices should not rely too heavily on any forecast. But when relying on some forecasting technique, it should be the forecast freely available in the futures market.

SPECULATION

Defining speculation or identifying the speculator in the futures market is always difficult. Many people say no such definitions can be given. For our purposes, the following definition of a speculator will prove useful. *A speculator is one who enters the futures market in search of profit and, by so doing, willingly increases his or her risk exposure.*[7]

Most individuals have no heavy risk exposure in most commodities. Consider an individual who is not a farmer or food processor who has an interest in the wheat market. If she trades a wheat futures contract, then she most likely is speculating in the sense defined above. She enters the futures market, willingly increasing her risk exposure, in the hope of profit.

One might object that this individual does have a pre-existing risk exposure in wheat. In fact, everyone who eats bread does. Our plans for consuming bread may change if wheat prices rise too high. This objection makes a good point. In order to know whether a particular action in the futures market is a speculative trade requires knowledge about the trader's current assets and future consumption plans. For an individual, however, entry into the futures market is most likely to be a case of speculation. For the woman who traded a wheat futures contract, the size of the wheat contract (5000 bushels) is so large relative to her needs for wheat, that the transaction increases her overall risk. Assuming that she, like most of us, is risk averse, she will not expose herself to the additional risk of entering the futures market unless she hopes to profit by doing so. This is what classifies her as a speculator.

Different types of speculators may be categorized by the length of time they plan to hold a position. The traditional classification recognizes three kinds of speculators: scalpers, day traders, and position traders.

Scalpers

Of all speculators, scalpers have the shortest horizon over which they plan to hold a position in the market. Scalpers aim to foresee the movement of the market over a very short interval, ranging from the next few seconds to the next few minutes. Many scalpers describe themselves as psychologists trying to sense the feel of the trading among the other market participants. In order to do this, they must be in the trading pit itself, otherwise they could not hope to see buying or selling pressure building up among the other traders.[8]

Since their planned holding period is so short, scalpers do not expect to make big profits. Instead, they hope to make a profit of one or two *ticks*—the minimum allowable price movement. Most of a scalper's trade will end with no profit or a loss. If the price does not move in the scalper's direction within a few minutes of his assuming a position, he will likely close out the position and begin looking for a new opportunity.

This type of trading strategy means that the scalper will generate an enormous number of transactions. Were he to make these transactions through a broker as an off-the-floor participant, any anticipated profit would be lost through high transaction costs. Since scalpers are members of the exchange, or lease a seat from a member, their transaction costs are very low. Scalpers probably pay less than $1 per round turn in most futures markets, in comparison to about $25–80 through a regular broker, and without these very low transaction costs, their efforts would be helpless. In order to sense the direction of the market and to conserve on transaction costs, the scalpers need to be on the floor of the exchange.

Although it may not be apparent at first glance, scalpers provide a valuable service to the market by their frenzied trading activity. By making so many trades, scalpers help supply the market with high liquidity. Their trading activity increases the ease with which other market participants may find trading partners. Without high liquidity, some traders would stay away from the market, which would decrease its usefulness further. A high degree of liquidity is necessary for the success of a futures market, and scalpers play an important role in providing that liquidity.[9]

Day Traders

Compared to scalpers, day traders take a very farsighted approach to the market. Day traders attempt to profit from the price movements that may take place over the course of one trading day. The day trader will close his position before the end of trading each day so that he has no position in the futures market overnight.

A day trader might follow a strategy such as concentrating his activity around announcements from the U.S. government. The Department of Agriculture releases production figures for hogs at intervals that are well known in advance. The day trader may think that the hog figures to be released on a certain day will indicate an unexpectedly high level of production. If so, such an announcement will cause the futures prices for hogs to fall, due to the unexpectedly large future supply of pork. To take advantage of this insight, the day trader would sell the hog contract prior to the announcement and then wait for prices to fall after the announcement. Such a strategy could be implemented without holding a futures market position overnight. Therefore, it is a suitable strategy for a day trader to pursue. (To avoid drastic effects on markets, government announcements are often made late in the day, after the affected market closes.)

The scalper's strategy of holding a position for a very short interval is clearly motivated, but it is not so apparent why the day trader should limit himself to price movements that will occur only during the interval of one day's trading. The basic reason is risk. Day traders believe that it is too risky to hold a speculative position overnight; too many disastrous price movements could occur.

To see the dangers in maintaining a position overnight, consider the following case of a position in orange juice concentrate traded by the Citrus Associates of the New York Cotton Exchange. In late November a trader held a short position in orange juice. The weather in Florida is crucial for the prices of orange juice, and the trader checks the weather forecast for Florida that day before the end of trading. There seems to be no possibility of damaging weather in the next few days, so he maintains his position overnight. Unexpectedly, a strong cold front pushes into Florida and destroys a large portion of the orange crop, which, in November, is still on the trees and not yet mature. Naturally, futures prices soar on the opening of trading the next day, and the trader who slept on his position suffers a large loss. In fear of sudden developments of this type, day traders close their positions each day before trading stops.

The overwhelming majority of speculators are either scalpers or day traders. This indicates just how risky it can be to take a position home overnight. As the close of trading approaches each day, the pace of trading increases. Typically, 25 percent of the day's trading volume will take place in the last half hour of trading. The last five minutes are particularly frenetic as traders attempt to close out any open positions that they may have.[10]

Position Traders

In spite of the apparent risks, some traders, called position traders, hold their positions overnight. On occasion they may hold them for weeks or even months. There are two varieties of Position traders—those holding an *outright position* and those holding a *spread position*. Of the two strategies, the outright position is far riskier.

Outright positions   An outright position trader might adopt the following strategy if she believed that long-term interest rates were going to rise more than the market expected over the next two months. As interest rates rise unexpectedly, the futures prices, representing the prices of bonds, must fall. However, the trader does not really know when during the next two months the rise in rates will occur. To take advantage of her belief about the course of interest rates, she could sell the futures contract on U.S. Treasury bonds traded on the Chicago Board of Trade and hold that position over the next two months. If she is correct, there will be a sharp rise in rates not correctly anticipated by the market, and futures prices will fall. She can then cover her position by executing a reversing trade and reap her profit.

The danger in this trader's outright position is clear. If she has made a mistake, and interest rates fall unexpectedly, then she will suffer a large loss. The outright position offers a chance for very large gains if she is correct, but it carries with it the risk of very large losses as well. For most speculators, the risks associated with outright positions are too large. The expected trading life of a new trader is about six months, but it is much shorter for outright position traders.

Spread positions   More risk-averse position traders may trade spreads. In the last chapter, an "intra-commodity" spread was considered for the heating oil contract. Intra-commodity spreads involve differences between two or more contract maturities for the same underlying deliverable good. By contrast, "inter-commodity" spreads are price differences between two or more contracts written on different, but related, underlying goods. For example, the difference between the July soybean and wheat contracts would be an inter-commodity spread. In trading a spread, one trades two contracts that are believed to be related in their price movements and tries to profit from changes in their relative prices.

Consider the case of a spread speculator who believes that the difference between the futures price of wheat and corn is too low. Such a trader believes that the inter-commodity spread between wheat and corn is inconsistent with the justifiable price differential between the two goods. Wheat normally sells at a higher price per bushel than corn does, but for this trader the differential in prices is too little. On November 10, the trader sees the futures prices for July wheat at 354 per bushel and for July corn at 254 cents per bushel. Believing that this differential is inappropriately small, he decides to trade to take advantage of this temporary mis-pricing, (see Table 3.1). Consequently, he buys one July wheat contract and sells one July corn contract. If his belief is correct, the difference of 100 cents between the wheat and corn should widen, and he can realize a profit. In this example, the speculator makes a profit. As shown in Table 3.1, the prices on June 10 of the following year, for the July delivery, are 370 cents per bushel for wheat and 265 cents per bushel for corn. The gap in prices has widened from 100 cents per bushel in November to 105 cents per bushel in June. As the table shows, the trader may now realize the profit by reversing his position in the two contracts. This is accomplished, and the profit is $250.

Figure 3.1 shows how the prices of the two goods moved over time. The gap in prices increased from 100 to 105 cents per bushel, just as noted in Table 3.1. But notice that the prices of both goods both went up. Since wheat and corn are close substitutes for each other, it is not surprising that their prices tend to rise and fall together. Prices of close substitutes tend to be positively correlated. Because of that positive correlation, a spread position will tend to be less risky than an outright position. An outright position in the corn contract would have incurred a price movement of $800 and in the wheat contract, a price movement of $550. In this situation, as is typically the case, the spread position suffered less price movement than either of the contracts considered individually. The lower risk of spread positions is realized by the market as well. The required margin for a spread position involving two contracts is typically lower than the margin required for two unrelated contracts.

In considering this difference in risk, it is important not to lose sight of the strategy the spread trader in the example was following. The spread position was initiated because the trader believed that the gap between wheat and corn prices was going to widen. Note that the speculator would make a profit even if both prices went down, as long as the price of corn fell more than the price of wheat. Consequently, the speculator did not need to have any beliefs about whether prices were going to rise or fall but only about the relative price performance of wheat and corn.

Other types of spread strategies are also possible. In an intra-commodity spread, one takes a position in two or more maturity months for the same good. The belief behind such a strategy is that the relative prices between delivery dates for the same commodity will change, generating a profit for the trader. Whereas an outright position only re-

TABLE 3.1

An Inter-Commodity Spread. The wheat and corn contracts are both for 5000 bushels.

Cash Market	Futures Market
November 10	Buy 1 July wheat contract at 354 cents per bushel on the CBT.
	Sell 1 July corn contract at 254 cents per bushel on the CBT.
June 10	Sell 1 July wheat contract at 370 cents per bushel.
	Buy 1 July corn contract at 265 cents per bushel.

Corn loss:	11 cents per bushel ($\times$ 5000 bushels) = $550 (loss)	
Wheat profit:	16 cents per bushel ($\times$ 5000 bushels) = $800 (gain)	
Total Profit:	$250	

quires a belief about the price movement of one commodity, a spread position focuses on the relative price movements between two or more commodities, or contract maturities.

The spread example considered previously was relatively simple, but spreads can be quite complex. One frequently mentioned complex spread is known as a *butterfly spread,* which is best illustrated by an example. Assume that today is November 10 and the prices for copper are as shown in Table 3.2. In comparing the price for September delivery, 67.5 cents per pound, with the prices on the adjacent delivery months of July and December, it seems that the September price is out of line. To this speculator, it appears that the September price should be about half-way between the July and December prices, but it is seriously below that level. Since the speculator does not really know whether copper prices are going to rise or fall in general, he only wants to attempt to take advantage of this apparent pricing discrepancy among the different maturity dates.

To do this, he initiates a futures transaction known as a butterfly spread, such as the one illustrated in Table 3.3. Since he expects the price of the September contract to rise relative to the July and December contracts, he sells 1 contract of each of the July and December maturities. To offset the sale of these two contracts, he buys two contracts for the September delivery. By April 15, the prices of all of the contracts have fallen, but their price relationships are much closer to what the speculator believed to be correct. On April 15, the September price has risen, relative to the other contracts, to a point about half-way between them. This is exactly what he expected to happen. The wings of the but-

FIGURE 3.1
Prices for July Delivery.

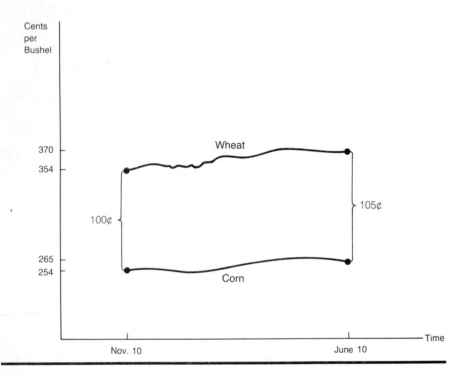

terfly spread (the July and December contracts) have flapped, bringing all the prices into line. As Table 3.3 reveals, this generates a total profit on the spread of $750.

The taxonomy of speculators into scalpers, day traders, and position traders is useful, but it should not obscure the fact that individuals can have multiple speculative strategies. A particular trader can easily merge his activities as a scalper and as a position trader. Those individuals actively trading in the pits would be expected to take advantage of all types of opportunities that might become available.

ARBITRAGE AND SPECULATIVE PROFITS

In describing the types and activities of speculators, no mention has been made of the kinds of success that speculators might anticipate. Speculative profits are difficult to identify, since one really is not concerned with whether they make accounting profits. The interesting question focuses on whether they make extraordinary profits. This section

TABLE 3.2
Copper Futures Prices on November 10.

Delivery Month	Price (cents per lb.)
July	67.0
September	67.5
December	70.5

specifies the meaning of extraordinary profits and tries to assess the magnitude of those profits.

Academic Arbitrage

The most exciting type of speculative opportunity occurs when one has a chance to engage in *arbitrage.* Speculation usually connotes riskiness, but if an arbitrage opportunity is available, one has the chance to make a sure profit with no investment. According to the academic conception, one engages in arbitrage when he or she transacts so as to guarantee a profit without investment.[11]

The prices in the gold futures market, as shown in Table 3.4 present a golden arbitrage opportunity. On January 1, an arbitrageur notes that the June futures price is $425.60 per troy ounce, and the September futures price is $445.40 per ounce. Further, the total storage cost for an ounce of gold per month is $5.00. This total storage cost includes shipping, warehousing, verification of purity, and the opportunity cost of using funds to store gold. In other words, if one stores gold, it requires money to finance that holding of gold. Since the money to cover the value of the gold cannot be used for anything else while the gold is in storage, it has a real cost. The $5.00 per ounce storage cost includes the opportunity cost of having one's money tied up in gold. For example, if gold costs $400.00 per ounce, and one wishes to store gold, then he or she must finance that $400, as well as pay all of the other storage costs. In this example, all of those costs are included in the $5.00 storage figure.

Confronted with the prices, as shown in Table 3.4 the arbitrage opportunity is clear. The difference between the June and September futures prices is large enough to cover the cost of storing gold from June to September, with a nice profit left over. Table 3.5 shows the transactions necessary to take advantage of the opportunity.

On January 1, the arbitrageur would buy the cheap June futures contract, while simultaneously selling the expensive September contract. At the same time, she would arrange for the storage of the gold from June to September, negotiating a $5.00 per ounce storage cost. On June 1, the arbitrageur could accept the delivery of gold on the June futures contract that she purchased and begin the storage. Having sold a September futures contract, the arbitrageur can deliver the stored gold in fulfill-

TABLE 3.3

A Butterfly Spread in Copper. The copper contract is traded on the Commodity Exchange, Inc. Each contract is for 25,000 lbs.

Cash Market	Futures Market
November 1	Sell 1 July copper contract at 67 cents per lb.
	Buy 2 September copper contracts at 67.5 cents per lb.
	Sell 1 December copper contract at 70.5 cents per lb.
April 15	Buy 1 July copper contract at 65 cents per lb.
	Sell 2 September copper contracts at 67 cents per lb.
	Buy 1 December copper contract at 68.5 cents per lb.

Profits and Losses

July:	2 cents profit
	× 25,000 lbs.
	= $500 (gain)
September:	.5 cents loss
	× 25,000 lbs.
	× 2 contracts
	= $250 (loss)
December:	2 cents profit
	× 25,000 lbs.
	= $500 (gain)
Total Profit:	$750

ment of her commitment. After the process is completed, the wisdom of the strategy is clear. The arbitrageur received $44,540 on September 1. Against this she had paid $42,560 on June 1 and a storage cost of $1500 on September 1. (This storage cost included the cost of financing the $42,560 from June to September.) This left her with a net profit of $480.

It is important to understand why this is an arbitrage situation. After the transactions were entered on January 1, the profit was assured. The transactions of June 1 and September 1 merely carry out the strategy that was executed on January 1. Therefore, the arbitrageur was certain that a profit would be made—there was no investment on her part. The $42,560 needed to pay for the June receipt of the gold was borrowed, and the financing costs for those funds were included in the total storage cost. These transactions represent the exploitation of a genuine arbitrage opportunity, since the arbitrageur secured a certain profit and made no investment.

TABLE 3.4

Gold Futures Prices on January 1. Gold is traded by the Commodity Exchange (COMEX) and by the International Monetary Market (IMM), part of the Chicago Mercantile Exchange (CME). For both exchanges, the contract size is 100 troy ounces.

Delivery Month	Price ($ per troy ounce)
June	425.60
September	445.40
Total storage cost for gold, per oz., per month = $5	

Risk Arbitrage

The concept of arbitrage as generating a sure profit without investent is largely an academic notion. Many active participants in the futures market use a very different idea of arbitrage and hold positions in their firm as arbitrageurs. These traders are typically involved in an activity known in the profession as *risk arbitrage*. Risk arbitrage involves taking a position in the futures market that involves some degree of risk exposure. Because of this risk, risk arbitrage does not fit the academic conception of arbitrage.

Among traders, the word "arbitrage" has so many different meanings that it is not useful to try to give a general definition. In the broadest sense, traders would say that arbitrage opportunities occur when attractive speculative opportunities involving an acceptable degree of risk are available. Somewhat more narrowly, risk arbitrage involves trading in two or more related instruments to take advantage of some perceived pricing discrepancy. Thus, market participants often speak of cash-futures arbitrage. In such a transaction, the risk arbitrageur will hold some position simultaneously in both the cash and futures market for a given commodity. Presumably, the expected return from the risk exposure makes undertaking the risk an attractive proposition for the risk arbitrageur.

The profits that speculators might hope for in the futures markets will come either from academic arbitrage opportunities or from some type of risk position. Academic arbitrage opportunities do not involve risk, so they are not really speculative opportunities at all. Since many futures market participants are speculators, it is important to understand the kinds of profit opportunities that they face. If the opportunities are really lucrative, more people should go into speculation. On the other hand, if the opportunities are chimerical, there may be too many speculators already.

TABLE 3.5

Arbitrage in Gold Futures. The total storage cost includes warehousing, insurance, shipping, etc. It also includes the financing cost of holding the gold.

Cash Market	Futures Market
January 1	
Arrange to store 100 ozs. of gold from June to September at a total storage cost of $5 per oz. per month.	Buy 1 June gold contract at $425.60 per oz. Sell 1 September gold contract at $445.40 per oz.
June 1	
Begin the storage of the gold.	Take delivery of 100 ozs. on the June contract; pay $42,560.
September 1	
Remove gold from storage. Pay storage fee of $1500.	Deliver gold against the September contract. Collect $44,540.

Profit:	$44,540
−	42,560
−	1,500 Storage
−	1,500 Storage
Net profit:	$ 480

FUTURES MARKET EFFICIENCY

To decide how well speculators are doing and the kinds of profits they are making is not easy. If there are spectacularly successful speculators, they should not be expected to be revealing their secrets. Consequently, one must expect any conclusions that can be drawn about speculative activity and its profits to be tentative.

Although not as fully explored as the stock market, the commodity futures markets have received considerable attention, and the level of attention has been increasing recently. Most of these studies attempt to determine whether futures markets are efficient in the sense that the prices in the futures market fully reflect all of the information contained in a given information set. This means that one can develop alternative concepts of efficiency by specifying alternative information sets. Three traditional versions of the efficient markets hypothesis are known as the weak, semi-strong, and strong versions.[12]

The weak form of the efficient markets hypothesis claims that prices in a market fully reflect all information contained in the history of volume and price. The semi-strong version claims that market prices fully reflect all publicly available information. The strong version states that market prices reflect all information, whether public or private. Private information includes information possessed only by corporate insiders and governmental officials.[13]

Weak Form Efficiency

The claims represented by these alternative versions of the efficient markets hypothesis are important since they have definite implications for the success that one can expect as a speculator. If the weak-form version is true, then no information about past or present prices or volume is useful for guiding a speculative strategy. If the futures market is weakly efficient, then one will not be able to find any academic arbitrage opportunities of the type analyzed in Table 3.5. The arbitrage example in the gold futures market required information about current gold futures prices and the price of storage. If prices in the futures market fully reflect all historical price information, then such arbitrage opportunities cannot exist.

Weak-form efficiency also rules out any trading strategies based on the analysis of price trends or other special sequences of prices. Technical analysis remains popular among futures market professionals, but if the futures market is weakly efficient, then technical analysis is without merit. In terms of the example of the Head and Shoulders pattern given in Chapter 2, weak-form market efficiency has a definite implication. If the futures market is weakly efficient, then the occurrence of a Head and Shoulders price pattern, or any other pattern, has no implication whatsoever about what prices are going to do subsequently. The weak-form version of the efficient markets hypothesis clearly presents a challenge to the practices of many working professionals.

Semi-Strong Form Efficiency

An even stronger challenge to current practice in the futures market is made by the semi-strong version. In claiming that all public information is fully reflected in futures prices, the semi-strong version asserts that analysis of any public information is worthless for directing a speculative strategy. This broader information set includes all historical price and volume information, but it also includes a much broader set of information, such as government economic reports, weather reports, political news, crop production statistics, speeches by economists, and so on. Bluntly, the semi-strong version asserts that no public information is useful for the direction of an investment strategy.

The semi-strong efficient markets hypothesis also attacks long-standing practices in the futures markets. Many analysts attempt to predict the movement of futures markets by researching the economic fundamentals. If the semi-strong hypothesis is true, then the analyst who researches crop and weather reports in the corn belt in order to guide trading in corn futures is wasting time. If the corn futures market is efficient in the semi-strong sense, then the corn futures price already reflects any information that could be gathered.

Strong Form Efficiency

The efficient markets hypothesis comes in an even more extreme version—the strong form. According to the strong version of the hypothesis, prices in the futures market fully reflect all information, whether public or private. The strength of this claim is best conveyed by an example. The Chairman of the Federal Reserve Board has continual access to non-public information, such as plans for the conduct of monetary policy. If the strong version of the efficient markets hypothesis is true, then the Chairman's privileged information is useless for earning speculative profits.

Relationship of the Efficient Markets Hypotheses

In understanding the relationship among the three versions of the efficient markets hypothesis, it is important to see the relationship among the three information sets. As one moves toward the strong version of the hypothesis, the information set is continually expanded and contains all of the information in its information set that the weak and semi-strong version do. So if the futures market is efficient in the strong sense, then the market is also efficient in the weak sense and the semi-strong sense.

It is not possible to appraise fully the evidence for and against each of these versions of the efficient markets hypothesis. In order to approach the futures market from a reasonable point of view, one needs to have some appreciation of the evidence regarding each of these claims of efficiency. This is difficult because there is little widespread agreement about the truth of some of the versions of the market efficiency hypothesis, particularly the semi-strong version. With this understanding, the following conclusions represent the current state of knowledge regarding market efficiency. Remember that each of the versions of the hypothesis is under continuing investigation and that revisions of current opinion continue to occur.

The strong form   Evidence supports the conclusion that markets in general, and the futures market in particular, are not efficient in the strong sense. Futures markets do not reflect all public and private information. Individuals or firms with privileged information can use that information to generate super-normal profits. Instead of reciting the litany of evidence against strong-form efficiency, the falsity of this version of market efficiency can be illustrated by examples. Previously, possible actions of the Chairman of the Federal Reserve Board were mentioned as a potential example of violations of strong-form inefficiencies. If the Chairman awakes one morning and decides to generate profits for himself in the interest rate futures market, it is fairly easy for him to do so. If interest rates rise, interest rate futures prices will fall. So, deciding to profit from a rise in interest rates, the Chairman could sell CD futures contracts and then announce a very sharp increase in the discount rate, the rate at which Federal Reserve Banks lend to commercial banks. In this example, this capricious decision is unexpected and would lead to a sharp rise in rates, generating a handsome profit for the Chairman.

As another example, consider a presidential decision to sell an unexpectedly large amount of wheat to the Soviet Union. The decision to sell so much wheat means that the demand for wheat in the coming months will be much larger than expected, and the announcement of the sale will drive spot and futures wheat prices higher. The President or one of his informed staff members could use this private information to obtain a windfall profit in the wheat futures market.

Both of the preceding examples depend on the use of private information by high government officials, but as the next example illustrates, the key point is that the information be private, not that the user be a particularly high official. The U.S. Department of Agriculture gathers data on the growth of crops, including information on the number of acres planted, the expected yields, and other factors that will help determine the final harvest. The collection and preparation of this data requires the efforts of numerous civil servants, some of whom have access to this important information before it is made public. Often the information is well-anticipated, and its announcement does not affect prices. On occasion, however, the information contained in the announcements is really news.

Consider a civil servant working on the report about the coming year's corn harvest who learns that the harvest promises to be spectacularly and unexpectedly successful. When this information becomes public, the futures markets participants will immediately realize that the future supply of corn will be larger than generally anticipated. The unexpected supply will have a negative impact on prices, and the futures price for corn will drop when the announcement is made. The civil servant, possessing the critical information in advance of the public, could sell corn futures and then wait until the announcement causes corn futures prices to fall. Such a strategy would be sure to generate a substantial profit.

In all of these examples, the crucial ingredient is access to private information that is not anticipated by the market. Without doubt, some individuals have access to such information and could use it to gain large profits in the futures markets. Because of this possibility, laws prohibit the use of such information to direct trading strategies. In most cases, the use of inside information is illegal, but some profitable and illegal inside trading occurs and escapes detection. Whether such activities are prevalent or not is not the important question for the strong-form version of the efficient markets hypothesis. The plausibility of these examples, coupled with a significant amount of empirical research, supports the conclusion that the futures market does not reflect all public and private information. Therefore, the futures market appears not to be strong-form efficient.

The weak form   At the other end of the spectrum of efficiency claims stands the weak-form version, which asserts that prices in futures markets fully reflect all previous price and volume data. Here the conclusion that can be drawn is not as sure as was the case for the strong-form version. In general, the bulk of empirical evidence supports the weak efficiency of futures markets, but the evidence is not totally one-sided. Some evidence suggests that small and rare opportunities for *arbitrage* may exist. Yet the case is not clear. Even though the small potential arbitrage profits appear to exist, the cost of continually searching for them may be prohibitive. If these search costs are too high, then there is no violation of weak-form efficiency.[14]

Evidence also exists that there are *trends* in futures prices. However, the strength of these trends is weak and attempts to take advantage of the trends by instituting the appropriate trading rule might not work. The problem with attempting to take advantage of the trends in futures prices lies in the high transaction costs that such strategies would incur. Some researchers believe that the transaction costs would wipe out the potential profits, while others believe that the strategies would still be profitable. If one includes all of the costs, including direct transaction costs and search costs, it is not clear that trend following offers real hope of super-normal profits.

Another recent kind of evidence, called *day-of-the-week* effects, points to another potential violation of weak-form efficiency. The returns on Monday tend to be low relative to returns on other days, particularly Wednesday. This day-of-the-week effect has been corroborated in the stock market, in the money markets, and in the futures market. It currently remains a *market anomaly*—an unexplained peculiarity of price behavior. The magnitude of this day-of-the-week effect appears to be small, particularly in the futures markets. Attempts to take advantage of the effect would generate high transaction costs that would apparently exceed the magnitude of the effect.[15]

From the discussion of these cases, arbitrage opportunities, trends, and day-of-the-week effects, it is clear that research in this area is uncertain. Yet a consistent pattern does emerge, not only in the cases mentioned, but in other research as well. The potential benefits seem to be small, and apparently do not cover the full costs of trying to exploit them. No case of a clearly profitable strategy for using price and volume information has become public. Perhaps such strategies exist and people use them to trade. This possibility makes it difficult to be sure that futures markets are efficient in the weak sense. Based on the research that has been published, it seems fair to conclude that futures prices do reflect all information contained in price and volume data and that the futures markets are efficient in the weak sense.

The semi-strong form   If the conclusion about the weak form of the efficient markets hypothesis was itself weak, the situation becomes even worse when considering the semi-strong version. First, every argument that counts against the weak form also counts against the semi-strong version, since the semi-strong version states that futures prices fully reflect all public information, and the set of public information includes the specific set of information for the weak form, namely, all price and volume data.

Evidence supports the semi-strong efficiency hypothesis. It does not seem possible to use publicly available information to gain a super-normal return. Evidence regarding the semi-strong version, as it specifically pertains to the futures market, is sketchy. In making inferences about semi-strong efficiency, it is necessary to lean on evidence from other markets that have been explored more fully than the futures market, particularly the stock market. An exhaustive amount of research in the stock market has failed to reject the efficiency of the stock market in the semi-strong form.

Even in the stock market, however, the efficiency issue is not resolved. Until a few years ago, the evidence strongly favored semi-strong efficiency. Recent years, by contrast, have witnessed the discovery of several other market anomalies, such as the *small-firm-effect,* the importance of quarterly earnings announcements, and the day-of-the-week effect already mentioned. The small-firm-effect notes that small New York Stock Exchange firms appear to have better returns than their riskiness warrants. If this conclusion is sustained, then one could earn a super-normal return by investing in small firms. The degree of inefficiency, if any, appears to be small, and many researchers deny that the small effect really constitutes a case of market inefficiency.[16]

Other research has focused on the information contained in quarterly earnings announcements. If the market prices fully reflect all public information, then one should not be able to earn super-normal returns by acting on that information when it becomes public. However, evidence suggests that when the quarterly earnings announcements are larger or smaller than their past trend, stock prices will rise or fall over the next few weeks in response to that information. While the use of quarterly earnings announcements may be the best reason to reject the semi-strong efficiency of the stock market, it is far from universally accepted. Most knowledgeable researchers in this field would probably reject the evidence on quarterly earnings announcements. In fact, the majority of researchers continue to support the semi-strong efficiency of the stock market. While the efficiency question is not really a voting matter, the continued support for the semi-strong efficiency of the stock market is a good measure of where the bulk of the evidence lies.[17]

These conclusions about the stock market have strong implications for the semi-strong efficiency hypothesis in the futures market. The stock market continues to be more closely watched by market professionals and continues to receive more research interest. This suggests that the stock market is at least as efficient as the futures market.[18] If we are convinced that the stock market is inefficient in some sense, we can probably conclude that the futures market is inefficient in the same sense. If one believes in the semi-strong efficiency of the stock market, it is reasonable to believe in the semi-strong efficiency of the futures market. More research is needed for a definitive resolution of the efficiency question.

The lack of certainty   The preceding discussion of the different types of market efficiency emerges from more than twenty years of serious research by a wide variety of skilled and highly trained individuals. It may appear odd that there is still no answer, but the lack of a resolution is due to the difficulty of the problem. The inefficiency of a market would be reflected in the chance to earn super-normal profits, as mentioned throughout the discussion of efficiency. To find inefficiencies one must measure the returns that can be earned by a particular strategy against what the normal returns ought to be. This requires some model or way of specifying what the normal returns are.

Since the mid-1960's, the dominant theory of what normal returns are has been the Capital Asset Pricing Model (CAPM). The CAPM says that one should expect to earn the risk-free rate of return on any asset, plus a risk-premium for any non-diversifiable, or unavoidable, risk that the holding of that asset entails. The amount of the non-diversifiable risk in this theory depends on the tendency of a particular asset's returns to vary in the same direction as the market in general. The theory, along with its empirical estimation, gives a market standard for the return one should expect on a particular asset, as a function of the risk-free rate and the asset's non-diversifiable risk.

Recently there has been an attack on the CAPM as the market standard itself.[19] With the appearance of the market anomalies mentioned previously, researchers have two choices. They may accept the CAPM as the standard of normal returns and admit that the market in question is inefficient, or they could maintain that the market is efficient and claim that the CAPM does not give the correct measure of the normal return. Faced with the conflict between the CAPM and market efficiency, many researchers reject the CAPM as providing a market standard.[20] This choice is not simply arbitrary and born of a desire to maintain market efficiency no matter what the cost. Independent and very serious attacks on the CAPM have cast its validity into doubt for other reasons.

Since any test of market efficiency also involves a test of the standard for a normal return, all tests of market efficiency really involve two simultaneous tests. If one finds apparent evidence of inefficiency, then one cannot be sure that the market is inefficient. The real explanation may be that the model of normal returns was at fault. This unfortunate, but apparently inescapable, feature of market efficiency tests accounts for the lack of certain knowledge about market efficiency.

"NORMAL" SPECULATIVE RETURNS

However difficult these tests may be in practice, the kernel idea is clear and sound. If markets are inefficient, then one can earn a super-normal return. In the futures market, the normal returns are clearly higher than is typically acknowledged, as the following reasoning process indicates.

To trade futures on a major exchange one must own a seat, or secure the use of a seat from one who does own one. Second, trading on the exchange involves a commitment of time and energy. Since the time and energy is being committed to trading, it canot be applied elsewhere to earn a return. Third, trading futures necessarily involves a degree of risk. Most people are unwilling to take risks with money unless they believe the potential returns from those risks are high enough to make the risks worthwhile. With these ideas in mind, consider a trader on a major exchange who owns her own seat and treats trading as a job, going to the exchange each working day. What kind of income must she expect to make the entire enterprise reasonable from a financial point of view?

The first consideration is the value of the seat that she needs to have in order to trade. As mentioned in Chapter 1, seats on the exchanges are traded in a market and have recently sold in the range of $200,000 to $340,000.[21] Taking a conservative figure of $200,000, it is clear that our trader loses the use of $200,000 in virtue of buying her seat. Assume that an equally risky investment would return a modest 12 percent. In order to cover the cost of her seat, the trader must make $24,000 per year. Second, it must also be acknowledged that the trader is committing her time to trading. After all, she could hold another job if she were not trading. Most of the traders are people of competence and executive ability, and trading is grueling and nerve-wracking work with long hours that go beyond the limited trading times. Our trader, having exhibited a willingness to work as hard as a trader must work and with the talents necessary to succeed as a trader, could expect to earn a relatively handsome salary in some other capacity, perhaps $50,000 per year would be realistic and conservative.

In addition to the foregone opportunities of investing the price of her seat elsewhere and of taking alternative employment, the high risk of trading must also be acknowledged. Relative to trading, a salaried position is very secure. Being risk-averse, the trader would reasonably expect some compensation for her additional risk exposure. The amount of compensation is very difficult to quantify and clearly depends on her personal risk tolerance. Finally, the character of a trader's work needs to be considered somewhat more fully. Trading is extremely demanding, both physically and mentally. A casual survey of the trading pits reveals few elderly participants. From conversations with many traders, it is clear that they do not generally expect to be trading past the age of forty.[22] As another indicator of the level of stress one need only consult the *Wall Street Journal,* which has frequent articles on the problems of traders.

They lose their voices from shouting and need voice coaches, they occasionally sustain physical injuries, and sometimes suffer mental disturbances as a result of the stress in their work.[23] While many traders are attracted by the excitement of the pits, many people would demand high compensation for working under such conditions. The extreme physical and psychic demands are difficult to value in terms of dollars, but they are real costs.

Table 3.6 summarizes these costs based on the figures used previously. If these figures are accepted as reasonable, then the full time trader with an income of anything less than $74,000 per year can be considered a failure. Included in the computation of her income must be the change in the value of the exchange seat. If the trader typically makes less than $74,000, she could do better by selling her seat, investing those funds, taking a secure job, and avoiding the high risk, stress, and strain associated with futures trading.

In thinking about trading, there is a tendency to regard any profit as having been obtained for free. In terms of efficiency, Table 3.6 shows that a trader should make at least $74,000 per year without there being the slightest hint that super-normal profits are being captured. Many traders make very handsome incomes and live quite well, when they are not on the trading floor. This fact alone does not warrant the conclusion that trading futures contracts is an easy way to get rich quickly. The traders have high costs to cover before they reach the point at which they start to make super-normal profits. The chance to speculate on futures may not be the way to easy street.

HEDGING

In contrast to the speculator. the hedger tries to reduce risk by entering the futures market with a pre-existing risk position. If he trades futures contracts on commodities in which he has no initial position, then he cannot be a hedger. Having a position, in this case, does not mean that he must actually own a commodity. An individual or firm who anticipates the need for a certain commodity in the future or a person who plans to acquire a certain commodity later also has a postion in that commodity.

An Anticipatory Hedge

The idea that you may be at risk in a certain commodity without actually owning it may be a confusing idea to some. Yet consider the following example. Silver is an essential input for the production of most types of photographic films and papers, and the price of silver is quite volatile. For a manufacturer of film, there is considerable risk that profits could be dramatically affected by fluctuations in the price of silver. If produc-

TABLE 3.6
Trader's Expected Income (annually).

Resource	Annual Amount
Use of money to secure seat	$24,000
Foregone alternative employment	50,000
Additional risk undertaken	?
Additional stress and strain	?
Total:	$74,000 + ?

tion schedules are to be maintained, it is absolutely essential that silver be acquired on a regular basis in large quantities. Assume that the film manufacturer needs 50,000 troy ounces of silver in two months and then confronts the silver prices shown in Table 3.7 on May 10. The current spot price is 1052.5 cents per ounce, and the price of the July futures contract lies above that at 1068., with the September futures contract trading at 1084.

Fearing that silver prices may rise unexpectedly, the film manufacturer decides that the price of 1068. is acceptable for the silver that he will need in July. He realizes that it is hopeless to buy the silver on the spot market at 1052.5 and to store the silver for two months. The price differential of 15.5 cents per ounce would not cover his storage cost. Also, the manufacturer will receive an acceptable level of profits even if he pays 1068. for the silver to be delivered in July. To pay a price higher than 1068., however, could jeopardize profitability seriously. With these reasons in mind, he decides to enter the futures market to hedge against the possibility of future unexpected increase in prices, and accordingly, he enters the trades shown in Table 3.8.

Taking the futures price as the best estimate of the future spot price, the manufacturer expects to pay 1068. cents per ounce for silver in the spot market two months from now in July. At the same time, he buys ten 5000 ounce July futures contracts at 1068. cents per ounce. Since he buys a futures contract in order to hedge, this transaction is known as a *long hedge*. Time passes and, by July, the spot price of silver has risen to 1071. cents per ounce, three cents higher than expected. Needing the silver, the manufacturer purchases the silver on the spot market, paying a total of $535,500, which is $1500 more than he had expected. Since the futures contract is about to mature, the futures price must equal the spot price, so the film manufacturer is able to sell his ten futures contracts at the same price of 1071. cents per ounce, making a three cent profit on each ounce, and a total profit of $1500 on the futures position. The cash and futures results net out to zero. In the cash market, the price was $1500 more than expected, but there was an offsetting futures profit of $1500, which generated a net wealth change of zero.

TABLE 3.7
Silver Prices, May 10. Silver futures are traded by the COMEX and the CBT in units of 5000 troy ounces per contract, and by the CBT and the MidAmerica Commodity Exchange for contracts of 1000 troy ounces. Additionally, the New York Mercantile Exchange trades a contract on U.S. silver coins.

Contract	Price (cents per troy oz.)
Spot	1052.5
July	1068.0
September	1084.0

The Reversing Trade

One peculiar feature of these transactions is that the manufacturer did not accept delivery on the futures contract but engaged in a reversing trade instead. Rather than accepting delivery on a contract, it usually is better to reverse the trade since this saves on transaction costs and administrative difficulties. The physical commodity can be obtained from the normal suppliers. Notice also that the same result could have been achieved in this example by accepting delivery. If delivery were accepted on the futures contract, the silver would have been secured at a price of 1068., which is what happened when the reversing trade was used.

A Short Hedge

Although this example involved the purchase of a futures contract, hedges do not necessarily involve long futures positions. To consider the advantages of a short hedge, in which one sells futures contracts, assume the same silver prices and a date of May 10. A Nevada silver mine owner is concerned about the price of silver, since she wants to be able to plan for the profitability of her firm. If silver prices fall, she may be forced to suspend production. Given the current level of production, she expects to have about 50,000 ounces of silver ready for shipment in two months. Considering the silver prices shown in Table 3.7, she decides that she would be satisfied to receive 1068. cents per ounce for her silver.

To assure that sale price for her silver, the miner decides to enter the silver futures market to avoid the risk that silver prices might fall in the next two months. The miner's transactions are shown in Table 3.9 and are simply the mirror image of the film manufacturer's transactions. Anticipating the need to sell 50,000 ounces of silver in two months, the mine operator sells 105,000 ounce futures contracts for the July delivery at 1068. cents per ounce. On July 10, with silver prices being at 1071. cents per ounce, the silver is sold and the miner receives $535,000, which is $1500 more than she originally expected. In the futures market, however, the miner suffers an offsetting loss. The futures contracts she sold at

TABLE 3.8

A Long Hedge in Silver.

Cash Market	Futures Market
May 10	
Anticipates the need for 50,000 troy ounces in two months and expects to pay 1068 cents per ounce, or a total of $534,000	Buys ten 5000 troy ounce July futures contracts at 1068 cents per ounce
July 10	
The spot price of silver is now 1071. The manufacturer buys 50,000 ounces, paying $535,000	Since the futures contract is at maturity, the futures and spot prices are equal, and the ten contracts are sold at 1071.
Opportunity Loss: ($1,500)	*Futures profit:* $1,500
Net Wealth Change = 0	

1068., she now buys back in July at 1071. cents per ounce. Once again, the profits and losses in the two markets offset each other, and result in a net wealth change of zero.

Viewing the results from the vantage point of July, it is clear that the miner would have been $1500 richer if she had not hedged. She would have received $1500 more than originally expected and would have incurred no loss in the futures market. However, it does not follow that she was unwise to hedge. In hedging, the miner and the film manufacturer both decided that the futures price was an acceptable price at which to complete the transaction in July, and that was exactly the price they got.

Do Hedgers Need Speculators?

Hedging is often viewed as the purchasing of insurance. Hedgers trade in the futures market and speculators bear the risk that the hedgers are trying to avoid. Naturally, the speculators demand some compensation for this service. In Chapter 2, the theories of normal backwardation and the contango were considered as explanations of the way in which speculators might receive their compensation. In considering the two sides of the silver example, no speculators were needed. The long and short hedgers balanced each other out perfectly. While the example is artificial, it illustrates an important point. Hedgers, as a group, need speculators to bear the risk only for the mismatch between the long and short hedgers. In most markets, some hedgers will be long and others short. To the extent that their positions match, the speculators are not needed for the job of bearing risk. This helps explain why the risk premia, if there are any, are not large. It does not suggest that speculators are not important. Even if they were not needed by the hedgers for risk bearing, speculators would still play an important role in the futures market by providing liquidity.

TABLE 3.9
A Short Hedge in Silver.

Cash Market	Futures Market
May 10	
Anticipates the sale of 50,000 troy ounces of silver in two months and expects to receive 1068. cents per ounce, or a total of $534,000.	Sells 10 5000 troy ounce July futures contracts at 1068. cents per ounce.
July 10	
The spot price of silver is now 1071., and the miner sells 50,000 ounces, receiving $535,000.	Buys 10 contracts at 1071.
Profit: $1500	*Loss:* ($1500)

Net Wealth Change = 0

Cross-Hedging

In the silver examples, the hedgers' needs were perfectly matched with the institutional features of the silver markets. The goods in question were exactly the same goods traded on the futures market, the amounts matched the futures contract amounts, and the hedging horizons of the miner and film manufacturer matched the delivery date for the futures contract. In actual hedging applications, it will be rare for all factors to match so well. In most cases the hedged and hedging positions will differ in (1) time span covered, (2) the amount of the commodity, or (3) the particular characteristics of the goods. In such cases, the hedge will be a *cross-hedge.* Cross-hedging is often particularly problematic in the interest rate futures market. Financial instruments are extremely varied in their characteristics, such as risk level, maturity, and coupon rate. By contrast, really active futures contracts are only traded on six different types of interest bearing securities.

When the characteristics of the position to be hedged do not perfectly match the characteristics of the futures contract used for the hedging, care must be taken to trade the right number and kind of futures contract to control the risk in the hedged position as much as possible. In general, we cannot expect a cross-hedge to be as effective in reducing risk as a direct hedge. To deal with problems in cross-hedging, more sophisticated techniques have been developed, and these are discussed and illustrated in Chapters 4 and 5.

Hedging Uncertain Quantities

Another simplifying feature of the silver example was the assumption that both parties were hedging a known quantity of silver. Realistically, the miner may not know with certainty how much silver will be available during the next two months. The uncertainty can be even more acute. Consider a farmer about to plant his wheat crop who wants to hedge his harvest in the futures market. The size of his harvest could be uncertain, and it might be very difficult for him to know how many futures contracts to trade. Caution is important in such cases because it is possible to increase the riskiness of one's position by poor planning of hedges.

The wheat farmer would be hedging against lower than expected wheat prices by selling futures contracts. Assume that he sells a number of contracts to cover his expected harvest. Then a drought strikes, and his harvest is worse than expected. As a result, he has sold too many futures contracts. If his harvest was poor due to the drought, then it is likely that the whole wheat harvest was poor, causing there to be less wheat available than was expected originally. This shortfall in the wheat harvest is likely to lead to higher than expected prices, which could have very disastrous consequences for the farmer. Since the harvest is poor, the farmer has obviously suffered a loss due to the drought. With futures prices rising unexpectedly and the farmer holding a short position, he will also suffer a loss in the futures market. In such a situation, the farmer has inadvertently increased the riskiness of his position by his attempt to hedge. While such occurrences are infrequent, they can be devastating.[24] The possibility of such disasters emphasizes a need for a thorough understanding of the markets in question and the risk characteristics of the position being hedged and the futures contracts used in hedging. The next chapter builds such an understanding by considering the traditional futures markets in agricultural and metalurgical commodities.

NOTES

1. This argument can be expressed more formally by using the theory of complete markets. A market is complete if we can transact for any desired pattern of payoffs. Complete market theory has often been developed by using a *state preference* framework of analysis. In the state preference approach, the objects of choice are defined as payoffs under certain *states of nature*. The states of nature are defined so that every possible occurrence falls under one, and only one, state of nature. In this framework, a market is complete if and only if we can contract for a payoff in any state, or combination of states, of nature. (For a development of the state preference framework, see S. Myers. "A Time State-Preference Model of Security Valuation," *Journal of Financial and Quantitative Analysis,* March, 1968.)

    If markets are complete, then we can freeely contract for the set of payoffs that best fits our needs. The more nearly complete markets are, the more society benefits from the ability to fit payoffs to individuals' desired outcomes. (For a highly mathematical development of complete markets under a state-preference approach, see G. Debreu.

Theory of Value, New Haven: Yale University Press, 1959. With this background, the argument for futures markets is clear: they contribute to the welfare of society by making financial markets more nearly complete.

2. Consistent with the discussion of Chapter 2, futures prices are regarded as market consensus forecasts.

3. The furniture manufacturer might also take the step of attempting to "lock-in" these "discovered" prices by buying futures contracts for plywood. Such a step is a small one and emphasizes the initimate connection between price discovery and hedging.

4. For a more formal treatment of the property of *unbiasedness* in estimators, see J. Kmenta. *Elements of Econometrics,* New York: Macmillan.

5. For an assessment of the accuracy of futures prices as forecasts of expected future spot prices, see R. Kolb, G. Gay, and J. Jordan. "Futures Prices and Expected Future Spot Prices," *Review of Research in Futures Markets,* 1983, *2,* 110–123.

6. See Richard Levich. "Currency Forecasters Lose Their Way," *Euromoney,* August 1983, 140–147. Chapter 6 discusses the forecasting accuracy of professional currency forecasters in more detail.

7. Some authors attempt to distinguish speculators from investors. The usual difference between the two definitions seems to lie in their respective attitudes toward risk and the length of time they expect to hold their positions. Here, speculators are contrasted only with hedgers, so any investor in the futures market, no matter how conservative, would be regarded as a speculator for the purposes of this book.

8. On the floor of the exchanges, different commodities are traded in different *pits.* A pit is really an area of the floor, surrounded by steps or risers, which are usually about five steps high. This arrangement allows traders to see and communicate with each other. The term "pit" is really synonomous with trading in futures, as indicated by the title of Frank Norris' novel, *The Pit,* which is the story of futures trading in wheat.

9. As discussed in Chapter 1, high liquidity is also crucial in the survival of a particular futures contract. In competing contracts, the one with the initially greater liquidity has a much higher probability of success.

10. In any event, visitors to the exchanges are allowed on the floor only for short periods of time and under the supervision of exchange personnel. Access to the floor near the close of trading is more highly restricted because as trading nears its close, the level of activity increases dramatically.

11. By the definition of speculation given here, arbitrageurs are not speculators. The true arbitrageur does not increase his risk by entering the futures market. Instead, he is trading to guarantee a riskless profit, with no investment.

12. These three versions of the efficient markets hypothesis were first articulated by E. Fama. "Efficient Capital Markets: Theory and Empirical Work," *Journal of Finance,* May 1970, 383–417. For a more recent survey of the efficient markets literature, see T. Copeland and F. Weston. *Financial Theory and Corporate Policy,* Second Edition Reading, MA: Addison Wesley, 1983.

13. As will become clear, the weak form efficient markets hypothesis attacks technical analysis, while the semi-strong version opposes fundamental

analysis. Since financial futures markets have been the subject of the most recent testing of the efficient markets hypothesis, a full discussion of efficient markets is reserved for Chapter 5. Some of the classic studies in futures market efficiency for non-financial futures are: K. Dusak. "Futures Trading and Investor Returns: An Investigation of Commodity Market Risk Premiums," *Journal of Political Economy,* November 1973, 1387–1406; R. Stevenson and R. Bear. "Commodity Futures: Trends or Random Walks?" *Journal of Finance,* March 1970, 65–81; S. Smidt. "A Test of the Serial Independence of Price Changes in Soybean Futures," *Food Research Institute Studies,* 1965, *5,* 41–49; Z. Bodie and V. Rosansky. "Risk and Return in Commodity Futures," *Financial Analysts Journal,* May–June 1980, 27–39; and T. Cargill and G. Rausser. "Temporal Price Behavior in Commodity Futures Markets," *Journal of Finance,* September 1975, 1043–1053. These are some of the most famous of many studies.

14. The concept of market efficiency entered the popular culture through the back door with the movie, *Trading Places,* starring Eddie Murphy and Dan Ackroyd. Murphy and Ackroyd acquire some private information about the size of the orange crop by getting early access to a government crop report. Their use of the crop report constitutes the use of private information to earn a super-normal profit trading orange juice futures and is a violation of strong form market efficiency. This information allows them to bankrupt the "bad guys" and to retire to a Pacific island paradise.

15. While many studies of the day-of-the-week effect for the stock market have appeared, there is only one for the futures market. See R. Chiang and C. Tapley. "Day of the Week Effects and the Futures Market," forthcoming in *Review of Research in Futures Markets.*

16. See M. Reinganum. "A Direct Test of Roll's Conjecture on the Firm Size Effect," *Journal of Finance,* March 1982, 27–35.

17. See O. Joy and C. Jones. "Earnings Reports and Market Efficiencies: An Analysis of Contrary Evidence," *Journal of Financial Research,* Summer 1979, 51–64.

18. This conclusion presupposes that active information gathering, and attempts to use that information in speculation, helps make a market efficient.

19. See R. Roll. "A Critique of the Asset Pricing Theory's Tests," *Journal of Financial Economics,* 1977, *4,* 129–176 and S. Ross. "The Current Status of the Capital Asset Pricing Model (CAPM)," *Journal of Finance,* June 1978, 885–901.

20. For a very frank statement of this choice, and a grasp of the market efficiency horn of the dilemma, see M. Reinganum. "Abnormal Returns in Small Firm Portfolios," *Financial Analysts Journal,* March–April 1981, 52–56.

21. Traditionally, the most highly valued seats have been those on the Chicago Board of Trade. In late 1982, a seat on the Chicago Mercantile Exchange cost more than a Chicago Board of Trade seat for the first time in history. The prices of these seats are very volatile. For example, seats on the International Monetary Market of the Chicago Mercantile Exchange ranged in price from $150,000 to $240,000 in 1981. The value of the seats responds very directly to the level of trading at the exchange, which is itself quite variable.

22. The youthfulness of the traders is particularly apparent in the new markets, such as the interest rate futures market. Relatively, the older, more traditional commodities are traded by older traders.

23. Many traders will not leave the trading pit during the six to seven hour trading session, even to go to the bathroom. It is simply too risky to leave the trading floor for even a short period of time. This indicates the level of stress in the pits.

24. See R. Conroy and R. Rendleman. "Hedging When Quantity is Uncertain," (an address presented at the Southern Finance Association, November 1982), for an elaboration and development of this idea.

4 Agricultural and Metallurgical Futures Contracts

INTRODUCTION

The first three chapters covered general information. With this chapter we begin analyzing particular segments of the futures market. In accordance with the pattern of historical development, we begin with the traditional futures contracts, those written on agricultural and metallurgical commodities. In spite of the fact that these types of contracts are typically regarded as "traditional" futures contracts, it will become apparent that there has been considerable innovation in this field, particularly with the development of contracts on perishable and growing commodities.

Much of this chapter, as well as those that follow, elaborates themes that were introduced in the first three chapters, and develops those themes with reference to specific commodities. The idea of storage was introduced in chapters 2 and 3 but in that discussion storage costs were implicitly assumed to be constant. Specifically, it was assumed that storage costs were constant at the margin, so that one could store as much as was desired without affecting the price of storage. Of course, that assumption is not always reasonable, so it must be relaxed for a full understanding of the role of storage in futures markets. Much of this chapter elaborates the concept of storage and differences in its application to particular commodities.

Also, the discussion of the first three chapters treated commodities as though they were constantly renewed and indefinitely storable. This is approximately true of petroleum products and metallurgical commodities, such as gold. Obviously, such a commodity is easier to understand than one that has the added complication of only seasonal availability, such as those whose supply is renewed periodically at harvest. Accordingly, we will focus first on such simpler commodities and then illustrate certain important features of the futures market with one of the most exciting of all commodities, gold.

After considering constantly renewable and indefinitely storable commodities, the next step is to consider those that are only periodically renewed, but that can be stored well for long periods. The best examples of this type of commodity are the grains, particularly corn, wheat, and the soya complex. Such commodities can be considered under the assumptions either that the crop size is constant or that it varies in size. Such variations in size have definite impacts of the price structure in these markets. One feature of the grains that makes them very interesting is their inter-substitutability. In a certain sense, grains are sold on the basis of their protein content, especially for their use as animal feeds. In animal feeding, taste and texture are not nearly as important as protein content, and the demand for animal feed depends very closely on factors such as the price per unit of protein.

Some commodities exhibit peculiar properties of storage. The storage life of fresh eggs is quite short, so it properly represents a perishable commodity.[1] Its storage characteristics also affect the price structure in its market in certain interesting ways. Most stored commodities lose some fraction of their value over the storage period. This could be due to rats eating grain, or eggs rotting, or simply a loss in moisture content. This "shrinkage" is a fact of life, but in at least one commodity the pattern is reversible. Futures contracts are traded on cattle, which raises the possibility that they could be accepted on delivery of a futures contract, and "stored," while being fed. They could then be delivered on a later contract. In such a case, it is possible that the increase in the value of the cattle could exceed the storage costs. One way of analyzing this phenomenon is to treat cattle as a commodity with possible negative storage costs.

All of these different types of commodities have their own peculiarities. In spite of the differences, these commodities are more alike than different. Understanding these commodities, including their similarities and differences, paves the way for an analysis of the truly different commodities to be considered in the subsequent chapters, such as bonds, currencies, and stocks.[2]

CONSTANTLY RENEWABLE AND INDEFINITELY STORABLE COMMODITIES

Cash and Futures Prices and Their Relationship

In addressing those commodities that are constantly renewable and indefinitely storable, the focus is clearly on metallurgical commodities and petroleum. Gold will be used as a particular commodity to consider, since it meets those characteristics of storability and renewability. Also, gold has a fascination unparalleled by any other good. In considering gold, or any other commodity, as constantly renewable and indefinitely storable, we must realize that two assumptions are being made. Nothing is indefinitely storable or constantly renewable. But gold, and similar

TABLE 4.1

High and Low Months of Cash Gold Prices.

Year	High	Low
1975	February	December
1976	December	August
1977	November	January
1978	October	January
1979	December	January
1980	September	May
1981	January	July

SOURCE: *Commodity Year Book,* 1982, 159. Prices are based on monthly averages.

commodities, approximate that ideal more closely than other goods, such as foodstuffs. In fact, the presumed "incorruptibility" of gold has been one of its primary characteristics that has made holding gold so attractive over the centuries.[3] Just as gold is not incorruptible, it is not constantly renewable, in a literal sense; the earthly supply of gold is finite. As is the case with virtually all extractive industries, gold mining started out exploiting the most available sources first. Whereas one might have been able to pick up gold nuggets in California rivers in the last century, current gold mining techniques are much less exciting. The easy gold is gone and must now be extracted by using painstaking and costly methods.

Nonetheless, gold is constantly renewable in a sense in which wheat is not. The extraction of gold follows a continuous process. Each hour of a mine's operation brings forth a relatively uniform quantity of gold. Similarly, each hour an oil well pumps or a refinery operates yields a fairly constant flow of crude oil or gasoline. By contrast, the production of wheat is very discrete. The wheat industry, or at least certain segments of it, pass months without the extraction of any product. Wheat production is lumpy in that it all comes to the market at the harvest. Whether production of a good follows a continuous or flowing process, like gold or petroleum, or a discrete process, like wheat, matters a great deal for the price structure in a market. If the production is continuous, prices will not tend to exhibit much of a seasonal pattern. Cash wheat prices, on the other hand, exhibit strong seasonal tendencies, as is illustrated in the next section.

One of the most important factors in causing seasonal price trends in a commodity is a production process that is discontinuous. Since gold does not depend on a harvest, its production is fairly smooth, at least on a world-wide basis. It is true that gold production does exhibit certain seasonal patterns, at least considering the United States in isolation. For example, Alaska's gold mines have virtually no production in the winter months. Table 4.1 shows the months which have had the highest and

FIGURE 4.1

Gold Cash Prices—London

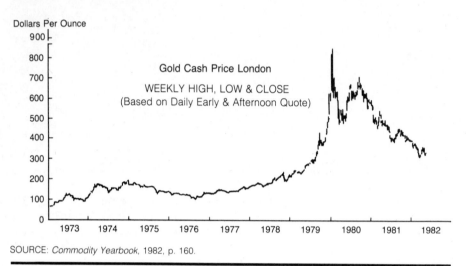

SOURCE: *Commodity Yearbook*, 1982, p. 160.

lowest average gold prices for the last few years. Out of seven years, the highest average price fell in six different months. For the lowest average monthly price, there was a tendency for January to have a disproportionately high number of occurrences, relative to a random distribution. However, this apparent tendency is easily explained. With gold prices tending to rise over this period, 1975–1981, it would be expected that lower prices would occur early in the year. In fact, if gold prices were constantly going up, then the low price would always occur in January and the high price in December. But that would still not be an indication of seasonality. Figure 4.1 shows the cash price of gold, based on London quotations, for the period 1973–1982. No apparent seasonal trend is revealed there.[4] Also, the tendency for January to have the lowest monthly average price in the years 1977–79 is easily explained by the major increase in price that occurred over this period.

If there is no reason to expect a seasonal fluctuation in the price of gold, what should the price of gold, and gold futures, look like over time? To answer this question, assume that the production of a commodity equals its consumption and there is no inflationary pressure on the price. For such a case, the theoretical price and inventory relationships are shown in Figure 4.2. The top panel shows the behavior of the inventory of the commodity over time. Since production is assumed to equal consumption, and production exhibits no seasonal component, the inventory level must remain constant. The society is consuming only what it produces. The corresponding price behavior is shown in the bottom panels. First, the cash price will remain constant. This is insured by

FIGURE 4.2

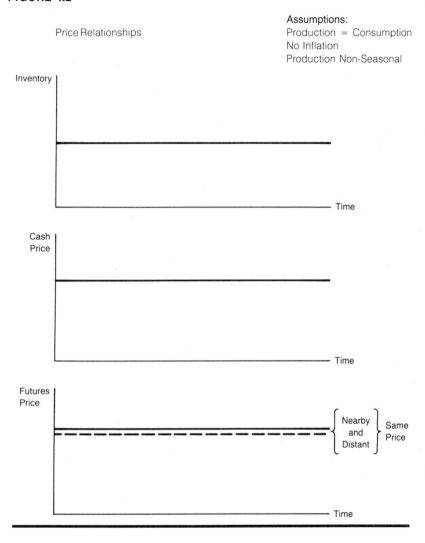

Price Relationships

Assumptions:
Production = Consumption
No Inflation
Production Non-Seasonal

the assumption that there is no inflation and that the future is certain. With no inflation, and no anticipated changes in the supply-demand relationship for the good being analyzed, there is no reason to expect the cash price of the commodity to change.

This expectation that cash prices will be relatively constant has an important impact on the futures prices, which are shown in the last graph. As argued in Chapter 2, futures prices are going to depend primarily upon expectations of future cash prices and the costs of storage. To reflect these different ideas, the graph for the futures prices shows both the nearby contract, indicated by the solid line, and a distant contract, whose price is shown by the dotted line. If cash prices are assumed to be constant, then one should also expect the futures prices to be constant and at the same level as the cash price. In the graph this is reflected by the nearby and distant futures contract having the same price level. Since it has been assumed that future prices are known with certainty, the cash and futures prices would have to be exactly equal.

What about the idea of storage? Why should any of the commodity be stored in such a situation? With no expectation of rising prices, there is no reason to hold the commodity for speculation. (Goods held in storage for speculation are referred to as *speculative balances,* particularly when the good stored is cash.) In these situations, the good is stored only for convenience.[5] Also, the spread between the distant and nearby futures contract should be very small or non-existent, as is reflected in the graph.

When some of these assumptions are relaxed, the price movements become more realistic, but also more complicated. Drop the assumption that production equals consumption, but continue to assume that the commodity in question has no seasonal fluctuation in production. Also, for the moment, assume that the changes in cash prices that are going to come about as a result of production exceeding consumption are known in advance. For such assumptions, the corresponding inventory and price movements over time are shown in Figure 4.3. With production exceeding consumption, the amount of the good in inventory must be increasing, as is shown in the first graph of the Figure. With supply rising relative to demand, and in the absence of any pervasive inflationary pressures, the price of the cash commodity should be falling, as reflected by the second graph.

Things become more interesting when the futures prices are considered. Assuming that the future price movements for the cash commodity are correctly anticipated, the futures prices should behave in a manner consistent with the third graph of the Figure. The nearby futures price should lie above the price of the distant contract. This is consistent with the fact that cash prices are expected to decrease over time. If futures prices are expected future spot prices, then the distant futures contract must trade at a lower price than the nearby contract. The spread between the two futures contracts is limited, of course, to the cost of carrying the commodity for the time between the maturity dates of the two futures contracts. Further, both futures prices should lie below the current cash price. The futures prices will be equal, under the present assumptions, to the cash prices that will prevail on their maturity dates. But since the cash price will be falling over this period, the current cash price must lie above the futures prices. One of the most interesting features of these price movements over the period under examination is the fact that the futures prices should not change, even though the cash price is falling. If the market has the correct price expectations, then the futures price should equal the future cash price, and need not change over time.

FIGURE 4.3

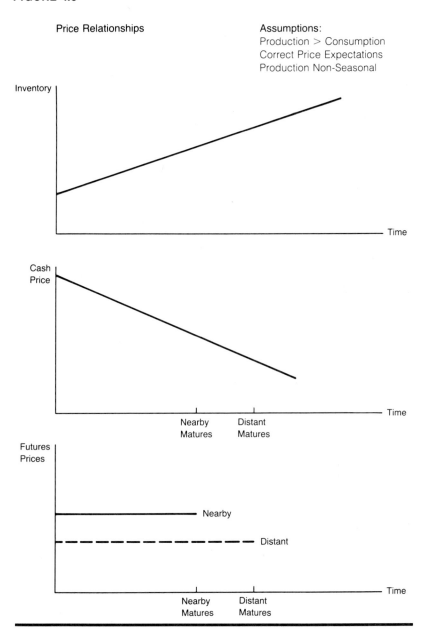

Price Relationships

Assumptions:
Production > Consumption
Correct Price Expectations
Production Non-Seasonal

Of course, as has already been considered in Chapter 2, price expectations are often in error. Figure 4.4 considers the influence of erroneous price expectations on the pattern of prices when the other assumptions remain in place. Assume that the prices that are initially expected prove to be lower than the actual prices that materialize. In the exhibit, this possibility is reflected by the actual accumulation of inventory being less than anticipated. This could, in turn, be due to many reasons, such as higher than anticipated demand, or poor production. In the inventory graph, this is reflected by the accumulated inventory falling below the originally expected inventory. This has an impact on the cash price of the commodity, such that the actual price of the good turns out to be higher than expected. The erroneous expectations about cash prices have an impact in the futures market also. Since the cash prices are higher than originally anticipated, the futures prices must rise as well, and this is reflected by the third graph. In general, futures prices will rise or fall over their life only when initial expectations are corrected or in the presence of a risk premium.

Gold Production and Inventories

Which scenario best fits the case of gold? As Table 4.2 shows, the non-Communist world has produced or bought slightly more gold than it has consumed over the period from 1969–1979. Gold statistics are often stated in terms of *fabrication,* rather than consumption. Here fabrication reflects the amount of gold that is transformed from *bullion* to some other application, such as jewelry, dental work, electronic components, coins, and medallions. Not all of such gold is lost from the world stock, since gold is so highly recoverable. Nonetheless, holdings of gold have varied considerably over the same period. As Figure 4.5 shows, non-communist holdings of both bullion and fabricated gold have fluctuated dramatically over the period 1969–1980. The tremendous rise in gold prices over this period cannot be attributed to drastically waning supplies, but rather, to two primary factors. First, the value of the dollar relative to other world currencies has fallen dramatically over the decade of the seventies, but with a strong comeback in the early 1980s. With strong demand from other countries, this insures that the price of gold will rise. A second and related factor is the high inflation experienced by the dollar; it is now clear that the price of gold should have risen over this period. Obviously, both of these trends were the result of a single underlying factor, the dramatic increase in the world price of oil.

If this premise is correct, how should the price of gold futures have behaved over the same period? The answer to this question depends crucially on the extent to which the price changes in gold were anticipated. Clearly, the dominant economic factor of inflation was poorly anticipated in the mid to late 1970s. (This is perhaps best reflected by the negative real returns on risk free bonds over this period.) If expectations of future gold prices were generally less than the subsequent actual prices, then gold futures prices should have risen over the period of the 1970s. As is well known and shown in Figure 4.6, gold futures prices exhibited the same dramatic increase in prices that was found in the cash

FIGURE 4.4

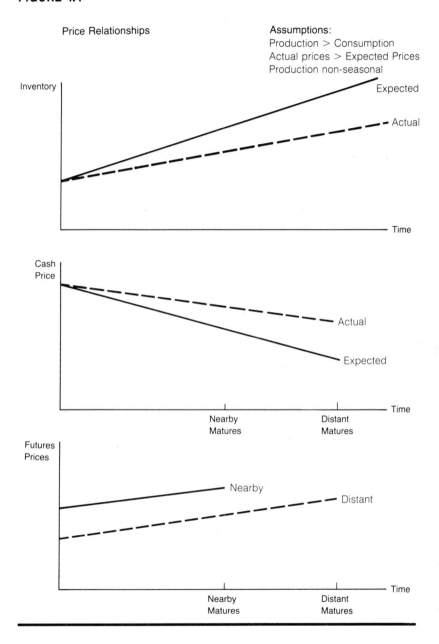

Price Relationships

Assumptions:
Production > Consumption
Actual prices > Expected Prices
Production non-seasonal

commodity. Figure 4.6 plots the price of the nearby futures contract, which is highly correlated with the cash price. Taking account of the difference in scale in the two graphs, it is apparent that their prices moved together very closely.

FIGURE 4.5
Gold Holdings, 1968–1980.

Gold holdings since 1968
(changes in fabricated gold and bullion
holdings within the non-communist private sector)

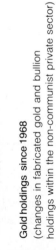

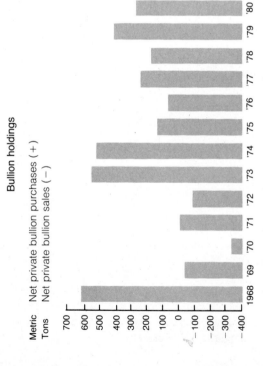

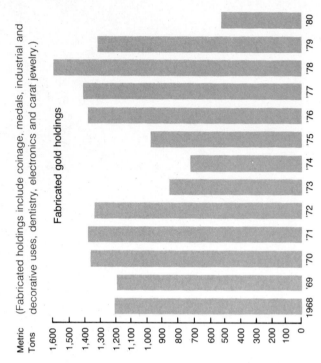

Source: *Commodities Magazine*, March 1982. p. 45.

TABLE 4.2
Gold Production and Usage, 1969–1980 (in metric tonnes).

Year	Production (non-communist)	East Bloc Trade	Fabrication
1969	1252.1	− 15	1200
1970	1273.6	− 3	1376
1971	1235.6	54	1388
1972	1183.6	213	1344
1973	1120.9	275	860
1974	1006.6	220	735
1975	953.9	149	983
1976	969.1	412	1384
1977	971.8	401	1420
1978	980.3	410	1596
1979	961.3	199	521
	12,851.8	2405	14,122

SOURCE: *IMM Yearbook*, 1981, 492–3.

Speculation in Gold and Gold Futures

As reflected in Figures 4.1 and 4.6, gold and gold futures offer chances for enormous profit and loss. This discussion considers two basically different speculative strategies and some ideas about how they might be implemented. First, an extended example of a technically based trading strategy is given, based on an article in *Commodities: The Magazine of Futures Trading.* Second, gold is considered in its role within a portfolio. After these two opportunities are considered, the best way to implement either strategy will be reviewed.

The discussion of technical analysis presented here relies on an article by Pamela Aden-Ayales and Mary Ann Aden-Harter, entitled, "Gold Holds Explosive Potential," which appeared in the April 1982 issue of *Commodities.*[7] The article is not strictly based on technical analysis, as it relies heavily on the expectation of continued increases in the U.S. national debt and a high level of accompanying inflation to support its conclusions. Against that background, the authors believe that gold prices follow certain cycles. "Each cyclical trough is higher than the previous trough, thus forming a large, upward-moving channel with each progressive inflationary cycle becoming more volatile" (p. 50). This idea is illustrated by a chart that appears in their paper and is here reproduced as Figure 4.7. The authors believe that gold follows a basically cyclical process and that strong similarities in the cycles persist, with the cycles lasting approximately 5.5 years. Each cycle consists of a *cyclical top area,* followed by a bull market in two phases, and then by a bear

FIGURE 4.6

Gold Futures Prices.

Dollars Per Ounce

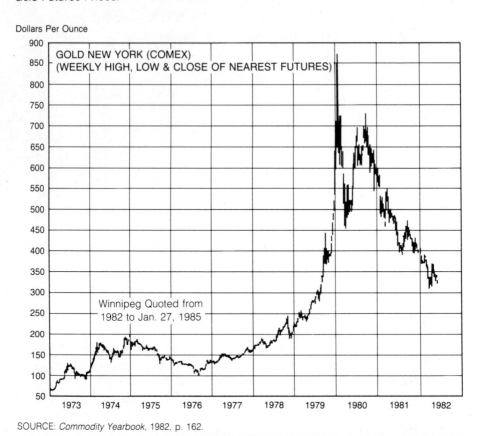

SOURCE: *Commodity Yearbook*, 1982, p. 162.

market. The article explains each of these components, but the key to profitable speculation is the ability to identify the crucial turning points. One technique for doing this is shown in their second chart, reproduced here as Figure 4.8. Gold prices moving above their 65-week moving average indicates a major bull market. Prices falling below their 65-week moving average signals a major market decline. Based on their analysis, the authors foresee that a peak in gold prices should occur sometime between September 1985 and September 1986, with prices in the neighborhood of $3750 to $4900 per ounce. This conclusion is based on the analysis that they print in their third chart, shown here as Figure 4.9.

This is an instructive example for two reasons. First, the mode of analysis is clear and indicates how practicing market professionals use technical analysis. Second, the predictions are very clear; the authors state that, "For the first two years of the bull market, we expect the price will be in a steady, quiet uptrend. In early to mid 1984, gold probably

FIGURE 4.7
Cycles in Gold Prices.

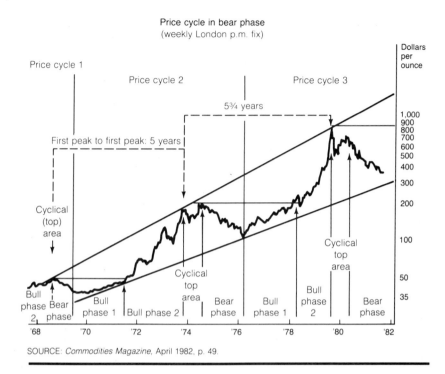

SOURCE: *Commodities Magazine,* April 1982, p. 49.

FIGURE 4.8
Moving Averages of Gold Prices.

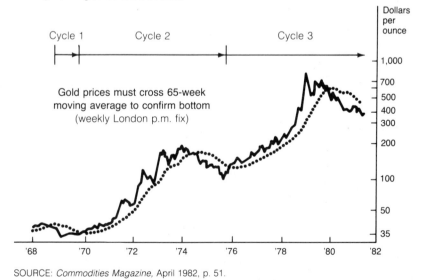

SOURCE: *Commodities Magazine,* April 1982, p. 51.

FIGURE 4.9
Gold Price Projections: 1982–1986.

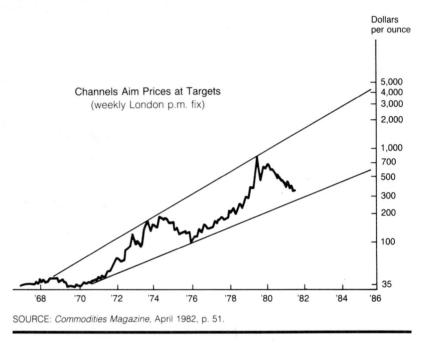

SOURCE: *Commodities Magazine*, April 1982, p. 51.

will be reaching its old high of $850 per oz. Price movements then will become far more dramatic until gold reaches its first price peak" (p. 51).

A second basic type of speculative strategy involving gold relies on its role within a broader portfolio. A number of authors have considered the potential role of gold in diversifying a stock portfolio, particularly in helping to make the portfolio perform better during inflationary periods. The attractiveness of gold is immediately reinforced by considering its investment performance relative to other assets, as shown in Table 4.3. For the ten year period ending in mid 1981, gold outperformed many other investments. Of those listed, only oil was superior, with gold clearly performing better than stocks, bonds, and a number of other commodities, as well as the inflation rate. Further, for a similar period, gold outperformed the stock indices for all major world exchanges. Whereas gold increased in value 820% in the decade that ended in 1981, the best performing stock index for any exchange was that of Hong Kong, which increased by 312%. By contrast, Japan's index grew in value by 183% and the S and P 500 by only 20%.[8] The inclusion of gold in virtually any stock portfolio during this period would have resulted in an improved performance, due solely to the high returns.

But the argument that some authors make for the investment role of gold is more subtle. It is not simply a matter of adding gold to a portfolio

TABLE 4.3

Asset Rates of Return.

Asset	Growth Rate (compounded annually)	
	May 1971–May 1981	May 1976–May 1981
Gold	28.0	30.7
S and P 500	5.8	9.8
CPI	8.3	9.7
BONDS (Salomon Bros. Index)	3.8	1.1
OIL (Saudi Arabian Light)	30.8	20.9
U.S. Coins	27.1	29.7
Silver	21.5	20.1
Farmland	14.6	14.8
Diamonds	14.5	16.9
Housing	10.3	11.6

SOURCE: Eugene J. Sherman. "Gold: A Conservative, Prudent Diversifier," *Journal of Portfolio Management,* Spring 1982, 24.

to increase the expected return of the portfolio, but to use gold to improve the risk-return characteristics of the whole portfolio. In modern portfolio theory, the desirability of any asset as a part of a portfolio depends upon its correlation with the other assets in the portfolio. The lower the correlation between a particular asset and the other assets in the portfolio, the more desirable that asset is, other things being equal. In fact, the well-known *Capital Asset Pricing Model* expresses the equilibrium price of an asset as a function of the risk-free rate of interest, the risk-level of the asset and of the market as a whole, and the correlation between the returns on the asset and the market as a whole.[9] Of these factors, the most important is the correlation between the asset and the rest of the portfolio. Other things being equal, the lower the correlation between the asset and the market, the more desirable the asset for inclusion in the portfolio.

The correlation can be as high as +1, or as low as −1. In stock portfolios, problems arise because most stocks tend to be very highly correlated with one another and with the market as a whole. It is rare to find a stock that has a correlation of less than 0.4 or 0.5 with the market as a whole. At this point, the special attraction of gold becomes even more evident, since the correlation between gold and stocks is preternaturally low. In fact, as Table 4.4 indicates, the observed correlation between gold and broad stock indices, such as the S and P 500, is often negative. This means that gold would be particularly useful as an addition to a stock portfolio, assuming that this correlation continues to be so low.

TABLE 4.4

Correlation Matrix for Gold and Other Assets, 1972–1980.

	Gold Bullion	**Silver Bullion**	**Crude Oil**	**S and P 500**
Gold Bullion	1.000			
Silver Bullion	.690	1.000		
Crude Oil	.565	.570	1.000	
S and P 500	− .056	.058	− .175	1.000

SOURCE: Anthony and Edward Renshaw, "Does Gold Have a Role in Investment Portfolios?" *Journal of Portfolio Management*, Spring 1982, 29.

While gold is a very interesting commodity in its own right, it is important not to lose sight of the fact that the discussion of gold here is intended to illustrate several points of interest that apply to other commodities as well. First, commodities that are constantly renewable and indefinitely storable, in the sense elaborated above, have their own peculiar price characteristics. Second, the discussion of technical analysis used gold as an example, but it is broadly applicable to other commodities as well. Finally, the idea of using a commodity to improve the performance of a portfolio of other assets extends beyond gold alone. Some authors believe that other commodities are important for diversifying stock portfolios as well.

PERIODICALLY RENEWABLE AND INDEFINITELY STORABLE COMMODITIES

In this section we turn our attention to those commodities that are periodically renewable and indefinitely storable. Periodically renewable commodities are those with harvests, such as wheat, corn, oats, barley, and soya products. The fact that new supplies of a commodity become available only periodically, and that the new increment to supply is large relative to existing stocks, has important consequences for the pattern that the cash price of the commodity will follow.

As we will see, the fact that such goods are harvested at a certain time introduces seasonality into the cash price; this has important implications for futures prices. Since the goods being discussed in this section are agricultural products, they are *indefinitely storable* in an even more limited sense than gold. These agricultural products are storable for some time, the essential point being that they can be stored for a long enough time to get to the next harvest, and even to be *carried over* into the new crop year. In this section we will use wheat, the soya complex, and palm oil to illustrate the essential features of pricing, including the effect of substitutions from one commodity to another and some advanced techniques for hedging.

TABLE 4.5

Gold Futures Prices, January 11, 1983. Estimated volume 68,000; open interest 124,565, +1,471.

Contract (COMEX)	Settlement Price	Open Interest
January 83	479.90	17
February	482.40	47,485
March	495.40	94
April	489.50	26,362
June	496.50	18,953
August	503.90	8,300
October	511.70	5,217
December	519.60	8,185
February 84	527.60	5,919
April	535.90	2,440
June	544.30	1,037
August	552.80	305
October	561.60	351

Availability

The single most important factor in determining prices, unique to periodically renewed commodities, is the erratic availability of the commodity. Imagine the most extreme kind of case, a delicate but plentiful fruit that can be harvested only one day a year and spoils in twenty-four hours. Such a product has bizarre inventory properties. Every day of the year, except for the harvest day, the world inventory is zero, but on the harvest day the fruit is widely available. Such a supply situation would have strong implications for the price of the fruit. On the harvest day, assume that the price is $.10. Although it would not be observable, the price of the fruit on any other day would be infinite; no matter what price is offered, no supply of the fruit would be forthcoming. In such a case, the price would fluctuate between infinity and $.10, the price movement coming on the day of harvest. Although there is no such commodity, this description emphasizes the importance of supply and sudden shifts in inventory in price determination.

Harvestable crops, such as wheat, are similar to the rare fruit, with the important exception that they can be stored and that their harvest is spread out over time. To see how the harvest patterns of such crops affect their price patterns, consider the following series of Figures, which pattern those for gold. To begin, consider the simplest case, shown in Figure 4.10. This Figure corresponds to Figure 4.2 for gold, with the important exception that the good now being considered has a seasonal harvest. For this first case, assume that long-term inventory is constant, that production equals consumption, and that there is no inflation. The commodity prices reflect no long term price trends. Also, for the sake of simplicity, assume that the harvest is instantaneous and that cash prices and inventory are certain.

In the graphs of Figure 4.10 the time line begins at the moment of the first harvest and extends through the fourth harvest. The inventory is at its peak at harvest and declines steadily until immediately before the next harvest. At the second harvest, the supply is immediately replenished and the inventory goes back to its peak level. The lowest point of inventory represents the amount of the commodity that is carried over from the previous crop year—the crop year running from one harvest to the next. This pattern of inventory can be expected to have a strong impact on the price of the cash commodity, which is also shown in Figure 4.10. Immediately upon harvest, there is a tremendous supply of the commodity and the price is correspondingly at its lowest point. As the harvest is consumed, the price of the good rises and reaches its zenith immediately before the next harvest. Upon the next harvest, the price plummets again. There is no mystery here; the price of the good simply varies inversely with its supply.

The pattern of the commodity's availability also has important implications for futures prices, as shown in the third graph of Figure 4.10. Under these conditions of certainty, the futures price will equal the cash price that will prevail at the time of the futures contract maturity. For a futures contract maturing just prior to a harvest, such as the contract maturing just before the fourth harvest, the futures price will be very high. When the contract matures, there will be little of the commodity available. By contrast, another contract that matures at the time of the second harvest will have a lower price. This is reasonable since there will be a low cash price at that time, consistent with the ample supplies brought about by the harvest. Under these conditions, the futures price should not change over the life of the contract. Instead, it will be priced to equal the cash price of the commodity at the time the contract matures. It is important to notice that the seasonal availability of the commodity will cause some futures contracts to have higher prices than others, depending upon the availability of the deliverable good at the time the futures contract matures.

It is also important to notice the difference in the cash-futures relationship between the gold case and the case of the seasonal good. With a constant inventory, as for gold in Figure 4.2, the cash price is constant, as is the futures price. But in Figure 4.10, the cash price is seasonal, varying inversely with supply. However, the seasonal pattern of cash prices need not make the futures price seasonal. As long as the market correctly anticipates the pattern that the cash price will follow, the futures price need not change. From this it is safe to conclude that a change in the cash price, by itself, will not cause changes in the futures price.

FIGURE 4.10

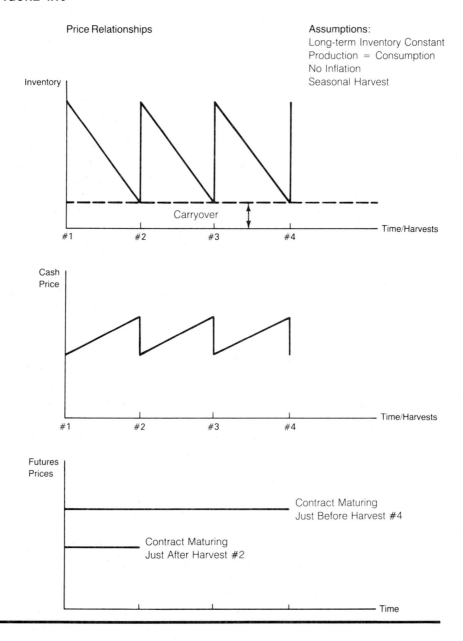

Price Relationships

Assumptions:
Long-term Inventory Constant
Production = Consumption
No Inflation
Seasonal Harvest

Figure 4.10 also shows a very important fact about *basis,* the difference between the cash and futures price. Recall that the inventories and price patterns are all presented under conditions of *certainty.* With certainty, the futures prices must remain constant, with the cash prices fluctuating in accordance with supply. This means that the basis must fluctuate, as shown in Figure 4.11. The graph of the basis in Figure 4.11 is consistent with the price patterns of Figure 4.10. Since the cash price is at the same level just before each harvest, and since the basis must be zero when the futures contract matures just before the fourth harvest, the basis must be zero or negative over the entire period. A fluctuating basis is often interpreted as a sign of high risk and unstable prices. In this example, there is no risk, since certainty has been assumed. This shows that the basis may fluctuate radically even under conditions of certainty. While a fluctuating basis often signals high risk, this is not always the case. It is important to separate fluctuations in the basis into the expected and unexpected components.[10]

Inventories

The next step in understanding the price behavior of periodically renewable goods is to relax the assumption of steady long-run inventories. For most crops, production exceeds consumption, and this difference is reflected in Figure 4.12. The assumptions of correct price expectations, no inflationary pressure, and a seasonal harvest remain. The key feature of this series of graphs is the continual increase in inventories, which might be due to very good harvests or a shift in consumer demand. In the absence of general inflationary pressures, the increase in supply should bring about a fall in prices. These two factors, the increase in inventory from harvest to harvest and the accompanying fall in price, are shown in the first two graphs of the Figure. The futures prices in the third graph show an interesting relationship, indicating that peculiar futures price relationships are really quite rational. Three futures contracts are shown. The futures contract with the highest price is for the contract maturing just prior to the third harvest. The next contract, maturing just prior to the fourth harvest, has a lower price. This is consistent with the expectation of generally falling prices as the inventory increases with each harvest. The last contract, for maturity just after the fourth harvest, reflects the drop in price that will occur with the change in the cash price due to the fourth harvest coming in. Notice that the time lines of all of the futures prices are straight lines. This reflects the assumption that the changes in prices were correctly anticipated from the outset and the absence of a risk premium.

Corresponding to the futures contracts in Figure 4.12 the basis for each of the three futures contracts is presented in Figure 4.13. Since the prices of the futures contracts were all constant over time, the path of the basis depends entirely on the movements in the cash price. The movements in the basis, as depicted in the Figure, are perfectly correlated. Note, however, that the basis differs radically from contract to contract. For some it fluctuates from negative to positive over each harvest cycle. For the last contract, maturing after the fourth harvest, the basis is always positive, returning to zero only at the maturity of the con-

FIGURE 4.11
The Basis for Seasonal Crops Under Certainty.

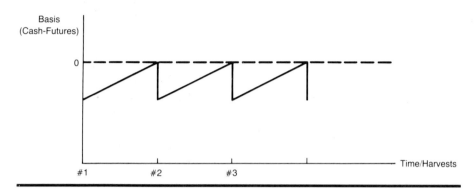

tract. This shows that radical swings in basis, and radical differences in basis for different contracts, can be observed even when the future prices are correctly anticipated. It also reveals the problem with looking at the basis on a particular contract to get a feel for the direction of the market.

The next step in the analysis is to drop the highly restrictive assumption of certainty, or the assumption of correct expectations regarding future prices. Consider the case of a crop with a seasonal harvest for which production exceeds consumption. Also, assume that actual prices turn out to be greater than expected prices. Such a situation could result when inventories get larger across crop years, but are not as large as expected. Prices could still be dropping, but they would not be dropping as rapidly as expected. Further, futures prices would have to adjust over time as the market realizes that its initial expectations were unfounded. These inventory and price patterns are shown in Figure 4.14.

Figure 4.14 reproduces the price and inventory patterns of Figure 4.12 for comparison. In addition, the actual inventory and prices are also shown as dotted lines. With actual inventory below its anticipated levels, actual prices exceed the originally expected cash prices. This means that futures prices must adjust to the new cash prices. The adjustment process that the futures price will follow depends upon the way in which the market adjusts its expectations. In the Figure, the futures prices adjust gradually over time. Such a pattern is consistent with a gradual realization on the part of the market that cash prices will differ from their originally anticipated prices. Had the market's realization been sudden, perhaps in reaction to a damaging freeze, the futures prices would have shifted suddenly. The pattern of futures prices that one normally sees, one of gradual and continuous change, reflects the ongoing process in the market of revised expectations. One of the most dramatic shifts in futures prices did, in fact, follow a sudden and unexpected freeze in Florida in January 1977. This freeze had a drastic effect on the price of the orange juice concentrate futures contract traded by the Orange Juice

FIGURE 4.12

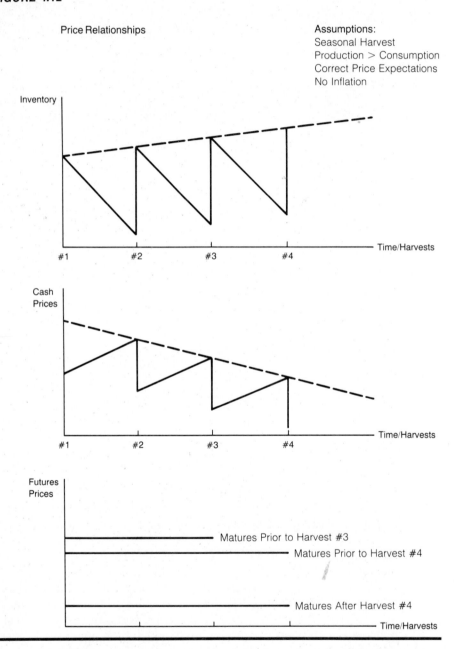

Price Relationships

Assumptions:
Seasonal Harvest
Production > Consumption
Correct Price Expectations
No Inflation

Inventory

Time/Harvests

#1   #2   #3   #4

Cash
Prices

Time/Harvests

#1   #2   #3   #4

Futures
Prices

Matures Prior to Harvest #3

Matures Prior to Harvest #4

Matures After Harvest #4

Time/Harvests

Associates of the New York Cotton Exchange. Within one week in January 1977 orange juice futures went from $.40 per pound to over $.70 per pound. Without doubt, the change in expectations that generates changes in futures prices can be dramatic as well as gradual.

FIGURE 4.13
The Basis with Falling Prices.

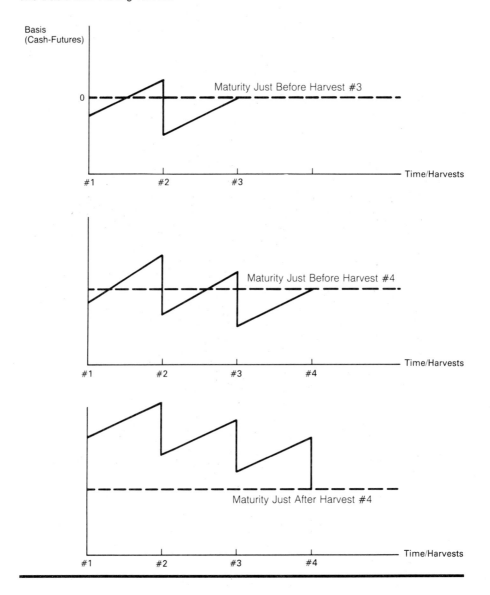

Wheat and Wheat Futures

Wheat is an extremely important crop that fits the description of a seasonally renewable commodity with long-term storage characteristics. Of course, wheat does not perfectly meet the simplified conditions of the preceding analysis. Wheat cannot be stored forever, and its harvest extends over some time. Examining the characteristics of prices for wheat,

FIGURE 4.14

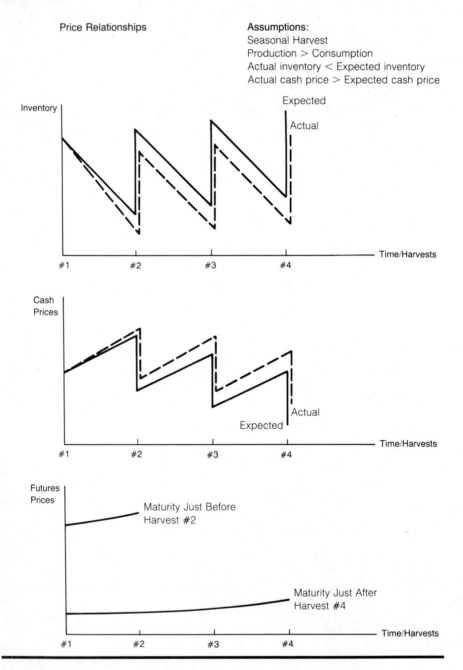

Price Relationships

Assumptions:
Seasonal Harvest
Production > Consumption
Actual inventory < Expected inventory
Actual cash price > Expected cash price

since it fits our model imperfectly, gives some idea of how sound the preceding way of thinking may be. If the preceding analysis is to be useful for wheat, then the performance of wheat should reveal several important tendencies. First, there should be a seasonal pattern to cash wheat prices. Other things being equal, wheat prices should tend to be high prior to harvests and low just following harvests. In this statement the cautioning phrase, "other things being equal," may have to bear a lot of weight. Also, other things being equal, futures prices should not tend to follow a seasonal pattern. The discussion that follows is intended to show the kinds of considerations that arise in addressing these problems of seasonality. As will become clear, continuing disputes characterize the discussion of these issues.

As discussed in Chapter 1, there are numerous varieties of wheat with different growing characteristics and different harvest times.[11] The harvest of winter wheat begins in late May in the southernmost region of the wheat belt and continues through mid-July. Spring wheat is harvested in August and September. In addition to the fact that the U.S. wheat harvest covers such an extended period, remember that important wheat producers below the equator, such as Argentina, have opposite harvest times, so wheat is continually coming to market.

In spite of this continuous world-wide supply of wheat, the seasonal factor in the availability of wheat in the United States is very strong. Table 4.6 presents the average stock of wheat in the United States by month for the crop years 1969–1982. (The U.S. Department of Agriculture defines the wheat crop year as running from June 1 to May 31.) In June, the carryover from the preceding harvest is nearly depleted, but the new harvest is just becoming available. The stock of wheat continues to grow over the harvest period, reaches its greatest level in October, and then begins to decline again. Notice that the largest surge in the wheat stock occurs in July and August, with increase of 31 to 38 percent.

According to this reasoning, the increase in supply should cause a drop in price, other factors held constant. With the persistent inflation of recent years, such price drops might be difficult to detect. This problem can be solved by using a longer period. Table 4.7 presents evidence about the seasonal trends in cash prices. Over the ninety year period 1892–1981, the Table shows the months in which the high and low cash prices for the calendar year occurred. The strongest regularity to be noted is that 37 of the 90 lowest prices occurred in the months of July and August. These months correspond, of course, to the months with the greatest percentage increase in wheat stocks. The highest prices had a similarly strong tendency to occur in December and January, when wheat stocks were low. These results confirm the view that cash prices should be high when inventories are low and that prices should be low when inventories are high. It must be acknowledged that wheat has not followed this pattern exactly, since the reasoning about the harvests would have led one to ex-

TABLE 4.6

Average U.S. Wheat Stocks, 1969–1982 Crop Years. Months are arranged in accordance with the USDA crop year.

Month	Stock (million bushels)	Percentage Change (from preceding month)
June	187.78	− 9.40%
July	246.37	31.20
August	339.65	37.86
September	380.19	11.94
October	398.40	4.79
November	379.40	− 4.77
December	346.41	− 8.70
January	314.28	− 9.28
February	284.21	− 9.57
March	257.42	− 9.43
April	236.14	− 8.27
May	205.44	− 13.01

pect the highest prices in May and June. But in periods of high inflation, we would expect low prices to be found in the early months of the year and the high prices to occur in the later months.

Table 4.8 shows the distribution of high and low futures prices for the May contract traded on the CBT over the 20 year period 1963–1982. There are several striking features of these data. First, there is a tendency for many extreme prices, both high and low, to be found in June. This is not surprising considering that the contract will not be maturing for almost a full year. When the maturity of the contract is distant, we would expect the futures prices to be farther from the price that will eventually prevail when the crop comes to harvest. Another concentration of extreme prices tends to occur in the delivery month itself. In particular, six of the lowest prices occurred in May. This is strange, but might be due to the unexpectedly large harvests that occurred in the decade of the sixties, as a product of the "Green Revolution." Three of these May lows occurred in the years 1963, 1967, and 1968, when the power of the Green Revolution was first being felt. Aside from these two peculiarities, the distribution of high and low futures prices is fairly evenly spread across the months, with a slight tendency for high futures prices to fall in the winter months.

Further interesting evidence on the behavior of futures prices is provided by Telser's classic study of wheat and cotton futures. Telser studied the behavior of wheat futures prices over the period 1927–1954, omitting the war years, and a portion of his results are presented in Table 4.9. As shown in that Table, he segregated these years into groups when

TABLE 4.7

Months in Which High and Low Cash Wheat Prices for the Year Occurred, 1892–1981. Data are for calendar years for #2 Winter Wheat.

Month	Number of Highs	Number of Lows
June	3	9
July	3	19
August	0	18
September	7	4
October	4	5
November	9	8
December	17	2
January	16	9
February	9	4
March	6	3
April	7	6
May	9	3

SOURCE: *Chicago Board of Trade, Statistical Annual,* 1981, 251.

the cash price of wheat rose, fell, or remained stable. He then examined the futures prices for these separate periods, noting the number of months when futures prices rose or fell. Over the entire period, futures prices rose about as often as they fell. But in periods of rising cash prices, futures prices tended to rise; when cash prices were falling, so were futures prices.

Such a phenomenon could be due to two factors. First, there could be seasonal trends in futures prices. Second, new information that caused the cash price to change could also have caused the futures price to change. Of these two explanations, the second is more reasonable. The seasonal pattern of cash wheat prices is well known and should be anticipated by the market. The fact that futures prices were moving in the opposite direction from cash prices over one-third of the time (35.17%), in conjunction with what has already been observed about the distribution of high and low futures prices, supports a conclusion that was stated by Telser. "The futures data offer no evidence to contradict the simple . . . hypothesis that the futures price is an unbiased estimate of the expected spot price."[12] As argued in Chapter 2, if futures prices are unbiased estimators of expected future spot prices, and if those expectations are themselves unbiased, the futures prices should neither rise nor fall over the life of a contract. On the whole, this is a fair interpretation of the movement of wheat futures prices.

It is important to realize that the relationships discussed above are all for the behavior of futures prices under idealized conditions. As a corrective to such abstraction, consider the wheat prices for January 17,

TABLE 4.8
*Months in Which High and Low Wheat Futures Prices Occurred for the Year,
1963–1982. Data are for the CBT May contract.*

Month	Number of Highs	Number of Lows
June	6	5
July	1	2
August	1	2
September	1	1
October	2	0
November	1	0
December	1	0
January	1	0
February	1	0
March	0	3
April	2	1
May	3	6

1983, reported in Table 4.10. For the delivery dates between March 1983
and March 1984, the futures prices increase steadily with length of time
to delivery. Further, each futures price lies above the current spot price
of $3.37 per bushel. Are these data inconsistent with the analysis of fu-
tures prices that has been developed above? Clearly not, but it is important to understand why. The futures prices reflect the expectation of rising prices over that entire period, even over the period of the harvest in
summer, 1983. Note, however, that the spread between the May and July
contract is the smallest of all. One interpretation is that this is due to the
harvest. This may seem plausible, but the preceding analysis leads one to
expect that the May futures should normally be priced higher than the
July futures, other factors being equal. This would be the case since the
May cash prices are normally higher than the July cash prices, as shown
in Table 4.7.

Other factors are seldom equal, and certainly not in the present case.
The price quotations are for January 17, 1983. The price pattern being
observed would be consistent with a high level of current stocks with the
expectation that the future harvests would not be so large. At that time,
January 17, 1983, the supply situation in wheat and other grains was very
unusual. The carryover of wheat into the 1982–83 crop year was the
highest in 21 years. Further, the carryover of corn and soybeans into the
1982–83 crop year both set all time records.[13] These facts, taken together,
suggest that supplies of grain were at very high levels in January, 1983,
which would account for the unusual pattern of futures prices that
prevailed at that time. The expectation of rising prices, reflected by the
structure of futures prices, is fully consistent with the high inventory

TABLE 4.9
Telser's Wheat Futures Results, 1927–41 and 1946–1954

	Number of Months Futures Rose	Number of Months Futures Fell
Years of Falling Cash Prices	19	42
Years of Stable Cash Prices	45	56
Years of Rising Cash Prices	52	32
Total	116 (47.15%)	130 (52.85%)

levels that prevailed in January, 1983, and the futures prices even have the smaller spread between the May and July contracts that reflects the arrival of the harvest.

Storage of Commodities and Heterogeneous Expectations

Thus far, we have analyzed the pattern of inventory and price changes over the crop year, but no real explanation of the reasons behind those patterns has been given. What makes inventories decline gradually over the crop year? Why do they decline only so far and at the speed they do?[14] The answer to these problems depends on the fact that market participants have different expectations about the future price movements of commodities, and these various parties are willing to store different amounts of a good, say wheat, at different price levels and with different storage costs.

To see the role of heterogeneous expectations in determining the consumption versus storage of commodities, assume first that homogeneous expectations prevail regarding the spot and future prices for wheat and that all market participants face the same storage costs. In such a simplified situation, every wheat speculator will have the same opinion about whether it is better to sell wheat immediately or to maintain title to it for delivery at a later time. But surely, not everyone can buy at the same time, and not everyone can sell. (Notice that the consumers are being left out here.) Two factors work together to eliminate this potential equilibrium: *divergent storage opportunities* and *heterogeneous expectations*. Not every potential holder of wheat faces the same marginal storage cost. The grain elevator owner has a very low marginal storage cost, since he has already incurred the capital costs and since he has knowledge superior to other market participants regarding the business of storage. When other market participants find storage costs too high to warrant the storage of wheat, it may still be possible for the

TABLE 4.10
Wheat Prices, Cash, and Futures, January 17, 1983.

	Futures	**Cash**	
		337.	*Soft-Red St. Louis*
March 83	342.25		
May	350.		
July	356.		
September	366.		
December	381.75		
March 84	396.50		

grain elevator owner to store wheat profitably, since his costs are lower. By the same token, the cost of storage is not constant for all amounts that are to be stored. The supply of storage facilities is fixed in the short run, so it is not possible to store any amount of wheat that one wishes without facing an increasing cost curve for storage. The equilibrium price of storage is determined competitively just like any other good.

If the spread between the cash price and the futures price is sufficiently large to justify storage of a great deal of wheat, the attempt to store so much wheat is bound to drive the price of storage up. But, as has already been observed, when the cost of carry is too high, it will be better to sell at the spot price for consumption, rather than to attempt to carry the good forward. So the increasing marginal cost of storage, as more and more storage is demanded, helps distribute the use of wheat between current consumption and storage for later sale.

The fact that people have different views about future costs of goods, such as wheat, helps adjust the spread between cash and futures prices. For most reasonable spreads and storage costs, some wheat speculators believe that storage is profitable, while others disagree. This disagreement, these heterogeneous expectations, will result in buying and selling in the spot and futures wheat until an equilibrium is reached. But the divergent storage costs faced by different speculators, and the rising marginal cost of storage as more wheat is held, mediate the equilibrium seeking process. Shifts in storage costs generate shifts in opinions about the relative profitability of selling (and consuming) versus the profitability of storing. Only as a result of this complex interaction of heterogeneous expectations and shifting storage costs can an equilibrium be achieved that gives the price patterns that have already been observed. Even if a consideration of storage costs for wheat helps to make the account of wheat price determination somewhat more realistic, it is very far from doing a complete job. By considering only the wheat market, even in conjunction with the market for the storage of wheat, one is still working only within a partial-equilibrium framework. There are important interactions between the wheat market and other diverse markets that are not even considered. Of course, it is not possible here to even make an attempt at any general-equilibrium analysis that would consider the equilibrium conditions in all markets, but the next sub-section briefly considers the interactions among wheat, corn, and the soya complex, treating all three kinds of goods as protein sources.

Substitution Among Commodities

At the end of the last sub-section, it was suggested that patterns of wheat futures prices might be partially explained by reference to other goods, such as corn and soybeans. It should be increasingly clear that prices of different commodities are set in a complex web of supply and demand relationships. Wheat, corn, and soybeans are, to some extent, substitutes for each other. However, when these products are viewed as feeds, then they are complements to poultry, hogs, and cattle. This subsection will explore some of these relationships very briefly, by focusing on the central role occupied by soybeans.

Perhaps it is misleading to attribute a crucial role to soybeans, since they are really not very useful as soybeans. The whole beans, as such, are mainly useful as seed and dairy animal feed. The real importance of soybeans stems from the two products that are made from the whole bean, soybean oil and soymeal. Most soybeans are crushed to produce meal or oil. The dominant use of soymeal is in animal feeds, with 70% of domestic production going to that purpose. Over 90% of soybean oil consumed domestically goes into the manufacture of cooking fats, salad and cooking oils, and margarine.

The importance of soymeal as an animal feed stems from its extremely high concentration of protein (44–49%). In a certain sense, livestock is fed protein, with the feeder attempting to secure the cheapest combination of feeds with the necessary requirement of protein. This means that feed lot operators will be very willing to trade from one form of feed to another, depending on price, as long as the nutritional components of the feed are cost-effective. The main competitors for soymeal as a feed are other meals of other oilseeds, such as rapeseed, cottonseed, flaxseed, and sunflower seeds. Also, soymeal competes with by-products of meat packing (tankage) and fish meal. When prices of substitute products are favorable, there is a tendency for substitution, but soymeal dominates the market on grounds of its protein/price ratio, and the fact that some other products are not at all suitable for certain uses. This substitutability leads us to expect close price relationships among corn, soybeans, and wheat, as reflected in Figure 4.15.

On one side, then, soymeal prices are tied to the prices of substitutes; but they are also tied to prices of complements. Hogs consume about one-third of all domestically used soymeal. This means that the demand for soymeal depends to a great extent on pork production. In

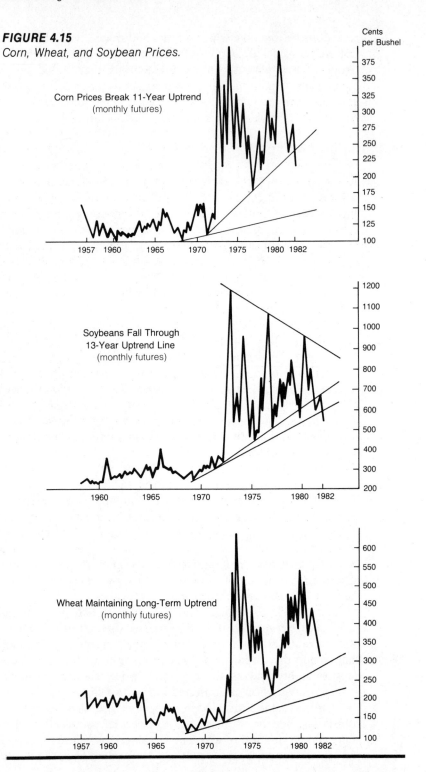

FIGURE 4.15

Corn, Wheat, and Soybean Prices.

Cents per Bushel

Corn Prices Break 11-Year Uptrend
(monthly futures)

Soybeans Fall Through
13-Year Uptrend Line
(monthly futures)

Wheat Maintaining Long-Term Uptrend
(monthly futures)

late 1981, pork production was on its way down, as was the size of the hog breeding herd. This fact, coupled with the record soybean harvest, was enough to have very serious consequences for soybean and soymeal prices throughout 1982.

The prices of soymeal and soybean oil are also tied very closely to the price of soybeans. The difference between the price of the soymeal and the soybean oil that can be produced from a 60-pound bushel of soybeans and the price of the bushel of beans is known as the *crush margin.* The proportion of meal and oil that can be produced is fixed, with a bushel of beans yielding about 48 pounds of soymeal and 11 pounds of soybean oil, with about 1 pound being lost in processing. Falling crush margins often stimulate export of beans, particularly to Western Europe, where the crush margin may be more favorable. While production costs tend to keep the crush margin uniform, demand for final soya products is highly variable and causes the crush margin to fluctuate quite radically.

In summary, then, the prices of goods that are substitutes for each other will typically exhibit close correlations in price movements. Also, goods that have the same complements will tend to have similar price movements. Both of these factors are at play for the corn, wheat, and soybean crops. Such close correlations are very useful in hedging, as becomes apparent in the discussion of hedging given in the final section of this chapter. But before turning to the hedging of physical commodities, it is best to finish the account of storage by considering commodities that are non-storable or transformable into other commodities.

NON-STORABLE AND TRANSFORMABLE COMMODITIES

While soybeans can be, and generally are, transformed into soymeal or soybean oil, there is not really a choice of what to do with them. If soybeans are not crushed, what can be done with them? Other goods, for which futures contracts are traded, can be transformed into some other good at the discretion of the owner. One prime example is the fact that young cattle can be transformed into more mature cattle by their retention and continued feeding. This particular case is of interest for students of futures markets, since the CME trades contracts on both *feeder cattle* and *live cattle,* the young and the more mature beef, respectively. The feed lot operator has the choice of holding the feeder cattle off the market in hopes of increasing profits by selling them later as live cattle. This choice has important implications for the price spread between the two futures contracts. This section briefly examines these two futures contracts for cattle as being representative of a commodity that is transformable and non-storable.

The dual contracts traded on cattle raise particularly interesting issues about storage and carrying charges in futures markets, since cattle deliverable on one contract can be carried forward and delivered on another contract, but with a difference. Whereas wheat or soybeans might be stored and carried forward to another contract, they do not gain in value; beef does. The decision about whether to deliver younger beef on the feeder cattle contract, or to carry them forward for delivery as live cattle, depends on the spread between the two futures contracts and the cost of feeding the cattle over the period represented by the spread on the two futures contracts.

To understand the pricing relationships that might reasonably prevail, it is necessary to know what the terms of the contracts are. The quality requirements for the feeder and live cattle contracts are similar. For the live cattle contract, the cattle must be of USDA grade 1, 2, 3, or 4 Choice quality, with a restriction on the number of head that may fall in grade 4. The delivery conditions for the feeder cattle are somewhat less stringent, allowing a certain percentage of the cattle to be of merely Good grade. Asise from this quality differential, the two contracts differ in the size of the cattle that may be delivered. The feeder cattle are the less mature and lighter cattle, with the average weight of the cattle in the 42,000 pound delivery unit averaging between 650 and 800 pounds. For the live cattle, the delivery unit is 40,000 pounds and the steers must average between 1050 and 1200 pounds. The specifications also permit various kinds of weight and quality deviations with certain price adjustments.[15]

These facts about the deliverable steers are enough to suggest the possibility that feeder cattle might be held off the market and delivered later against a live cattle contract. The incentive to do so would depend upon the spreads in the prices between the two contracts. If the live steers would bring sufficiently more than the feeder cattle, then one could continue to feed the animals until they reached the weight range of 1050 to 1200 pounds. Obviously, this possibility restricts the price spread between the two contracts. This kind of relationship is already familiar from the discussion of spreads in Chapters 2 and 3. In those earlier discussions, we noted that the restriction merely limited the amount by which a distant contract could diverge from the price of a nearby contract. The difference could not be sufficiently large to generate an arbitrage opportunity. But this relationship implied no minimum differential between the two contracts. After all, one cannot transform wheat that will be harvested in September into a deliverable commodity for a May contract in the same calendar year. In other words, in this limited case, reverse arbitrage is not possible.

This brings up an important difference between contracts, such as wheat, and the beef contracts. Under some circumstances, steers deliverable on a live cattle futures contract at one time might be deliverable against the feeder contract at an earlier time. If the spread between the feeder contract and the live cattle contract is too small, then it would indicate that a feed lot operator could not profit by continuing to feed the cattle up to the higher weight level. The calf that would be of sufficient weight for delivery against the live cattle contract might better be slaughtered when its weight matches that of feeder cattle. In a certain sense, this means that cattle that would be of live cattle size in the more distant future could be *transformed* into feeder cattle in the less distant future. Such an opportunity would help keep the spread between the feeder cattle contract and the live cattle contract from getting too small. If the spread is so small that it does not pay to keep feeding cattle, then they will be slaughtered earlier. More and more cattle will be slaughtered earlier, thereby reducing the distant supply of the larger live cattle, until the spread is sufficiently wide to make continued feeding profitable for the most efficient feeders.

In wheat, market forces exist to keep the spread between two maturities from getting too large. But with the two cattle contracts, the spread can be neither too large nor too small without calling forth corrective action from feed lot operators, as will be expressed by their decisions to slaughter or continue feeding younger cattle. This relationship is made more explicit by Figure 4.16, which shows a time line for cattle production. If a calf is born at month 0, then it might be deliverable as a feeder steer at month 12. If kept on feed, then it might be deliverable as live cattle at month 18. Assume that the owner of the newborn calf sold two futures contracts for the calf, one for delivery as a feeder in 12 months, and one for delivery against the live cattle contract in 18 months. For this owner of the calf approaching its twelfth month, there is a basic choice. The owner may deliver the calf against the feeder contract, and close the live cattle contract. Alternatively, he might close the feeder contract, maintain the live cattle contract and plan to deliver the 18 month steer against the live cattle contract when it matures.[16] His decision will be motivated, to a large extent, by the profitability of keeping the cattle on feed from month 12 to month 18. This profitability, in turn, is largely a function of the cost of corn in this interval. As feed rises in price, the profitability of feeding is reduced, other things being equal. In such a case, we would expect the spread between the cash (or nearby futures) price of feeder cattle and the futures price for live cattle (to be delivered six to seven months later) to narrow as corn prices rise. With rising corn prices, holding feeder cattle off the market to mature is less and less attractive.

To see how this works in practice, consider the data presented in Table 4.11. The data are for calendar year 1980, a period of sharply rising corn prices. Corn rose a full dollar per bushel between January and December, 1980. For the corresponding period, the futures prices for the nearby feeder cattle contract, the nearby live cattle contract, and the six to seventh month distant live cattle contract are shown. Based on the reasoning about spreads, one would expect some relationships to show up in these data. First, the spread between nearby feeder and nearby live

FIGURE 4.16
Time Line for Cattle.

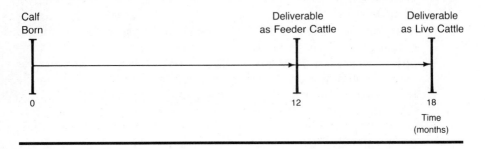

cattle should be inversely related to the price of corn. Second, the spread between nearby feeder and the distant live cattle contract should also be inversely related to the price of corn. Third, the second of these spreads should be more strongly negatively correlated with the price of corn. After all, the spread between the two nearby contracts is not too important, since feeder cattle cannot be instantaneously transformed into more mature animals for near-term delivery. The data support these hypotheses. The correlation of the spread between the two nearby contracts and cash corn is negative, but it is not statistically significant. The spread between the nearby feeder and distant live cattle is also negatively correlated with the price of corn. This relationship is statistically significant, the correlation being −.78045. In fact, fluctuations in the cash price of corn explain 60 percent of the variance in the nearby feeder versus distant live cattle spread.

From what has been observed about the rationality of futures prices in other contexts, such a result should not be at all surprising. In fact, this kind of relationship has been substantiated in much more formal tests than the one presented in Table 4.11 and the discussion of the last paragraph. These relationships have been confirmed in varying contexts by a number of authors.[17]

HEDGING PHYSICAL COMMODITIES

The rational and regular price relationships between futures and cash prices, and between pairs of futures prices, that have been emphasized throughout this chapter are very important for hedging. In Chapter 3, the role of the futures market hedger was discussed along with the kinds of activities that he or she might pursue in order to avoid unwanted risk. The discussion there assumed an ideal world of commodity needs and time commitments that exactly matched the goods underlying futures contracts. In Figures 3.8 and 3.9, the two hedges in silver exhibited these

TABLE 4.11
*Cattle Futures Prices and Corn Cash Prices, 1980. Cattle prices are quoted in cents per lb. Corn is quoted in cents per bushel. *Given the pattern of delivery months, as shown here, this column represents the contract maturing about 6 months after the nearby contract. This difference approximately equals the feeding time to turn feeder cattle into cattle deliverable against the live cattle contract.*

Month	Nearby Feeder Futures	Nearby Live Futures	6–7 Month Live Futures*	Cash Corn Price
January 80	83.05	68.15	75.25	254
February	83.40	65.47	72.37	265
March	82.70	69.92	71.27	260
April	68.47	60.55	60.67	261
May	66.80	64.12	61.95	270
June	70.90	64.27	63.92	270
July	75.85	69.50	69.22	308
August	78.92	72.27	71.30	336
September	77.10	69.32	73.97	344
October	75.10	67.57	73.07	343
November	76.35	69.77	74.82	343
December	76.60	65.72	74.57	354

fortuitous characteristics. Such a perfect hedging situation is the rare exception, rather than the rule. In the normal event, the hedged and hedging positions will differ with respect to:

1. The time the positions are terminated;
2. the amount of the good;
3. the type of good.

Mismatches in one or more of these characteristics mean that the hedge will be a *cross hedge*. Cross hedges require more careful analysis if they are to be made to perform correctly. The following example illustrates the problems encountered in cross hedges and prepares the way for yet more difficult hedging situations to come.

Upon inspecting the ingredients label of snack food today, one may notice that the exact kind of edible oil that the product contains is not always shown. Often the label will list a number of oils, one or more of which might actually be present in the product. Three typical oils that might show up in such a list are soybean oil, coconut oil, and palm oil. These oils are fairly close substitutes for one another in many uses, so it is not difficult to guess that the food processors list different oils so that they may use whichever is most economical. The producer of palm oil, however, cannot switch so easily among the three products. So, the palm oil producer might reasonably wish to hedge the price that he could hope to obtain for his palm oil production. About 60% of the world's palm oil is produced in Malaysia, and palm oil is traded on the Kuala Lampur futures exchange. The producer in question prefers, however, to use United States financial markets wherever possible and decides that trading on the Kuala Lampur exchange is not for him.

With this background, the palm oil producer fears that prices will fall from their current level of 24.7 cents per pound in September, 1980. He expects to be able to deliver 1,000,000 pounds to the U.S. by May, 1981, and he wishes to protect against falling prices in the interim. One alternative is to attempt to hedge his position by using a cross hedge with a related product for which there is a U.S. futures contract traded, and he settles on the soybean oil contract, since soybean oil is close to palm oil in its uses. If this kind of hedging plan is to be successful, then there must be a correlation in price movements between the soybean oil contract and the palm oil that he wishes to hedge.

As Table 4.12 shows, the correlations between the cash price of palm oil and soybean oil products are not too high. In fact, the correlation between palm oil and soybean oil is negative ($-.0759$). The correlations between the palm oil and the soybean oil futures contracts are low, but positive. The calculated correlation between the cash price of palm oil and the nearby soybean oil futures contract is 0.44485. The correlation between cash palm oil and the May 1981 soybean oil futures contract is still lower, at 0.37422. These correlations are important for hedging, since they indicate the extent to which the prices of the good to be hedged (palm oil) and the potential hedging instruments (nearby soybean futures and the May 1981 contract) tend to move together.

These two futures contracts are shown here, since the cash price of a good will tend to move most closely with the futures contract that is closest to delivery. That general tendency is substantiated here. Also, the correlation with the May 1981 futures contract is examined; it is a potential hedging vehicle as well, particularly since the hedge will be terminated in May 1981.

The proper technique for using this kind of analysis was developed independently by two scholars in about 1960. Johnson and Stein both show that the way to choose a *hedge ratio* to minimize risk is to find the hedge ratio that minimizes the sum of squared errors when the good to be hedged is regressed on the hedging vehicle and a constant. The argument for this conclusion is rather complex, but the results and the means for obtaining them are clear. See the Appendix to this Chapter for the mathematics behind the Johnson-Stein strategy. In our case, one would use historical data available at the time the hedge is going to be entered and estimate the following regression, where the variables are expressed as percentage price changes from the preceding period:

$$\textbf{Cash Palm Oil} = \textbf{a} + \textbf{b (Soybean Futures)} + \textbf{e} \qquad \textbf{(4.1)}$$

TABLE 4.12

Correlation Matrix, Palm Oil and Soybean Oil.

	Cash Palm Oil	Cash Soybean Oil	Nearby Soybean Oil	May 1981 Soybean Oil
Cash Palm Oil	1.000			
Cash Soybean Oil	− .076	1.000		
Nearby Soybean Oil	.445	.738	1.000	
May 1981 Soybean Oil	.374	.715	.885	1.000

Using data from 1980, this was done, with the results being shown in Table 4.13. The results are clearly miserable; palm oil and soybean oil experience poorly related price movements. As measured by the t-statistic or the R-square, the results are better for the use of the nearby futures contract. This is consistent with the correlation matrix. For this case, the most important feature of the example is the interpretation of the beta-coefficient and of the R-square statistic. The beta-coefficient gives the hedge ratio that minimizes the variability of the combined palm oil and futures position. It is saying that the price of palm oil moves 0.445 for every one unit move in the price of the nearby futures contract. But this relationship is not very regular, as is reflected by the low value for the R-square. The R-square can be interpreted as giving the amount of variance in the palm oil position alone that can be eliminated by taking on the futures position consistent with the hedge ratio of 0.445. No other hedge ratio will do better in terms of getting rid of price variability in the palm oil position. Since the prices of both the palm oil and the soybean oil futures are measured in cents per pound, this result tells us to take a futures position based on the hedge ratio of 0.445. Such a position will minimize the variance over the coming hedge period, assuming that the past relationship between the two price series continues to hold as it has in the past.

Since the palm oil producer cannot stand the idea of trading on the Kuala Lampur exchange, he decides to attempt the hedge using the soybean oil contract, even in spite of its anticipated poor performance. Since he anticipates having 1,000,000 pounds of palm oil in May 1981 and the hedge ratio is 0.445, he needs to sell 445,000 pounds of soybean oil futures. Since soybean oil is traded in contracts of 60,000 pounds, he needs to sell 7.4 contracts. Since one cannot trade in fractional contracts, he decides to sell 7 nearby contracts.

Still more practical problems face our palm oil producer. Since the

TABLE 4.13
Results of Regressing Cash Palm Oil on Soybean Oil Futures.

Cash Palm Oil = −.486 + .445 nearby soybean oil futures
t-statistic = 1.2166
R-square = .1979

Cash Palm Oil = −.344 + .374 May 1981 soybean oil futures
t-statistic = .9884
R-square = .1400

---

hedge is going to be entered in September, 1980, the nearby contract is for October. But the producer knows that one does not want to hold a contract as it approaches maturity, so he decides not to trade the October contract, but the December, 1980 contract instead.[18] The December contract will expire, of course, in December, 1980, so he will have to *roll the hedge forward* into a later contract as the December contract approaches maturity. In accordance with this plan, he decides to roll forward on the last trading day of November, 1980 into the January, 1981 contract. Then, he will roll forward on the last day of December, 1980 into the March, 1981 contract, and then, finally, into the May, 1981 contract. His transactions, and the results of his hedge, are shown in Table 4.14. The producer takes no action in the cash market over the entire hedge period. In each of his futures market transactions, he merely trades according to his plan of rolling the hedge forward. Notice that he lost on the December contract, but he maintained the strategy, the final results of which are tabulated in Table 4.15.

The results reported in Table 4.15 prove the producer to be among the most fortunate of hedgers: he was hedged to protect against the possibility of a loss on his harvest of palm oil. But the palm oil actually increased in price. There is no information given about what the expected price of palm oil was for May, 1981, but he shows an accounting gain on the cash good of $29,000.[19] The futures positions, on the whole, turned out quite favorably as well. He made money on every futures contract, except for the December futures. Recall that he used the soybean oil contract because its price movements were positively correlated with palm oil prices. But, for the period of the hedge, the correlation was generally negative. As his palm oil increased in price, the soybean oil futures decreased. This pleasing result gave him a gain on both the cash and futures transactions.

Although these results were pleasing, this hedge was a bad hedge in an important sense. The purpose of the hedge was to protect against falling prices for palm oil. This means that futures gains were anticipated to offset potential palm oil losses, and vice versa. These gains did not hap-

TABLE 4.14
Palm Oil Short Hedge.

Cash Market	Futures Market
September 15, 1980	
Producer anticipates having 1,000,000 lbs. of palm oil to deliver. Current price of palm oil = 24.7 cents per lb.	Producer sells 7 December, 1980 soybean oil contracts at 27.45 cents per lb.
November 28, 1980	Buys 7 December, 1980 soybean oil contracts at 28.30
	Sells 7 January, 1981 soybean oil contracts at 28.90
December 31, 1980	Buys 7 January, 1981 soybean oil contracts at 24.30
	Sells 7 March, 1981 soybean oil contracts at 25.15
February 27, 1981	Buys 7 March, 1981 soybean oil contracts at 24.00
	Sells 7 May, 1981 soybean oil contracts at 24.82
April 30, 1981	
Sells 1,000,000 lbs. of palm oil on the spot market at 27.6	Buys 7 May, 1981 soybean oil contracts at 23.85

TABLE 4.15
Palm Oil Hedge Results.

	Original Price	Final Price	Amount	Profit (Loss)
Cash Palm Oil	24.7 (held)	27.6 (sold)	1,000,000	$29,000

Soybean Oil Futures	Selling Price	Purchase Price		
December 80	27.45	28.30	420,000	− 3,570
January 81	28.90	24.30	420,000	19,320
March 81	25.15	24.00	420,000	3,570
May 81	24.82	23.85	420,000	4,074

	Cash Result	+ $29,000
	Futures Result	23,394
		+ $52,394

pen. It is not surprising that the hedge did not perform as hoped, when one recalls the poor correlation between the palm oil and the soybean oil futures. This fact emphasizes two important rules about hedging:

1. Any unexpected gain could just as easily have been a loss.
2. One should attempt to hedge a good with a futures contract as similar as possible to the item being hedged.

The next chapter develops the concept of hedging further and applies it to interest rate futures, which have their own special characteristics.

CONCLUSION

In this chapter, the focus has been on the relationship between the storage and production characteristics of commodities, on the one hand, and the behavior of their cash and futures prices on the other. The inescapable conclusion of this analysis is that futures prices are rational in an important sense; they clearly conform to the underlying economic realities specific to the characteristics of the deliverable goods. This is true for goods with quite varied storage and production characteristics, whether they be gold, wheat, soybeans, or cattle.

This rationality of futures prices has two very important implications. First, it indicates that participants in the futures markets for these commodities know the underlying goods and the factors that determine their prices. Second, it implies that the potential speculator in futures contracts must be prepared to pit his knowledge of these goods against the collected wisdom of the other futures traders, as represented in the market-determined futures prices. One may still believe, and after all it may be true, that with so many diverse commodities, there must be opportunities for speculative profits for the discerning trader. In the next chapter, we turn our attention to a much more homogeneous commodity—money carried over time. In such a case, the law-like relationships that have begun to appear here become even more apparent. These relationships have important implications for both speculation and hedging.

NOTES

1. Contracts for fresh eggs are listed on the Chicago Mercantile Exchange. However, current trading interest is virtually nil.
2. It needs to be emphasized repeatedly that the analysis of this chapter will proceed under the assumption (defended in Chapter 3) that there is no risk premium in the futures market. To a certain extent, the very character of the analysis makes that clear, since much of the analysis is conducted under conditions of certainty.

3. Not only is gold noted for its incorruptibility, and prized as a store of value, but some have noted a perverse economic role for the metal. John Maynard Keynes observed, "Never in history was there a method devised of such efficacy for setting each country's advantage at variance with its neighbours' as the international gold (or, formerly, silver) standard. For it made domestic prosperity directly dependent on a competitive pursuit of markets and a competitive appetite for the precious metals." *The General Theory,* p. 349.

4. Exact detection of seasonal factors typically requires extended statistical analysis using relatively complex techniques. For the analysis of time series data, see G. E. P. Box and G. M. Jenkins. *Time Series Analysis,* San Francisco: Holden-Day, 1970.

5. The case of rising marginal storage costs is considered later in this chapter.

6. See R. G. Ibbotson and R. A. Sinquefield, *Stocks, Bonds, Bills, and Inflation: The Past and the Future,* Charlottesville, VA: The Financial Analysts Foundation, 1982. Their study shows negative real returns for Treasury Bills for each year in the period 1973–1980, with the exception of 1976 (p. 30).

7. See Pamela Aden-Ayales and Mary Anne Aden-Harter. "Gold Holds Explosive Potential," *Commodities: The Magazine of Futures Trading,* April 1982, 49–51.

8. See E. Sherman. "Gold: A Conservative, Prudent Diversifier," *Journal of Portfolio Management,* Spring 1982, 21–27. See also, A. and E. Renshaw. "Does Gold Have A Role in Investment Portfolios?" *Journal of Portfolio Management,* Spring 1982, 28–31.

9. Although the Capital Asset Pricing Model will be discussed in Chapter 7, a complete and readable treatment is provided by D. Harrington. *Modern Portfolio Theory and the Capital Asset Pricing Model: A User's Guide,* Englewood Cliffs, NJ: Prentice-Hall, 1983.

10. The distinction between expected and unexpected changes in the basis is extremely important for interest rate futures, as explained in Chapter 5. For an extended discussion of this point, see R. Kolb. *Interest Rate Futures: A Comprehensive Introduction,* Richmond, VA: Robert F. Dame, Inc., 1982.

11. For more on the characteristics of the wheat market, see the *Commodity Trading Manual,* Chicago: Chicago Board of Trade, 1982 and D. Morgan. *Merchants of Grain,* New York: Penguin Books, 1982.

12. See the following works, all reprinted in A. Peck. *Selected Writings on Futures Markets,* Chicago: Chicago Board of Trade, 1977. L. Telser, "Futures Trading and the Storage of Cotton and Wheat;" L. Telser and P. Cootner, "Returns to Speculators: Telser vs. Keynes;" R. Gray, "The Search for a Risk Premium;" and H. Working, "Financial Results of Speculative Holding of Wheat."

13. See S. Abbot. "Grain Bulls' Worst Fears Become Reality," *Commodities,* November 1982, 43–47.

14. It is tempting to say that inventories decline since people eat the wheat. But the issue concerns how prices prevail which lets some wheat be eaten and the rest stored.

15. For more details on the contract specifications, see the various "Statistical Yearbooks of the Chicago Mercantile Exchange."

16. The feedlot operator could obviously pursue strategies not involving the futures market. Those strategies are not considered here.

17. See R. Leuthold and W. Tomek, "Developments in the Livestock Futures Literature," and W. Purcell, D. Flood and J. Plaxico, "Cash-Futures Interrelationships in Live Cattle: Causality, Variability, and Pricing Processes," both in R. Leuthold and P. Dixon. *Livestock Futures Research Symposium.* Chicago: Chicago Mercantile Exchange, 1980; R. Leuthold. "The Price Performance on the Futures Market of a Nonstorable Commodity; Live Beef Cattle," *American Journal of Agricultural Economics, 56,* 1974, 271–279; J.Helmuth. "A Report on the Systematic Downward Bias in Live Cattle Futures Prices," *Journal of Futures Markets, 1,* 1981, 347–358; L. Palme and J. Graham. "The Systematic Downward Bias in Live Cattle Futures: An Evaluation," *Journal of Futures Markets, 1,* 1981, 359–366; and R. Kolb and G. Gay. "The Performance of Live Cattle Futures as Predictors of Subsequent Spot Prices," *Journal of Futures Markets, 3,* 1983, 55–63.

18. As a futures contract approaches maturity, the open interest declines dramatically. This means that the market for that contract is losing liquidity. For this reason, most traders will close a position in a maturing contract, and roll forward into a later maturity.

19. The theoretically correct measure of a hedge's success depends on what the price of the hedged good is expected to be when the hedge is to be terminated. In the absence of any information about that, the accounting profit or loss was used. This is equivalent to assuming that the expected price of the hedged commodity, when the hedge is lifted, is equal to its price when the hedge is initiated.

Chapter 4 Appendix

This appendix shows the solution for finding the hedge ratio to minimize the total variance of a spot plus futures position where the spot position is determined in advance. For simplicity's sake, we assume that one unit of the spot currency is to be held. The variance of the spot plus futures combined position is given by:

$$\sigma_p^2 = b^2 \, \sigma_f^2 + 2b \, \sigma_f \, \sigma_s \, \rho_{f.s} + \sigma_s^2 \qquad \textbf{(A4.1)}$$

where,

σ_p^2 = **variance of combined futures and spot position**

σ_f^2 = **variance of the futures instrument**

σ_s^2 = **variance of the spot instrument**

b = **the number of futures contracts to trade**

$\rho_{f.s}$ = **correlation between the futures and spot instruments**

The hedging problem is to choose b to minimize σ_p^2.

$$\frac{d\sigma_p^2}{db} = 2b \, \sigma_f^2 + 2 \, \sigma_f \, \sigma_s \, \rho_{f.s} \qquad \textbf{(A4.2)}$$

Setting the derivative of (A4.2) equal to zero, and solving for b gives,

$$b^* = - \frac{\sigma_s}{\sigma_f} \, \rho_{f.s} \qquad \textbf{(A4.3)}$$

where b^* is the variance minimizing futures position. The negative sign in (A4.3) indicates that the futures position should be opposite that in the spot market. A long position in the spot commodity requires a short futures position, for example.

The b^*, it should be noted, is the same quantity one would estimate for $\tilde{\beta}$ from the following regression:

$$\textbf{Spot} = \tilde{\alpha} + \tilde{\beta} \, \textbf{Futures} + \tilde{\varepsilon} \qquad \textbf{(A4.4)}$$

The "futures" and "spot" variables should be measured as percentage price changes in order to avoid problems of statistical estimation, such as auto-correlation and spuriously inflated coefficient of determimantion (R^2). When (A4.4) is estimated correctly, the R^2 may be interpreted as a measure of hedging effectiveness, if the hedge had been implemented during the period over which the hedge ratio was estimated.

5 Interest Rate Futures

INTRODUCTION

This chapter explores one of the most successful and exciting innovations in the history of futures markets—the emergence of interest rate futures contracts. Since the first contracts were traded on October 20, 1975, the market has expanded rapidly. In spite of a number of relatively unsuccessful contracts that have been introduced, such as commercial paper and Certificate Delivery GNMA contracts, the market has been a huge success.[1] By early 1983, a typical day saw an open interest representing over 100 billion dollars (face value) of underlying financial instruments, and this amount was only from the most important six contracts listed. From inception, the interest rate futures market has come to represent about one-third of the entire futures market, and most industry observers expect the continued growth of the futures market to center around interest rate futures and the other financial instruments.

Almost all of the activity in interest rate futures is concentrated in two exchanges, the Chicago Board of Trade and the International Monetary Market of the Chicago Mercantile Exchange. The Board of Trade specializes in contracts at the longer end of the maturity spectrum, with active contracts on long-term Treasury Bonds, GNMAs (pools of 30 year residential mortgages), and ten-year Treasury Notes. By contrast, the International Monetary Market has successful contracts with very short maturities, trading contracts for three-month Treasury Bills, Certificates of Deposit, and Eurodollar Deposits. Of all of these, the two most successful contracts are for Treasury Bonds and Treasury Bills, and this chapter focuses on these two futures instruments.

But before turning to a discussion of the futures instruments themselves, a review of the principles of bond pricing will help pave the way for a full understanding of the futures contracts. Since the interest rate futures contracts represent claims based on financial instruments, the price movements of the futures contracts are closely related to the factors that influence the value of the underlying securities. With a background in bond pricing, the specific contract features of the Treasury Bill and Treasury Bond contract are examined, and the speculative and hedging opportunities of the interest rate futures market are assessed.

INTEREST RATES AND BOND PRICING PRINCIPLES

The Bond Pricing Equation and Principles of Bond Price Movements

The value of any debt instrument depends on two factors: the promised payment stream of that instrument and the rate of discount that is applied to the payment stream. In this sense, the price of any debt instrument is the present value of the promised stream of payments and is expressed by the *Bond Pricing Equation:*

$$P_0 = \sum_{t=1}^{M} \frac{Ct}{(1 + r)^t} \qquad (5.1)$$

Equation (5.1) simply says that the price of a bond at time $= 0$, P_0, equals the discounted present value of all of the payments promised by the bond. These payments are represented by *C(t)*, where *t* indicates the time at which the payment is promised. Many bonds are coupon bonds and have two types of promised payments, the coupons and the return of principal. The coupon payments are periodic payments made over the life of the bond. For most corporate bonds and many U.S. government bonds, these payments occur every six months. The other type of payment, the return of principal, occurs when the bond matures. The principal, or par value of the bond, is the trading unit of the bond. Since most corporate bonds have a par value of $1000, the examples that will follow focus on bonds of this type. The ratio of the annual coupon payment to the par value of the bond is called the coupon rate. In spite of the fact that most bonds pay coupons semi-annually, it will be much more convenient to focus on bonds that make their coupon payments annually. Each of these promised future payments is converted into its present value equivalent by dividing it by its discount factor. The discount factor equals $1/(1 + r)^t$, where *r* is the discount rate. The price of the bond is the sum of the present values of all promised payments. Consider a bond that promises to pay an annual coupon of $100 for each of the next two years, has a discount rate of 12%, and will return its principal of $1000 in two years.

$$P_0 = \frac{100}{1.12} + \frac{1100}{(1.12)^2} = 89.29 + 876.91 = \$966.20 \qquad (5.2)$$

As is shown in equation (5.2), such a bond would be worth $966.20. Any bond can be valued in the same way.

Just as the price of any bond is given by equation (5.1), there are rules that govern the price movements of all bonds. These five rules were proven by Burton Malkiel.[2] They are given here without proof, but with examples.

RULE 1: Bond prices move inversely with yields.

If the yield of the bond of equation (5.2) were suddenly to rise, Rule 1 says that the price of the bond would fall, and this is illustrated by allowing the interest rate to suddenly jump from 12% to 16%, and then valuing the payment stream promised by the bond of equation (5.2):

$$P_o = \frac{100}{1.16} + \frac{1100}{(1.16)^2} = 86.21 + 817.48 = \$903.69 \qquad (5.3)$$

With the new discount rate of 16%, the bond's value drops from $966.20 to $903.69, confirming Rule 1.

RULE 2: For two bonds that differ only in their coupon size, the bond with the smaller coupon will have a greater percentage price change, for a given change in yields.

The bond in equation (5.4) is just like the bond of equation (5.2) except it has a coupon of $40 per year, not $100.

$$P_o = \frac{40}{1.12} + \frac{1040}{(1.12)^2} = 35.71 + 829.08 = \$864.79 \qquad (5.4)$$

With a discount rate of 12%, the bond is worth $864.79. When rates change from 12 to 16%, the bond in equation (5.4) drops in value just as one would expect.:

$$P_o = \frac{40}{1.16} + \frac{1040}{(1.16)^2} = 34.48 + 772.89 = \$807.37 \qquad (5.5)$$

The increase in rates has driven the bond price from $864.79 to $807.37. For the change in yields from 12 to 16%, the bond with the large coupon dropped in value by 6.47%, from $966.20 to $903.69. The lower coupon bond had a price drop of 6.64%; when its price fell from $864.79 to $807.37. In accordance with Rule 2, the lower coupon bond had the greater percentage price drop. The difference here, between a price drop of 6.47% and 6.64% may not seem significant, but as will become apparent, coupon differences can be very important, particularly in conjunction with other factors, such as maturity.

RULE 3: For two bonds that differ only in their time to maturity, the bond with the longer time to maturity will have a greater percentage price change than the shorter maturity bond, for a given change in yields.

Still using the two year 10% coupon bond as a standard of comparison, consider a similar bond that merely has a longer maturity of five years, with the coupon payments being made annually. With the discount rate at 12%, the bond's price is $927.91, as shown in equation (5.6):

$$P_O = \frac{100}{1.12} + \frac{100}{(1.12)^2} + \frac{100}{(1.12)^3} + \frac{100}{(1.12)^4} + \frac{1100}{(1.12)^5}$$

$$= \$927.91 \tag{5.6}$$

But if rates suddenly changed to 16%, the new price of the bond would be $803.55. For this longer maturity bond, the price would fall by 13.4% for a change in yields from 12 to 16%. For the shorter maturity bond of equation (5.2), the same yield change only generated a drop in price of 6.47%. Other things being equal, the longer the maturity, the greater the effect of any change in yields.

Thus far, all of the bonds that have been considered have had one feature in common. Their prices were less than their par values. A bond with its market price below its par value is known as a *discount bond*. If the market price exceeds the par value, it is a *premium bond*. Some bonds pay no coupons whatsoever, so their market prices are always below their par value, the difference being the promised interest, since such bonds promise to pay their par value at maturity. Such bonds without coupon payments are known as *pure discount* bonds or as *zero coupon* bonds.

smaller denominator

> *RULE 4: For any given change in yields, the percentage of price change will be greater for a discount, rather than a premium, bond.*

With interest rates at 12%, the 5-year 10% coupon bond of equation (5.6) is naturally a discount bond. For comparison consider the 5-year premium bond of equation (5.7):

$$P_O = \frac{150}{1.12} + \frac{150}{(1.12)^2} + \frac{150}{(1.12)^3} + \frac{150}{(1.12)^4} + \frac{1150}{(1.12)^5}$$

$$= \$1108.15 \tag{5.7}$$

With a coupon rate (15%) in excess of the discount rate (12%), the bond must sell at a premium, its price being $1108.15. If rates were to suddenly rise to 16%, its new price would be $967.25, for a price drop of 12.71%. However, the discount bond of equation (5.6) had a drop in price of 13.40% from the same yield change, illustrating the greater sensitivity of discount bonds to yield changes.

95   100   105

> *RULE 5: For any bond, a given increase in yields will cause a smaller price change than a decrease in yields of the same magnitude.*

Rule 5 can be illustrated by using the bond of equation (5.7), where it has already been shown that an increase in yields caused a price drop of 12.71%, from $1108.15 to $967.25. According to Rule 5, a similar drop in yields of 4% should cause a larger price change. As equation (5.8) indicates, a drop in yields of 4%, from 12 to 8%, will cause the bond to sell for $1279.48.

$$P_o = \frac{150}{1.08} + \frac{150}{(1.08)^2} + \frac{150}{(1.08)^3} + \frac{150}{(1.08)^4} + \frac{1150}{(1.08)^5}$$

$$= \$1279.48 \tag{5.8}$$

The drop in yield caused a price change from $1108.15 to $1279.48, a gain of 15.46%. The same size increase in yields, however, caused a price drop from $1108.15 to $967.25, or a loss of 12.71%. As Rule 5 states, a given decrease in yields has a greater price effect than the same size increase in yields.

These five rules summarize a great deal of information about the price movements of bonds, but they do not reveal everything about bond price sensitivity. For example, which of the following two bonds has the greater price sensitivity to changes in interest rates, an 8% coupon, 20-year bond yielding 13.73% with a price of $632.50, or an 8% 15-year bond yielding 11.94% and priced at $746.56? The five rules do not give any immediately obvious answer to such a question. In fact, as Table 5.1 shows, the two bonds have almost exactly the same price sensitivity, in that their prices change by the same percentage amounts for given change in yields. What is needed is some single measure of a bond's overall price sensitivity, a measure that summarizes the impact of all five of the rules. Such a measure is known as *duration.*

Duration

The concept of duration was first introduced by Frederick Macaulay in 1938, and since that time it has achieved a position of considerable importance in bond analysis and bond portfolio management.[3] Duration measures the elasticity of a bond's price with respect to a change in the discount rate. For any given bond, the duration of the bond is given by equation (5.9):

$$D = \frac{\sum_{t=1}^{M} \frac{t\, C\, (t)}{(1 + r)^t}}{P} \tag{5.9}$$

The numerator in equation (5.9) is just like the regular bond pricing equation, except that each payment is multiplied by t, the time until the payment is received. This means that the longer until the payments are received, the greater will be the bond's duration. The denominator is simply the price of the bond, as given by the Bond Pricing Equation. The duration of a bond is easy to compute. As an example, consider the 5-year bond of equation (5.7) that pays an annual coupon of $150, yields 12%, and has a price of $1108.15. Table 5.2 shows how to compute the duration for this particular bond. Multiplying each of the cash flows by

TABLE 5.1

Price Sensitivities of Disparate Bonds.

Yield Change	Bond 1 (8%, 15-year maturity)			Bond 2 (8%, 20-year maturity)		
	Yield	Price	% Price Change	Yield	Price	% Price Change
− 2%	9.94%	$869	+ 16.01	11.73%	$734	+ 16.01
Original Position	11.94	747	———	13.73	633	———
+ 2%	13.94	651	− 12.87	15.73	552	− 12.80

the time in years until it is received, and discounting those weighted cash flows at the bond's yield of 12%, gives a stream of present values. Summing all of these gives the numerator of $4337.46. Dividing this result by the price gives duration, D, which is 3.91 for this bond.

Since the duration is an elasticity measure, it can be expressed in a different way, as indicated by equation (5.10):

$$D = - \frac{\dfrac{\Delta P}{P}}{\dfrac{\Delta(1 + r)}{(1 + r)}} \qquad (5.10)$$

Equation (5.10) says that duration equals the negative of the elasticity of the bond's price with respect to a change in the discount factor $(1 + r)$. But a more useful expression can be obtained by rearranging the terms of equation (5.10) to isolate the change in the bond price, as in the **Duration Price Change** equation (5.11):

$$\Delta P = -D \times \frac{\Delta (1 + r) \times P}{(1 + r)} \qquad (5.11)$$

Equation (5.11) says that the change in a bond's price will equal the negative of duration times the percentage change in $(1 + r)$ times the original price of the bond. To illustrate this relationship, consider again the bond of equation (5.7), for which the duration has already been calculated. If yields on this bond were to suddenly fall from 12 to 11%, the new price of the bond given by the Bond Price Equation would be $1147.84. Applying equation (5.11) to this situation gives a price change of $38.69, as is shown in equation (5.12):

$$\Delta P = (-3.91) \frac{-.01}{1.12} (\$1108.15) = \$38.69 \qquad (5.12)$$

With an increase in the price of $38.69, the new price would be $1146.84, which is almost equal to the price given by the bond pricing equation of

TABLE 5.2

Calculation of Duration.

Time (t)	1	2	3	4	5
Cash Flow (for t)	150	150	150	150	1150
Cash Flow × t	150	300	450	600	5750
Present Value of [cash flow × t]	133.99	239.16	320.30	381.31	3262.70

Sum of Present Values = $4337.46
  (to form numerator)

Bond Price   = $1108.15
  (to form denominator)

$$D = \frac{4337.46}{1108.15} = 3.91$$

$1147.84. The difference is due to two factors. Duration is an idea drawn from the calculus, so equation (5.12) holds exactly only for infinitesimal changes in r. Since a change of 1% is a discrete change, equation (5.12) holds only as an approximation. A second, and more mundane, reason for the $1.00 discrepancy is due to rounding error.

The concept of duration is very useful for bond managers attempting to manage their portfolio risk. If they anticipate falling rates, then they can trade low duration securities away in favor of long duration securities to try to take advantage of the fall in rates. If there is a perceived high risk of rising rates, which would cause the value of the bond portfolio to fall, the loss can be minimized by shortening the duration of the portfolio. One of the major uses of duration is to try to make a portfolio insensitive to changes in interest rates. If a portfolio's value does not change when interest rates change, then the portfolio is said to be *immunized* against changes in interest rates. Immunization plays an important role in the management of financial institutions, as the following simplified example indicates.

Consider a small bank with a simple balance sheet as given in Table 5.3, where the values are actual market values. Assuming that the commercial loans and the CDs are both pure discount instruments, the duration of the assets will be two years and the duration of the liabilities will be .5 years. (This is the case since the duration of a pure discount bond equals its time to maturity.) If interest rates rise 2% on both instruments, the values of both the assets and liabilities will fall, and the bank will have a new balance sheet as given in the bottom panel of the Table. (Remember that the values are market values.) Using the Duration Price Change Equation to compute the new balance sheet gives a total asset value of $964.29 and a liability value of $991.07. The bank is now insolvent with equity being −$26.78. The bank could have avoided this by establishing an immunized position at the outset. If the bank had traded 2 year CDs, the duration of the asset and liability portfolios would have been equal, and the 2% rise in rates would have had the same effect on both sides of the balance sheet, leaving equity unchanged.[4] In briefest terms, Table 5.3 reveals the story of the savings and loan industry's crisis in the early 1980s. Duration, as will be shown below, has many uses for managing interest rate risk, and it plays an important role in hedging interest rate risk with interest rate futures as well.

Yield Curve Analysis

To understand interest rates and bond analysis, it is also essential to understand the *term structure of interest rates,* a relationship between bond yields and the time to maturity for bonds. Graphically, this relationship is expressed by the yield curve, an example of which is presented in Figure 5.1. The yield curve can be drawn for many different kinds of instruments, but to isolate the effect of maturity from other factors, it is necessary that the bonds used to construct a yield curve be as similar as possible in all respects except for maturity. Ideally, they should be identical in coupon, tax status, callability, and risk level. Investors' choices about what kinds of instruments to hold are often influenced by the shape of the yield curve. A sharply upward sloping yield curve means that rates on long-term bonds are higher than rates on short-term instruments, and this gives investors a reason to prefer the longer maturity instruments.

One of the most interesting and important facts about the term structure of interest rates is what it reveals about the expected future course of interest rates. If the yield curve is sharply upward sloping, then the market as a whole believes that interest rates will be rising, as seen in the following. Consider two Treasury Bills with yields as follows:

3-month	**8%**
6-month	**9%**

In order to hold Treasury bills for six months, we have two choices. It is easy to invest in the 6-month bill and earn 9%, or we could invest in the 3-month bill at 8% and then roll the investment over after three months into a second 3-month bill at some rate which is not known at the beginning of the 6-month holding period. If the market for Treasury bills is in equilibrium, then the two strategies should give the same return after six months, unless there is some strong preference for holding bills of one maturity rather than another. What would the rate on the second 3-month bill have to be in order to give the same final return from either strategy?

Assume that $1 is invested in the 6-month bill and that the invest-

TABLE 5.3

Simple National Bank.

Assets		Liabilities	
Commercial Loans (12%, 2 year maturity)	$1000	CDs (10%, six month maturity)	$1000
		Equity	0
Total Assets	$1000	Total Liabilities	$1000

Rates rise by 2% on all instruments.
All balance sheet items are shown at market value.

Assets		Liabilities	
Loans	$964.29	CDs	$991.07
		Equity	− 26.78
Total Assets	$964.29	Total Liabilities	$964.29

ment is held for six months. The investor's final wealth is given by equation (5.13):

$$\$1 \; (1.09)^{.5} = \$1.0440 \qquad (5.13)$$

If there is no reason to prefer holding two 3-month bills in a row to holding one 6-month bill for six months, or vice versa, then the two strategies should give the same return. This is shown in equation (5.14):

$$\$1 \; (1.08)^{.25} \; (1 + x)^{.25} = \$1.0440 \qquad (5.14)$$

In equation (5.14) the $1 is first invested at the rate of 8% for one-fourth of a year. The investment is then rolled over into a new 3-month bill at some rate x, which is not known at the outset. But, if the two strategies are to be equally desirable, then they must both give the same final end return of $1.0440 for an initial investment of $1. This is only possible if the second rate, x, equals 10%. These rates, implied by pairs of spot market instruments of different maturities, are called *forward rates*. In the absence of any strong preferences for holding particular maturities, the forward rates should be equal to the market's expectation of future spot rates.

If the forward rates did not equal expected future spot rates, then anyone planning to hold an investment for six months would have a reason to prefer the long-term bill or the sequence of short-term bills, depending on which gave the higher return. But this yield difference would cause investors to switch from the low yielding instrument to the high yielding instruments. As they did so, the price of the low yielding instrument would fall, raising its yield. This process would continue until there was no reason to prefer one strategy to the other.

In the example of equation (5.14), the current rate on 3-month bills

FIGURE 5.1
Yield Curves.

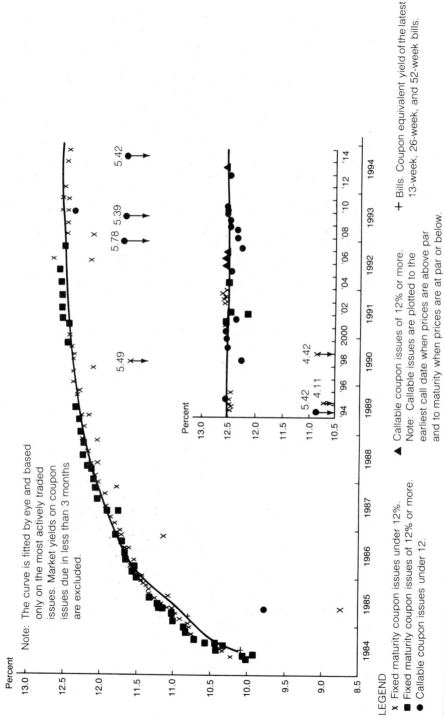

Note: The curve is fitted by eye and based only on the most actively traded issues. Market yields on coupon issues due in less than 3 months are excluded.

LEGEND

x Fixed maturity coupon issues under 12%.
■ Fixed maturity coupon issues of 12% or more.
● Callable coupon issues under 12.

▲ Callable coupon issues of 12% or more.
   Note: Callable issues are plotted to the earliest call date when prices are above par and to maturity when prices are at par or below.

+ Bills. Coupon equivalent yield of the latest 13-week, 26-week, and 52-week bills.

is 8%, and the forward rate for 3-month bills, to begin in three months, is 10%. If forward rates are expected future spot rates, then the market is expecting the three month bill rate to rise from 8 to 10% over the next three months. In general, whenever the yield curve is upward sloping, the forward rates must exceed the spot rates for a given maturity instrument. Exactly the opposite relation holds if the yield curve is downward sloping.

All of the preceding discussion of forward rates and expected future spot rates of interest was predicated on the assumption that market participants had, on the whole, no strong maturity preference. This is the belief of those who support the *pure expectations* theory of the term structure. Such theorists simply believe that forward rates equal expected future spot rates of interest. Others, naturally enough, disagree. According to the argument of the liquidity premium theorists, market participants prefer to hold short-term instruments. This means that yields will normally be lower on short-term instruments, so the yield curve will naturally slope upward. A consequence of this theory is that forward rates do not equal expected future spot rates. The conflict between these two theories has yet to be resolved. If there is a liquidity premium, causing forward rates and expected future spot rates to diverge, it is probably quite small. At any rate, both parties agree that forward rates are intimately related to expected future spot rates.[5]

This situation is analogous to the situation with futures prices as estimators of expected future spot prices. There may be some difference between futures prices and expected future spot prices, and there may be some difference between forward rates and expected future spot rates of interest. But the differences, if they do exist, are small and will be ignored. As will become clear, the two controversies turn out to be exactly the same, at least where interest rate futures are concerned. This is the case since yields on futures contracts should be equal to corresponding forward rates of interest and to expected future spot interest rates.

The Risk Structure of Interest Rates

So far, any differences in risk between bonds have been ignored. These risk differences, however, are very important. Analogous to the term structure of interest rates, there is also a risk structure of interest rates. The risk structure of interest rates is a schedule showing the difference in yield between instruments that are the same in all respects, except for their risk level. For example, corporate bonds have a higher level of default risk than U.S. government bonds and must pay correspondingly higher rates of interest to bondholders to compensate them for bearing the additional risk. Figure 5.2 shows the risk structure of interest rates, by comparing Treasury issues with non-government issues. The yield differential between any two issues is normally larger when interest rates are

FIGURE 5.2

The Risk Structure of Interest Rates.

Average Yields of Long-term Treasury, corporate, and municipal bonds, 1970-1980. SOURCE: Treasury Bulletin January 1981, p. 73.

high, and this tendency is reflected in the graph. There is a tendency to ignore the risk structure of interest rates in many discussions of interest rate futures, since the futures contracts tend to be written on only the safest instruments, such as government securities and top quality bank obligations. But differences in risk between two instruments become very important in hedging, as will become apparent later.

This brief review of interest rates reflects only the most important factors in bond price determination and bond portfolio management. There are many more important ideas that are useful to anyone interested in interest rate futures. The treatment of interest rates to this point merely gives the reader the essential core of knowledge necessary to understand interest rate futures. All of the ideas developed to this point will be put together to develop a grasp of interest rate futures. Consequently, a mastery of this minimal set of bond pricing concepts is essential to understanding the next sections.

INTEREST RATE FUTURES

To understand the special features of the interest rate futures market, it is important to understand the specific contract features for the different instruments. Among all the different types of futures contracts, interest rate futures exhibit the most variety, with the characteristics of the futures contracts being tailored to the particular attributes of the underlying instruments. By analyzing two of the interest rate futures contracts in some detail, the other available contracts will be much easier to understand. Accordingly, this section focuses on the two most important contracts, the Treasury-Bill contract and the Treasury-Bond contract. After analyzing these two contracts, their specific features are used to illustrate other important conceptual issues pertaining to the interest rate futures market.

Treasury-Bills and Treasury-Bill Futures

Treasury-Bills are obligations of the U.S. Government, issued by the Treasury Department, and backed by the *full faith and credit* of the Government and its taxing powers. As such, Treasury obligations are usually regarded as being the world's safest investment, and when people speak of the "risk-free rate of interest," they usually are referring to the rate on some Treasury issue. Treasury-Bills, or *T-Bills,* are auctioned each business Monday for delivery on the Thursday of the same week. They are always for a maturity of one-year or less and are pure discount instruments, having no cash flow until their maturity. Bills that mature in 91 and 182 days are auctioned every week, and 52-week bills are auctioned monthly, with minimum denominations of $10,000, and with increments above this minimum of $5000. Starting from very modest beginnings in 1929, T-Bills have grown in importance. By early 1983, $311.8 billion of marketable T-bills were outstanding, with a very active secondary market. This active secondary market, and the great size of the outstanding issues, is important for the futures market, since it insures a large and readily available deliverable supply of the T-Bills for delivery against the futures contract.[6]

One important feature of T-Bills is the method by which they are priced. Quotations for T-Bills take the form shown in Table 5.4. For each maturity date, both a *bid* and asked *discount yield* are shown, along with a bond-equivalent yield in the "yield" column. The discount yield is a function of the face value, the price (which may be either the bid or asked price to give the bid or asked discount yield), and the number of days to maturity, based on a 360-day year. It can be computed according to equation (5.15):

$$\text{Discount Yield} = \frac{(\text{Face Value} - \text{Price}) \times 360}{\dfrac{\text{Days to Maturity}}{}} \qquad (5.15)$$

$$\text{Discount Yield} = \frac{\dfrac{(\text{Face Value} - \text{Price}) \times 360}{\text{Days to Maturity}}}{\text{Face Value}} \qquad (5.15)$$

TABLE 5.4
Treasury Bill Quotations. February 14, 1983.

Maturity Date	Bid (Discount)	Asked (Discount)	Yield
—1983—			
2–17	7.88	7.76	7.87
2–24	7.95	7.83	7.95
•			
•			
•			
5–26	8.28	8.18	8.48
•			
•			
10–6	8.38	8.26	8.76
•			
•			
•			
—1984—			
1–26	8.42	8.36	9.02

The bond equivalent is computed on a somewhat similar basis. Although the bond equivalent yield is based on a 365-day year, the main difference between the discount yield and the bond equivalent yield appears in the divisors. As equation (5.16) shows, the bond equivalent yield uses the price of the instrument in the divisor:

$$\text{Bond Equivalent Yield} = \frac{\dfrac{(\text{Face Value} - \text{Price}) \times 365}{\text{Days to Maturity}}}{\text{Price}} \qquad (5.16)$$

This means that the bond equivalent yield will tend to be higher than the yield based on the mean of the bid-asked spread, since the price will always be less than the face value. One other way of evaluating the yield of a T-Bill is based on the Bond Pricing Equation, which is given for a T-Bill as equation (5.17):

$$\text{Price} = \frac{\text{Face Value}}{(1 + r)^t} \qquad (5.17)$$

These are three different measures of the yield on T-Bills, with the first two being more important in the actual institutional practice of the T-Bill market and the last being useful for allowing more direct yield comparisons with other instruments.

The T-Bill futures contract, traded by the International Monetary Market (IMM) of the Chicago Mercantile Exchange (CME), calls for the delivery of T-Bills having a face value of $1,000,000 and a time to maturity of 90 days at the expiration of the futures contract. The contracts trade for delivery in March, June, September, and December, with trading ending on the Wednesday following the third Monday of the delivery month. Delivery normally occurs on Thursday of the same week.

Price quotations are made according to the IMM-Index, which is a function of the discount yield:

$$\text{IMM Index} = 100.00\% - \text{Discount Yield} \qquad (5.18)$$

As an example, a discount yield of 8.32% would imply an IMM-index value of 91.68. This method of price quotation was adopted to insure that the bid price would be below the asked price, the usual relationship prevailing in most markets. Price fluctuations may be no smaller than one tick, or one *basis point*. Given the fact that the instruments are priced by using a discount yield and a contract size of $1,000,000, a movement of one basis point translates into a price change of $25.00. The price to be paid at delivery can be found by rearranging equation (5.15) to give equation (5.19):

$$\text{Bill Price} = \$1,000,000 - \frac{\text{Discount Yield} \times \$1,000,000 \times 90}{360} \qquad (5.19)$$

With a discount yield of 8.32% on the futures contract, the price to be paid for the T-Bill at delivery would be $979,200. If the futures yield rose to 8.35%, the delivery price would be $979,125, changing $25 for each basis point. As is the case with most futures contracts, there is a limit on the amount by which the price may move in one day, and for the T-Bill contract, that limit is 60 basis points, or $1500, in either direction from the previous day's settlement price. In times of volatile price movements, this daily limit may be expanded to 90 or even 120 basis points, in accordance with the rules of the exchange. Although the contract specifications call for the delivery of a T-Bill having 90 days to maturity, delivery of 91- or 92-day bills is also permitted with a price adjustment. In any event, all of the delivered T-Bills must be of the same maturity, and the value of the delivery unit is calculated according to equation (5.20):

$$\text{Value of Delivery Unit} =$$

$$\frac{\$1,000,000 - \begin{array}{c}\text{days from delivery}\\\text{date to maturity}\end{array} \times \text{T-Bill Yield} \times \$1,000,000}{360} \qquad (5.20)$$

The T-bill contract can exhibit considerable volatility in its price. Figure 5.3 shows the pattern and range of the June and December 1981 T-Bill futures contracts over their lives. The June 1981 contract ranged from a low IMM index value of 83.35 to a high of 92.64, while the December contract traded in the range from 84.72 to 92.17. In terms of dollars per contract, the June contract had a price range of $23,225 and the December contract had a price range of $18,625. In spite of the well known high volatility of interest rates during the period these contracts existed, the figures show substantial opportunity for gain and a high risk of loss. For the nearby T-Bill contract, over the life of the market, the standard deviation of the daily price fluctuation has been about $475 per contract. With a low initial margin in the range of $2000–3000, there is ample excitement in trading T-Bill futures.

Treasury-Bonds and Treasury-Bond Futures

Treasury-Bonds, like Treasury-Bills, are also issued by the Treasury Department and have the same backing by the Government. T-Bonds and T-Bills differ in their maturity and the structure of the instruments. T-Bonds are issued with an initial maturity of at least ten years. In practice, the initial time-to-maturity is much greater, usually 25–30 years. T-Bonds pay semi-annual coupon payments, with the coupon rate being set to make the initial price of the bonds close to their par value. Most T-bonds are callable, with the first call date coming five years before the bond matures. Reference to a particular bond might often be made in the form "ten-and-three-eighths of 2007 to 2012." This would refer to a bond with a 10–3/8% coupon rate that matures in 2012 and is callable beginning in 2007. Most T-Bonds mature in the months of February, May, August, or November, with the maturity falling on the 15th. But that generalization is not a hard and fast rule.

T-Bond price quotations show the bid and asked prices quoted as a percent of par, where the digits appearing after the decimal point are expressed in 32nds of one percentage point. A price quotation of 98.20 reflects a price of 98 plus 20/32 percent of the par value. Quotations also show a yield to maturity. T-Bond prices and yields may be calculated by the Bond Pricing Equation. Since coupon payments are made semi-annually, application of the formula will yield a semi-annual yield which must be doubled to give the annual yield on the T-Bond. To obtain a T-Bond one must pay the asked price, which is quoted, and the *accrued interest,* which is not reflected in the bond price quotation. The accrued interest is the interest that has been earned on the bond since the last coupon payment and its value is given by equation (5.21):

$$\textbf{Accrued Interest} = \frac{\textbf{Days Since Last Interest Payment}}{\textbf{Days in Half-year}} \times \textbf{Semi-Annual Interest Payment} \quad \textbf{(5.21)}$$

Short-term rates of interest are more volatile than long-term rates. From the analysis of the preceding section, however, it is clear that a long-term instrument has a greater sensitivity to any given change in interest rates than does a short-term instrument. This difference in sensitivity can be expressed by analyzing the relative durations of the short-

FIGURE 5.3

T-Bill Futures Prices.

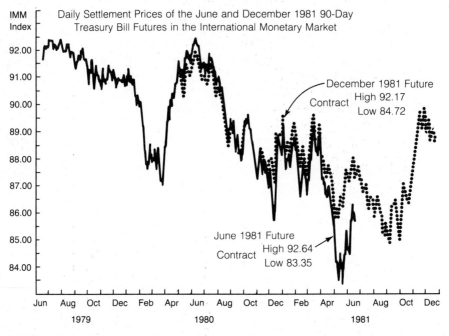

SOURCE: *IMM Yearbook*, 1981, p. 538.

and long-term instruments. The difference in the volatility of T-Bills and T-Bonds is demonstrated in Table 5.5. Consider a 3-month T-Bill and a 20-year 8% coupon T-Bond, both with face values of $1000 and initial yields of 14%. A given change in yields has a much greater effect on the T-Bond's price in comparison with the price of the T-Bill. For small yield changes of .5%, the price of the T-Bond changes about three times as much as that of the T-Bill. For later changes, however, the relative volatility of the T-Bond is greatly increased. For a drop in rates from 14% to 8.5%, for example, the percentage price change for the T-Bond is more than 45 times as large as that for the T-Bill. From the mere fact that long-term rates are relatively stable, it does not follow that prices of long-term bonds are relatively stable.

The volatility of T-Bond prices is emphasized by Figure 5.4, which shows the price volatility of the 12-3/4% T-Bond of 2005–10. In the period from December, 1980 to August, 1981, the price ranged from 108% of par (approximately) to almost as low as 95%. This high price volatility, which is stimulated by rather modest changes in interest rates, promises considerable price action for the T-Bond futures contract.

TABLE 5.5
Relative Volatility of T-Bills and T-Bonds.

	3 mos. Treasury-Bill			20 yr. 8% coupon Treasury Bond		
Yield	Price	% Price Change		Price	% Price Change	% △ Corporate % △ T-Bill
.14	967.77	—		$620	—	—
.145	966.72	− .108%		600	− 3.23%	3.02
.12	972.07	+ .44		718.75	+ 15.93	36.20
.10	976.45	+ .90		806.14	+ 30.04	33.38
.085	979.81	+ 1.24		968.75	+ 56.25	45.36

Of all of the futures contracts currently traded, the T-Bond contract is one of the most difficult to understand, as well as one of the most interesting. The complexity of the contract stems from the delivery rules under which it is traded and from the wide variety of bonds that can be delivered in fulfillment of the contract. For the T-Bill contract, delivery takes place within a very narrow span of time, but the Chicago Board of Trade (CBT), which trades the T-Bond contract, employs a radically different delivery procedure.

Delivery against the T-Bond contract is a several day process that can be triggered at the initiative of the short position to cause delivery on any business day of the delivery month. Like the T-Bill contract, the T-Bond contract is traded for delivery in March, June, September, and December. But delivery can be made on any business day of the delivery month, with the exact date of delivery being specified by the short position. To effect delivery, the short trader initiates a delivery sequence that extends over three business days. Figure 5.5 shows the delivery procedure for T-Bond futures, a procedure which is also followed for other Board of Trade contracts, such as GNMAs and T-Note futures. The *First Position Day* is the first permissible day for the short trader to declare his or her intention to make delivery, with the delivery taking place two business days later. The first permissible day for such an announcement will fall in the month preceding the delivery month, since actual delivery is permitted on the very first day of the delivery month. If the short declares his or her intention to deliver on any other day besides the First Position Day, then that day is called *Position Day*. On Position Day, the short trader announces his or her intention to deliver on the second business day thereafter.

The second day in the delivery sequence is the *Notice of Intention Day*. On this day, the Clearing Corporation matches the short trader with the long trader having the longest outstanding position, and identifies the short and long traders to each other.[7] The short trader will then be obligated to make delivery to that particular long trader on the next

FIGURE 5.4

Volatility of Treasury Bond Prices.

U.S. Treasury Bond 12¾
Dec. 1980-Aug. 1981

32nds of 100 PCT.

12¾ of 2005-10

business day. The third and final day of the delivery sequence is *Delivery Day,* when the actual transaction takes place. On this day the short delivers the financial instrument to the long trader and receives payment. The long trader then has all rights of ownership in the T-Bonds that were delivered in fulfillment of the contract.

For the T-Bond futures contract, a wide variety of bonds may be delivered against the contract at any one time. The rules of the Board of Trade call for the delivery of $100,000 worth of T-Bonds that have at least 15 years remaining until maturity or to their first permissible call date. Table 5.6 shows all of the twenty-one bonds that were deliverable against the March, 1983 contract, as of February 14, 1983. Notice the tremendous range of coupons and maturities on these bonds. In the past, there have not been so many deliverable issues, but with all of these bonds outstanding, it is clear that quite a few bonds will be deliverable against the T-Bond contract for some time to come. One of these bonds merits special mention, the 3–1/2s of 1998. This bond matures in May,

FIGURE 5.5

The Delivery Sequence for T-Bond Futures. SOURCE: Chicago Board of Trade.

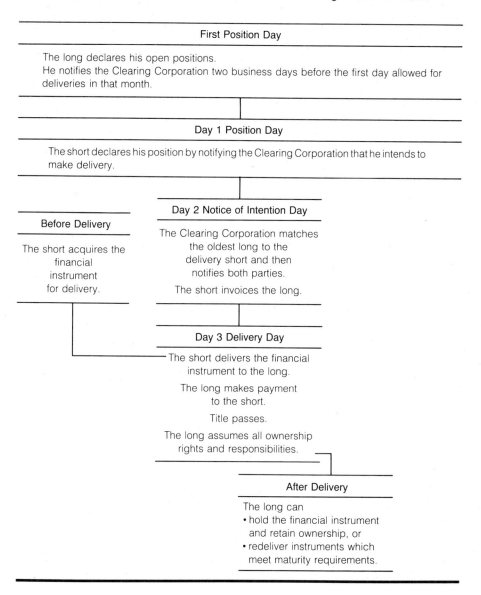

First Position Day
The long declares his open positions. He notifies the Clearing Corporation two business days before the first day allowed for deliveries in that month.

Day 1 Position Day
The short declares his position by notifying the Clearing Corporation that he intends to make delivery.

Before Delivery	Day 2 Notice of Intention Day
The short acquires the financial instrument for delivery.	The Clearing Corporation matches the oldest long to the delivery short and then notifies both parties. The short invoices the long.

Day 3 Delivery Day
The short delivers the financial instrument to the long. The long makes payment to the short. Title passes. The long assumes all ownership rights and responsibilities.

After Delivery
The long can • hold the financial instrument and retain ownership, or • redeliver instruments which meet maturity requirements.

1998, so it is deliverable against the March, 1983 contract, but not the June, 1983 contract. Also, this particular bond is a *flower bond,* which is acceptable at face value in payment of Federal Estate Tax. Due to this special tax status, it has a very low coupon and trades at a relatively high price.

TABLE 5.6
Deliverable T-Bonds for March, 1983 (as of February 14, 1983).

Coupon	Maturity
3–1/2s	1998
11–3/4s	2001
13–1/8s	2001
13–3/8s	2001
15–3/4s	2001
14–1/4s	2002
11–5/8s	2002
10–3/4s	2003
8–1/4s	2000–05
7–5/8s	2002–07
7–7/8s	2002–07
8–3/8s	2003–08
8–3/4s	2003–08
9–1/8s	2004–09
10–3/8s	2004–09
11–3/4s	2005–10
10s	2005–10
12–3/4s	2005–10
13–7/8s	2006–11
14s	2006–11
10–3/8s	2007–12

The fact that some bonds are cheap, and some expensive, suggests that there may be an advantage to delivering one bond rather than another. If there is such an advantage, why did the CBT allow several bonds to be delivered against the contract? These considerations are intimately related, and have an important impact on the contract design. Given the significant difference in maturity and coupon rates, there are large price differences among these bonds. But, in the absence of any further consideration, one of the bonds would be cheapest to deliver. Since the short trader chooses whether to make delivery, and which bond to deliver, we might expect that only the cheapest bond would ever be delivered.

To eliminate an incentive to deliver just one particular bond, the CBT initiated a system of *conversion factors* which alters the delivery values of different bonds as a function of their coupon rate and term-to-maturity. The conversion factors are based on the assumed normal bond having 20 years to maturity and an 8% coupon rate. A quick glance at Table 5.6 shows that no such bond even existed for delivery on the

March, 1983 contract. Every bond's price would be adjusted by the conversion factor specific to its maturity and coupon rate.

For purposes of delivery, the invoice amount is calculated according to equation (5.22):

Invoice Amount = Decimal Settlement Price × Conversion Factor + Accrued Interest (5.22)

Each term requires comment. The *Decimal Settlement Price* is simply the quoted price, which is quoted in "points and 32nds of par" just as the spot instrument, converted to its decimal equivalent. The $100,000 reflects the contract amount. The conversion factor is the technique for adjusting the differences in value for bonds of different coupon rates and maturities. The conversion factor for any bond can be found by following two rules:

1. Assume that the face value of the bond to be delivered is $1.
2. Discount the assumed cash flows from the bond at 8% using the Bond Pricing Equation.

The result will be the conversion factor for the bond in question. A sample of conversion factors is shown in Table 5.7[8]. Reflecting on these two rules, and the conversion factors of Table 5.7 makes several points clear. In general, the closer the coupon rate is to 8%, the closer the conversion factor will be to 1. For a bond with an 8% coupon, the conversion factor will always be 1, no matter what the maturity of the instrument. This makes sense, given the rules which would be telling one to discount an 8% coupon instrument at 8%. For bonds with coupon rates above 8%, the shorter the maturity, the closer the conversion factor will be to 1. Just the opposite holds for bonds with coupon rates below 8%.

In general, if yields are 8% across all maturities, the conversion factors will be proportional to the bonds' market prices. This is exactly the desired situation, since the delivery value of a bond should be proportional to its market value. With a flat term structure and yields at 8%, there is no advantage to delivering any bond rather than another. The correlative of this proposition is somewhat disturbing and very important for T-Bond futures. If the term structure is not flat, or if yields are not equal to 8%, then there will be some bond that is better to deliver than the other permissible bonds. This bond is known as the *cheapest to deliver*. Among T-Bond futures traders, the concept of the cheapest to deliver bond is well known. Most brokerage houses have computer systems that show the cheapest to deliver T-Bonds on a real time basis. Since this feature is well known, it is not surprising that the futures prices tend to price the cheapest to deliver bond, which may change over time.

Why did the CBT adopt this cumbersome system of conversion factors, particularly since it introduces biases into the marketplace? As men-

TABLE 5.7
T-Bond Conversion Factors.

DELIVERABLE TREASURY BONDS

Coupon	Maturity	Dec 83	Mar 84	Jun 84	Sep 84	Dec 84	Mar 85	Jun 85
8¼	May 15 2000-05	1.0223	1.0223	1.0220	1.0220	1.0216	1.0216	
7⅝	Feb. 15 2002-07	0.9645	0.9646	0.9650	0.9651	0.9655	.9655	.9660
7⅞	Nov. 15 2002-07	0.9878	0.9880	0.9879	0.9882	0.9881	.9883	.9882
8⅜	Aug. 15 2003-08	1.0367	1.0363	1.0363	1.0359	1.0359	1.0355	1.0355
8¾	Nov. 15 2003-08	1.0736	1.0734	1.0728	1.0726	1.0720	1.0718	1.0711
9⅛	May 15 2004-09	1.1117	1.1113	1.1105	1.1102	1.1093	1.1089	1.1081
10⅜	Nov. 15 2004-09	1.2383	1.2374	1.2360	1.2350	1.2336	1.2326	1.2310
11¾	Feb. 15 2005-10	1.3785	1.3764	1.3749	1.3727	1.3711	1.3689	1.3672
10	May 15 2005-10	1.2025	1.2019	1.2007	1.1999	1.1987	1.1979	1.1967
12¾	Nov. 15 2005-10	1.4856	1.4838	1.4813	1.4794	1.4768	1.4748	1.4722
11¾	Feb. 15 2001	1.3452	1.3425	1.3403	1.3374	1.3351	1.3322	1.3298
13⅛	May 15 2001	1.4747	1.4718	1.4681	1.4650	1.4612	1.4580	1.4541
13⅞	May 15 2006-11	1.6058	1.6036	1.6007	1.5984	1.5954	1.5930	1.5898
13⅜	Aug. 15 2001	1.5016	1.4979	1.4948	1.4910	1.4877	1.4837	1.4804
15¾	Nov. 15 2001	1.7276	1.7233	1.7180	1.7134	1.7080	1.7032	1.6976
14	Nov. 15 2006-11	1.6238	1.6216	1.6187	1.6165	1.6135	1.6111	1.6080
14¼	Feb. 15 2002	1.5909	1.5868	1.5833	1.5790	1.5753	1.5709	1.5671
11⅝	Nov. 15 2002	1.3487	1.3470	1.3446	1.3427	1.3402	1.3383	1.3357
10⅜	Nov. 15 2007-12	1.2505	1.2499	1.2487	1.2480	1.2468	1.2461	1.2448
10¾	Feb. 15 2003	1.2663	1.2645	1.2632	1.2614	1.2600	1.2581	1.2566
10¾	May 15 2003	1.2675	1.2663	1.2645	1.2632	1.2614	1.2600	1.2581
12	Aug. 15 2008-13	1.4268	1.4251	1.4234	1.4221	1.4209	1.4190	1.4177
11⅛	Aug. 15 2003	1.3060	1.3041	1.3026	1.3006	1.2991	1.2970	1.2954
11⅞	Nov. 15 2003	1.3812	1.3794	1.3771	1.3753	1.3728	1.3709	1.3683

Courtesy Chicago Board of Trade

tioned above, a substantial deliverable supply of the spot commodity is a necessary condition for a successful futures contract. If there is an insufficient supply of the deliverable commodity, then the chance for *market corners* and *squeezes* of traders obligated to make delivery can arise. To insure a large deliverable supply, the CBT allowed a wide range of bonds to qualify for delivery. Once this decision was made, it was necessary to attempt some adjustment of the bond prices for the purpose of assessing their delivery value.

One other feature of the delivery procedure is less well known, but potentially very important, and that is the *wild card play*. On position day, the short trader may announce her plan to deliver until the early evening, after the spot and futures market have closed. The amount she may invoice the long trader depends on the bond she selects to deliver and the settlement price on the futures on the position day. On certain occasions, news that causes a significant fall in the value of bonds can come to light after the market closes, but before the deadline for announcing plans to deliver. The short trader can then announce her intention to deliver, thereby *locking-in* the settlement price for that day, a price that does not reflect the bearish information for bonds. The next day, the bond will open at a lower price, and the short trader simply acquires the now cheaper bond for delivery at the old higher price. The chance of being victimized by a wild card play is an additional risk that the long trader must bear, and it is presumably impounded in the price of the futures contract. Notice finally that there are a number of chances for the short trader to make the wild card play, since any position day is a possibility. Many of the features of the delivery process for both T-Bills and T-Bonds are important for arbitrage attempts, speculation, and hedging.

In spite of the peculiarities of the T-Bond contract, it is the single most successful futures contract ever introduced. Starting in August, 1977, its success has been amazing. Figure 5.6 reflects that amazing growth, both in trading volume and the level of open interest. With open interest of 170,000 contracts in February, 1983, T-Bond futures represent claims for a total face value of T-Bonds in excess of $17 billion dollars.

As for all futures contracts, the basis is important for interest rate futures. Figure 5.7 depicts the basis for the June, 1981 futures contract, where the basis is computed against the 10-3/8s of 2004–09. When the price is adjusted to reflect the conversion factor, the difference between the spot and futures position is stable and close to zero. The closeness of the basis to zero in this Figure indicates that the conversion factors often do a good job in equilibrating the cash T-Bond and the T-Bond futures. However, the basis in the interest rate futures market has some special features that require attention. Given the virtual costlessness of storing financial instruments, the basis in the interest rate futures market also has a special interpretation.

FIGURE 5.6
Growth of the T-Bond Futures Contract.

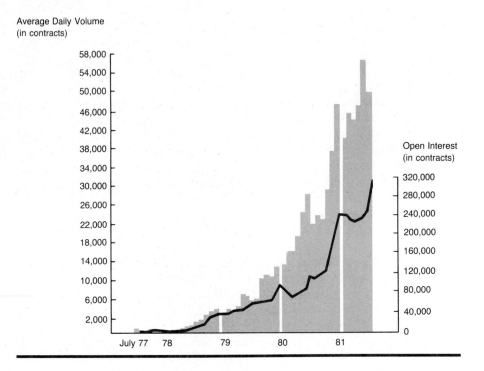

Average Daily Volume
(in contracts)

Open Interest
(in contracts)

Basis, the Cost of Carry, and Implied Repo Rates

In futures markets, the *basis* represents the difference between the futures price and the cash market price. It receives, and deserves, attention because it indicates the likely future direction of cash prices. From the earlier discussion of basis in Chapters 3 and 4, it is clear that certain restrictions exist on the permissible size of the basis. If the basis exceeds the financing cost of acquiring and storing the cash market asset, then an arbitrage opportunity exists. In the interest rate futures market, the cost of storing an asset, or the cost of carry, is sometimes negative. If a trader purchases and stores a U.S. T-Bill or T-Bond, then the cost of storing that asset equals the interest rate on the funds being used to buy the bill or bond, minus the bill or bond's yield. (This neglects the cost of *warehousing* the bill or bond while it is in *storage,* since such costs are virtually zero.)[9]

These facts have strong implications for the basis. In the case of interest rate futures, the basis can be expressed in terms of dollars or the difference in yields between the spot and futures instruments. The same non-arbitrage condition that has been explored in varying contexts

FIGURE 5.7
The Basis for T-Bond Futures.

means that the yield differential between the spot instrument and the futures contract cannot exceed a given amount. This relationship is best illustrated by an example. Table 5.8 summarizes the pertinent data for this example of arbitrage. The yields used in the Table are not the discount yields of the IMM Index, but the yields calculated according to the Bond Pricing Formula. The example assumes the usual unrealistic case of perfect markets, including the assumption that one can either borrow or lend at any of the riskless rates represented by the T-Bill yields. These restrictive assumptions will be relaxed momentarily. The data presented in Table 5.8, and the assumptions just made, mean that an arbitrage opportunity is present. Since the futures contract matures in 77 days, the spot 77-day rate represents the financing cost to acquire the 167-day T-Bill, which can be delivered against the March, 1984 futures contract on March 22, 1984. This will work, because the T-Bill that has 167 days to maturity on January 5, 1984 will have exactly 90 days to maturity on March 22, 1984.

As the transactions presented in Table 5.9 indicate, an arbitrage opportunity is present since the rates on the three instruments are mutually inconsistent. The basic strategy is to acquire the 167-day T-Bill on January 5 and hold it for delivery against the March, 1984 futures, which is sold. The transaction must be financed for the 77-day interval from January 5 to delivery on March 22. To take advantage of the rate discrepancy, one borrows at the short term rate of 6%, and uses the proceeds to acquire the long-term T-Bill. At the maturity of the futures, the long-term T-Bill has the exactly correct maturity and can be delivered against the futures contract. Doing so generates a profit of $2,235 on each contract. Relative to the short term rate, the futures yield and the long-term T-Bill yield were too high. In this example, one is able to acquire short-term funds at a low rate (6%) and reinvest those funds at a higher rate (10%). It may appear that this difference generates the arbitrage profit, but that is not completely accurate, as the next example shows.

Consider the same situation, except allow the rate on the 77-day T-Bill to be 8%. Now the short-term rate is too high relative to the long-term rate and the futures yield. To take advantage of this situation, the procedure of Table 5.9 is reversed, as is shown in Table 5.10. With the rates reversed, the procedure is slightly more complicated, since it involves holding the T-Bill that is delivered on the futures contract. In this situation, the arbitrageur will borrow $955,131 for 167 days at 10%, and invest these funds at 8% for the 77 days until the March futures matures. The payoff from the 77 day investment of $955,131 will be $970,984. This is exactly enough to pay for the delivery of the T-Bill on the futures contract. This bill is held for 90 days until June 20, 1984, when it matures and pays $1,000,000. On June 20, the loan the arbitrageur took out on the 167-day T-Bill is also due, and equal to $998,308. This debt is paid off out of the $1,000,000, yielding a profit of $1,692. Notice in this second example, that one borrowed at 10% and invested the funds at 8% temporarily. This shows that it is the entire set of rates that must be consistent, and that arbitrage opportunities need not only involve misalignment between two rates.

From the two examples of Tables 5.9 and 5.10, it is apparent that there must be a very exact relationship among these rates on the different instruments if arbitrage opportunities are not permitted. Taking the March futures yield and the 167-day spot yield as fixed, there is only one yield for the 77-day T-Bill that will not give rise to an arbitrage opportunity, and that rate is 7.15%. To see why that is the case, consider the two ways of holding a position for the full 167 day period of the examples. One could either hold the 167-day T-Bill, or one could hold a 77-day T-Bill followed by the 90-day T-Bill that is delivered on the

TABLE 5.8

Interest Rate Futures and Arbitrage. Today's Date: January 5, 1984.

Futures	Yield According to the Bond Pricing Formula
March Contract (Matures in 77 days on March 22)	12.50%
Cash Bills	
167-Day T-Bill (Deliverable on March futures)	10.00
77-Day T-Bill	6.00

futures contracts. Since these two ways of holding cover the same time period and have the same risk level, the two positions must have the same yield if arbitrage is not permitted. This conclusion holds, given our perfect market assumptions and the fact that we are ignoring the daily-resettlement feature of the futures contract. For the examples, the necessary yield on the 77-day T-Bill can be found by using the same type of equation as (5.14), which expresses the yield on a long term instrument as being equal to the yield on two short term positions:

$$(1.10)^{167/360} \;=\; (1 + x)^{77/360} \qquad\qquad (1.1250)^{90/360} \qquad (5.23)$$

167-day Bill   77-day T-Bill   90-day T-Bill underlying T-Bill futures

Equation (5.23) will hold only if the rate, x, on the 77-day T-Bill is 7.15%.

These examples might seem unrealistic, since we cannot borrow at the T-Bill rate. This objection is an important one and requires an extension of the example to reflect realistic market conditions more adequately. Consider again the transactions of Table 5.9 and consider that a trader could transact exactly as indicated if his or her borrowing cost for a 77-day period were 6%. Major participants in the futures markets can borrow and lend at the *repo rate,* the rate on repurchase agreements. In a repurchase agreement, one party sells a financial instrument, usually a Treasury issue or a Federal Agency issue, and agrees to repurchase it later at a given price. The difference between the sale price and the promised repurchase price give rise to an interest rate, the rate on the repurchase agreement or the repo rate. In the example of Table 5.9, if one faced a repo rate of 6%, then one could transact as indicated.[10]

In a broader context, the relationship between futures yields and yields on spot instruments imply a rate on repurchase agreements at which it is not profitable to transact. In the example, the *implied repo rate* equals 7.15% for a 77-day instrument. If one can borrow for 77 days at a rate lower than 7.15%, or if one can lend for the same period at a rate higher than 7.15%, then a potential arbitrage opportunity exists. The arbitrage opportunity is only potential, since the trader must be able

TABLE 5.9
Arbitrage Transactions.

January 5, 1984

Borrow $956,750 for 77 days by issuing a 77-day T-Bill at 6%.

Buy 167-day T-Bill yielding 10% for $956,750.

Sell March, 1984 T-Bill futures contract with a yield of 12.50% for $970,984.

March 22, 1984

Deliver the originally purchased T-Bill against the March futures contract and collect $970,984.

Repay debt on 77-day T-Bill that matures today for $968,749.

Profit: $970,984
        −   968,749
           $ 2,235

---

to pay for all transaction and search costs out of the proceeds of the arbitrage transaction if there is really to be a profit. This practice of calculating implied repo rates may seem rather arcane. However, virtually every major participant in the interest rate futures market will have complete information for all implied repo rates for the whole array of interest rate futures contracts. This information is kept constantly current by computer. In other words, major traders have access to implied repo rates based on current futures and spot market prices. Their motivation is clear; they are seeking arbitrage opportunities.

Are arbitrage opportunities available? This question will be addressed more fully later, but you may notice that everything here hinges on a relationship involving the implied repo rate. One problem with the repo market is that the market is extremely thin for *term repo agreements*. A term repo is a repurchase agreement for a span of time longer than a few days. Most repo agreements are only for one day, and are called *overnight repos*. This means that traders often know the implied repo rate exactly, but they may well not know their actual repo rate for an extended period. This situation is probably enough to frustrate arbitrage in the academic sense of an opportunity generating a sure profit without investment.

Tables 5.9 and 5.10 also reveal important points about the concept of basis in the interest rate futures market. On January 5, 1984 how would one measure the basis for the March, 1984 futures contract? The basis is supposed to be the difference between the futures price (or yield) and the spot price (or yield). But what is the relevant spot instrument to use in the calculation of the basis? An obvious candidate is to use the current 90-day T-Bill yield, since the futures contract is written for the delivery of a 90-day Bill. The futures contract, however, calls for the

TABLE 5.10
Arbitrage Transactions.

January 5, 1984
    Borrow $955,131 by issuing a 167-day T-Bill yielding 10%
    Buy a 77-day T-Bill yielding 8% for $955,131 that will pay $970,984 on March 22.
    Buy one March, 1984 futures contract with a yield of 12.50% for $970,984.

March 22, 1984
    Collect $970,984 from the maturing 77-day T-Bill.
    Pay $970,984 and take delivery of a 90-day T-Bill from the March, 1984 futures contract.

June 20, 1984
    Collect $1,000,000 from the maturing 90-day T-Bill that was delivered on the futures contract.
    Pay $998,308 debt on the maturing 167-day T-Bill.

Profit: $1,000,000
    −   998,308
    $ 1,692

---

delivery of a T-Bill having 90 days to maturity as of March 22, 1984. A T-Bill that has 90 days to maturity on January 5, 1984 will have only 13 days to maturity on March 22. A second choice might be to change the spot T-Bill every week for purposes of calculating the basis. There is always a T-Bill with just about 90 days to maturity, so one could figure the basis using whichever T-Bill currently has 90 days to maturity. This strategy, which involves changing the spot bill, has certain drawbacks. If we examine the basis over time, then we can compare a futures contract with a whole series of spot bills. The proper interpretation of this information is by no means obvious. A third choice might calculate the basis using a longer-term bill, perhaps one maturing at about the same time as the bill deliverable on the futures contract. In the example, this would mean comparing the futures yield with a 167-day bill on January 5, a 166-day bill on January 6, and so on. The interpretation of such information is, again, not clear. No obviously superior method of calculating the basis exists, so diverse strategies are followed. The basis might be calculated against a diverse collection of spot instruments, such as a bill maturing when the bill deliverable on the futures contract matures, current 90-day bills, current 180-day bills, and current 1-year bills.

For the Treasury-Bond futures contract, the basis is even more problematic. With more than 20 different deliverable spot instruments, there are more than 20 prime alternatives for calculating the basis. If one uses the conversion factor to adjust the value of the spot instrument to reflect its value in delivery against the futures contract, there are more than 40 alternatives. Again, there is no obviously correct choice. Unlike a

physical commodity such as gold, the bills and bonds are always changing their characteristics. This requires additional watchfulness and inter-
pretive skill from the participants in the interest rate futures market.

Futures Yields and Expected Future Spot Yields

In Chapters 3 and 4, the idea that futures prices may be taken as
estimates of future spot prices was developed. In the interest rate futures
market, a similar relationship is reasonable, but the emphasis is often
placed on futures market yields as estimates of future spot market yields.
With the background on forward rates presented in the first section of
this chapter, we now see more clearly the extent to which futures rates
may be taken as estimates of future spot rates. As has been shown, forward rates of interest may be calculated from the set of spot market yield
data. The interpretation of these forward rates is undecided, since many
scholars believe that there is a liquidity premium which causes forward
rates to be somewhat higher than expected future spot rates. If this possible liquidity premium is ignored, if perfect market conditions are assumed, and if the feature of daily resettlement is assumed to have no effect, then forward rates should equal futures rates, which should equal
expected future spot rates. The problem is whether this relationship, expressed as a question in equation (5.24), actually holds:

$$\textbf{Forward Rates} \overset{?}{=} \textbf{Futures Rates} \overset{?}{=} \textbf{Expected Future Spot Rates} \quad \textbf{(5.24)}$$

The difficulty, of course, is to evaluate how closely the three assumptions, upon which (5.24) is based, conform to reality. As mentioned in
the discussion of forward rates, there does seem to be evidence for the existence of a small liquidity premium.[11] Yet the issue is not yet settled.
This state of affairs suggests that any liquidity premium must be so small
that competent and disinterested scholars fail to find it. Whatever its
size, evidence supports the existence of a liquidity premium, and that is
enough to render (5.24) suspect. The condition of perfect markets is only
approximated in the futures market, since information is costly and one
must pay transaction costs to participate in the market. The economic
mechanism that would make (5.24) true is the seeking of profit by arbitrageurs and other traders. With wide discrepancies in rates, such as
those in Tables 5.9 and 5.10, the mechanism will surely operate to drive
rates toward the condition stated in (5.24). However, (5.24) need not
hold exactly if transaction and information costs exist. To see why this
must be the case, consider a very small difference between the futures
yield and the relevant forward rate. If the difference is too small to
generate a profit, then there will be no incentive for traders to trade in
such a way to bring the two rates back into exact equality. Therefore, we
can be fairly certain that (5.24) does not hold exactly as stated.

One other reason that (5.24) might not hold exactly is only beginning to be understood, and that is the influence of daily resettlement in

the futures market.[12] In comparing two sides of an arbitrage strategy, such as the strategies of Tables 5.9 and 5.10, both a futures position and a combination of spot market positions can be seen. The futures market position is subject to the requirements of daily resettlement, however. It has recently been shown that the variability of the daily cash flow due to resettlement can cause a divergence between forward and futures rates. The magnitude of this divergence between forward and futures rates and the stochastic character of interest rates is not yet known. Preliminary evidence, however, shows the effect to be extremely small.[13] Even an extremely small effect, however, is enough to render (5.24) false.

These three reasons, the possibility of a liquidity premium, the market imperfections that characterize all financial markets, and the impact of daily resettlement, mean that equation (5.24) cannot be maintained. This is the case, despite the fact that any differences among these rates due to these individual factors are small. Might these three small differences. however, add up to a sizeable difference? The answer to this question is not fully determined, but there is no reason to believe that the effects of the three factors are correlated. In general, then, one may expect any divergences among forward rates, futures rates, and expected future spot rates to be small. This state of affairs justifies belief in the following proposition:

Forward Rates $\approx$ **Futures Rates** $\approx$ **Expected Futures Spot Rates** (5.25)

For practical applications, it is justifiable to treat expression (5.25) as stating an equality. If these three rates are not nearly equal, then unwarranted profit opportunities exist, and the interest rate futures market is not efficient.

The Efficiency of the Interest Rate Futures Market

The concept of *market efficiency* comes in several forms, as we saw in Chapters 3 and 4. A minimal standard of market efficiency requires that prices in a market fully reflect all market information, including past and present prices. Opportunities for arbitrage profit, such as those in Tables 5.9 and 5.10 would show that the market is inefficient, even in the weak form. Large divergences between forward and futures rates of interest would be the kind of pricing discrepancy that would generate important arbitrage opportunities. If forward and futures rates are not approximately equal to each other, then they are not likely to be near the expected future spot rate. Large divergences among forward rates, futures rates, and expected future spot rates would signal the opportunity for some market participants to make large profits. Since the futures market is a *zero sum game,* in the absence of transaction costs, one participant's large profits would mean large losses for someone else. Further, if futures rates are greatly different from expected future spot rates, it would mean that hedging interest rate risk could often be a very costly venture.

For these reasons, the efficiency of the interest rate futures market should be an important topic of concern to all potential users of the market, whether speculators or hedgers. The importance of the concept of efficiency has been widely recognized by researchers. This section reviews the development of research on interest rate futures market efficiency and attempts to draw some conclusions about the efficiency based on the state of research to date. In spite of the attention that has been focused on the efficiency question, only T-Bill and T-Bond futures contracts have been subjected to analysis in published works. Almost all of these analyses focused on divergences between forward rates implied by spot market positions and futures market positions. This focusing on divergences means that the tests have been looking for evidence of arbitrage opportunities in the interest rate futures market.[14] Also, many of the early tests were based on a less than full understanding of the conditions under which the market could be judged efficient or not.

Early tests of futures market efficiency focused exclusively on differences between forward rates and futures rates on T-Bills. Differences between these rates were often found, and these differences were sometimes interpreted without further ado as evidence of market inefficiency. Immediate difficulties with this conclusion arose because different researchers arrived at radically different conclusions, some finding efficiency and others finding gross inefficiencies. From the discussion of the preceding section, it is clear that forward and futures rates could diverge for two basic reasons: market imperfections or the influence of daily resettlement. Many of the earliest researches into efficiency did not take these two factors into adequate consideration, yet both are important.[15]

Attempts to evaluate arbitrage opportunities in the T-Bill futures market involve taking complementary positions in the futures market and in the spot market. The difference in the futures and forward yields must be sufficiently large to cover considerable transaction costs if there is to be genuine arbitrage. While many studies neglected the full magnitude of these transaction charges, the best evidence to date renders the existence of genuine arbitrage opportunities very unlikely. Depending on the exact way in which the arbitrage attempt is constructed, a trader must incur a variety of transaction costs. To see this, consider again the arbitrage transaction of Table 5.9. The expenses incurred in implementing the strategy of Table 5.9 depend on whether the trader has an initial position in the spot or futures market. If he has no position in either market, then all transaction costs must be paid out of the profits in order for there to be an arbitrage profit. If an opportunity is attractive enough to show a profit, even after paying transactions costs, it can be considered a case of *pure arbitrage.* If he already holds a portfolio of T-Bills, for example, then he need not incur all of the transaction costs anew. Some of them have already been paid, and they should be considered as sunk costs for the analysis of the arbitrage. If he can successfully engage in arbitrage, assuming an initial portfolio of T-Bills that can be traded out of inventory, then the case is one of *quasi-arbitrage.*[16]

In Table 5.9 there are many transactions costs to be paid for engaging in pure arbitrage. The following are some of the costs:

1. To issue a 77-day T-Bill is equivalent to borrowing the same bill. The most creditworthy traders can borrow a T-Bill for about 50 basis points above its current yield. For $956,750 for 77 days, this would cost about $1023. Consider also that the acquisition of the $956,750 might be through the issuance of a term repo agreement.
2. To buy a 167-day T-Bill, a trader will have to pay the asked price for the bill, even if she is a market participant. This might involve an additional cost of about $100. If she is not a participant in the spot T-Bill market, then she will have to trade through a broker and pay a commission as well.
3. To sell the March futures contract, a trader can expect to receive only the bid price, thereby increasing costs about $25. If she is not a trader on the IMM, there are commission costs to incur as well.
4. To deliver the Bill also costs money, since the short trader in the futures market bears all costs of delivery. These costs might be about $50.
5. Paying off the due bill also involves transactions costs of the wire transfer and record keeping, which might all cost $25.

This list of transaction charges is only an indication of the additional expenses that might be incurred in an arbitrage attempt. Many of the charges shown in the list are difficult to gauge and different market participants face different levels of expense. Nonetheless, the expenses are large and can offset a substantial difference between forward and futures yields. In addition, a trader also faces a cost that is not shown in the list. To find an arbitrage opportunity, a trader must search for it, and the cost of searching for the opportunity must be reckoned into the calculation of the arbitrage profit. From the list of transaction costs, we can see that some market participants are in a much better position than others. If a participant has a portfolio of spot T-Bills, has a very good credit rating, is a trader on the futures exchange, and has a network of computerized information sources already in operation, then the transactions costs incurred in attempting to carry out an arbitrage operation are much smaller. That is the difference between pure arbitrage and quasi-arbitrage. For pure arbitrage, the yield discrepancy must be large enough to cover all transaction costs faced by a market outsider. For quasi-arbitrage, the trader does not face full transaction costs.

One of the most thorough and carefully conducted studies of T-Bill futures efficiency was conducted by Rendleman and Carabini, using daily data for the period from January 6, 1976 to March 31, 1978. The analysis focused on the three futures contracts closest to maturity at any one time. By a careful analysis of the transaction costs faced by a market

FIGURE 5.8
Pure Arbitrage in T-Bill Futures.

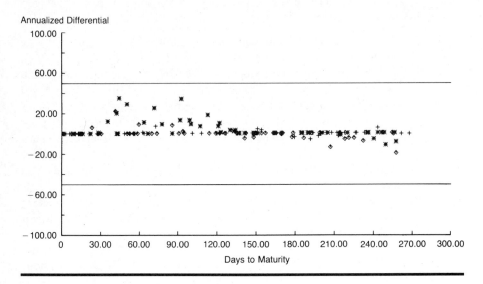

outsider, Rendleman and Carabini were able to define a band of difference between the forward rate and the futures rate that would still not support pure arbitrage. In other words, if forward and futures rates diverged only slightly, by 50 basis points or less, the difference would not cover transaction costs. Their results are shown in Figure 5.8. The divergences between actual and theoretical yields for T-Bill futures always fall within the band, set at 50 basis points, which denotes the no-profit limits. This was true for all 1606 observations in their sample, justifying their conclusion that the T-Bill futures market was efficient—in the sense of excluding opportunities for pure arbitrage. Regarding quasi-arbitrage opportunities, Rendleman and Carabini found that some occasions did exist in which a trader could improve the return on a portfolio of spot T-Bills. The quasi-arbitrage opportunities were found only infrequently, and no attempt was made to factor in search costs needed to discover the opportunities. About these quasi-arbitrage opportunities, Rendelman and Carabini conclude: " . . . the inefficiencies in the Treasury bill futures market do not appear to be significant enough to offer attractive investment alternatives to the short-term portfolio manager."[17]

The T-Bond futures market has not received nearly the attention that has been devoted to the T-Bill futures market. Part of the reason for this difference is the extreme complexity of the contract, particularly the

FIGURE 5.9

Potential Arbitrage in T-Bond Futures.

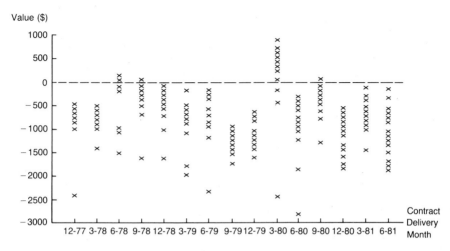

Values of eq. (2) for each deliverable bond: Invoice Amount — (Bond Price + Accrued Interest) − Financing Cost (values less than −$3000 not reported).

diversity of deliverable instruments. Since the short trader chooses which bond to deliver in fulfillment of the contract, the long position has no opportunity for arbitrage. The short trader could conduct an arbitrage operation if it were profitable to (1) buy a bond, (2) sell a futures contract on the bond, and (3) store the bond until delivery. Even such a strategy is limited in its effectiveness, however, because the bond that the short trader might hold will pay a coupon, in most cases, on the 15th of the month preceding delivery. The rate at which that coupon could be invested will be uncertain, so the short trader cannot really count on an arbitrage profit if he or she must rely on the cash flow from the reinvested coupons. These conditions restrict the possible arbitrage strategies to a very short time span just prior to delivery. In the only paper on T-Bond futures efficiency published to date, Kolb, Gay, and Jordan investigated the possibility of arbitrage for all T-Bond futures contracts in existence from December, 1977 through June, 1981.[18] The analysis was conducted for one day on each instrument, the last business day of the month preceding the delivery month.

To conduct arbitrage in such a situation, the cash flow to the short trader is given by equation (5.26):

Cash Flow = Invoice Amount − (Bond Price + Accrued Interest)
$$\textbf{− Financing Cost} \tag{5.26}$$

The short trader will receive the invoice amount upon delivery, with the invoice amount depending on the futures price, the conversion factor, and the accrued interest as shown in equation (5.22). Out of this, he must pay the cost of acquiring the bond, and the financing cost of holding the bond from the time of acquisition until it can be delivered. Since the short trader can choose which bond to deliver, he need find only one bond that is profitable. Figure 5.9 shows the value of expression (5.26) for all deliverable bonds for fifteen contract maturities, as calculated for the last business day of the month preceding the delivery month. Only three contract maturities had a bond that promised a positive cash flow: September, 1978, September, 1980, and March, 1980. For the September, 1978 contract, the positive cash flow was $49.07 and for the September, 1980 contract, the positive cash flow was $27.57. Out of these potential profits, the arbitrageur would have had to pay transaction and search costs, so these two occasions do not represent any chance for an arbitrage profit.

For the March, 1980 contract, there was one bond that would have yielded a cash flow as large as $591.34. If there is to be hope of arbitrage, it must rest with this contract. This hope, however, appears to be illusory. Prices reported for this date vary widely from source to source, with reported futures prices differing by as much as $1625. The uncertainty over the actual prices at which one could contract requires that this apparent arbitrage opportunity not be regarded as genuine. Kolb, Gay, and Jordan conclude that their results are fully consistent with the efficiency of the T-Bond futures market.

These studies support a conclusion that the interest futures market is efficient, but efficiency is far from proven. To date, all published studies of interest rate futures efficiency have focused only on the existence of arbitrage opportunities. Arbitrage, however, is the grossest kind of inefficiency. A market may well have no arbitrage opportunities and still be inefficient. If there are risky positions that could be taken in the futures market, and those risky positions earn returns in excess of a risk-adjusted normal return, then the futures market would still be inefficient. No tests of such possibilities have been conducted, probably due to the difficulty in defining a risk-adjusted normal return. In spite of this possibility of inefficiency, it is important to note that the actual evidence supports interest rate futures market efficiency. For those areas not covered by actual evidence, it seems likely that subsequent analysis will tend to support the conclusion of efficiency, as it has generally in other markets.

Speculation and Risk Arbitrage in Interest Rate Futures

To the academic ear, the term *risk arbitrage* sounds like a contradiction in terms. For the trader in the pits, risk arbitrage, or equivalently, just *arbitrage,* is the name of his or her daily activity. According to the parlance of the market, arbitrage involves the trading of one position against another. For the academic, by contrast, arbitrage means the act of achieving a riskless profit without investment. Risk arbitrage is really a form of speculation, in that it involves taking a risky position in hope of a profit. As is the case in other segments of the futures market, speculative strategies in interest rate futures can take on a variety of forms, from outright holding to complex spread strategies.

If futures yields equal expected future spot yields, consistent with equation (5.25), then the expected return from holding a futures market position is zero, ignoring transaction costs. This would mean that the speculator is betting against the combined wisdom of the rest of the market, as it expresses itself through futures prices. If futures prices do not equal expected future spot prices, due to the presence of a liquidity premium or some other kind of risk premium, then the chance for speculative profits may be improved. The term *speculative profits* is a slippery expression. A speculator might earn accounting profits that would constitute a justifiable return to the application of his capital and energies. This is different from economic profit or an economic rent, which would be a profit in excess of return for the use of capital and the bearing of risk. Accounting profits are consistent with market efficiency, but economic profits are not. As the speculative strategies of this section are considered, it is important to keep these different conceptions of profit in mind.

Speculative strategies in the interest rate futures market, other than outright positions, tend to be spreads to speculate on maturity differentials or spreads to speculate on shifting risk differentials between two or more kinds of instruments. In terms of the earlier discussion of interest rates, the maturity spreads are speculations on the term structure of interest rates, while inter-commodity spreads are speculations on the risk structure of interest rates. Of course, a given spread could combine features of both term structure and risk structure speculations.

The first example of a speculative strategy is for a time-spread in the T-Bill futures contract. Table 5.11 presents a series of spot rates and futures rates for T-Bills. As the spot rates show, the yield curve is upward sloping, on March 20, with 3-month bills yielding 10% and 12-month bills yielding 12%. Three futures contracts are shown, with the nearby contract maturing in three months. For the futures contracts, the futures yields are consistent with the terms structure given by the spot rates, in the sense that the futures yields equal the forward rates from the term structure. Faced with such circumstances, particularly with a very steep upward sloping yield curve, a speculator might believe that the term structure would flatten out within the six months. Even if one were not sure whether rates were going to rise or fall, the speculator could still profit from a T-Bill futures spread by entering the transactions shown in Table 5.12.

If the yield curve is to flatten, the yield spread between successively

TABLE 5.11

Spot and Futures T-Bill Rates for March 20.

Spot Rates

Time to Maturity	Rates
3	10.00%
6	11.00
9	11.50
12	12.00

Futures Rates

Time to Expiration (months)		Rate	IMM Index
June Contract	3	12.00%	88.00
September	6	12.50	87.50
December	9	13.50	86.50

maturing futures contracts must narrow. Currently, the yield spread between the December and September futures contracts is 100 basis points.
By selling the more distant December contract and buying the September
contract, the trader is betting that the yield differential will narrow. If
the yield curve flattens, no matter whether the general level of rates rises
or falls, then this spread strategy will give a profit. As Table 5.12 shows,
the yields have fallen dramatically by August 30. The yield on the
December contract has fallen from 13.50% to 11.86% and the
September yield has moved from 12.50% to 10.98% For the profits on
this speculative strategy, the important point is that the yield spread has
changed from 100 basis points to 88 basis points. This generates a profit
on the spread of 12 basis points, which would be $300, since each basis
point change represents $25. The same kind of result could have been ob-
tained in a market with rising rates, as long as the yield curve was flatten-
ing. From this example, it is apparent that all time-spreads, or *intra-
commodity spreads,* in the interest rate futures market are speculations
on the changing shape of the yield curve. No matter what change in the
shape of the yield curve is anticipated, there is a way to profit from that
change by trading the correct interest rate futures spread.

To illustrate the use of spreads more completely, consider a situation in which the yield curve is flat, as depicted in Table 5.13. Here all
rates, spots and futures, are at 12%, representing a yield curve that is
perfectly flat. If a trader believes that the yield curve is going to become
upward sloping, two strategies could take advantage of this belief. First,
the trader could use an intra-commodity spread, similar to the spread of
Table 5.12. Since the speculator anticipates a positively sloping yield

TABLE 5.12
Speculation on T-Bill Futures.

Cash Market	Futures Market
March 20	Buy the December T-Bill futures at 86.50.
	Sell the September T-Bill futures at 87.50.
August 30	Sell the December T-Bill futures at 88.14.
	Buy the September T-Bill futures at 89.02.

Profits:

December	September
88.14	87.50
− 86.50	− 89.02
1.64	− 1.52

Total Gain:

12 basis points × $25 = $300

TABLE 5.13
Assumed Spot and Futures Yields. (June 20, 1984).

Spot Rates		Futures Rates		
Instrument	Yield	Instrument	Yield	Price
3-month T-Bill	12.00%	SEP T-Bill	12.00%	88.00
6-month T-Bill	12.00	DEC T-Bill	12.00	88.00
10–3/8s 2007–12	12.00	SEP T-Bond	12.00	
		DEC T-Bond	12.00	

curve, he or she could sell the distant T-Bill futures and buy the nearby T-Bill futures. Doing so would be speculating that the yield curve would become upward sloping for the very low maturity instruments represented by the T-Bills. With an upward sloping yield curve, however, we would expect the greatest difference in yields between short maturity and long maturity instruments, that is, between T-Bills and T-Bonds. This implies that long-term yields are expected to rise relative to short-term yields. To take advantage of this anticipated change in yields, the trader might use an inter-commodity spread, in accordance with the transactions of Table 5.14.

If long-term yields are expected to rise relative to short-term yields, then the best spread strategy calls for selling the futures contract on a long-term instrument while buying a futures on a short-term instrument. This is exactly the course pursued by a speculator whose transactions are shown in Table 5.14. With yields at 12%, the T-Bond instrument has a price of 69–29, and the T-Bill futures price is 88.00. By October 24, 1984,

TABLE 5.14

Inter-Commodity Spread Speculation. Each 32nd on the T-Bond contract is equivalent to $31.25 and each basis point on the T-Bill contract is equivalent to $25.00.

Cash Market	Futures Market
June 20, 1984	Sell the December T-Bond futures at 69–29 with a yield of 12%.
	Buy the December T-Bill futures at 88.00 with a yield of 12%.
October 24, 1984	Buy the December T-Bond futures at 65–24 with a yield of 12.778%.
	Sell the December T-Bill futures at 87.80 with a yield of 12.20%.

Profits:

T-Bond	T-Bill
69–29	87.80
− 65–24	− 88.00
4–05	− .20
= $4156.25	= − $500

Total Profit: $3656.25

yields have moved as anticipated, with T-Bond futures yields at 12.778% and the T-Bill futures at 12.20%. For the T-Bond contract, this gives a price change of 4–05. Since each 32nd of a point of par represents $31.25 on a T-Bond futures contract, this gives a total profit on the T-Bond contract of $1456.25. On the T-Bill side, rates have risen, but not as rapidly, so that there was only a movement of 20 basis points. Since each basis point represents $25, there is a loss on the T-Bill futures of $500. When the T-Bill loss is offset against the T-Bond gain, the net profit from the speculation is $3656.25.

In this example we assumed that one T-Bond and one T-Bill contract were traded. Often such a procedure will not be the best, since different futures contracts have different price volatilities. In this case, the T-Bond yield moved almost four times as much as the T-Bill yield, but the T-Bond price moved more than eight times as much in terms of dollars. This difference in the sensitivity of prices can be very important, both for speculating and for hedging. Notice, also, that both contracts were traded for the same futures delivery month. This shows that a speculative strategy focusing on yield curve changes need not employ different futures maturities. It will be necessary, however, to use either different futures expiration months, or different contracts.

Another basic kind of speculation that is possible in the interest rate futures market is a speculation on the changing risk structure of interest rates. Late 1982 and 1983 was a time of crisis for banks heavily engaged in international lending, with great fear of widespread default on the part of many third world nations. In the interest rate futures markets there

TABLE 5.15

Inter-Commodity Spread in Short-Term Rates.

Cash Market	**Futures Market**
February 17	Sell 1 December CD futures contract yielding 9.71% with an IMM Index value of 90.29.
	Buy 1 December T-Bill futures contract yielding 8.82% with an IMM Index value of 91.18.
October 14	Buy 1 December CD futures contract yielding 10.09% with an IMM Index value of 89.91.
	Sell 1 December T-Bill futures contract yielding 8.93% with an IMM Index value of 91.07.

Profits:

CD	T-Bill
90.29	91.07
− 89.91	− 91.18
.38	− .09

Total Profit:

29 basis points × $25 = 725

are widely traded contracts on 3-month CDs and 3-month Eurodollar deposits, as well as on 90-day T-Bills. A speculator might have well viewed this situation and seen a potential opportunity. If the crisis developed, we might expect to find a widening of the yield spread between T-Bill deposits and CDs, for example. This widening yield spread would reflect the changing perception of the risk involved in holding CDs in the face of potentially very large loan losses. In February, 1983, one might have found yields for the December, 1983 T-Bill contract at 8.82% and CDs at 9.71%. If the full riskiness of the banks' position had yet to be understood, it might be reasonable to expect the yield spread to widen. This would be the case whether interest rates were rising or falling in general. To take advantage of this belief, a trader could sell the December CD contract and buy the December T-Bill contract, as shown in Table 5.15.

Since the trader expects the yield spread to widen, he or she sells the CD contract and buys the T-Bill contract for IMM Index values of 90.29 and 91.18, respectively. Later, on October 14, 1983, the yield spread of the example has, in fact, widened, with T-Bill yields having moved up slightly to 8.93% and CDs moving from 9.71 to 10.09%. The spread has widened by 29 basis points, which means a profit of $725 on the speculation.

Perhaps the single most important point about speculation can be emphasized using this example. In early 1983, virtually everyone was aware of the problems being faced by banks involved in international

TABLE 5.16
Short-Term Interest Rates on March 20, 1984.

Spot	90-day T-Bill	12.00%
Futures	June T-Bill contract	11.50
	September T-Bill contract	11.00

lending, with articles on the problem appearing almost daily in the *Wall Street Journal*. Therefore, the futures prices must already have imbedded in them the market's expectation of the future yield spread between T-Bills and CDs. By engaging in the speculative strategy discussed here, a trader was speculating against the rest of the market. It was not enough to expect yield spreads to widen, but he must have expected them to widen by more than the market expected. And he must have been right, in order to make a profit.

HEDGING WITH INTEREST RATE FUTURES

Of all the potential participants in the futures market, financial institutions have perhaps the most to gain by the use of the interest rate futures market. The very nature of banks, savings and loans, insurance companies, and finance companies requires exposure to interest rate risk in the ordinary conduct of business. The advent of the interest rate futures market has provided such institutions with a technique for controlling that risk by hedging. In many respects, the same techniques of hedging that were applicable to the traditional commodities pertain to interest rate hedging as well. While the basic ideas are the same, there are many important differences. This section presents a number of hedges using interest rate futures. They are organized to go from the most straightforward kind of hedge to some that are fairly complicated.

An anticipatory hedge. As an initial example, consider the situation of a government bond portfolio manager, who learns on March 20, 1984 that she will receive $972,500 in six months to invest in short-term U.S. Treasury issues. She fears that interest rates may fall unexpectedly during the next six months and that the current high yield opportunities might be lost. Since she knows that she will have money to invest in six months, she can protect her client against an unexpected drop in interest rates by entering the futures market. For purposes of the example, assume that the rates of Table 5.16 prevail on March 20. The current spot rate is a very attractive 12%, in the judgment of the bond manager, and that rate could be captured if the funds were currently available for investment. Given the rates of Table 5.16, and the fact that the funds will not be available for investment until September, the current 12% invest-

TABLE 5.17

A Long Hedge with T-Bill Futures

Cash Market	Futures Market
March 20, 1984 Anticipates having $972,500 for short-term investment in six months.	Buys 1 September T-Bill futures yielding 11%.
September 20, 1984 Receives $972,500 for short-term investment.	Futures contract matures and the manager takes delivery. With yields now at 11%, the invoice amount is $972,500.
December 19, 1984 Bill matures, paying $1,000,000.	

ment rate cannot be guaranteed for funds that only become available in September. By entering the futures market, however, the bond manager can trade to guarantee a rate of 11%, and her transactions are shown in Table 5.17.

On March 20, the manager buys one T-Bill futures for delivery in September, with a yield of 11%, on a discount yield basis. Similar to hedges in other commodities, this is a long hedge, since the hedger buys a futures contract. It is necessary to buy a futures in this situation since there will be a supply of funds later that the hedger wants to be able to commit at the futures rate. Time passes until September 20, 1984 and yields have not changed on the futures contract at all, still being at 11%. The bond manager decides to take delivery, and pays the invoice amount of $972,500. She then holds the spot bill until its maturity on December 19, realizing a return of 11% on the investment.

This highly artificial example avoids a number of potential difficulties by arranging the hedging context in a way such that:

1. the original futures yield is the same as the futures yield when the hedge is lifted;
2. the hedging period matches the futures maturity exactly;
3. the size of the cash flows between the spot and futures positions match perfectly;
4. the maturity and coupon characteristics of the hedged and hedging instruments match perfectly.

In normal hedging situations, one or more of these four simplifying conditions will not prevail.

It would be a very unusual event if the futures yield did not change over the life of the hedge. Assume that all of the facts of the previous hedge example continued to hold, except for the yield at the end of the

TABLE 5.18

A T-Bill Futures Hedge with Shifting Rates.

March 20, 1984	
Anticipates having $972,500 for short-term investment in six months.	Buys 1 September T-Bill futures yielding 11%.
September 20, 1984	
Spot yields are now 10%, so a 3-month T-Bill is purchased. But with yields at 10%, a 3-month bill costs $975,000.	The futures yield is 10.00%. This means that the futures trade has earned 100 basis points since March, or $2500.

hedging period. The transactions and results for this new situation are shown in Table 5.18. Consistent with her fears, yields did fall below the futures rate over the six-month hedging period, lying at 10% in September. In the cash market, the purchase of the $1,000,000 T-Bill costs $975,000, not the originally anticipated $972,500. Since the futures contract is at maturity, the futures and spot yields must be equal. With a futures yield of 10.00%, the futures side of the transaction has generated a profit of 100 basis points, or $2500. This means that the gain in the futures market has exactly offset the loss in the spot market caused by the fall in rates. The bond portfolio manager can still add the $1,000,000 bill to the portfolio. Notice that this example retains many simplifying assumptions, notably that the spot and futures instruments are of the same maturity and coupon and that the time period of the futures contract and the desired spot market positions match. This insures that the futures yield and the spot yield converge at the end of the hedging horizon.

A cross hedge. The next example concerns a bank that plans to come to market with a large issue of CDs, but wishes to hedge the interest rate risk inherent in that situation. Fearing that the CD futures market is not sufficiently liquid, the bank decides to hedge the CD issuance using T-Bill futures. The position of the bank and the hedging transactions are shown in Table 5.19. On January 13, 1984 the bank finalizes its plans to issue $100,000,000 face value of CDs in mid-May, and hedges this transaction by selling 100 June T-Bill futures. They plan to issue the CDs at 11.83% and the T-Bill futures are currently yielding 11.10%. If all goes according to the plan, the CDs should provide $97,042,500 to the bank. By May 11, yields have risen, just as the bank feared when the hedge was established. The CDs are issued at a yield of 12.25%, bringing $96,937,500 to the bank. This represents $105,000 less than originally anticipated, a shortfall that is partially offset by the hedge in the futures market. Over the same interval, the T-Bill futures yield rose from 11.10% to 11.47%, generating a profit on the futures transaction of $92,500. This still leaves a net shortfall in the funds received by the bank

TABLE 5.19

Banker's Hedge of a CD Issuance.

Cash Market	Futures Market
January 13, 1984	
The banker plans to issue 90-day CDs in 4 months at a yield of 11.83%, with a face value of $100,000,000, to realize $97,042,500.	Sells 100 June 1984 T-Bill futures with a yield of 11.10%.
May 11, 1984	
The CDs are issued at 12.25%, and the bank realizes $96,937,500.	Buys 100 June 1984 T-Bill futures with a futures yield of 11.47%.
Shortfall: $105,000	*Futures Profit:*
	37 basis points × $25 × 100 contracts = $92,500

Net Shortfall or Hedging Error:

$$\begin{array}{r} \$105{,}000 \\ -\ \underline{92{,}500} \\ \$\ 12{,}500 \end{array}$$

of $12,500. Put in other terms, it means that the CDs were issued at an effective rate of 11.88%, instead of the desired 11.83%.

This hedge was largely effective, but not perfect, in controlling the risk of the CD issuance. The hedge was less than perfect because the change in the CD yields exceeded that of the change in the T-Bill futures yield. Put in other terms, the anticipated spread between the CDs and T-Bills widened by 5 basis points. Since the futures position and the cash market position were not perfectly matched, this kind of outcome is no surprise. The hedge worked well, but not perfectly, and that is normal with cross hedges. Had the bank not hedged, it would have issued the CDs with an effective rate exactly equal to the prevailing spot rate at the time of issuance, namely 12.25%. Using the hedge saved the bank $92,500 of the cash market shortfall of $105,000.

One of the most important factors in determining how well a hedge in the interest rate futures market will work is the relationship between the characteristics of the spot and futures market position. In the preceding example, there was not an exact match, but the characteristics of CDs and T-Bills are very similar. The only reason the preceding hedge did not work perfectly was due to a difference in yield movements on the CDs and the T-Bill futures. For many situations, one could have exactly the same yield change on the cash and futures sides of the hedge, yet have drastically different gains and losses. This could occur when the coupon and maturity characteristics of the hedged and hedging instruments are dissimilar.

TABLE 5.20

Yields on Futures and AAA Corporate Bonds.

	T-Bill Futures	T-Bond Futures	AAA
March 1	8.00%	8.50%	9.50%
June 1	7.58	8.08	9.08

The importance of coupon and maturity. To illustrate the dangers of coupon and maturity mismatches in interest rate heding consider the following example. A portfolio manager learns on March 1 that he will receive $5 million on June 1 to invest in AAA corporate bonds with a coupon rate of 5% and a maturity of 10 years. The coupon and maturity of the AAA bonds matches neither the T-Bill nor the T-Bond futures instruments. For that matter, the AAA bond is dissimilar in coupon and maturity to all currently traded interest rate futures instruments. Assume that yields for the T-Bill futures, the T-Bond futures, and the AAA instruments are as shown in Table 5.20. The yields are all calculated according to the Bond Pricing Formula, and the AAA yield for March 1 is the yield which the portfolio manager expects to prevail on the bonds on June 1, when the funds become available for investment.

One strategy for hedging this future purchase of corporate bonds might be to buy either five T-Bill futures contracts or fifty T-Bond futures contracts, both strategies giving a face value position in the futures market that matches the $5 million in bonds that the manager expects to purchase. Notice in Table 5.20, the yields on all three instruments fall by 42 basis points over the period from March 1 to June 1. The fall in yields will generate a loss on the cash market position, but gains on the futures positions. The gains and losses on these two alternative hedging strategies are shown in Table 5.21. The first row of the Table shows the initial dollar value of each of the three positions. Between March 1 and June 1, the 42 basis point drop in rates on each of the instruments causes all prices to rise. The price rise generates a gain on the two long futures positions that are being considered, but since one plans to buy the AAA bonds, the drop in rates causes a loss. For the T-Bill futures the profit is $4780, while the T-Bond futures enjoy a gain of $193,750. The AAA bond price increases by a total of $150,742 on the 6969 corporate bonds the portfolio manager was planning to buy with $5,000,000.

The final row of the Table shows the hedging error that would have been incurred from hedging with either the T-Bill or the T-Bond futures. For the T-Bill futures hedge, the same 42 basis point change in yields caused a $150,742 change in the price of the AAA bonds, but only a $4780 change in the futures price. This means that the portfolio manager would still have lost $145,962, even taking the profits from the hedge into account; 97% of the loss remains. For the hedge with T-Bond

TABLE 5.21
Naive Hedging Results.

	T-Bill Futures (5 contracts)	T-Bond Futures (50 contracts)	AAA (6969 bonds)
Prices Based on March 1 Yields	$4,904,718	$4,843,750	$5,000,000
Gain or Loss on Individual Instruments	$4780	$193,750	− $150,742
Hedging Error	− $145,962	+ $43,008	

futures, the futures gain is $193,750, generating a total profit on the hedge of $43,008, since the futures gain more than offsets the loss on the bonds.

One hedge left a loss of $145,962, the other produced a gain of $43,008, but both performed miserably. The goal of the hedge was to have neither a gain nor a loss. Hedging is a technique to reduce uncertainty, so the goal was to have futures gains offset any cash market loss, may have had a fortuitous outcome, but it could equally well have had a disastrous outcome, if yields had risen instead of fallen. The well-executed hedge would have given a very small hedging error, not big gains and not big losses. The large errors shown in Table 5.21 were due to the mismatch between the coupon and maturity on the futures instruments and on the AAA bonds. The potential hedger in the interest rate futures market must adjust the hedge ratio to account for differences in coupon and maturity.

The portfolio approach to hedge ratios.   One way of calculating a hedge ratio for interest rate futures is the regression technique based on the work of Johnson and Stein. In Chapter 4, the example of the palm oil hedge applied that basic framework to find the hedge ratio. The hedge ratio found by the regression technique was the optimal hedge ratio. Optimal here means that it reduced the variance of the combined futures-cash position, given the assumption that the correlation of the cash and futures instruments stayed the same during the period of the hedge as it was during the period used to estimate the hedge ratio. This is an important point. The regression technique finds the hedge ratio that gives the lowest sum of squared errors for the data used in the estimation. Since price changes are usually regressed on price changes, it gives a way of finding the hedge ratio that minimizes the sum of squared price change errors for the estimation data. Using the estimated hedge ratio for an actual hedge assumes that the relationship between the price changes on the futures and cash instruments does not change between the sample period and the actual hedging period.

This is a practical assumption. If the relationship is basically unchanged, then the estimated hedge ratio will perform well in the actual hedging situation. Fundamental shifts in the relationship between the price of the futures contract and the cash market good can lead to serious hedging errors. This danger is present in all hedging situations, but may be exacerbated in interest rate hedging. Without doubt, the regression approach has proven its usefulness in the market for the traditional futures contracts, and it has been adapted for use in the interest rate futures market by Louis Ederington, Charles Franckle, Joanne Hill and Thomas Schneeweis.[19]

However, there are some problems with this approach in its application to interest rate hedging. First, since the technique involves statistical estimation, a data set is required for both cash and futures prices. This data may sometimes be difficult to acquire, particularly for an attempt to hedge the issuance of a new security. In such a case, no cash market data would even exist, and a proxy would have to be used. Second, the regression technique does not explicitly consider the differences in the sensitivity of different bond prices to changes in interest rates. As the example of Table 5.21 indicates, this can be a very important factor. The regression approach does include the different price sensitivities indirectly, since their differential sensitivities will be reflected in the estimation of the hedge ratio. Third, any cash bond will have a predictable price movement over time. Any instrument will have to have a price at maturity that is equal to its par value. The regression technique does not consider this change in the cash bond's price explicitly, but again it is included implicitly in the sample data that is used for the estimation. Fourth, the hedge ratio is chosen to minimize the variability in the combined futures-cash position over the life of the hedge. Since the regression hedge ratio depends crucially on the planned hedge length, one might reasonably prefer a hedging technique that focuses on the wealth position of the hedge when the hedge is terminated. After all, the wealth change from the hedge depends on the gain or loss when the hedge is terminated, not on the variability of the cash-futures position over the life of the hedge. In spite of these difficulties, the regression technique is a useful way of estimating hedge ratios, both for traditional commodities and, to a lesser extent, for interest rate hedging.

The price sensitivity approach to hedging.

Another approach has been developed that is designed explicitly for interest rate hedging. It is called the Price Sensitivity (PS) approach.[20] The PS approach comes from a different definition of the hedging goal and focuses on the unexpected wealth change that the hedger incurs. This is expressed more formally in equation (5.27):

$$\Delta Pi + \Delta Pf (N) = 0 \qquad (5.27)$$

Equation (5.27) expresses the goal that the change in the value of the spot instrument, denoted by i, and the futures position, denoted by f, should together equal zero. This would correspond to a wealth change, or a hedging error, of zero in terms of Table 5.21. The problem for the hedger

TABLE 5.22
Data for the Price Sensitivity Hedge.

Cash Instrument		T-Bill Futures		T-Bond Futures	
P(i)	$717.45	FP(f)	$980,944	FP(f)	$96,875
D(i)	7.709	D(f)	.25	D(f)	10.143
R(i)	1.095	R(f)	1.08	R(f)	1.085
		N	.022244	N	.005577
		Number of Contracts to Trade 155		Number of Contracts to Trade 39	

is to choose the correct number of contracts, denoted by N in equation (5.27), to make the equation hold. As a result of adopting this hedging goal, the PS approach focuses on the final wealth change that will occur. The correct number of contracts to trade (N), per spot market bond, is given by equation (5.28):

$$N = \frac{R_f\, P_i\, D_i}{R_i\, FP_f\, D_f} \qquad (5.28)$$

where:

R_f = 1 + the rate expected to obtain on the asset *underlying* futures contract *f*;

R_i = 1 + the expected yield to maturity on asset *i*;

FP_f = the price agreed upon in the futures contract for title to the asset *underlying f*;

P_i = the price of asset *i* expected to prevail on the planned termination date of the hedge;

D_i = the duration of asset *i* expected to prevail on the planned termination date of the hedge; and

D_f = the duration of the asset *underlying* futures contract *f* expected to prevail on the planned termination date of the hedge.

This expression is derived mathematically in the Appendix to this chapter. In non-technical terms, equation (5.28) says that the number of futures contracts to trade for each cash market instrument to be hedged is the number that should give a perfect hedge, assuming that yields on the cash and futures instrument change by the same amount. To explore the meaning and application of this technique, consider again the case of the AAA bond hedge of Tables 5.20 and 5.21. The large hedging errors of Table 5.21 were due to a failure to consider the difference in the price sensitivities between the futures instruments and the AAA bonds.

Table 5.22 presents all of the data needed to calculate the hedge ratios for the two hedging instruments. As shown, one could hedge the AAA bonds by buying 155 T-Bill futures or by buying 39 T-Bond futures

TABLE 5.23
Performance Analysis of Price Sensitivity Future Hedge.

	Cash Market	T-Bill Hedge	T-Bond Hedge
Gain/Loss	− $150,742	+ $148,203	+ $150,608
Hedging Error	——	$2539	$134
Percentage of Cash Market Loss Hedged		98.32%	99.91%

contracts. With either of these hedges in place, the same shift in yields on the AAA bonds and the futures instrument should give a perfect hedge. The performance of these two hedges, for the same 42 basis point drop in rates used above, is given in Table 5.23.

With the given hedges and the same drop in yields, the T-Bill hedge gave a futures gain of $148,203 to offset the loss on the AAA bonds of $150,742. The futures gain on the T-Bond hedge was $150,608. The next row of Table 5.23 shows the size of the hedging error for the T-Bill and T-Bond hedges, while the final row gives the percentage of the cash market loss that was hedged. For the T-Bill hedge, the hedge was 98.32% effective and for the T-Bond hedge, it was 99.91% effective. In each case, a near perfect hedge was achieved. The slight errors were due to rounding error and to the fact that the change in interest rates was large in size. In these examples, the PS approach worked very effectively. In actual hedging situations, one could not hope for such near perfect results, since yields need not change by the same amount on all instruments all of the time.

CONCLUSION

Interest rate futures constitute one of the most exciting and complex financial markets. Part of what makes it interesting is the newness of the market and the complexity of the instruments. The uses of the market are only now being explored. But interest rate futures have very wide applicability for a number of applications, including bond portfolio management, foreign interest rate risk management, the management of public utilities and insurance companies, mortgage financing, and the control of risk in creative financing arrangements. Other uses abound and are just starting to be explored. This chapter constitutes only an introduction to the topic.[21]

NOTES

1. A recent spectacular failure was the introduction of a two-year T-note contract in January 1982 that went from its opening to zero volume in nine trading days. See "Two-Year T-Notes: A Bungled Opening," *Commodities: The Magazine of Futures Trading,* March 1982, 100.

2. See B. Malkiel. "Expectations, Bond Prices, and the Term Structure of Interest Rates," *Quarterly Journal of Economics, 76,* 1962, 197–218.

3. Some good treatments of duration are: F. Macaulay. *Some Theoretical Problems Suggested By the Movements of Interest Rates, Bond Yields, and Stock Prices in the United States Since 1856,* New York: Columbia University Press, 1938; R. McEnally. "Duration as a Practical Tool for Bond Management," *Journal of Portfolio Management, 3,* Summer 1977, 53–57; G. Bierwag and C. Khang. "Duration and Bond Portfolio Analysis: An Overview," *Journal of Financial and Quantitative Analysis,* November 1979, 671–681; J. Ingersoll, J. Skelton and R. Weil. "Duration Forty Years Later," *Journal of Financial and Quantitative Analysis,* November 1978, 627–650; and F. Reilly and R. Sidhu. "The Many Uses of Bond Duration," *Financial Analysts Journal, 36,* 1980, 58–72.

4. The change will not be exactly equal, due to the fact that the yields on the two sides of the balance sheet are different. One could find the optimal duration for the liabilities by using the Duration Price Change formula, such that the dollar price change on the assets and liabilities would be exactly equal.

5. For more on the theory and measurement of the term structure, see W. Sharpe. *Investments,* Englewood Cliffs, NJ: Prentice-Hall, 1981. For the importance of the term structure to interest rate futures in particular, see R. Kolb. *Interest Rate Futures: A Comprehensive Introduction,* Richmond, VA: Robert F. Dame, Inc., 1982.

6. For a more thorough discussion of the characteristics of Treasury Bills, see T. Cook and J. Monhollon. "Treasury Bills," *Instruments of the Money Market,* Richmond, VA: Federal Reserve Bank of Richmond, 1981.

7. By doing so, the Clearing Corporation fulfills its obligation of being buyer to every seller and seller to every buyer. At the actual delivery, the Clearing Corporation supervises the exchange of T-Bonds and cash, but need not enter the process itself. It should also be noted that fewer than 1% of all futures contracts are satisfied by delivery, the others being completed by reversing trades.

8. A complete table of these conversion factors is published in booklet form by the Financial Publishing Company.

9. Note that the shape of the yield curve will have a strong impact on the delivery behavior in the T-Bond contract. Assume that the yield curve is strongly upward sloping, so that short-term rates are much lower than long-term rates. For a trader with a short position in the T-Bond contract, this provides an incentive to delay delivery. If this trader holds the long-term bond in inventory, and finances that holding at a lower short-term rate, then he has every incentive to wait as long as possible to make delivery.

10. For a further discussion of repos, see N. Bowsher. "Repurchase Agreements," *Instruments of the Money Market,* Richmond, VA: Federal Reserve Bank of Richmond, 1981.

11. For a recent discussion of this perennial issue see B. Friedman. "Interest Rate Expectations Versus Forward Rates: Evidence From An Expectations Survey," *Journal of Finance,* September 1979, 965–974.

12. For the impact of daily resettlement on the difference between forward and futures rates see G. Morgan. "Forward and Futures Pricing of Treasury Bills," *Journal of Banking and Finance,* December 1981,

483–496; J. Cox, J. Ingersoll and S. Ross. "The Relation Between Forward Prices and Futures Prices," *Journal of Financial Economics,* December 1981, 321–346; and R. Jarrow and G. Oldfield. "Forward Contracts and Futures Contracts," *Journal of Financial Economics,* December 1981, 373–382.

13. See B. Cornell and M. Reinganum. "Forward and Futures Prices: Evidence from the Foreign Exchange Markets," *Journal of Finance,* December 1981, 1035–1045.

14. Some of the more important studies of interest rate futures markets, other than those to be discussed specifically, include: W. Poole, "Using T-Bill Futures to Gauge Interest-Rate Expectations"; D. Puglisi, "Is the Futures Market for Treasury Bills Efficient?"; A. Vignola and C. Dale, "Is the Futures Market for Treasury Bills Efficient?"; R. Lang and R. Rasche, "A Comparison of Yields on Futures Contracts and Implied Forward Rates;" B. Branch, "Testing the Unbiased Expectations Theory of Interest Rates"; D. Capozza and B. Cornell, "Treasury Bill Pricing in the Spot and Futures Markets"; and "The Efficiency of the Treasury Bill Futures Market: An Analysis of Alternative Specifications." All of these articles are reprinted in G. Gay and R. Kolb. *Interest Rate Futures: Concepts and Issues,* Richmond, VA: Robert F. Dame, Inc., 1982. One very recent important paper is E. Elton, M. Gruber and J. Rentzler, "Intra-Day Tests of the Efficiency of the Treasury Bill Futures Market," a working paper from the Columbia University School of Business.

15. The importance of various institutional factors was brought to attention by E. Kane, "Market Incompleteness and Divergences Between Forward and Futures Interest Rates," *Journal of Finance,* May 1980, 221–234.

16. See R. Rendleman and C. Carabini. "The Efficiency of the Treasury Bill Futures Market," 191–212, in G. Gay and R. Kolb, *Interest Rate Futures: Concepts and Issues,* Richmond, VA: Robert F. Dame, Inc., 1982. In this article, they develop the idea of quasi-arbitrage.

17. R. Rendleman and C. Carabini. "The Efficiency of the Treasury Bill Futures Market," 211–212, in G. Gay and R. Kolb, *Interest Rate Futures: Concepts and Issues,* Richmond, VA: Robert F. Dame, Inc., 1982.

18. See R. Kolb, G. Gay, and J. Jordan. "Are There Arbitrage Opportunities in the Treasury-Bond Futures Market?" *Journal of Futures Markets,* Fall 1982, 217–230.

19. See L. Ederington. "The Hedging Performance of the New Futures Market," *Journal of Finance,* March 1979, 157–170; C. Franckle. "The Hedging Performance of the New Futures Market: Comment," *Journal of Finance,* December 1980, 1273–1279; and J. Hill and T. Schneeweis. "Risk Reduction Potential of Financial Futures," in G. Gay and R. Kolb, *Interest Rate Futures: A Comprehensive Introduction,* Richmond, VA: Robert F. Dame, Inc., 1982.

20. See R. Kolb and R. Chiang. "Improving Hedging Performance Using Interest Rate Futures," *Financial Management, 10,* 1981, 72–79 and "Duration, Immunization, and Hedging with Interest Rate Futures," *Journal of Financial Research,* Summer 1982, 161–170.

21. For a more complete treatment of these and other topics, see R. Kolb. *Interest Rate Futures: A Comprehensive Introduction,* Richmond, VA: Robert F. Dame, Inc., 1982.

Chapter 5 Appendix

Using the notation developed in the body of the chapter, the Price Sensitivity (PS) strategy takes as its goal the condition of zero wealth change as expressed by:

$$\Delta P_i + (\Delta P_j) N = 0 \qquad \text{(A.1)}$$

where:

$$P_j = \sum_{t=1}^{J} \frac{C_{jt}}{(R_j)^t} - \sum_{t=1}^{J} \frac{C_{jt}}{(R_j{}^*)^t} \qquad \text{(A.2)}$$

In A.2 $R_j{}^*$ is the future yield prevailing at the time of contracting and R_j is the current yield on the futures contract. P_j is the gain or loss on the futures contract. Notice also that the C_{jt} terms are the cash flows promised on the instrument underlying the futures contract and that the time index has $t = 0$ as the time of delivery on the futures contract.

To find the optimal value of N, one must substitute for P_i and P_j into (A.1) and take the derivative of the left-hand side with respect to the risk-free rate R_f.

$$\frac{d \sum_{t=1}^{I} \frac{C_{it}}{(R_i)^t}}{d R_f} \times \frac{d R_i}{d R_j} + \frac{d \left[\sum_{t=1}^{J} \frac{C_{jt}}{(R_j)^t} - \sum_{t=1}^{J} \frac{C_{jt}}{(R_j{}^*)^t} \right]}{d R_j}$$

$$\times \frac{d R_j}{d R_i} = 0 \qquad \text{(A.3)}$$

From (A.3), it follows that:

$$\frac{1}{R_i} \sum_{t=1}^{I} \frac{-t\, C_{it}}{(R_i)^t} \times \frac{d R_i}{d R^f} + \frac{N}{R_j} \sum_{t=1}^{J} \frac{-t\, C_{jt}}{(R_j)^t} \times \frac{d R_j}{d R_f} = 0 \qquad \text{(A.4)}$$

Solving for N gives:

$$N = - \frac{R_j}{R_i} \frac{\sum_{t=1}^{I} \dfrac{t\, C_{it}}{(R_i)^t} \dfrac{d R_i}{d R_f}}{\sum_{t=1}^{J} \dfrac{t\, C_{jt}}{(R_j)^t} \dfrac{d R_j}{d R_f}} \qquad \text{(A.5)}$$

Using the definition of Macaulay's duration, and substituting into (A.5) produces:

$$N = - \frac{R_j P_i D_i}{R_i FP_j D_j} \times \frac{\dfrac{d R_i}{d R_f}}{\dfrac{d R_j}{d R_f}} \tag{A.6}$$

since $R_j = R_j*$ at the time of contracting for the hedge, and the futures price, FP_j, is given by:

$$FP_j = \sum_{t=1}^{J} \frac{C_{jt}}{(R_j)^t} \tag{A.7}$$

Equation (A.6) is a general expression for the hedge ratio. However, if one is willing to assume that R_i and R_j respond in the same way to R_f, then $d R_i / d R_f = d R_j / d R_f$ and the hedge ratio becomes:

$$N = - \frac{R_j P_i D_i}{R_i FP_j D_j} \tag{A.8}$$

For a more complete elaboration of the hedging rule, see Robert W. Kolb *Interest Rate Futures: A Comprehensive Introduction.*

6 *Foreign Exchange Futures*

INTRODUCTION

The market for foreign exchange has a peculiar organization. It is the only market in which a successful futures market has grown up in the face of a robust forward market. The forward market for foreign exchange existed for a long time, but the foreign exchange futures market developed only in the early 1970s, with trading beginning on May 16, 1972. Without doubt, the presence of such a strong and successful forward market retarded the development of a futures market for foreign exchange. This dual market system means that the futures market cannot be understood in isolation from the forward market. The conceptual bond arises both from the similarity of the two markets and from the fact that the forward market continues to dominate the futures market in size by a wide margin. Since many traders are active participants in both markets, there is a strong mechanism at hand to insure that the proper price relationships between the two markets are maintained. That mechanism, as you may have guessed, is the desire for profit by participants in the market.

As discussed in Chapters 2 and 3, the forward and futures markets for a given commodity are similar in many respects. A consequence of this similarity is that tight relationships must hold between prices in the two markets if arbitrage opportunities are not to arise. While any observer might be more impressed by the similarities in the two markets, it must also be recognized that the markets differ in several key respects. Particularly important are the differences in the cash flow patterns (due to daily resettlement in the futures market) and the different structures of the contracts with respect to their maturity.

To understand foreign exchange futures trading, this chapter begins with a brief discussion of the markets for foreign exchange: the spot, forward, and futures markets. The analysis then turns to a review of some of the most important factors in determining exchange rates between two currencies, including the exchange rate regimes of fixed versus floating rates, the question of devaluation, and the influence of balance-of-payments. With this institutional background, we will discuss the more rigorous pricing relationships, such as the Interest Rate Parity Theorem (IRP) and the Purchasing Power Parity Theorem (PPP). The relationship between forward and futures prices will also be discussed, and the importance of forecasting in foreign exchange analyzed. As always in the futures market, the twin issues of speculation and hedging play an important role. Both of these principal aims in the use of foreign exchange futures will be considered, with a number of examples.

PRICE QUOTATIONS

In the foreign exchange market, it is important to realize that every price, or exchange rate, that is quoted is a relative price. To say that $1.00 is worth DM 2.5 is also to imply that DM 2.5 will buy $1.00, or that DM 1 is worth $ .40. All foreign exchange rates are related to each other as reciprocals, a relationship that is quite apparent in Figure 6.1, which shows the foreign exchange quotations as they appear daily in the *Wall Street Journal*. The quotations consist of two double columns of rates, one for the "U.S. Dollar Equivalent" of the foreign currency, and one set of two columns for the amount of foreign currency per U.S. dollar. Each set of quotations shows the rates for the current day and the preceding business day. This makes it possible, for purposes of discussion, to focus only on the two columns pertaining to the current quotation. The first point to notice is that the rate in one column has its reciprocal in the other column. The value of $/DM ($ per DM) is just the reciprocal of the value of DM/$ (DM per $). For some countries, such as Australia, only one rate is shown, and that is the spot rate, the rate at which Australian and U.S. dollars may be exchanged at the moment.

For many of our major trading partners, such as Germany, England, Japan, and Canada, there are also forward rates quoted for periods of 30, 90, and 180 days into the future. The 30-day forward rate, for example, indicates the rate at which a trader can contract for the delivery of some foreign currency 30 days hence. If the trader buys the foreign currency, then he or she agrees to pay the 30-day forward rate in 30 days for the currency in question, with the actual transaction taking place in 30 days. This exactly fits the description of forward markets that was given in Chapter 1.

The quotations shown in Figure 6.1 are provided by Bankers' Trust Company, a major participant in the foreign exchange market. The market from which these quotations are drawn is largely made up of large banks in the U.S. and abroad. As the Figure notes, the quotations shown pertain to transactions in amounts of $1 million or more. As is typical of forward markets, there is no physical location where trading takes place. Instead, banks around the world are linked electronically with each other. The large banks in the market are equipped with trading rooms elaborately equipped with electronic communications devices. A

FIGURE 6.1
Foreign Exchange Quotations.

Foreign Exchange

Thursday, March 1, 1984

The New York foreign exchange selling rates below apply to trading among banks in amounts of $1 million and more, as quoted at 3 p.m. Eastern time by Bankers Trust Co. Retail transactions provide fewer units of foreign currency per dollar.

Country	U.S. $ equiv. Thurs.	Wed.	Currency per U.S. $ Thurs.	Wed.
Argentina (Peso)	.03569	.03569	28.015	28.015
Australia (Dollar)	.9447	.9442	1.0585	1.0591
Austria (Schilling)	.05444	.05447	18.37	18.36
Belgium (Franc)				
Commercial rate	.01875	.01887	53.345	53.000
Financial rate	.01810	.01801	55.250	55.530
Brazil (Cruzeiro)	.0008665	.0008665	1154.00	1154.00
Britain (Pound)	1.4795	1.4890	.6759	.6716
30-Day Forward	1.4804	1.4900	.6755	.6711
90-Day Forward	1.4837	1.4932	.6740	.6697
180-Day Forward	1.4892	1.4982	.6715	.6675
Canada (Dollar)	.7990	.7993	1.2516	1.2511
30-Day Forward	.7991	.7994	1.2514	1.2509
90-Day Forward	.7994	.7997	1.2510	1.2505
180-Day Forward	.7999	.8003	1.2501	1.2496
Chile (Official rate)	.01135	.01135	88.12	88.12
China (Yuan)	.4898	.4898	2.0417	2.0417
Colombia (Peso)	.01090	.01090	91.81	91.81
Denmark (Krone)	.1046	.1047	9.5625	9.5475
Ecuador (Sucre)				
Official rate	.01748	.01748	57.22	57.22
Floating rate	.01125	.01125	88.85	88.85
Finland (Markka)	.1775	.1781	5.6350	5.6150
France (Franc)	.1245	.1244	8.0325	8.0375
30-Day Forward	.1239	.1238	8.0715	8.0745
90-Day Forward	.1225	.1224	8.1600	8.1700
180-Day Forward	.1208	.1208	8.2775	8.2750
Greece (Drachma)	.009908	.009926	100.93	100.75
Hong Kong (Dollar)	.1285	.1284	7.7792	7.7860
India (Rupee)	.0935	.0935	10.6952	10.6952
Indonesia (Rupiah)	.001006	.001006	994.00	994.00

Country	Thurs.	Wed.	Thurs.	Wed.
Ireland (Punt)	1.1790	1.1860	.8482	.8432
Israel (Shekel)	.007263	.007614	137.68	131.33
Italy (Lira)	.0006165	.0006165	1622.00	1622.00
Japan (Yen)	.004285	.004287	233.37	233.38
30-Day Forward	.004297	.004297	232.72	232.74
90-Day Forward	.004325	.004325	231.19	231.71
180-Day Forward	.004369	.004367	228.90	228.97
Lebanon (Pound)	.1621	.1621	6.17	6.17
Malaysia (Ringgit)	.4288	.4290	2.3320	2.3310
Mexico (Peso)				
Floating rate	.005865	.005865	170.50	170.50
Netherlands (Guilder)	.3398	.3401	2.9425	2.9400
New Zealand (Dollar)	.6661	.6670	1.5013	1.4993
Norway (Krone)	.1330	.1335	7.5170	7.4925
Pakistan (Rupee)	.07576	.07519	13.20	13.30
Peru (Sol)	.0004084	.0004084	2448.11	2448.11
Philippines (Peso)	.07133	.07133	14.02	14.02
Portugal (Escudo)	.007547	.007547	132.50	132.50
Saudi Arabia (Riyal)	.2851	.2850	3.5075	3.5085
Singapore (Dollar)	.4715	.4715	2.1210	2.1210
South Africa (Rand)	.8320	.8350	1.2019	1.198
South Korea (Won)	.001255	.001255	796.70	796.70
Spain (Peseta)	.006671	.006702	149.90	149.22
Sweden (Krona)	.1283	.1285	7.7950	7.7800
Switzerland (Franc)	.4599	.4606	2.1745	2.1710
30-Day Forward	.4625	.4631	2.1623	2.1590
90-Day Forward	.4675	.4684	2.1391	2.1350
180-Day Forward	.4750	.4759	2.1053	2.1013
Taiwan (Dollar)	.02488	.02488	40.19	40.19
Thailand (Baht)	.04351	.04351	22.985	22.985
Uruguay (New Peso)				
Financial	.02180	.02180	45.88	45.88
Venezuela (Bolivar)				
Official rate	.1941	.1941	5.15	5.15
Floating rate	.07734	.07734	12.93	12.93
W. Germany (Mark)	.3836	.3836	2.6070	2.6070
30-Day Forward	.3850	.3850	2.5975	2.5976
90-Day Forward	.3879	.3879	2.5783	2.5782
180-Day Forward	.3923	.3922	2.5490	2.5496

SDR	1.06023	1.06013	.943196	.948280

Special Drawing Rights are based on exchange rates for the U.S., West German, British, French and Japanese currencies. Source: International Monetary Fund.
z-Not quoted.

trader in such a room may have access to 60 telephone lines and 5 or more video quotation screens.[1] The market has no regular trading hours and is open somewhere in the world 24 hours per day. In addition to banks, some large corporations may have access to the market through their own trading rooms.

Regional banks are not likely to have trading rooms themselves. Instead, they will clear their foreign exchange transactions through correspondent banks, with whom they have the appropriate arrangements. Corporations, as well as individuals, that are too small to have their own trading room will engage in foreign exchange transactions through their own banks. As the Figure notes, the rates shown cannot be expected to be obtained by small retail traders. Instead, retail transactions will be subject to a larger bid-asked spread that allows the bank providing the foreign exchange service to make a profit.

GEOGRAPHICAL AND CROSS-RATE ARBITRAGE

A number of pricing relationships exist in the foreign exchange market, the violation of which would imply the existence of arbitrage opportunities. The first two to be considered involve *geographical arbitrage* and *cross-rate arbitrage.* One of the best ways to learn about these kinds of relationships that must exist among currency prices is to explore the potential arbitrage relationships that would arise if the pricing relationships were violated.

Geographical arbitrage occurs when one currency sells for two prices in two different markets. As an example, consider a situation in which the following prices were quoted in New York and Frankfurt for the exchange rate between Deutschemarks (DM) and dollars (These are 90-day forward rates.)

- New York $/DM   .42
- Frankfurt   DM/$ 2.35

The New York price, quoted as $ per DM, implies a DM/$ price equal to the inverse of the $/DM price:

$$\frac{1}{.42} = \text{DM/\$} = 2.381$$

In New York the DM/$ rate is 2.381, but in Frankfurt, it is 2.35. Since these are not equal, an arbitrage opportunity exists. The preceding example shows how to test for a geographical arbitrage opportunity. One can simply take the inverse of the price prevailing in one market, and see if it matches the price quoted in another market.

The next step is to determine the market in which a given currency is relatively cheaper. The currency will be purchased where it is cheap and sold where it is expensive. In New York, a trader can receive 2.381 DM per $, but only 2.35 DM per $ in Frankfurt. Therefore, the DM is cheaper, relatively speaking, in New York. To take advantage of this pricing discrepancy, the trader can enter the arbitrage transactions shown in Figure 6.2. These transactions represent the exploitation of an arbitrage opportunity since they insure a profit with no investment. At the outset, there is no cash flow. The only cash flow involved in the transactions occurs simultaneously when the commitments initiated at time = 0 are completed at time = 90. The profit, however, was certain from the time of the initial transactions.

The second kind of arbitrage opportunity involves cross rates, which may be defined as follows. In a given market, exchange rates for currencies A and B and for currencies A and C imply an exchange rate, called a *cross rate,* between currencies B and C. If the rate implied for B and C does not match the rate between B and C in some other market, an arbitrage opportunity exists. The cross rate is an implied rate, since the rate

FIGURE 6.2

Geographical Arbitrage. This is an arbitrage transaction since it has a certain profit with no investment. Notice that the arbitrage is not complete until the transactions at t = 90 are completed.

The Arbitrage Transaction:

t = 0 (the present)

    Buy DM 1 in New York 90 days forward for $.42.
    Sell DM 1 in Frankfurt 90 days forward for $.4255.

t = 90

    Deliver DM 1 in Frankfurt; collect $.4255.
    Pay $.42; collect DM 1.

Profit: $.4255
      −   .42
        .0055

for B in terms of C will not be explicitly stated in the market. As an example, assume that the following rates are observed, where SF indicates the Swiss Franc, and all of the rates are 90-day forward rates.

- New York $/DM   .42
                       $/SF   .49
- Frankfurt   DM/SF   1.2

In New York, rates for the DM/SF or SF/DM are not stated. Not surprisingly, rates in the U.S. are stated in terms of dollars, with the value of each currency being expressed in dollars, just as shown in the quotations. But the two rates shown in New York imply a cross rate in New York for the DM/SF:

Cross Rate in New York $$\text{DM/SF} = \frac{1}{\$/\text{DM}} \times \$/\text{SF} = \text{DM/SF}$$

$$= \frac{1}{.42} \times .49 = 1.167$$

Since the rates for DM/SF are different in New York and Frankfurt, an arbitrage opportunity exists. Notice, again, that no quotation for DM/SF is explicitly available in New York. Further, to take advantage of the arbitrage opportunity, one can trade only the exchange rates actually shown. For example, in New York there may not be a market for DM in terms of the Swiss Franc.[2] To convert DM to SF in the New York market will involve two transactions, first from DM to $, and then, from $ to SF.

    To know how to trade, one must know which currency is relatively cheaper in a given market. In New York one receives DM 1.167 per SF, but in Frankfurt SF 1 is worth DM 1.2. The DM, therefore, is cheaper in Frankfurt than it is in New York. Figure 6.3 shows the transactions required to take advantage of this arbitrage opportunity.

FIGURE 6.3
Cross-Rate Arbitrage Transactions.

---

t = 0

    Sell SF 1 90 days forward in Frankfurt for DM 1.2.
    Sell DM 1.2 90 days forward in New York for $.504.
    Sell $.504 90 days forward in N. Y. for SF 1.0286.

t = 90

    Deliver SF 1 in Frankfurt; Collect DM 1.2.
    Deliver DM 1.2 in New York; Collect $.504.
    Deliver $.504 in New York; Collect SF 1.0286.

Profit: SF   1.0286
          − 1.00
        SF   .0286

FORWARD AND FUTURES MARKET CHARACTERISTICS

The institutional structure of the foreign exchange futures market is similar to that of the forward market, with a number of notable exceptions. While the forward market is a world-wide market with no particular geographical location, the futures market is located at the International Monetary Market (IMM) of the Chicago Mercantile Exchange (CME). In the futures market, contracts are traded on only a few important currencies, such as the German Mark, the British Pound, the Canadian Dollar, the Swiss Franc, the Japanese Yen, and the Mexican Peso.[3] As is typical with other futures markets, contracts are traded for specific maturity dates. For foreign exchange futures, the maturity dates occur on the third Wednesday of March, June, September, and December. This is different from the forward market, where quotations are for a stated number of days into the future.[4] In the futures market, the maturity date of a given contract is fixed by the rules of the exchange. With each passing day, one comes closer to that maturity date. In the forward market, one can always contract for 30, 90 or 180 days into the future. In the futures market, contracts mature on only four days of the year; in the forward market, contracts mature every day.

In the forward market, the amount of currency to be covered by a given contract is determined by negotiation. In the futures market, the amount of a currency represented by one contract is fixed by the rules of the exchange. The price quotations, including the contract amounts, are shown in Figure 6.4. Active contracts exist on the British Pound, Canadian Dollar, Japanese Yen, Swiss Franc, and the German Mark. All prices are quoted in terms of dollars per unit of the foreign currency. Notice for the yen that two zeroes have been suppressed. Contract

FIGURE 6.4

Foreign Exchange Futures Quotations for March 1, 1984.

```
        BRITISH POUND (IMM)−25,000 pounds; $ per pound
Mar    1.4855 1.4870 1.4750 1.4830 − .0055 1.6010 1.3930 16,651
June   1.4900 1.4920 1.4800 1.4880 − .0055 1.5520 1.3950 10,342
Sept   1.4855 1.4920 1.4855 1.4935 − .0025 1.5240 1.3980    373
Dec    1.4920 1.4970 1.4910 1.4990 − .0040 1.5100 1.3990     85
Mar85  1.5010 1.5050 1.5000 1.5050 − .0035 1.5170 1.4000    112
    Est vol 12,524; vol Wed 8,566; open int 27,563, −388.
        CANADIAN DOLLAR (IMM)−100,000 dlrs.; $ per Can $
Mar     .8003  .8004  .7988  .7995  ....  .8169  .7969  2,552
June    .8004  .8007  .7991  .7997 − .0002 .8168  .7971  2,509
Sept    .8011  .8012  .8000  .8003 − .0001 .8147  .7980    326
Dec     ....   ....   ....   .8010 + .0002 .8040  .7985    160
Mar85   ....   ....   ....   .8012  ....   .8038  .7993     60
    Est vol 881; vol Wed 1,992; open int 5,607, +138.
        JAPANESE YEN (IMM) 12.5 million yen; $ per yen (.00)
Mar     .4290  .4293  .4288  .4292  ....   .4396  .4125 23,515
June    .4331  .4335  .4331  .4334 + .0002 .4435  .4180  9,691
Sept    .4376  .4378  .4376  .4378 + .0002 .4450  .4354    929
Dec     ....   ....   ....   .4418  ....   .4493  .4395    321
    Est vol 3,290; vol Wed 6,332; open int 34,456, −788.
        SWISS FRANC (IMM)−125,000 francs-$ per franc
Mar     .4620  .4629  .4608  .4626 + .0006 .5230  .3702 17,175
June    .4694  .4706  .4684  .4702 + .0007 .5045  .3742 13,394
Sept    .4775  .4780  .4763  .4770 + .0005 .5020  .3782    277
Dec     .4860  .4860  .4830  .4841 + .0005 .4880  .3818     93
Mar85   .4935  .4935  .4900  .4900 + .0006 .4962  .4755      9
    Est vol 18,808; vol Wed 26,162; open int 30,948, −440.
        W. GERMAN MARK (IMM)−125,000 marks; $ per mark
Mar     .3841  .3859  .3933  .3857 + .0017 .4552  .3537 21,138
June    .3882  .3905  .3876  .3901 + .0019 .4628  .3568 16,443
Sept    .3936  .3947  .3922  .3947 + .0020 .4695  .3602    709
Dec     .3981  .3892  .3974  .3992 + .0017 .4755  .3640    271
Mar85   ....   ....   ....   .4040  ....   .4040  .3699      8
    Est vol 22,600; vol Wed 35,137; open int 338,569, +124.
        EURODOLLAR (IMM)−$1 million; pts of 100%
                                       Yield      Open
```

amounts are quite divergent in terms of the units of the foreign currency, and in terms of their dollar equivalents.

The columns of quotations follow the pattern set for other types of contracts, showing the open, high, low, and settlement prices, and the change in the settlement price since the preceding day. The next two columns present the high and low lifetime prices for each contract, while the final column shows the open interest in each contract. The final line of data for each contract shows the estimated volume of the current day, the actual volume of the preceding day, the current open interest across all contract maturities for each contract, and the change in the open interest since the preceding day. For most contracts, four or five maturities are listed. This indicates that there is a fairly active market with a longer time horizon than that shown for the forward market.

While the differences between forward and futures markets were delineated in Chapter 1, it is interesting to consider these differences more closely for the case of foreign exchange, since it represents a good that is traded on two thriving markets, both forward and futures. These differences between the two types of markets in foreign exchange are tabulated in Table 6.1. For purposes of analysis, the most important differences are the standardized contract, the standardized delivery dates, and the differences in the ways contracts are closed. It is particularly interesting to note that less than 1% of all foreign exchange futures are

TABLE 6.1
Futures vs. Forward Markets.

	Forward	**Futures**
Size of Contract	Tailored to individual needs.	Standardized.
Delivery Date	Tailored to individual needs.	Standardized.
Method of Transaction	Established by the bank or broker via telephone contact with limited number of buyers and sellers.	Determined by open auction among many buyers and sellers on the exchange floor.
Participants	Banks, brokers, and multinational companies. Public speculation not encouraged.	Banks, brokers and multinational companies. Qualified public speculation encouraged.
Commissions	Set by ''spread'' between bank's buy and sell price. Not easily determined by the customer.	Published small brokerage fee and negotiated rates on block trades.
Security Deposit	None as such, but compensating bank balances required.	Published small security deposit required.
Clearing Operation (Financial Integrity)	Handling contingent on individual banks and brokers. No separate clearing house function.	Handled by exchange clearing house. Daily settlements to the market.
Marketplace	Over the telephone worldwide.	Central exchange floor with worldwide communications.
Economic Justification	Facilitate world trade by providing hedge meachanism.	Same as forward market. In addition, it provides a broader market and an alternative hedging mechanism via public participation.
Accessibility	Limited to very large customers who deal in foreign trade.	Open to anyone who needs hedge facilities, or has risk capital with which to speculate.
Regulation	Self-regulating.	April 1975—Regulated under the Commodity Futures Trading Commission.
Frequency of Delivery	More than 90% settled by actual delivery.	Theoretically, no deliveries in a perfect market. In reality, less than 1%.
Price fluctuations	No daily limit.	Daily limit imposed by the exchange with a rule provision for expanded daily price limits.
Market liquidity	Offsetting with other banks.	Public offset. Arbitrage offset.

SOURCE: *IMM*, ''Understanding Futures in Foreign Exchange Futures,'' 6–7.

completed by delivery, but delivery occurs on more than 90% of all forward contracts.

The forward market for foreign exchange dates back to beyond the reaches of history, while the futures market began only in the 1970s. The major center for the forward market continues to be London, but New York has been gaining in importance, as the market for foreign exchange in the U.S. has grown dramatically. Table 6.2 presents Turnover Statistics for the U.S. foreign exchange market, which focus on the activity of the largest U.S. banks. By March 1980, the total turnover of 90

TABLE 6.2
Turnover Statistics.

	In billions of dollars		
	April 1977 **44 banks**	**March 1980** **41 banks**	**March 1980** **90 banks**
Total	106.3	325.8	491.3
Spot	58.7	216.0	315.4
Interbank	54.0	206.1	300.4
of which: brokers	23.1	104.3	162.5
Customer	4.7	10.1	15.1
Outright forwards of which: . . .	5.6	22.4	29.4
International Monetary Market	*	4.5	6.3
Swaps	42.1	87.2	146.5

*Not available
SOURCE: Federal Reserve Bank of New York: Foreign Exchange Turnover Surveys (April 1977 and March 1980).

large U.S. banks was $491 billion, with most of that activity, $315 billion, occurring in the spot market. Activity in the forward market, which is here defined to include futures contracts, accounted for about $176 billion. Futures contracts played only a minor role for these banks, with a turnover of only $6.3 billion. Since banks are the major participants in the forward market, it is not too surprising that their level of activity in the futures market is rather limited.

Foreign exchange activity by U.S. banks is concentrated among only a few currencies, as Table 6.3 shows. The German Mark leads, followed by British Pounds, Canadian Dollars, Swiss Francs, and Japanese Yen. Notice that these currencies of heavy trading are exactly the currencies on which active futures contracts are traded. The Table also presents the concentration ratios of the larger banks in the markets for each of the currencies.

In spite of its smaller size, the foreign exchange futures market has been growing rapidly, a growth that is depicted by Figure 6.5. From a level of only 436,000 contracts in 1973, the total trading volume on foreign exchange futures climbed to over 6 million by 1981. The volume of trading in the various currencies on the futures market matches that of the forward market fairly closely. As Figure 6.6 shows, the German Mark is also the volume leader in the futures market, and the five futures market currencies match the top five currencies in the forward market. The Mexican Peso, French Franc, and Dutch Guilder have so little volume that they are not viable currencies for trading in the futures market.

TABLE 6.3
Trading Activity of Active Banks by Currency.

Currency	Turnover (billions of United States dollars)	Share of 4 most active banks (percent)	Share of 8 most active banks (percent)	Share of 20 most active banks (percent)
German mark	155.8	28.0	45.6	73.9
Pound sterling	111.5	24.3	43.9	74.9
Canadian dollar	60.0	30.3	50.8	82.8
Swiss franc	49.7	38.0	62.5	89.0
Japanese yen	50.0	32.4	51.8	82.2
French franc	33.6	51.8	73.8	95.0
Netherlands guilder	9.3	48.4	72.9	97.4
Belgian franc	5.1	50.0	77.4	98.6
Italian lira	4.2	69.2	85.5	97.7
Other	10.7	60.4	78.4	96.0
Total	490.1	24.9	39.0	67.3

Data based on the Federal Reserve Bank of New York's Foreign Exchange Turnover Survey (March 1980).

DETERMINANTS OF FOREIGN EXCHANGE RATES

The differences between the forward and futures markets notwithstanding, the fundamental determinants of foreign exchange prices are the same in both markets. As the fundamental factors of supply and demand for agricultural commodities are important, there are likewise fundamental factors that shape the exchange rate that prevails between the currencies of two countries. These factors are numerous and quite complex, with entire books being written on the subject.[5] Consequently, the brief discussion that follows merely indicates some of the most important influences on exchange rates.

One way of thinking about currencies is to regard them as essentially similar to other assets, subject to the same basic laws of supply and demand.[6] When a particular currency is unusually plentiful, its price might be expected to fall. Of course, the price of a given currency, in terms of some other currency, is merely the exchange rate between the two currencies. In foreign exchange, the flow of payments between residents of one country and the rest of the world gives rise to the concept of a balance of payments.[7] The balance of payments is generally calculated on a yearly basis. If expenditures by a particular country exceed receipts, then that country has a deficit in its balance of payments; if receipts exceed expenditures, then the country has a surplus. The balance of payments encompasses all kinds of flows of goods and services among nations, including

FIGURE 6.5

Growth in Trading on the International Monetary Market.

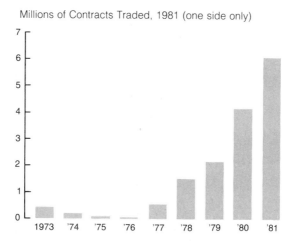

Millions of Contracts Traded, 1981 (one side only)

SOURCE: IMM Division of Chicago Mercantile Exchange
SOURCE: Chalupa, "Foreign Currency Futures: Reducing Foreign Exchange Risk," p. 5.

the movement of real goods, services, international investment, and all types of financial flows.

To understand how considerations of the balance of payments influence exchange rates, consider the following simple example. A country, Importeria, engages in trade with other countries and always imports more goods than it exports. This means that there is always a net flow of real goods into Importeria. These goods must be paid for in some way, so assume that the government of Importeria simply prints additional currency in an amount sufficient to allow payment for the extra goods that are imported. Such a situation cannot go on indefinitely without causing a change in the exchange rates between Importeria and its trading partners. As the trading partners continue to send more and more goods to Importeria, they collectively have fewer and fewer real goods themselves, but a growing supply of the currency of Importeria. As the world supply of Importeria's currency swells, it becomes apparent that it has only a few uses. It can be used to acquire other currencies, or it can be used to purchase goods from Importeria. However, the accumulation of Importeria's currency continues until there is an excess supply at the prevailing exchange rate, so the value of Importeria's currency must fall. Just as Importeria cannot continually import more than it exports without the value of its currency falling, no country can continually consume more than it creates without causing a fall in the value of its currency.

FIGURE 6.6

Trading in Diverse Currencies on the International Monetary Market.

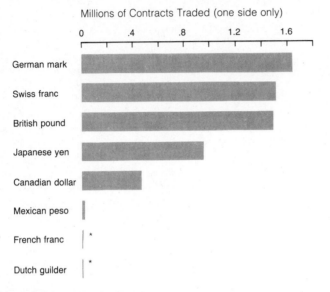

*Fewer than 5,000 contracts.
SOURCE: IMM Division of Chicago Mercantile Exchange
SOURCE: Chalupa, "Foreign Currency Futures: Reducing Foreign Exchange Risks," p. 7.

Fixed Exchange Rates

The kind of adjustment that a country such as Importeria might have to suffer in the value of its currency depends upon the kind of exchange rate system that is in effect. For most of the history of the United States, there has been a system of *fixed exchange rates*. A fixed exchange rate is a stated exchange rate between two currencies at which anyone may transact. A country, such as Importeria, might import more than it exports for quite some time without causing a change in the fixed exchange rate. However, even fixed exchange rates are only fixed in the short run and are subject to periodic adjustments. In the case of Importeria, the continual excess of imports over exports puts pressure on the value of Importeria's currency as the world supply of Importeria's currency continues to grow. Eventually, the fixed exchange rate between Importeria's currency and that of other nations will be adjusted. In the case of Importeria, it is clear that the value of the currency will have to fall and be *devalued*. The value of other currencies will increase, relative to that of Importeria's, so they are said to have been *revalued*. Devaluations and revaluations, when they occur, are usually large in size. It is not uncommon for the value to change by 25 to 50%, or even more.

It may seem perplexing that the value of the currencies would not adjust smoothly over time, as Importeria continued its program of excess imports. Under a fixed exchange rate regime, however, there are forces that prevent gradual adjustment. Rates are fixed through the intervention of the central banks of Importeria and other countries. As excess supplies of Importeria's currency accumulate, central banks may use their reserves of other currencies to buy Importeria's, thereby easing the imbalance between supply and demand that would arise at the fixed level of rates. In effect, central banks would be "sopping up" the excess supply of Importeria's currency which would otherwise exist at the fixed level of exchange rates. If the pressures against the currency of Importeria are not too severe, such action by the central banks may be able to maintain the fixed level of exchange rates. Often, however, the excess supply of a currency, at a given exchange rate, may become excessive so that the central banks are unable, or unwilling, to hold all of the currency that is supplied. In such a situation, a country like Importeria would be forced to devalue its currency and set a new rate of exchange as the official rate. If the value of the Importeria unit of currency was one-tenth of a U.S. dollar before the devaluation, it might be reset at one-twelfth of a dollar after the devaluation. Then the procedure of trying to defend that level of the exchange rate would be followed. If Importeria were to continue its practice of trying to import much more than it exports, it is likely that it would again face another devaluation. One obvious, and apparently disadvantageous, feature of a fixed exchange rate system is that changes in exchange rates continue to occur, but when they do, the changes are rather large.

There are, however, considerable advantages to a fixed exchange rate system. First, planning exchange transactions is simplified considerably in the normal situation. If we could count on a fixed exchange rate for the next year, then we need not take any particular action to control the risk of a change in the exchange rate. Such a situation promotes international trade. Second, for multinational firms, a fully functioning fixed exchange rate system means that accounting income is not sensitive to exchange rate fluctuations. Third, a system of fixed exchange rates may constitute a form of discipline for economic policies by the participating countries. This would be the case, since the countries would realize that pursuit of certain policies would be likely to lead to devaluation.

Perhaps for these reasons, and also as a signal of financial probity, the industrialized West pursued a fixed exchange rate policy from the end of World War II until 1971. Even stronger than a fixed exchange rate, the dollar was convertible into gold at a rate of $35 per ounce, according to the Bretton Woods Agreement. Other major currencies fixed their value in reference to the U.S. dollar. In August, 1971, faced with a weakening dollar and a soaring balance of payments deficit in the U.S., the U.S. went off the gold standard. In spite of attempts to re-establish some semblance of a fixed rate system, notably the Smithsonian Agreement of 1971, March 1973 witnessed a new era in international foreign exchange. Most currencies were allowed to float, with daily fluctuations in exchange rates becoming the norm.

Other Exchange Rate Systems

This new system of exchange rates, or free market, prevails today, but there are a number of important exceptions and variations that the foreign exchange trader must consider. With the breakdown of the Bretton Woods system and the failure of the Smithsonian Agreement, countries were free to adopt a variety of strategies where their exchange rates were concerned. This has led to such strategies as free floats, managed or dirty floats, pegs, and joint floats. A currency is *freely floating* if it has no system of fixed exchange rates and if the central bank of the country in question does not attempt to intervene in the foreign exchange market to influence the value of the currency. Few countries have truly freely floating exchange rates, as central banks seem unable to resist the temptation to intervene. When the central bank of a country engages in market transactions to influence the exchange value of its currency, but the rate is basically a floating rate, the policy is called a *managed float* or a *dirty float*. As opposed to this floating system, a number of countries continue to use a *pegged* system of exchange rates. The value of one currency might be pegged to the value of another currency, that itself floats. For example, Importeria might try to maintain a fixed exchange rate with the dollar, but the dollar itself floats against most of the world's currencies. In such a situation, the currency of Importeria would be said to be pegged to the value of the dollar. Of those currencies that are pegged, some may be pegged to a single currency, while others could be pegged to a basket, or portfolio, of currencies.[8]

One other policy for exchange rate management is particularly important for the foreign exchange futures market, and that is the policy of a *joint float*. In a joint float, currencies in a particular group have a fixed exchange value in terms of each other, but the group of currencies floats in relation to other currencies that are not within the group. The prime example of the joint float technique comes from the European Economic Community (EEC), or the common market. The nine member nations formed the European Monetary System (EMS) in 1979, with full participation by Belgium, Denmark, France, Germany, Ireland, Luxembourg, and the Netherlands. The United Kingdom and Italy, while members of the EMS, do not participate in the joint float. The basic strategy of the EMS agreement is to maintain very narrowly fluctuating exchange rates among the currencies of the participating countries.[9]

In theory, such a system means that the values of the currencies of the participating countries will be fixed relative to one another, but will float relative to external countries, such as the U.S. This has important implications for speculation and hedging in all of these currencies, particularly where the futures market is concerned. In spite of the fact that only the mark is actively traded on the IMM, one may speculate on the other currencies by using the mark contract, since the other currencies in the group will have a fixed value relative to the mark. Such a scheme does not always work out in practice, however. Recent experience has shown that some countries may be forced to devalue their currency relative to those of the group. Italy has faced the problem several times since the inception of the EMS. More recently, France has devalued several times. In such cases, it is apparent that one could not successfully use the German Mark as a cross hedge against the Italian Lire or the French Franc.[10]

MORE PRICE RELATIONSHIPS

The arbitrage opportunities that were noted before, for geographical or cross-rate arbitrage, were opportunities that occur when foreign exchange rates are improperly aligned among single contracts. Both of the arbitrage examples of Figures 6.2 and 6.3 arose from a pricing discrepancy in the foreign exchange rates for a single maturity 90 days forward. Other price relationships are equally important and determine the permissible spreads that may exist between contracts of differing maturities. These relationships are expressed as the *Interest Rate Parity Theorem* (IRP) and the *Purchasing Power Parity Theorem* (PPP).

Interest Rate Parity Theorem

The interest rate parity theorem asserts that interest rates and exchange rates form one system. A trader will earn the same rate of return by investing in risk free instruments of any currency, assuming that the proceeds from investment are converted back into the home currency by a forward contract initiated at the outset of the holding period. Interest rate parity may be illustrated by considering the rates of Table 6.4. In this situation, if interest rate parity holds, the trader must earn the same return by following either of these two strategies:

> *Strategy 1:*   *Hold an investment in the U.S. for 180 days*
> *Strategy 2:*   *(a)*   *Convert funds from $ to DM at the spot rate.*
>   *(b)*   *Invest for 180 days in Germany.*
>   *(c)*   *Convert the proceeds of German investment back into dollars by means of a forward contract initiated at the outset of the investment horizon.*

The two strategies may be expressed by the following equation as well:

$$\$1(1.20)^{.5} = [\$1/.42 \, (1.323)^{.5}] \, (.40)$$

TABLE 6.4
Interest Rates and Exchange Rates to Illustrate Interest Rate Parity.

Exchange Rates	$/DM	Interest Rates	
		U.S.	Germany
Spot	.42	--	--
30-day	.41	.18	.576
90-day	.405	.19	.33
180-day	.40	.20	.323

The equation represents Strategy 1 on the left hand side, where one dollar is invested at the 20% U.S. rate for ½ year. On the right hand side, the dollar is first converted into marks at the spot rate of .42. These proceeds are invested at the rate appropriate to the mark for ½ year of .323. The funds to be generated are converted back into dollars by multiplying the entire bracketed amount by .40, the 180-day forward exchange rate to convert marks into dollars. The equation holds, so no arbitrage opportunity is available.

This example shows, however, only that there is not an arbitrage opportunity in the 180-day contract. If interest rate parity is to hold in general, then the same must be true for all available contracts. In the rates of Table 6.4, there is an arbitrage opportunity in the 90-day contract. This is apparent when one realizes that the strategy of holding the U.S. and DM investment does not yield the same terminal wealth in U.S. dollars when the marks are converted back into dollars by using a forward contract. This is shown by the fact that the following strategies yield different terminal dollar values, depending on the currency in which one holds an investment.

> *Strategy 1: (hold in U.S.) $1 (1.19)^{.25} = $1.0444*
> *Strategy 2: (convert to DM, invest, and use forward*
> *contract) $1/.42 (1.33)^{.25} (.405) = $1.0355*

Strategy 1, investing in the U.S., gives a higher return and means that an arbitrage opportunity is available. It is clearly better to invest funds in the U.S. rather than Germany. Figure 6.7 shows the transactions necessary to take advantage of this discrepancy. Arbitrage of this type is known as *covered interest arbitrage,* since the position in the DM investment is covered by the forward contract to convert the DM proceeds back into dollars. The transaction is a genuine arbitrage opportunity, since one guarantees a profit without risk and without investment. Simply stated, interest rate parity asserts that such opportunities do not exist. Whether interest rate parity actually holds is a topic to be explored in the section on efficiency.

FIGURE 6.7
Covered Interest Arbitrage.

---

t = 0

    Borrow DM 2.3810 in Germany for 90 days at 33%.
    Sell DM 2.3810 spot for $1.00.
    Invest $1.00 in the U.S. for 90 days at 19%.
    Buy DM 2.5570 90 days forward for $1.0355.

t = 90

    Collect $1.0444 on investment in U.S.
    Pay $1.0355 on forward contract; Collect DM 2.5570.
    Pay DM 2.5570 on DM 2.3810 that was borrowed.

Profit: $1.0444
     − 1.0355
      $ .0089

Purchasing Power Parity Theorem

Purchasing power parity is intimately tied to interest rate parity, as will become clear later. The purchasing power parity theorem asserts that the exchange rates between two currencies must, at all times, be proportional to the price level of goods in the two currencies. Violations of PPP can lead to arbitrage opportunities, such as the following example of "Croissant Arbitrage." Assume, for the purposes of this example, that transportation and transaction costs do not exist and that there are no trade barriers, such as quotas or tariffs. The French Franc is worth $.10 and the cost of a croissant in Paris is FF 1, as shown in Figure 6.8. Also, a croissant sells for $.15 in New York. This situation leads to the obvious arbitrage situation of Figure 6.8., and a trader can exploit this opportunity by engaging in the arbitrage transactions as shown. The only price for a croissant in New York that is consistent with the other values is $.10. If an opportunity such as the one presented in the Figure were to exist, then arbitrageurs would engage in the transactions shown until the discrepancy was eliminated.

    The behavior of exchange rates over time must also be consistent with the dictates of PPP. In the left panel of Figure 6.9, the prices and exchange rates are now all consistent with PPP. The right-hand side panel shows the situation one year later, after a year of inflation in France and the United States. For this year, the French inflation rate was 20%, so a croissant now sells for FF 1.2. In the U.S. the inflation rate was 10%, so the croissant price is now $.11. To be consistent with PPP, the exchange rates must also have adjusted so that their relative value remains consistent with the change in the relative purchasing power of the dollar and the Franc. As a consequence, the dollar is now worth FF

FIGURE 6.8
Croissant Arbitrage.

	FF/$	**Cost of One Croissant**
Paris	10	FF 1
New York	10	$.15

Arbitrage Transactions:

    Sell $1 for FF 10 in the spot market.
    Buy 10 croissants in Paris.
    Ship the croissants to New York.
    Sell 10 croissants in New York at .15 for $1.50.

Profit: $1.50
        − 1.00
           .50

10.91. Any other exchange rate would give rise to an arbitrage opportunity. The requirement that PPP holds at all times means that the exchange rate must change proportionately with the relative price levels in the two currencies.

The intimate relationship that exists between the purchasing power parity theorem and the interest rate parity theorem originates from the link between interest rates and inflation rates. According to the analysis of Irving Fisher, the nominal, or market, rate of interest is composed of two elements, the *real* rate and the *expected* inflation rate. This relationship can be expressed mathematically as follows:

$$(1 + R) = (1 + r^*) (1 + E(I)) \qquad (6.1)$$

where, R is the market interest rate, r^* is the real rate of interest, and $E(I)$ is the expected inflation rate over the period in question. Since the expected inflation is nothing other than the expected change in purchasing power, purchasing power parity may be interpreted as a view about the linkage between exchange rates and relative inflation rates. If nominal interest rates differ between two countries, that is most likely to be due to differences in expected inflation. This means that interest rates, exchange rates, price levels and foreign exchange rates form a single integrated system.[11]

FOREIGN EXCHANGE FUTURES PRICES
AND EXPECTED FUTURE EXCHANGE RATES

Throughout this book, and particularly in Chapter 2, the theme that futures prices represent expected future spot prices has appeared

FIGURE 6.9
Purchasing Power Parity over Time.

t = 0		t = 1	
FF/$	10	FF/$	10.91
Croissant Prices		Inflation over the Last Year	
Paris	FF 1	FF	20%
New York	$.10	$	10%
		Croissant Prices	
		FF	1.2
		$	.11

repeatedly, and the case of foreign exchange is no exception. The linkages among interest rates, price levels, expected inflation, and exchange rates merely emphasize the fundamental relationship that exists between forward and futures foreign exchange prices, on the one hand, and the expected future value of the currencies, on the other.

To investigate these relationships, consider the now familiar situation of exchange rates and price levels depicted in Table 6.5. In the left panel, a set of consistent exchange rates, interest rates, expected inflation rates, and croissant prices are presented for March 20, 1984. The right panel presents the expected spot exchange rate for March 20, 1985, along with expected croissant prices, consistent with the expected levels of inflation in France and the U.S.

Assume now that everything is exactly as shown, except that the expected spot exchange rate in one year is FF 11 per U.S. dollar. With the March 1985 futures price of 10.45 FF/$, a strong opportunity exists as follows. A speculator might buy a futures contract for the delivery of U.S. dollars in one year at a price of FF 10.45 per dollar. If the expectation that the dollar will be worth FF 11 in one year is correct, then he or she will earn a tidy profit. This will result from acquiring a dollar via the futures market for FF 10.45 and selling it for the price of FF 11. If we assume that avaricious speculators are present in the foreign exchange market, then such a discrepancy between the futures price of 10.45 FF/$ and an expected spot exchange rate of 11 FF/$ (at the time the futures contract matures) cannot exist. In fact, with perfect market conditions in place, the only expected spot exchange rate to prevail on March 20, 1985 which would eliminate the incentive to speculate, would be 10.45 FF/$. Of course, different market participants have different expectations regarding inflation rates and expected future spot exchange rates, and this difference in expectations is the necessary requirement for the continuance of speculation.

TABLE 6.5
Price Levels, Interest Rates, Expected Inflation and Exchange Rates.

March 20, 1984		March 20, 1985	
Exchange Rates FF/$			
Spot	10.00	Expected Spot Exchange Rate	10.45
March 1985 Futures	10.45		
Interest Rates (1 year maturities)			
U.S.	.12		
France	.17		
Expected Inflation (for the next year)			
U.S.	.10		
France	.15		
Croissant Prices		*Expected Croissant Prices*	
U.S.	$.10	$ .11	
France	FF 1	FF 1.15	

DIFFERENCES BETWEEN FORWARD
AND FUTURES MARKETS FOR FOREIGN EXCHANGE

Most of the discussion of the theoretical relationships among exchange rates, inflation rates, interest rates, and price levels has been conducted without specific reference to the futures market for foreign exchange. Most of these concepts were developed prior to the emergence of the foreign exchange futures market, so it is important to know how closely related the futures and forward market for foreign exchange really are. This is particularly crucial, due to a recent challenge to any easy identity between forward and futures prices.

The challenge to any simple identification between forward and futures contracts arises from the important differences in the timing of cash flows that one would incur on forward versus futures contracts. Due to the daily resettlement feature of the futures market, there are intermediate cash flows on the futures contract between the time of contracting and the maturity of the contract. This is not true of a forward contract. It has been proven mathematically that this difference can generate a difference in market prices if the pattern of future interest rates is not known at the time one enters a forward or futures contract. Since one can never know what interest rates will be doing with any certainty, the conditions for there to be differences between futures and forward prices definitely are met. Because of the time value of the daily cash flows on the futures contract, the higher the correlation between futures prices and spot bond prices, the lower will be the futures price relative to the forward price.[12]

If the futures and forward price are significantly different from one another, then they cannot both be equal to the expected future spot exchange rate. Such a consequence would have serious implications for the understanding of the economic meaning of these prices. Since most of the research on foreign exchange has focused on the forward market, a large difference between forward and futures prices for foreign exchange would mean that one could not infer very much about the futures market for foreign exchange based on research conducted on the forward market for foreign exchange.

The relationship between foreign exchange forward and futures prices has been examined empirically, however. The results seem to be rather clear: "The foreign exchange data reveal that mean differences between forward and futures prices are insignificantly different from zero, both in a statistical and economic sense."[13] In view of these findings, results based on research in the forward market will be regarded as holding for the futures market as well. Such a procedure is justifiable, but we must still interpret these cross market results with caution. Nonetheless, understanding the foreign exchange futures market can be greatly enhanced, particularly in regard to questions of market efficiency and forecasting accuracy, by using research conducted with forward market data.

THE EFFICIENCY OF FOREIGN EXCHANGE MARKETS

The efficiency of the foreign exchange market has been explored by numerous researchers over an extended time period. In spite of this attention, the efficiency of the market remains an open question. This situation is not unusual when a complex empirical issue in finance is at stake. While the question remains open, it must also be acknowledged that the bulk of evidence to date strongly supports the view that the market is efficient. There may be some exceptions to this general conclusion, particularly in the minor currencies, but the evidence in support of efficiency is quite strong for the major currencies. Since futures contracts are traded on only the major currencies, there is also strong evidence that the futures market for foreign exchange is efficient.

If arbitrage opportunities such as geographical, cross-rate, or covered interest arbitrage exist, then the foreign exchange market is inefficient. Reflection on the structure of the market helps support the case for efficiency. With a worldwide network of active traders, all linked together by sophisticated information systems and all aware of the profits implied by arbitrage opportunities, we might expect any incipient arbitrage opportunities to be detected very early. A result of near arbitrage, or quasi-arbitrage opportunities appearing, would be that traders would alter their trading patterns slightly to take advantage of even the slightest opportunity. A result of this activity would be the non-existence of any observable arbitrage opportunities.

As a single example of the effect of this kind of activity, consider the case of the interest rate parity theorem. In the marketplace, it would not be necessary for the interest rate parity theorem to hold exactly, since the existence of transaction costs would make it unprofitable for traders to attempt to take advantage of minor discrepancies. The arbitrage opportunity depends upon finding deviations from interest rate parity that are large enough to cover all transaction costs and still leave a profit. As a result, one way of searching for the existence of violations of interest rate parity is to look for the occurrence of large deviations from interest rate parity. Table 6.6 presents evidence regarding the size of the deviations from interest rate parity that one might expect for some of the major currencies on which futures contracts are traded. Richard M. Levich selected .25% as a permissible deviation from interest rate parity, which would still be consistent with the absence of arbitrage opportunities. As the Table shows, a high percentage of the observations fall within that band. From this, Levich concludes, "Therefore, the Eurocurrency market is efficient in that there are few unexploited opportunities for risk-free profit through covered interest arbitrage."[14]

To what extent do deviations outside the band of .25% represent arbitrage opportunities? If we find only few opportunities, it may still be worthwhile to look for them. Based on the Table, it seems potentially worthwhile to follow the Swiss Franc, since over 20% of the observations appear to lie outside the stated boundaries. The critical question here is the selection of the no-arbitrage boundaries. If traders have transactions costs in excess of .25%, then the bounds are too narrow. By the same token, perhaps transactions costs are really less than .25%, and the no-arbitrage boundaries are too lax. These questions are not easy to answer, since it is virtually impossible to know what measure of transaction costs to use. The most striking feature of Table 6.6, however, appears to be the very high tendency for so many opportunities to fall within .25% of exact interest rate parity. While it may not be possible to say that no arbitrage opportunities are to be found in the foreign exchange market, it is much more impressive to note how closely the observations tended to correspond to interest rate parity.[15]

Another type of potential inefficiency in the foreign exchange market could arise, not from arbitrage opportunities, but from risky strategies. Perhaps the future spot exchange rates could be predicted better than the forward market. In such a situation, we could assume a position in the forward market, based on the prediction, and profit when the forecast proved to be correct. As a consequence, risky trading opportunities depend upon being able to make superior forecasts of future exchange rates. To profit from a trading strategy, a trader must make a better prediction of the future spot exchange rate than that provided by the forward or futures market. Because of this, opportunities for super

TABLE 6.6
Percentage of Deviations from Interest Parity Within +/− .25%. All assets are for 3-month maturities.

	External Deposits
Canada	93.43
United Kingdom	96.68
Germany	98.82
Switzerland	78.59

SOURCE: Richard M. Levich, "The Efficiency of Markets for Foreign Exchange: A Review and Extension." Reprinted in Kolb and Gay, *International Finance: Concepts and Issues.*

normal returns in foreign exchange depend upon the forecasting accuracy of the futures and forward exchange rates. If we cannot reasonably hope to give a better forecast than the market forecast provided by the forward and futures exchange rates, then we cannot hope to engage in successful speculative trading. For purposes of assessing the efficiency of the foreign exchange market, the forecasting accuracy of the forward or futures exchange rate becomes critical.

MARKET BASED FORECASTS OF FUTURE EXCHANGE RATES

One of the recurring themes of this book asserts that futures prices and forward prices may be treated as estimators of future spot prices. As has already been argued, the forward and futures exchange rates may be treated as forecasts of future exchange rates. This is not to say that these market based forecasts will not have large errors; it is a fact that they do. The usefulness of market based forecasts of future exchange rates depends, however, on a whole range of factors, including availability, cost, extent of bias, size of the forecast error, and performance of the forecast relative to other methods. As will become apparent, in spite of their limitations, the forward and futures forecasts have important advantages in all of these dimensions.

Clearly, the forward and futures forecasts have an advantage in availability and cost. Both are readily available every day for the price of the *Wall Street Journal.* If forward and futures prices may be treated as equivalent to expected future spot prices, then they are unlikely to have any serious bias. Over time, the forward and futures prices will turn out to have values that are equal to subsequently observed spot prices.[16]

It remains to be seen whether the market based forecasts can stand up to other forecasting methods in terms of performance as measured by the size of the forecasting error. Perhaps the most severe challenge to the market based forecasts comes from the forecasting services that prepare

TABLE 6.7
Percentage Forecast Errors for the 1980/1981 Period.

	Y/$	CS/$	£/$	DM/$	Average error
1. Berkeley Consulting Group	7.4	1.2	15.1	29.1	13.2
2. European American Bank/Forex Research	3.5	1.2	17.2	31.2	13.2
3. Henley Centre/Manufacturers Hanover	7.4	6.0	11.5	28.3	13.3
4. Economic Models	8.3	4.5	14.1	28.7	13.9
5. Amex Bank	5.2	1.2	19.3	30.0	13.9
6. BI Metrics	*	1.2	10.9	32.9	15.0
7. Brown Brothers Harriman	9.6	4.5	16.7	30.4	15.3
8. Chemical Bank	7.4	6.0	18.3	31.2	15.7
9. Predex	12.3	3.6	18.3	29.1	15.8
10. Citibank	12.7	8.0	14.1	29.1	15.9
11. ContiCurrency	9.6	8.0	17.8	30.0	16.3
12. Phillips and Drew	12.7	8.0	17.8	29.1	16.9
13. Marine Midland	16.2	4.5	19.3	29.1	17.2
14. Data Resources	22.0	6.0	18.8	29.5	19.0
15. Harris Bank	12.3	8.0	25.6	33.3	19.8
16. Security Pacific	13.2	4.5	29.8	32.9	20.1
The Forward Rate	4.0	6.0	18.8	28.3	14.2

SOURCE: *Euromoney*, August 1981, 45.

and disseminate forecasts of exchange rates. *Euromoney* conducts an annual survey of a number of foreign exchange rate forecasting services and their performances over the recent year. Table 6.7 presents the results of the survey for the 1980–81 forecast period. It shows the average percentage forecast errors, for each of 16 forecasting firms, where the errors are averaged over the forecasts for the Yen, Canadian Dollar, British Pound, and German Mark. Only five of the sixteen services had an average error smaller than the average error for the forward rate forecast, and the best forecast beat the forward rate by only one percentage point.

Several competing explanations of these results may seem plausible. First, it may be that some firms do a good job, while others are incompetent. After all, five firms did do better than the forward rate. This explanation might be more persuasive if there were good evidence to support the consistent accuracy of some firms. Unfortunately, such evidence has not been forthcoming to date. A second explanation might be that this particular year was especially bad for the forecasting firms, but this conclusion does not stand up to examination either, as will become apparent. Third, it may be that the accuracy of the forecasts is in some way related to the cost of the forecast. This seems not to be the case. There is no apparent correlation between prediction accuracy and cost of the forecast.

TABLE 6.8
Recent Performance of a Group of Professional Forecasters.

	1980–1981	*1981–1982*	*1982–1983*
Forecasters vs. Chance	won	lost	not reported
Forecasters vs. the Forward Rate	lost	lost	lost

SOURCE: *Euromoney*, August 1981, 45; August 1982, 111; August 1983, 140–147.

Nor does it seem that the data presented in Table 6.7 is simply an isolated instance. In evaluating the performance of forecast accuracy, one might evaluate the forecasts against alternative simple models. The simplest model simply says that the present exchange rate is the forecast of the exchange rate to prevail at a later time. To beat such a forecast, one need only know whether the exchange rate is going to rise or fall. Since someone completely ignorant of exchange rates could just guess, and be correct 50% of the time, a test of a forecasting service against this simplest model is just a test against the tossing of a coin. The prediction results from just tossing a coin would be correct 50% of the time.

Testing the accuracy of forecast services against the forecast provided by the forward rate is a more stringent test, since the forward rate reflects a great deal of information. Yet it seems to be a minimal test for forecast services to meet. If the forecast service cannot even beat the forward rate forecast, why should anyone be interested in what forecasters have to say? These two alternative models present a standard of comparison against which professional forecast services should be able to compete. Table 6.8 gives the performance results of the professional forecast services vs. the chance prediction model of no change and the forward rate model. From Table 6.7 it is already clear that the forecasters lost to the forward rate forecast in the 80–81 prediction period. The same was true for the 81–82 period. What is more surprising is the failure of the forecasters to outperform the chance or the no change model on a consistent basis. The forecasters, as a group, did better than chance for the 80–81 forecast, but actually under-performed the no change forecast for the 81–82 forecast period.

While it would be a mistake to lay too much emphasis on these results from just a few years, they certainly do not inspire confidence in the ability of the forecasting firms. If the professional forecasting firms cannot outperform the forward or futures rate forecast, and cannot even outperform the no change forecast on a regular basis, then there is little reason to believe that a private individual could do better. For a speculator to earn money, he or she must be able to outperform the forward rate forecast. For private individuals, there is little reason to believe that they can do better than a forecasting service with its considerably greater resources.

TABLE 6.9

Foreign Exchange Prices—Spot and Futures. April 7, 1984.

	$/DM
Spot	.4140
June Futures	.4183
September Futures	.4211
December Futures	.4286

SPECULATION IN FOREIGN EXCHANGES FUTURES

In view of the last two sections, where it has been argued that the foreign exchange market is highly efficient and that forecasts of future foreign exchange rates are unlikely to perform better than forecasts based on the forward rate, it appears that speculation in foreign exchange is a hazardous enterprise. From a statistical point of view, a trader cannot expect great success. For exactly the same reason, the trader should not expect tremendous losses to speculation either, at least not statistically speaking. These conclusions would hold for a large number of speculative transactions over an extended period of time. Spectacular speculations, disasters and triumphs alike, occur when transaction amounts are large relative to wealth or when the speculative positions are assumed within a short span of time.

In contemplating speculation, the most important single point to remember is that one is opposing the opinion of the entire market, since prices available in the market reflect the consensus opinion of all participating parties. The dependence of speculative profits on superior estimation of future exchange rates is demonstrated in Tables 6.9 and 6.10. Imagine yourself as a speculator who confronts the exchange rates of Table 6.9 between the U.S. dollar and the German Mark on April 7, 1984. As an expression of the market's beliefs, these exchange rates imply that the mark will gain in value relative to the dollar. You, however, strongly disagree and believe that the price of the mark, in terms of dollars, will actually fall over the rest of the year. Table 6.10 shows the speculative transactions that you might use to take advantage of your belief.

Since you expect the price of the mark to decline over time, you simply sell the December futures contract at an initial price of .4286. If the subsequent price is below that level, you will make a profit. It is not necessary that you actually be correct in the stated belief that the value of the mark will fall over the next eight months. A profit is assured if the mark is worth less than the December futures price. On December 10, as is shown in the Table, the December futures is trading at 0.4218 and the spot exchange rate is 0.4211. Notice that the belief that the mark would

TABLE 6.10

Speculation in Foreign Exchange.

Cash Market	Futures Market
April 7	
Anticipates a fall in the value of the DM over the next 8 months.	Sell 1 December DM futures contract at .4286.
December 10	
Spot Price $/DM = .4211	Buy 1 December DM futures contract at .4218.

	Profit:	
		$ .4286
		− .4218
	Profit per DM	$ .0068
	Times DM per contract	× 125,000
	Total Profit	$ .850

fall in value was incorrect. The December 10 spot price still exceeds the original spot price, as does the price of the December futures contract. Nonetheless, the drop in the futures price from .4286 to .4218 generates a profit of $.0068 per Mark. Since the DM contract calls for delivery of 125,000 Marks, the total profit is $850.

In addition to outright positions, such as the one just described, various spread strategies are possible, including *intra-* and *inter-commodity* spreads. Some of the inter-commodity spreads are important, since they allow positions that might not be attainable easily in other markets. The only futures market for foreign exchange is the IMM market, and in this market all prices are stated in terms of dollars. A speculator might believe that the Swiss Franc will gain in value relative to the German Mark, but might also be uncertain about the future value of the dollar relative to either of these currencies. It is possible to speculate on the SF/DM exchange rate by trading on the IMM futures market.

Table 6.11 presents market prices on the IMM for June 24, 1984 for the $/DM and $/SF spot and future exchange rates. The rates for futures contracts quoted in the left panel imply a system of exchange rates between the mark and franc as well, and these are shown in the right hand panel. Here the structure of rates is peculiar, with the DM/SF rate dipping first, and then rising. In particular, the implied cross-rate for December 1984 appears to be too low to the speculator in question, who believes that the Swiss Franc will tend to appreciate against the dollar over the coming year. Even though it is impossible to trade the Mark against the Swiss Franc directly, it is possible to use a spread position in the futures market to achieve the desired speculative position.

TABLE 6.11
Spot and Futures Exchange Rates.

	June 24, 1984		Implied DM/SF
	$/DM	*$/SF*	
SPOT	.3853	.4580	1.1887
SEP 84	.3915	.4616	1.1791
DEC 84	.4115	.4635	1.1264
MAR 85	.4163	.4815	1.1566
JUN 85	.4180	.5100	1.2201

Since the speculator believes that the value of the mark will fall relative to the Swiss Franc, he must also believe that the value of the mark relative to the dollar will perform worse than the value of the Swiss Franc relative to the dollar. In other words, even if the mark appreciates against the dollar, his belief about the relative value of the Swiss Franc implies that the Swiss Franc would appreciate even more against the dollar. Likewise, if the mark falls against the dollar, the speculator would believe that the Swiss Franc would either gain or not fall as much as the mark. It is important to realize that the speculator need not have any belief regarding the performance of the dollar relative to either of the European currencies. He is merely going to trade through the dollar in order to establish the desired position in the DM/SF exchange rate.

The transactions necessary to take advantage of the belief that the December implied cross-rate is too low are shown in Table 6.12. If the speculator is correct, the price of the mark will fall relative to the Swiss Franc, so she sells one December mark contract at a price of 0.4115 and buys one December Swiss Franc contract at .4635. This is equivalent to speculating that the implied cross-rate of 1.1264 is too low, or that it will require more than 1.1264 DM to buy 1 SF in December. By December 11, 1984 the two contracts are approaching their maturity, and the speculator closes her position by initiating two reversing trades. She buys the December DM contract at a price of 0.3907 and sells the SF contract at 0.4475. This generates a profit of $.0208 per DM and a loss of $.0160 per SF. Both contracts are written for 125,000 units of the foreign currency, so the net profit on the spread transaction is $600.

As a final example of currency speculation, consider the spot and futures prices for the British Pound presented in Table 6.13. A speculator notes these relatively constant prices, but believes that the British economy is even worse than generally appreciated. Specifically, he anticipates a worsening of British inflation relative to that in the U.S. and so believes that the value of the British pound will fall. One easy way to act on this belief would be to sell a distant futures contract, but this speculator is very risk averse and decides to trade a spread instead of taking the outright position. He believes that the equal prices for the

TABLE 6.12
A Speculative Cross-Rate Futures Spread.

Cash Market	Futures Market
June 24, 1984	Sell 1 December DM futures contract at .4115.
	Buy 1 December SF futures contract at .4635.
December 11, 1984	Buy 1 December DM futures contract at .3907.
	Sell 1 December SF futures contract at .4475.

Futures Trading Results:

	DM	SF	
Sold	.4115	.4475	
Bought	− .3907 −	− .4635	
	$.0208	− $.0160	
	× 125,000		
	= $ 2600	− $ 2000	= $600

December 1984 and March 1985 contracts will not be sustained, so he trades as shown in Table 6.14, selling what he believes to be the relatively overpriced March contract and buying the relatively underpriced December contract. By December 1984, the speculator's expectations have been realized and the value of the British Pound has fallen relative to the dollar, with the more distant futures contract falling even more. The speculator then closes his position on December 5, and realizes a total profit of $150, as is shown in the Table. The result of his extreme conservatism has been the limitation of his profit to only $150. Had he taken an outright position by selling the March contract, he would have had a profit of $517.50 by the same point in time.

In these examples of successful speculations it must be recognized that each involves pitting the speculator's knowledge against the collective opinion of the entire market, as that opinion is expressed in market prices.

HEDGING WITH FOREIGN EXCHANGE FUTURES

Many firms, and some individuals, find themselves exposed to foreign exchange risk. Firms engaged in importing and exporting, for example, often need to make commitments to buy or sell goods for delivery at some future time, with the payment to be made in a foreign currency. Likewise, multinational firms operating foreign subsidiaries receive payments from their subsidiaries that may be denominated in a foreign

TABLE 6.13
Spot and Futures Prices. August 12, 1984.

	$/British Pound
Spot	1.4485
September 1984	1.4480
December 1984	1.4460
March 1985	1.4460
June 1985	1.4470

TABLE 6.14
Time Spread Speculation in the British Pound.

Cash Market	**Futures Market**
August 12, 1984	Buy 1 December 1984 BP futures contract at 1.4460.
	Sell 1 March 1984 BP futures contract at 1.4460.
December 5, 1984	Sell 1 December 1984 BP futures contract at 1.4313.
	Buy 1 March 1985 BP futures contract at 1.4253.

	December	March
Sold	1.4313	1.4460
− Bought −	1.4460	− 1.4253
−	.0147	.0207
× 25,000 = −	$369.50	+ $517.50
	Total Profit:	$150

currency. A wealthy individual may be planning an extended trip abroad and may be concerned about the chance that the price of a particular foreign currency might rise unexpectedly. All of these different parties are potential candidates for hedging unwanted currency risk by using the foreign exchange futures market.

Hedging Transaction Exposure

The simplest kind of example arises in the case of someone like Moncrief Snobbody, who is planning a six month trip to Switzerland. Moncrief plans to spend a considerable sum during this trip, enough to make it worthwhile to attend to exchange rates, which are shown in Table 6.15. With the more distant rates lying above the nearby rates, Moncrief fears that the rates may be even higher, so he decides to *lock-in* to the existing

TABLE 6.15
Swiss Exchange Rates. January 12, 1984.

Spot	.4935
March 1984	.5034
June 1984	.5134
September 1984	.5237
December 1984	.5342

TABLE 6.16
Moncrief Snobbody's Swiss Franc Hedge.

Cash Market	Futures Market
January 12, 1984	
Moncrief plans to take a six-month vacation in Switzerland, to begin in June, and to cost about SF 250,000.	Moncrief buys 2 June 1984 SF futures contracts at .5134 for a total cost of $128,350.
June 16, 1984	
The $/SF spot rate is now .5211, giving a dollar cost of $130,275 for SF 250,000.	Moncrief delivers $128,350 and collects SF 250,000.
Savings on the Hedge = $130,275 − 128,350 = $1925	

rates by securing the future delivery of Swiss Francs for his trip at the currently available prices. Since he plans to depart for Switzerland in June, he buys two June Swiss Franc futures contracts at the currently available price of .5134. He anticipates that the SF 250,000 will be enough to cover his six month stay, as shown in Table 6.16. By June 6, Moncrief's fears have been realized, and the spot rate for the Swiss Franc is now .5211. Moncrief, consequently, delivers $128,350 and collects his SF 250,000. Had he waited and transacted in the spot market on June 6, the SF 250,000 would have cost $130,275. In virtue of having hedged his foreign exchange risk, Moncrief has saved $1925, which is enough to finance an extension of his stay in Switzerland for a few extra days.

In this example, Moncrief had a pre-existing risk in the foreign exchange market, since it was already determined that he would acquire the Swiss Francs. By trading in the futures market, he guaranteed a price for himself of $.5134 per Franc. Had he waited, the price he would have had to pay would have been higher. But it just as easily could have been lower. The advantage of entering the futures market was to eliminate the uncertainty regarding the price that he would have to pay to acquire the needed Francs. Of course, the futures market can be used for purposes even more serious than reducing the risk surrounding Moncrief Snobbody's Swiss vacation.

TABLE 6.17
$/Yen Foreign Exchange Rates. April 11.

Spot	.004173
June Futures	.004200
September Futures	.004237
December Futures	.004265

Hedging Import/Export Transactions

Consider the case of a small import/export firm that is negotiating a large purchase of Japanese watches from a firm in Japan. The Japanese firm, being a very tough negotiator, has demanded that payment be made in yen upon delivery of the watches. (If the contract had called for payment in dollars, rather than yen, the exchange risk would be borne by the Japanese firm.) Between the present and the time of delivery there is to be approximately a seven month delay, but the price of the watches is agreed today to be Yen 2850 per watch, and the transaction will be for 15,000 watches. This means that the purchaser will have to pay Yen 42,750,000 in about seven months. Current exchange rates, assuming that it is now April 11, are given in Table 6.17. With the current rate of .004173 dollars per yen, the purchase price for the 15,000 watches would be $178,396. If the futures prices on April 11 are treated as a forecast of future exchange rates, it seems that the dollar is expected to lose ground against the yen. With the December futures trading at .004265, it seems that the actual dollar cost might be closer to $182,329. If delivery and payment are to occur in December, the importer might reasonably estimate his actual dollar outlay in the $182,000 range instead of the $178,000 range.

To avoid any worsening of his exchange position, the importer decides to hedge the transaction by trading in the foreign exchange futures market. Delivery is expected in November, so the importer decides to trade the December futures. This will avoid any problem with having to *roll over* a nearby contract, so that transaction costs will be kept to a minimum. Also, the December contract has the advantage of being the first contract to mature after the hedge horizon, so the December futures exchange rate should be close to the spot exchange rate prevailing in November when the yen are needed.

The importer's next difficulty stems from the fact that the futures contract is written for Yen 12.5 million. If he trades three contracts, his transaction will be for 37.5 million. If he trades four contracts, however, he would be trading 50 million, when he really only needs coverage for 42.75 million. No matter which way he trades, the importer will be left

TABLE 6.18

The Importer's Hedge.

Cash Market	Futures Market
April 11	
The importer anticipates a need for Yen 42,750,000 in November, the current value of which is $178,396, and which have an expected value in November of $182,329.	The importer buys 3 December Yen futures contracts at .004265 for a total commitment of $159,938.
November 1	
Receives watches; buys Yen 42,750,000 at the spot market rate of .004273 for a total of $182,671.	Sells 3 December Yen futures contracts at .004270 for a total value of $160,125.

	Spot Market Results:		Futures Market Results:
	Anticipated Cost	$182,329	Profit = $187
	− Actual Cost	− 182,671	
		− $ 342	
	Net Loss:	− $155	

with some unhedged exchange risk. Finally, he decides on three contracts and his transactions are shown in Table 6.18. On April 11 he anticipates that he will have to have the Yen 42.75 million, with a current dollar value of $178,396 and an expected future value of $182,329, where the expected future worth of the yen is measured by the December futures price. This expected future price is the most relevant price for measuring the success of the hedge. In the futures market, the importer buys three December yen contracts at the prevailing price of .004265 dollars per yen.

On November 18, the watches arrive, and the importer purchases the yen on the spot market at a rate of .004273. Relative to his anticipated cost of yen, he has to pay $342 more than expected. Having fulfilled his need for yen, the importer also closes his futures position by executing a reversing trade. Since the price of the futures has moved only .000005, the profit on the futures is only $187. This gives a total loss on the entire transaction of $155. Had there been no hedge, the loss would have been the full change of the price in the cash market, or $342. This hedge was only partially effective for two reasons. First, the futures price did not move as much as the cash price. The cash price changed by .000008 dollars per yen, but the futures price changed by only .000005 dollars per yen. Second, the importer was not able to fully hedge his position, due to the fact that his needs fell between two contract amounts. Since he needed Yen 42.75 million and only traded futures for Yen 37.5 million, he was left with an unhedged exposure of Yen 5.25 million.

TABLE 6.19
Exchange Rates for the German Mark.

	January 2	December 15
Spot	.4233	.4017
December Futures	.4211	.4017

Hedging Foreign Subsidiary Earnings

Many corporations in international business have subsidiaries that earn revenue in foreign currencies and remit their profits to a U.S. parent company. The U.S. parent company reports its income in dollars, so the reported earnings of the parent company wil fluctuate with the exchange rate between the dollar and the currency of the foreign country in which the subsidiary is operating. For many firms, fluctuating earnings are anathema, and one way to avoid variability in earnings, stemming from exchange rate fluctuations, is to hedge in the foreign exchange futures market.

Table 6.19 shows exchange rates in the futures market and spot market for the German Mark as of January 2 and December 15. Faced with these exchange rates is the Schropp Trading Company of Neckarsulm, a subsidiary of an American firm. Schropp Trading expects to earn DM 4.3 million in this year, and to remit those funds to its American parent. With the December futures trading at .4211 dollars per DM on January 2, the expected dollar value of those earnings is $1,810,730. If the value of the mark fall, however, the actual dollar contribution to the earnings of the parent will be lower.

The firm can either hedge or leave unhedged the value of the earnings in marks, as is shown in Table 6.20. With the rates shown in Table 6.19, the 4.3 million marks turn out to be worth only $1,727,310 on December 15. This shortfall could have been avoided by selling the expected earnings in marks in the futures market in January at the December futures price of .4211. This possibility is also shown in Table 6.20. With each contract being for DM 125,000, the firm might have sold 35 contracts at the price prevailing on January 2. This would have generated a profit in the futures market of $84,875 (35 contracts × 125,000 marks × $.0194 profit per mark). This futures profit would have almost exactly offset the loss in the value of the mark, and Schropp Trading could successfully make its needed contribution to the American parent, by remitting $1,812,185.[17]

TABLE 6.20
Schropp Trading Company of Neckarsulm.

The Situation of January 2:

| Expected earnings in Germany for the year: | DM 4.3 million |
| Anticipated value in U.S. dollars:
(computed @ .4211 $/DM) | $1,810,730 |

Schropp Trading Company's Contribution to Its Parent's Income:

Unhedged		Hedged
Futures Market Action on January 2	None	Sells 35 December DM futures contracts at .4211.
Contribution to Parent's Income in U.S. Dollars from DM 4.3 million earnings (Assumes spot rate of .4017)	$1,727,310	$1,727,310
From futures (Closed at the spot rate of .4017)	0	$ 84,875
Total	$1,727,310	$1,812,185

CONCLUSION

The market for foreign exchange is one of the more complex and interesting financial markets. The dual system that has emerged between forward and futures markets is unique. In no other market has such a dual system developed to the extent that one finds in foreign exchange. Another feature of foreign exchange markets is that all prices are relative prices in a stronger sense than is usually realized. Everyone is familiar with the idea of buying a loaf of bread for a dollar, but such a transaction is also the buying of a dollar with a loaf of bread. In the market for foreign exchange, the fact that every transaction is a sale and purchase from both sides is brought to the forefront.

With the volatility of foreign exchange and the fact that exchange rates are subject to the whims of governments, the foreign exchange market provides an arena for sophisticated speculation. Superior insight into geopolitical trends and world economic developments can be translated directly into speculative profits, for the lucky possessor of such wisdom. By the same token, the same factors that make foreign exchange such an attractive speculative arena also stimulate the desire to hedge for many participants.

NOTES

1. One such trading room was featured in the film, *Rollover,* starring Kris Kristofferson and Jane Fonda. In this story of international financial intrigue and panic, Kristofferson played the brilliant hard-nosed manager of the trading room, who saves the world from financial collapse.

2. Actually, in major foreign exchange centers, such as New York, some traders will make markets in the major cross-rates. For many currencies in many markets, however, there will not be a separate quotation available for cross-rates.

3. Contracts on other currencies have also been traded, but the contracts on Dutch Guilders, French Francs, and Italian lire have expired from lack of trading interest.

4. Although maturities of 30, 90, and 180 days are normally listed, forward market transactions may be arranged with different maturities to suit the needs of the customer.

5. For more on foreign exchange see J. Frenkel. *The Economics of Exchange Rates,* Reading, MA: Addison-Wesley, 1978; or R. Kolb and G. Gay. *International Finance: Concepts and Issues,* Richmond, VA: Robert F. Dame, Inc., 1982.

6. Consistent with the general monetarist approach, money is analyzed as one among many assets. See, for example, T. Humphrey. "Explaining Exchange Rate Behavior: An Augmented Version of the Monetary Approach," R. Kolb and T. Schneeweis, *International Business: Concepts and Issues,* Reston, VA: Reston Publishers, 1984.

7. For more on the balance of payments, see the International Monetary Fund's *Balance of Payments Statistics.*

8. For more on the history of exchange rate policies, see D. Eiteman and A. Stonehill. *Multinational Business Finance,* Reading, MA: Addison-Wesley, 1982, 49–90.

9. The origins and structure of the European Monetary System are discussed by N. Pinsky and J. Kvasnicka. "The European Monetary System," R. Kolb and G. Gay, *International Finance: Concepts and Issues,* Richmond, VA: Robert F. Dame, Inc., 1982.

10. The alignment of rates within the European Monetary System has been altered as recently as March 1983 and is likely to be changed again before this book appears.

11. For a more formal discussion of Interest Rate Parity, Purchasing Power Parity, and the linkages between the two theorems, see I. Giddy. "An Integrated Theory of Exchange Rate Equilibrium," R. Kolb and G. Gay, *International Finance: Concepts and Issues,* Richmond, VA: Robert F. Dame, Inc., 1982.

12. A number of papers have dealt with this issue, including G. Morgan. "Forward and Futures Pricing of Treasury Bills," *Journal of Banking and Finance,* December 1981, 483–496; and J. Cox, J. Ingersoll and S. Ross. "The Relation Between Forward Prices and Futures Prices," *Journal of Financial Economics,* December 1981, 321–346.

13. See B. Cornell and M. Reinganum. "Forward and Futures Prices: Evidence from the Forward Exchange Markets," *Journal of Finance,* December 1981, 1035–1045.

14. See R. Levich. "The Efficiency of Markets for Foreign Exchange: A Review and Extension," R. Kolb and G. Gay, *International Finance: Concepts and Issues,* Richmond, VA: Robert F. Dame, Inc., 1982, 406.

15. Many other empirical tests tend to confirm the conclusion of efficiency reached by Levich, and a number of these are included in the bibliography to his article.

16. Whether the futures price constitutes an unbiased estimator of the spot exchange rate at the time the futures contract matures remains an open question. See, as examples, F. Papadia. "Forward Exchange Rates as Predictors of Future Spot Rates and the Efficiency of the Foreign Exchange Market," *Journal of Banking and Finance, 5,* 1981, 217–240; S. Kohlhagen. "The Forward Rate as an Unbiased Predictor of the Future Spot Rate," *The Columbia Journal of World Business,* Winter 1979, 77–85; L. Hansen and R. Hodrick. "Forward Exchange Rates as Optimal Predictors of Future Spot Rates: An Econometric Analysis," *Journal of Political Economy, 80,* 1980, 829–853; and T. Agmon and Y. Amihud. "The Forward Exchange Rate and the Prediction of the Future Spot Rate," *Journal of Banking and Finance, 5,* 1981, 425–437.

17. For more on hedging foreign exchange risk see, J. Westerfield, "How U.S. Multinationals Manage Currency Risk;" L. Jacque, "Management of Foreign Exchange Risk: A Review Article;" and I. Giddy, "Why It Doesn't Pay to Make a Habit of Forward Hedging," all of which appear in R. Kolb and G. Gay, *International Finance: Concepts and Issues,* Richmond, VA: Robert F. Dame, Inc., 1982. Giddy argues that frequent small risks should not be hedged. His argument first assumes that there are no transaction costs. Since the futures exchange rate is equal to the expected future spot rate, a trader expects neither a gain nor a loss on a given hedge. If the trader makes many hedges, then he is almost certain to have a result very close to a zero gain or loss. In such an event, there is no benefit or detriment, except, perhaps, a reduction in variance. If transactions costs are considered, however, he would expect to lose the amount of the transaction costs on a given hedge. With many hedges, the net expected result is to lose the amount of the transaction costs, so the trader would be well advised not to make a habit of forward hedging. When the risk is large or will occur only infrequently, then he may reasonably hedge. Giddy intends his argument to apply only to the hedging of numerous small transactions.

7 Stock Index Futures

INTRODUCTION

Although stock index futures have been the most recent major futures contracts to emerge, they are the easiest to understand, at least at a superficial level. Everyone who follows the financial news is used to hearing predictions about the future of the stock market, which often refer to the future movement of some stock market index. With the advent of stock index futures, these pundits now have the opportunity to trade to take advantage of their insights. (Perhaps they should be required to do so.) In addition to the opportunity for speculation, stock index futures also have a role in hedging various kinds of portfolio risk.

This chapter explores stock index futures and the indices upon which they are based. Currently, futures are actively traded on three broad market indices: the Standard and Poor's 500 (S and P 500), the New York Stock Exchange Index (NYSEI), and the Value Line Index (VLI). As of June, 1984, the CME also trades a contract on the S&P 100 Index, but it has only about 10% of the activity of the S&P 500 contract. Accordingly, this chapter considers only the three broad indices mentioned. Without too much doubt, the future will bring other kinds of stock index contracts.

At first glance, it might seem that the three indices are very similar, since each is a broad market index. Important differences exist among the three indices, however. Successful trading of the index contracts requires a thorough understanding of the composition of the indices. When the differences and inter-relationships among the indices are understood, it is easier to understand the differences among the futures contracts that are based on those indices. As we will see, in bull markets one of the indices can be expected to rise faster than the others. One index is more conservative than the other as a function of its calculation and the stocks it includes.

The differences among the indices should not be exaggerated, however. While the three may differ in some respects, they are all subsumed under capital market theory. The kinds of risk and the expected changes in the levels of the indices are predicted by the theory of *capital asset pricing*. The Capital Asset Pricing Model (CAPM) also expresses the relationship between individual stocks and partially diversified portfolios, on the one hand, and the broad indices on the other. As is the case with all futures contracts, the exact construction of the contracts is very important for the trader.

Since the stock index futures are so new, there are many unsettled issues regarding the proper pricing of these futures. As was the case with other futures contracts, there are some non-arbitrage conditions that constrain the possible deviations between the price of the futures contract and the level of the underlying index. In other words, the basis is constrained for stock index futures as it is for other types of contracts. As will become apparent, the relationship between the spot index level and the futures price is complicated by the impossibility of actual delivery. This fact has important implications for the two ways of thinking about futures pricing—the *cost-of-carry* model and the *expected future price* model.

Largely because these index futures are so new, there is very little empirical evidence regarding the behavior of the futures prices. Not surprisingly, the evidence supports the view that the stock index futures market is performing efficiently now, although there may be some doubt as to whether it did so when first introduced.

More exciting than the study of price performance is the wide range of uses for stock index futures. Both speculative and hedging opportunities abound. With three closely related futures contracts, it is possible to fit one's trading to many different kinds of expectations about the future of stock prices. By the same token, stock index futures provide rich hedging alternatives. The uses of stock index futures for portfolio management are just now being explored, and it is reasonable to expect that the uses of the futures contracts will expand beyond those currently appreciated.

THE THREE INDICES

The three indices, the Standard and Poor's 500, the Value Line Composite Index, and the New York Stock Exchange Index, are all familiar, but few people are actually acquainted with their calculation and method of composition. For an understanding of stock index futures, however, a thorough knowledge of the indices is indispensable. This section reviews the make-up of the three indices, moving from the most specific to the most general.

TABLE 7.1

Calculation of S and P 500.

	Outstanding Shares		Price		Value
Company ABC	100	×	$50	=	$ 5,000
Company DEF	300	×	40	=	12,000
Company GHI	200	×	10	=	2,000
	Current Market Valuation			=	$19,000

If the 1941–43 value was $2,000, then $19,000 is to $2,000 as X is to 10.

$$\frac{\text{Current market valuation}}{\text{1941-43 market valuation}} \quad \frac{\$19,000}{\$2,000} = \frac{X}{10}$$

$$\$190,000 = \$2,000X$$

$$95.00 = X$$

SOURCE: *CME*, "Inside S AND P 500 Stock Index Futures," 5.

The S and P 500

The S and P 500 index is the most narrow, yet the best known of the three indices. The index is based on 400 industrial firms, 40 utilities, 20 transportation firms, and 40 financial institutions, all of which are listed on the New York Stock Exchange. Together, these 500 firms comprise approximately 80% of the total value of the stocks listed on the New York Stock Exchange.

Each of the stocks in the index has a different weight in the calculation of the index, and the weight is proportional to the total market value of the stock (the price per share times the number of shares outstanding). The value of the index is reported relative to the value during the period of 1941–1943, which was assigned an index value of 10. As a simplified example of the way the index is computed, assume that the index is composed of only three securities, ABC, DEF, and GHI. Table 7.1 shows how the value of the three firms would be weighted to calculate the index. For each stock, the total market value of the outstanding shares is computed, and these market values are summed across all shares. In the Table, the three firms' shares have a total value of $19,000. If the value in the 1941–1943 period had been $2000, the current level of the index would be calculated as shown in the Table, where X is the current index level and would have a value of 95.00. Mathematically, the calculation of the index is given by:

$$\text{S and P Index}_t = \frac{\sum_{i=1}^{500} N_{i,t} P_{i,t}}{\text{O.V.}} \times 10 \qquad (7.1)$$

FIGURE 7.1
The S and P Index: 1965–1982.

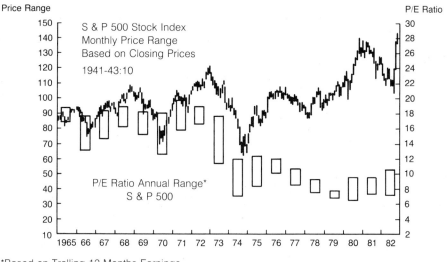

*Based on Tralling 12 Months Earnings

where:

O.V. = **original valuation in 1941–43**

$N_{i,t}$ = **number of shares outstanding for firm** i

$P_{i,t}$ = **price of shares in firm** i

In 1983, during the market rally, the S and P 500 reached the 150–160.00 range, but it was as low as 62.28 in 1974. Figure 7.1 presents the history of the index during the period from 1965 through 1982.

Table 7-2 presents all of the firms in the index, along with their relative weights and betas. Of course, the weights of each firm change as their prices rise and fall relative to other firms represented in the index. Firms such as Exxon, AT&T, and IBM represent large shares of the index, while other firms have only a miniscule impact. The index is computed on a continuous basis throughout the trading day and reported to the public. One reason that the S and P 500 makes a good index for a financial futures contract is due to its importance to professional portfolio managers. Many portfolio managers have their performance measured relative to the S and P 500, so it serves as an industry standard for many purposes.

As the graph in Figure 7.1 shows, there is considerable variability in the performance of the index over time, even though it is a large port-

TABLE 7.2
Stocks in the S and P 500.

TICKER	NAME	PERCENT OF S&P 500	BETA	TICKER	NAME	PERCENT OF S&P 500	BETA
AA	ALUMINUM CO AMER	0.220	0.911	BUD	ANHEUSER BUSCH COS INC	0.220	0.704
ABC	AMERICAN BROADCASTING COS	0.110	0.691	BUR	BURLINGTON INDS INC	0.080	0.795
ABT	ABBOTT LABS	0.380	0.889	BX	BENDIX CORP	0.130	0.987
AC	AMERICAN CAN CO	0.080	0.756	BY	BUCYRUS ERIE CO	0.040	1.038
ACCOB	COORS ADOLPH CO	0.040	1.118				
ACF	ACF INDS INC	0.040	1.213	C	CHRYSLER CORP	0.030	1.186
ACK	ARMSTRONG WORLD INDS INC	0.050	1.013	CAF	CNA FINL CORP	0.080	1.805
ACV	ALBERTO CULVER CO	0.010	1.644	CAT	CATERPILLAR TRACTOR CO	0.560	1.098
ACY	AMERICAN CYANAMID CO	0.160	1.138	CBE	COOPER INDS INC	0.260	1.128
AD	AMSTED INDS INC	0.040	1.372	CBM	CHESEBROUGH PONDS INC	0.180	0.670
ADM	ARCHER DANIELS MIDLAND CO	0.150	1.523	CBS	CBS INC	0.150	0.871
AEP	AMERICAN ELEC PWR INC	0.300	0.283	CCB	CAPITAL CITIES COMMUNICATIONS	0.110	0.989
AET	AETNA LIFE & CAS CO	0.410	0.721	CCC	CONTINENTAL GROUP INC	0.130	0.924
AGC	AMERICAN GEN CORP	0.120	1.073	CCK	CROWN CORK & SEAL INC	0.050	0.916
AGM	AMALGAMATED SUGAR CO	0.010	1.179	CDA	CONTROL DATA CORP DEL	0.150	0.519
AH	ALLIS CHALMERS CORP	0.020	1.015	CFD	CONSOLIDATED FOODS CORP	0.100	0.408
AHM	AHMANSON H F & CO	0.040	1.231	CG	COLUMBIA GAS SYS INC	0.120	0.656
AHP	AMERIAN HOME PRODS CORP	0.66u	0.551	CGG	CHICAGO PNEUMATIC TOOL CO	0.010	0.731
AHS	AMERICAN HOSP SUPPLY CORP	0.190	0.987	CGN	CONNECTICUT GEN CORP	0.240	0.953
AIGR	AMERICAN INTL GROUP INC	0.480	0.860	CHA	CHAMPION INTL CORP	0.130	1.222
AL	ALCAN ALUM LTD	0.220	1.271	CHH	CARTER HAWLEY HALE STORES	0.050	0.770
ALD	ALLIED CORP	0.170	1.489	CHL	CHEMICAL NER YORK CORP	0.100	0.600
ALS	ALLIED STORES CORP	0.060	0.586	CHM	CHAMPION SPARK PLUG CO	0.030	0.945
AMB	AMERICAN BRANDS INC	0.230	0.421	CHU	CHURCHS FRIED CHICKEN INC	0.040	1.022
AMF	AMF INC	0.070	1.013	CHUB	CHUBB CORP	0.070	0.616
AMI	AMERICAN MED INTL INC	0.100	2.021	CIC	CONTINENTAL CORP	0.160	0.761
AMO	AMERICAN MTRS CORP	0.020	0.859	CIL	CONTINENTAL ILL CORP	0.150	0.652
AMP	AMP INC	0.210	0.960	CKL	CLARK EQUIP CO	0.040	0.742
AMR	AMERICAN AIRLS INC	0.040	1.198	CL	COLGATE PALMOLIVE CO	0.160	0.690
AMT	ACME CLEVELAND CORP	0.010	1.289	CLU	CLUETT PEABODY & CO INC	0.020	1.069
AMX	AMAX INC	0.340	1.760	CLX	CLOROX CO CALIF	0.030	0.901
ANR	AMERICAN NAT RES CO	0.110	1.041	CMB	CHASE MANHATTAN CORP	0.200	0.766
APC	ALPHA PORTLAND INDS INC	0.000	1.355	CMK	CARNATION CO	0.120	0.746
AR	ASARCO INC	0.080	2.036	CMZ	CINCINNATI MILACRON INC	0.070	1.967
ARA	ARA SVCS INC	0.030	0.764	CNF	CONSOLIDATED FREIGHTWAYS INC	0.060	1.285
ARC	ATLANTIC RICHFIELD CO	1.310	1.318	CNG	CONSOLIDATED NAT GAS CO	0.120	1.069
AS	ARMCO INC	0.200	1.469	COE	CONE MILS CORP	0.020	0.854
ASA	ASA LTD	0.050	0.942	COX	COX BROADCASTING CORP	0.120	0.665
ASC	AMERICAN STORES CO NEW	0.030	0.846	CPB	CAMPBELL SOUP CO	0.110	0.211
ASR	AMSTAR CORP	0.030	1.138	CPC	CPC INTL INC	0.200	0.651
AST	AMERICAN STD INC	0.090	1.005	CPH	CAPITAL HLDG CORP DEL	0.070	0.585
AUD	AUTOMATIC DATA PROCESSING	0.100	0.841	CPS	COLUMBIA PICTURES INDS INC	0.040	1.655
AVP	AVON PRODS INC	0.210	0.691	CR	CRANE CO	0.040	1.324
AXO	AKZONA INC	0.010	1.057	CRK	CAMPBELL RED LAKE MINES LTD	0.080	0.968
AXP	AMERICAN EXPRESS CO	0.470	0.692	CS	CITIES SVC CO	0.450	1.534
				CSC	COMPUTER SCIENCES CORP	0.020	1.394
BA	BOEING CO	0.250	1.326	CSP	COMBUSTION ENGR INC	0.140	1.604
BAC	BANKAMERICA CORP	0.360	0.536	CSR	CENTRAL & SOUTH WEST CORP	0.130	0.352
BAX	BAXTER TRAVENOL LABS INC	0.270	0.764	CSX	C S X CORP	0.280	NA
BBL	BLUE BELL INC	0.040	0.641	CTC	CONTINENTAL TEL CORP	0.120	0.459
BC	BRUNSWICK CORP	0.040	1.134	CTU	CENTRAL TEL & UTILS CORP	0.100	0.301
BCC	BOISE CASCADE CORP	0.110	1.384	CTX	CENTEX CORP	0.040	2.312
BCR	BARD C R INC N J	0.030	1.404	CUM	CUMMINS ENGINE INC	0.030	1.094
BDK	BLACK & DECKER MFG CO	0.070	1.237	CWE	COMMONWEALTH EDISON CO	0.280	0.295
BDX	BECTON DICKINSON & CO	0.110	1.073	CZ	CELANESE CORP	0.100	0.915
BFI	BROWNING FERRIS INDS INC	0.070	1.529				
BG	BROWN GROUP INC	0.040	0.733	DAL	DELTA AIR LINES INC	0.110	0.928
BGE	BALTIMORE GAS & ELEC CO	0.090	0.368	DCN	DANA CORP	0.120	0.455
BGG	BRIGGS & STRATTON CORP	0.040	0.700	DD	DU PONT E I DE NEMOURS & CO	1.020	0.924
BGH	BURROUGHS CORP	0.170	0.926	DE	DEERE & CO	0.280	1.019
BKI	BEKER INDS CORP	0.010	1.664	DEC	DIGITAL EQUIP CORP	0.150	1.250
BKO	BAKER INTL CORP	0.300	1.834	DEN	DENNYS INC	0.030	0.645
BMS	BEMIS INC	0.010	0.750	DG	ASSOCIATED DRY GOODS CORP	0.040	0.835
BMY	BRISTOL MYERS CO	0.410	0.812	DGN	DATA GEN CORP	0.170	1.605
BN	BORDEN INC	0.100	0.371	DH	DAYTON HUDSON CORP	0.170	0.690
BNI	BURLINGTON NORTHN INC	0.260	2.083	DI	DRESSER INDS INC	0.300	1.184
BNL	BENEFICIAL CORP	0.050	0.897	DIS	DISNEY WALT PRODTNS	0.200	1.237
BNS	BROWN & SHARPE MFG CO	0.010	1.400	DJ	DOW JONES & CO INC	0.180	0.990
BOR	BORG WARNER CORP	0.130	0.919	DKI	DART & KRAFT INC	0.320	0.187*
BRY	BEATRICE FOODS CO	0.210	0.544	DM	DOME MINES LTD	0.120	1.170
BS	BETHLEHEM STL CORP	0.120	1.264	DN	DIAMOND INTL CORP	0.060	1.095
BT	BANKERS TR N Y CORP	0.100	0.682	DNB	DUN & BRADSTREET CORP	0.210	0.991
BU	BROOKLYN UN GAS CO	0.020	0.283	DOC	DR PEPPER CO	0.030	1.220

TICKER	NAME	PERCENT OF S&P 500	BETA
DOW	DOW CHEM CO	0.580	1.123
DPT	DATAPOINT CORP	0.120	2.068
DR	NATIONAL DISTILLERS & CHEM	0.090	0.919
DTE	DETROIT EDISON CO	0.120	0.326
DUK	DUKE PWR CO	0.210	0.075
EAF	EMERY AIR FGHT CORP	0.020	0.964
ECH	ECHLIN INC	0.030	0.907
ECK	ECKERD JACK CORP	0.110	0.979
ED	CONSOLIDATED EDISON CO N Y	0.240	0.301
EDS	ELECTRONIC DATA SYS CORP	0.080	1.261
EFU	EASTERN GAS & FUEL ASSOC	0.060	1.831
EK	EASTMAN KODAK CO	1.330	0.938
ELG	EL PASO CO	0.140	1.474
EMR	EMERSON ELEC CO	0.340	0.741
ENS	ENSERCH CORP	0.160	1.328
ESM	ESMARK INC	0.070	1.098
ETN	EATON CORP	0.100	0.818
EVY	EVANS PRODS CO	0.030	1.179
F	FORD MTR CO DEL	0.230	0.511
FB	FIRST NATL BOSTON CORP	0.070	0.613
FBG	FABERGE INC	0.010	1.678
FBO	FEDERAL PAPER BRD INC	0.020	1.171
FCF	FIRST CHARTER FINL CORP	0.040	1.501
FDS	FEDERATED DEPT STORES INC	0.200	0.578
FDX	FEDERAL EXPRESS CORP	0.140	2.225
FG	USF&G CORP	0.140	0.692
FIR	FIRESTONE TIRE & RUBR CO	0.080	0.985
FJQ	FEDDERS CORP	0.010	1.724
FLE	FLEETWOOD ENTERPRISES INC	0.020	1.654
FLR	FLUOR CORP DEL	0.270	1.704
FMC	FMC CORP	0.100	1.195
FNB	FIRST CHICAGO CORP	0.090	1.002
FNC	CITICORP	0.360	0.859
FPA	FIRST PA CORP	0.010	0.525
FPL	FLORIDA PWR & LT CO	0.140	0.338
FRM	FIRST MISSISSIPPI CORP	0.040	2.022
FTR	FRUEHAUF CORP	0.030	0.792
FWC	FOSTER WHEELER CORP	0.060	1.716
GAO	GENERAL AMERN OIL CO TEX	0.110	1.881
GAP	GREAT ATLANTIC & PAC TEA INC	0.020	1.209
GCI	GANNETT INC DEL	0.220	0.647
GCN	GENERAL CINEMA CORP	0.050	1.419
GCO	GENESCO INC	0.010	1.335
GD	GENERAL DYNAMICS CORP	0.150	1.778
GE	GENERAL ELEC CO	1.520	0.854
GEB	GERBER PRODS CO	0.030	0.729
GET	GETTY OIL CO	0.620	1.612
GF	GENERAL FOODS CORP	0.180	0.584
GID	GIDDINGS & LEWIS INC	0.030	1.955
GIS	GENERAL MLS INC	0.210	0.319
GLD	GOULD INC	0.100	0.908
GLM	GLOBAL MARINE INC	0.080	2.722
GLW	CORNING GLASS WKS	0.110	0.990
GM	GENERAL MTRS CORP	1.350	0.509
GO	GULF OIL CORP	0.780	1.244
GP	GEORGIA PAC CORP	0.230	1.139
GPC	GENUINE PARTS CO	0.100	0.678
GQ	CRUMMAN CORP	0.030	1.438
GR	GOODRICH B F CO	0.050	1.083
GRA	GRACE W R & CO	0.250	1.241
GS	GILLETTE CO	0.120	0.722
GSX	GENERAL SIGNAL CORP	0.120	0.998
GT	GOODYEAR TIRE & RUBR CO	0.160	0.771
GTE	GENERAL TEL & ELECTRS CORP	0.600	0.437
GW	GULF & WESTN INDS INC	0.140	1.247
GWF	GREAT WESTN FINL CORP	0.040	1.465
GWW	GRAINGER W W INC	0.060	0.740
HAL	HALLIBURTON CO	0.710	1.559
HBJ	HARCOURT BRACE JOVANOVICH	0.020	1.078
HBL	HEUBLEIN INC	0.090	0.762

TICKER	NAME	PERCENT OF S&P 500	BETA
HCA	HOSPITAL CORP AMER	0.210	1.254
HD	HUDSON BAY MNG & SMLT LTD	0.020	1.181
HDL	HANDLEMAN CO DEL	0.010	1.488
HI	HOUSEHOLD INTL INC	0.080	0.792
HIA	HOLIDAY INNS INC	0.100	1.736
HLR	HELLER WALTER INTL CORP	0.030	1.126
HLT	HILTON HOTELS CORP	0.120	1.556
HLY	HOLLY SUGAR CORP	0.010	1.847
HM	HOMESTAKE MNG CO	0.070	1.498
HNZ	HEINZ H J CO	0.150	0.685
HON	HONEYWELL INC	0.180	1.285
HPC	HERCULES INC	0.110	0.977
HR	INTERNATIONAL HARVESTER CO	0.030	1.213
HRS	HARRIS CORP DEL	0.150	1.472
HSM	HART SCHAFFNER & MARX	0.020	1.137
HSY	HERSHEY FOODS CORP	0.070	0.547
HT	HUGHES TOOL CO	0.260	1.620
HUM	HUMANA INC	0.150	1.693
HWP	HEWLETT PACKARD CO	0.560	1.356
HWR	WALKER HIRAM RES LTD	0.160	0.293*
HYST	HYSTER CO	0.020	0.996
I	FIRST INTST BANCORP	0.160	1.005
IAD	INLAND STL CO	0.060	0.772
IBM	INTERNATIONAL BUSINESS MACHS	3.900	0.725
ICX	IC INDS INC	0.070	1.315
ID	IDEAL TOY INC DEL	0.000	1.187
IDL	IDEAL BASIC INDS INC	0.030	1.500
IFC	INTERFIRST CORP	0.140	0.743
IFF	INTL FLAVORS & FRAGRANCES	0.080	0.787
IGL	INTL MINERALS & CHEM CORP	0.100	1.122
IK	INTERLAKE INC	0.030	1.092
INA	INA CORP	0.200	0.971
INI	INTERNORTH INC	0.160	1.347
INTC	INTEL CORP	0.110	1.531
IP	INTERNATIONAL PAPER CO	0.230	1.467
IQ	QUESTOR CORP	0.010	1.493
IR	INGERSOLL RAND CO	0.130	0.984
ISS	INTERCO INC	0.080	0.641
ITT	INTERNATIONAL TEL & TELEG CO	0.440	1.150
JCP	PENNEY J C INC	0.230	0.561
JNJ	JOHNSON & JOHNSON	0.800	0.681
JOL	JONATHAN LOGAN INC	0.010	1.307
JOY	JOY MFG CO	0.080	1.235
JP	JEFFERSON PILOT CORP	0.070	0.600
JPM	MORGAN J P & CO INC	0.240	0.412
JWC	WALTER JIM CORP	0.040	1.180
JWL	JEWEL COS INC	0.050	0.665
K	KELLOGG CO	0.200	0.705
KB	KAUFMAN & BROAD INC	0.010	1.925
KCC	KAISER CEMENT CORP	0.020	1.581
KFM	KROEHLER MFG CO	0.000	0.719
KLU	KAISER ALUM & CHEM CORP	0.080	1.144
KM	K MART CORP	0.230	0.521
KMB	KIMBERLY CLARK CORP	0.170	0.663
KO	COCA COLA CO	0.500	0.548
KR	KROGER CO	0.080	1.039
KRN	KNIGHT RIDDER NEWSPAPERS INC	0.110	1.051
LCE	LONE STAR INDS INC	0.040	1.203
LIT	LITTON INDS INC	0.260	1.502
LKS	LUCKY STORES INC	0.080	0.666
LLX	LOUISIANA LD & EXPL CO	0.130	1.426
LLY	LILLY ELI & CO	0.490	0.723
LNC	LINCOLN NATL CORP IND	0.100	0.981
LOF	LIBBEY OWENS FORD CO	0.030	0.700
LPX	LOUISIANA PAC CORP	0.070	1.438
LST	LOWENSTEIN M CORP	0.010	1.053
LVI	LEVI STRAUSS & CO	0.130	0.950
MA	MAY DEPT STORES CO	0.090	0.808
MAI	M A COM INC	0.110	2.224
MAN	MANVILLE CORP	0.040	1.148

TABLE 7.2 (cont.)
Stocks in the S and P 500.

TICKER	NAME	PERCENT OF S&P 500	BETA
MAS	MASCO CORP	0.110	1.686
MAT	MATTEL INC	0.020	1.662
MB	BILTON BRADLEY CO	0.020	1.511
MCA	MCA INC	0.110	1.097
MCD	MCDONALDS CORP	0.310	0.580
MD	MCDONNELL DOUGLAS CORP	0.130	1.714
MDC	MARYLAND CUP CORP	0.030	1.203
MDE	MCDERMOTT INC	0.160	2.052
MDP	MEREDITH CORP	0.020	1.324
MEA	MEAD CORP	0.070	1.514
MEL	MELLON NATL CORP	0.080	0.670
MES	MELVILLE CORP	0.110	0.648
MET	METROMEDIA INC	0.070	1.160
MF	MARSHALL FIELD & CO	0.020	1.094
MGM I	METRO GOLDWYN MAYER FILM CO	0.050	0.157*
MGR	MCGRAW EDISON CO	0.070	1.264
MHC	MANUFACTURERS HANOVER CORP	0.140	0.570
MHP	MCGRAW HILL INC	0.150	1.042
MHS	MARRIOTT CORP	0.110	1.435
MIS	MISSOURI PAC CORP	0.150	1.488
ML	MARTIN MARIETTA CORP	0.160	1.333
MLL	MACMILLAN INC	0.020	1.146
MLN	MCLEAN TRUCKING CO	0.000	0.274
MMM	MINNESOTA MNG & MFG CO	0.740	0.668
MMO	MONARCH MACH TOOL CO	0.010	1.597
MNC	MASONITE CORP	0.040	1.213
MO	PHILIP MORRIS INC	0.710	0.655
MOB	MOBIL CORP	1.200	1.135
MOH	MOHASCO CORP	0.010	1.136
MOT	MOTOROLA INC	0.210	1.314
MRK	MERCK & CO INC	0.730	0.628
MSA	MESA PETE CO	0.160	2.537
MSE	MASSEY FERGUSON LTD	0.010	0.874
MSU	MIDDLE SOUTH UTILS INC	0.180	0.223
MTC	MONSANTO CO	0.320	1.079
MYG	MAYTAG CO	0.040	0.520
MZ	MACY R H & CO INC	0.100	0.996
N	INCO LTD	0.130	1.180
NAC	NATIONAL CAN CORP	0.020	1.433
NB	NABISCO BRANDS INC	0.230	0.210*
NC	NORTH AMERN COAL CORP	0.010	1.488
NCB	NCNB CORP	0.030	1.068
NCR	NCR CORP	0.140	1.223
NEM	NEWMONT MNG CORP	0.130	1.679
NES	NEW ENGLAND ELEC SYS	0.060	0.475
NFK	NORFOLK & WESTN RY CO	0.200	1.314
NG	NATIONAL GYPSUM CO	0.040	1.180
NL	NL INDS INC	0.310	1.792
NLT	NLT CORP	0.090	1.413
NME	NATIONAL MED ENTERPRISES INC	0.090	1.760
NMK	NIAGARA MOHAWK PWR CORP	0.120	0.287
NOB	NORTHWEST BANCORPORATION	0.070	0.628
NS	NATIONAL STL CORP	0.050	0.625
NSI	NORTON SIMON INC	0.090	0.877
NSM	NATIONAL SEMICONDUCTOR CORP	0.050	2.014
NSP	NORTHERN STS PWR CO MINN	0.080	0.328
NT	NORTHERN TELECOM LTD	0.200	1.079
NWA	NORTHWEST AIRLS INC	0.070	1.731
NWT	NORTHWEST INDS INC	0.210	1.315
OAT	QUAKER OATS CO	0.080	0.701
OCF	OWENS CORNING FIBERGLAS CORP	0.080	0.898
OEC	OHIO EDISON CO	0.110	0.369
OI	OWENS ILL INC	0.100	1.041
OKE	ONEOK INC	0.030	1.391
OM	OUTBOARD MARINE CORP	0.020	1.622
P	PHILLIPS PETE CO	0.720	1.257
PABT	PABST BREWING CO	0.010	1.168
PB	PHIBRO CORP	0.200	0.349*
PBD	PEABODY INTL CORP	0.010	1.607
PBI	PITNEY BOWES INC	0.050	1.049
PCAR	PACCAR INC	0.080	1.388

TICKER	NAME	PERCENT OF S&P 500	BETA
PCG	PACIFIC GAS & ELEC CO	0.310	0.081
PCH	POTLATCH CORP	0.050	1.331
PCO	PITTSTON CO	0.110	1.707
PD	PHELPS DODGE CORP	0.080	2.063
PE	PHILADELPHIA ELEC CO	0.170	0.292
PEG	PUBLIC SVC ELEC & GAS CO	0.180	0.402
PEL	PANHANDLE EASTN CORP	0.170	1.345
PEP	PEPSICO INC	0.390	0.637
PFE	PFIZER INC	0.460	0.749
PG	PROCTER & GAMBLE CO	0.770	0.523
PGL	PEOPLES ENERGY CORP	0.030	1.152
PIN	PUBLIC SVC CO IND INC	0.090	0.264
PKN	PERKIN ELMER CORP	0.130	1.615
PLT	PACIFIC LTG CORP	0.080	0.341
PN	PAN AMERN WORLD AWYS INC	0.020	1.450
PPG	PPG INDS INC	0.150	0.893
PRD	POLAROID CORP	0.080	1.358
PRX	PUREX INDS INC	0.030	0.659
PSY	PILLSBURY CO	0.100	0.662
R	UNIROYAL INC	0.020	1.184
RAD	RITE AID CORP	0.050	1.396
RAL	RALSTON PURINA CO	0.150	0.750
RAM	RAMADA INNS INC	0.020	1.535
RB	READING & BATES CORP	0.080	2.601
RCA	RCA CORP	0.160	1.003
RCC	ROYAL CROWN COS INC	0.010	0.464
RD	ROYAL DUTCH PETE CO	1.090	0.898
RDS	REVCO D S INC	0.060	0.956
RE	REDMAN INDS INC	0.010	2.079
REV	REVLON INC	0.110	0.879
REX	REXNORD INC	0.040	0.870
RJR	REYNOLDS R J INDS INC	0.570	0.670
RLM	REYNOLDS METALS CO	0.050	1.189
RM	ROLM CORP	0.060	1.797
ROAD	ROADWAY EXPRESS INC	0.090	1.832
ROK	ROCKWELL INTL CORP	0.290	1.214
ROP	ROPER CORP	0.000	0.999
RS	REPUBLIC STL CORP	0.050	0.881
RTN	RAYTHEON CO	0.370	1.553
RVS	REEVES BROS INC	0.010	0.390
S	SEARS ROEBUCK & CO	0.590	0.688
SA	SAFEWAY STORES INC	0.080	0.558
SAFC	SAFECO CORP	0.090	0.817
SCE	SOUTHERN CALIF EDISON CO	0.290	0.271
SD	STANDARD OIL CO CALIF	1.700	1.409
SED	SEDCO INC	0.140	2.031
SFA	SCIENTIFIC ATLANTA INC	0.070	1.658
SFF	SANTA FE INDS INC	0.220	1.665
SFN	SFN COS INC	0.030	0.955
SGN	SIGNAL COS INC	0.210	1.793
SGP	SCHERING PLOUGH CORP	0.170	0.759
SHW	SHERWIN WILLIAMS CO	0.030	1.414
SKL	SMITHKLINE BECKMAN CORP	0.520	0.863
SKY	SKYLINE CORP	0.020	1.403
SLB	SCHLUMBERGER LTD	1.880	1.238
SLZ	SCHLITZ JOS BREWING CO	0.040	0.963
SMF	SINGER CO	0.030	1.132
SMI	SPRINGS MLS INC	0.020	1.189
SN	STANDARD OIL CO IND	1.790	1.377
SNT	SONAT INC	0.160	1.071
SO	SOUTHERN CO	0.260	0.321
SOC	SUPERIOR OIL CO	0.540	1.499
SOH	STANDARD OIL CO OHIO	1.180	1.592
SPP	SCOTT PAPER CO	0.080	1.050
SQB	SQUIBB CORP	0.190	0.655
SQD	SQUARE D CO	0.090	1.057
SR	SOUTHERN RY CO	0.170	1.000
SRL	SEARLE G D & CO	0.190	1.218
SRT	ST REGIS PAPER CO	0.130	1.110
STF	STAUFFER CHEM CO	0.110	0.781
STK	STORAGE TECHNOLOGY CORP	0.120	1.860
STN	STEVENS J P & CO INC	0.030	0.934

TICKER	NAME	PERCENT OF S&P 500	BETA
STPL	ST PAUL COS INC	0.120	0.725
STY	STERLINE DRUG INC	0.160	0.716
SUN	SUN INC	0.630	1.944
SUO	SHELL OIL CO	1.580	1.558
SVC	STOKELY VAN CAMP INC	0.010	0.517
SX	SOUTHERN PAC CO	0.130	1.238
SY	SPERRY CORP	0.170	1.561
T	AMERICAN TEL & TELEG CO	5.560	0.132
TA	TRANSAMERICA CORP	0.170	1.161
TAN	TANDY CORP	0.400	2.026
TDY	TELEDYNE INC	0.330	1.923
TEK	TEKTRONIX INC	0.120	1.182
TET	TEXAS EASTERN CORP	0.160	1.438
TFB	TAFT BROADCASTING CO	0.040	1.088
TGR	TIGER INTL INC	0.030	1.715
TGT	TENNECO INC	0.500	1.313
TIC	TRAVELERS CORP	0.220	0.657
TKA	TONKA CORP	0.010	1.546
TKR	TIMKEN CO	0.080	1.046
TL	TIME INC	0.210	1.137
TMC	TIMES MIRROR CO	0.180	1.157
TNB	THOMAS & BETTS CORP	0.050	1.002
TRA	TRANE CO	0.030	1.090
TRW	TRW INC	0.210	1.283
TX	TEXACO INC	0.990	1.277
TXB	TEXAS GAS TRANSMISSION CORP	0.080	1.643
TXN	TEXAS INSTRS INC	0.220	1.362
TXO	TEXAS OIL & GAS CORP	0.390	1.747
TXT	TEXTRON INC	0.110	1.233
TXU	TEXAS UTILS CO	0.240	0.315
TYM	TYMSHARE INC	0.040	1.856
UAL	UAL INC	0.060	1.167
UCC	UNION CAMP CORP	0.140	1.058
UCL	UNION OIL CO CALIF	0.760	1.570
UH	U S HOME CORP	0.020	2.233
UK	UNION CARBIDE CORP	0.410	0.791
UN	UNILEVER N V	0.220	0.579
UNP	UNION PAC CORP	0.580	1.598
UPJ	UPJOHN CO	0.190	0.951
USG	UNITED STATES GYPSUM CO	0.060	0.937

TICKER	NAME	PERCENT OF S&P 500	BETA
UT	UNITED TELECOMMUNICATIONS	0.190	0.583
UTX	UNITED TECHNOLOGIES CORP	0.250	1.391
VEL	VIRGINIA ELEC & PWR CO	0.140	0.253
VFC	V F CORP	0.040	1.024
VO	SEAGRAM LTD	0.230	1.317
W	WESTVACO CORP	0.070	1.124
WAG	WALGREEN CO	0.040	1.058
WAN B	WANG LABS INC	0.230	2.489
WCI	WARNER COMMUNICATIONS INC	0.390	1.401
WEN	WENDYS INTL INC	0.040	1.731
WFI	WHEELABRATOR FRYE INC	0.090	1.361
WHR	WHIRLPOOL CORP	0.110	0.851
WHX	WHEELING PITTSBURGH STL CORP	0.010	1.670
WIN	WINN DIXIE STORES INC	0.090	0.196
WLA	WARNER LAMBERT CO	0.210	0.787
WMB	WILLIAMS COS	0.090	1.624
WMOR	WESTMORELAND COAL CO	0.020	1.159
WMX	WASTE MGMT INC	0.170	1.509
WPC	WISCONSIN ELEC PWR CO	0.070	0.198
WPM	WEST POINT PEPPERELL INC	0.030	0.515
WSN	WESTERN CO NORTH AMER	0.120	2.145
WSW	WHITE CONS INDS INC	0.040	0.678
WWY	WRIGLEY WM JR CO	0.030	0.431
WX	WESTINGHOUSE ELEC CORP	0.250	1.447
WY	WEYERHAEUSER CO	0.430	1.357
X	UNITED STATES STL CORP	0.310	1.103
XLO	EX CELL O CORP	0.040	1.763
XON	EXXON CORP	3.120	0.980
XRX	XEROX CORP	0.400	0.936
YELL	YELLOW FGHT SYS INC	0.030	0.773
Z	WOOLWORTH F W CO	0.060	0.920
ZB	CROWN ZELLERBACK CORP	0.090	1.234
ZE	ZENITH RADIO CORP	0.020	1.304
ZRN	ZURN INDS INC	0.020	1.181

*Beta measures were calculated using a period shorter than five years because of mergers or spin-offs

folio of the very largest and most stable firms. Table 7.3 shows the frequency distribution of daily changes in the S and P 500 index where the daily change is defined as daily high–daily low. As the Table indicates, for half of the days in the sample, the daily fluctuation in the index was 2.50 or less, while the average fluctuation was 2.58 points. During this recent period, from February 1981 through March 12, 1982, the minimum fluctuation in any given day was 1.49 points and the maximum was 5.64 points.

To give an indication of the performance of the index over a longer period of time, Table 7.4 shows the performance of the index from 1968 through early 1982. Here the daily change is defined as the difference from closing price to closing price. As is clear from the Table, the variability of the index appears to be considerably smaller with this second kind of computation. Later the variability of the S and P 500 index will be compared to that of the other indices.

TABLE 7.3
Frequency Distribution of Daily* Price Changes in the S and P 500.
February 2, 1981–March 12, 1982.

Percentile	Number Observations**		Value in Points of S&P 500 Index
.50	1	◄	1.49
1.00	2	◄	1.63
2.00	5	◄	1.85
3.00	6	◄	1.94
4.00	11	◄	1.97
5.00	13	◄	1.98
10.00	27	◄	2.07
20.00	55	◄	2.20
25.00	69	◄	2.24
30.00	83	◄	2.29
40.00	111	◄	2.39
50.00	140	◄	2.50
60.00	167	◄	2.60
70.00	195	◄	2.77
75.00	209	◄	2.84
80.00	223	◄	2.92
90.00	251	◄	3.15
95.00	265	◄	3.31
96.00	267	◄	3.40
97.00	270	◄	3.66
98.00	273	◄	3.80
99.00	276	◄	4.03
99.50	277	◄	4.13
99.90	278	◄	5.26
Number of Observations	279		
Median Value	2.50		
Mean Value	2.58		
Standard Deviation	0.50		
Minimum Value	1.49		
Maximum Value	5.64		

*Daily change is defined as S&P High–S&P Low

**Number of days on which the difference between the maximum and the minimum value of the S&P is *less than or equal to* the number of points of the S&P 500 Index indicated in the right-hand column.

SOURCE: *CME*, "Inside S AND P 500 Stock Index Futures," 7.

TABLE 7.4
Absolute Value of Daily Changes in the S and P 500.

Year	Mean	Standard Deviation	Maximum
1968	.32	.34	1.71
1969	.37	.37	1.90
1970	.44	.50	3.48
1971	.35	.37	1.73
1972	.36	.35	2.26
1973	.65	.63	3.07
1974	.69	.67	3.27
1975	.54	.49	2.14
1976	.47	.42	1.60
1977	.37	.37	1.72
1978	.47	.51	3.70
1979	.41	.48	3.25
1980	.74	.72	3.63
1981	.64	.64	3.24
1982**	.59	.66	3.18

*Daily changes are defined as the difference between the closing price for the S&P 500 Index on one day and the closing price on the next day

**Through March 31, 1982.

SOURCE: *CME*, "Inside S and P 500 Stock Index Futures," 7.

Another very important point about the S and P 500 index, and a point that pertains to the other indices as well, is the fact that all of them exclude dividends. This naturally means that the indices do not reflect the full appreciation that the market has enjoyed over any given period. The omission of dividends is also very important for understanding the pricing of the futures contracts as well.

The New York Stock Exchange Composite

The New York Stock Exchange Composite Index is broader than the S and P 500, since it includes all stocks listed on the New York Stock Exchange. This means that the S and P 500 is a subset of the stocks in the NYSE Composite Index. As of May 27, 1982, there were 1520 stocks traded on the NYSE and, therefore, included in the index. Figure 7.2 shows the composition of the index. Three firms, IBM, Exxon, and AT&T make up more than 10% of the total value of the NYSE listed securities. The largest 50 companies account for about 40% of the value of the NYSE capitalization, with the smallest 1470 making up the remaining 60%.

FIGURE 7.2
The Composition of the NYSE Index.

Market Profile of the 1520 NYSE Common Stocks (as of 5/27/82)

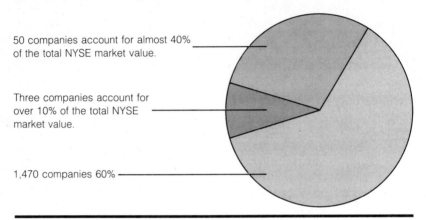

50 companies account for almost 40% of the total NYSE market value.

Three companies account for over 10% of the total NYSE market value.

1,470 companies 60%

The weight of each stock in the index is proportional to its value, just as was the case with the S and P 500 Index. The method of calculating the index is essentially similar in both cases, but with some slight differences. The NYSE Composite Index takes its base date as December 31, 1965. At any subsequent point in time, the value of the NYSE Index is given by:

$$\textbf{(NYSE) Index}_t = \frac{\sum_{i=1}^{1520} N_{i,t} P_{i,t}}{\textbf{O.V.}} \times 50 \qquad (7.2)$$

where:

O.V. = original value of all shares on the NYSE as of December 31, 1965

Equation (7.2) says that the value of the NYSE Index equals the current value of all shares listed on the NYSE divided by the December 1965 base value, with the result being multiplied by 50 as a simple scaling device. This gives an initial value of 50.00 for the index. By late 1974, the index stood at 32.89, was as high as 81.02 in 1980, and was in the range of 90.00 in 1983.

On occasion, the volatility of the NYSE Index can be quite high, as emphasized by Table 7.5. Notice that the longer the time interval, the larger the moves in the index. In spite of these large moves, the average move over a long period of time has been about one-half point (.51) per day. Figure 7.3 shows the range of movement in the index over an extended period of time. One may compare it with Figure 7.1 to see a basic similarity. As will be considered in more detail later, the indices do tend to track one another with a high degree of accuracy.

TABLE 7.5
Maximum Changes in the NYSE Index.

	1 day	1 week	1 month
Up	2.12	4.59	5.91
Down	2.05	4.17	7.30

FIGURE 7.3
NYSE Index Weekly Ranges: 1978–1983. Provided by the New York Futures Exchange.

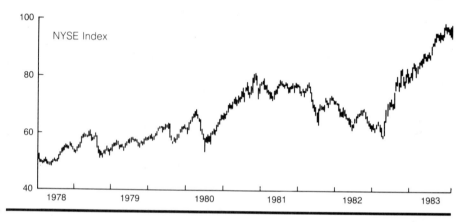

Value Line Composite Index

The broadest of the three indices for which futures contracts are traded is the Value Line Composite Index. It is composed of more than 1700 stocks, including all stocks listed on the NYSE. In addition, it includes some stocks from the American Stock Exchange and some over-the-counter issues as well. Compared to the S and P 500 Index and the NYSE Composite Index, the Value Line Index differs radically in the weighting of the securities that are included and in the method by which the index values are computed. Whereas the S and P 500 and the NYSE indices were based on arithmetic averages, the Value Line Index is computed as a geometric average. The base value of the Value Line Index comes from June 30, 1961, and was assigned a value of 100. The Index is computed according to the following formula:[1]

$$\textbf{Value Line Index}_t = \sqrt[n]{\prod_{i=1}^{n}\left(\frac{P_{i,t}}{P_{i,t-1}}\right)} \times \textbf{Value Line Index}_{t-1} \quad (7.3)$$

where:

$P_{i,t}$ = price of stock i on day t

Value Line Index$_t$ = value of index on day t

FIGURE 7.4
Value Line Index: 1965–1983.

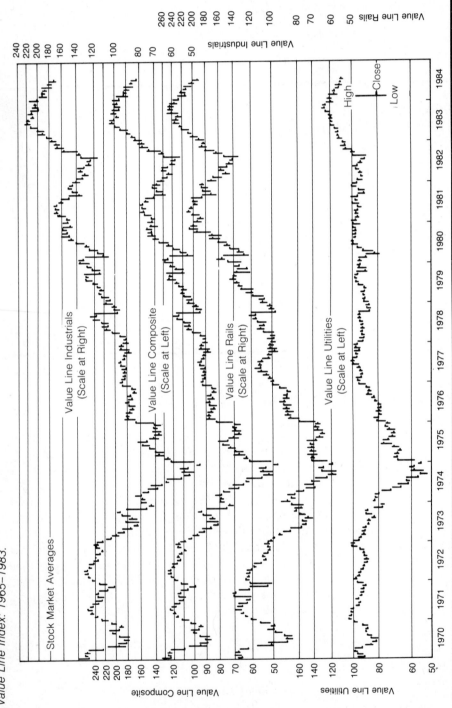

FIGURE 7.5

Four Stock Indices Compared.

Major Market Averages

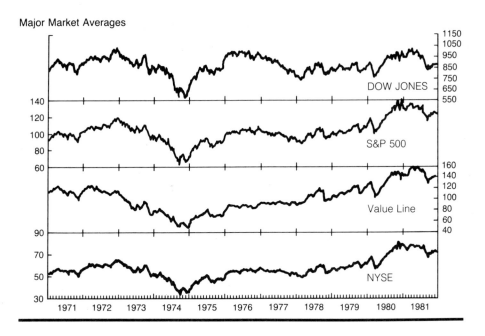

This method of calculation means that each security receives an equal weight. The importance of the firm in the marketplace has nothing to do with its impact on the Index value. Also, as will become clear later, the procedure of multiplying all of the prices together means that the Index is very sensitive to high variability in prices. Consider, for example, the effect of a security in the Index approaching a zero price.

Figure 7.4 shows the performance of the Value Line Index over the period from 1965 through early 1983 in the top panel, and the bottom panel shows the weekly performance of the Index over the recent past. During the period covered by the chart, the Index hit its low near year end 1974 at about 50.00 and reached its highs of about 185 in 1968 and 1983. Over the first half of 1982, the Value Line Index experienced average daily fluctuations of about .77 points.

COMPARISON OF THE INDICES

Since there are three futures contracts, it is important to understand the relationships among the three underlying indices, since such knowledge is important in choosing the most appropriate contract for speculation or hedging. Figure 7.5 shows the performance of all three indices over the

FIGURE 7.6

NYSE vs. Value Line and S and P 500 Indices.

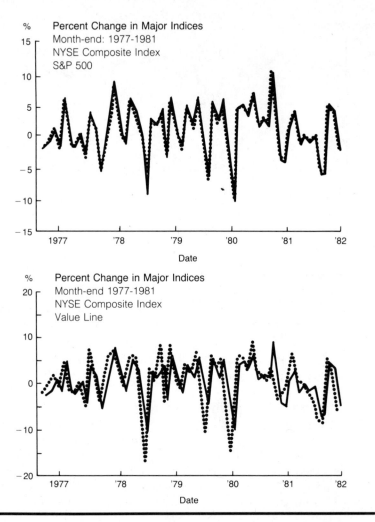

decade of the 1970s and also includes the Dow-Jones Industrial Average for purposes of comparison. Clearly, there is a very strong tendency for the indices to track one another. This is emphasized graphically by the two panels of Figure 7.6, which show the close relationship between the NYSE Index and the S and P 500 Index and the Value Line Index. While the different indices are highly correlated, there are some tendencies for the different measures to diverge. For example, over the 1970s the NYSE Index moved up 56%, while the S and P Index was up only 47% and the Value Line Index gained only 39%. Over the same period, the Dow Jones

TABLE 7.6

Correlations Among the Indices. Based on data from the period February 1, 1971–March 31, 1982.

	S and P 500	Value Line	NYSE	Dow-Jones
S and P 500	1.000			
Value Line	.882	1.000		
NYSE	.989	.928	1.000	
Dow-Jones	.729	.507	.644	1.000

SOURCE: *CME,* "Inside S and P 500 Stock Index Futures," 6.

Index gained only 15%. Given the stocks included in each index and the diverse methods of calculation, this result should not be surprising. Table 7.6 presents a correlation matrix for the four indices computed over the period from February 1, 1971 through March 31, 1982. In the last half of 1982, the correlation among the three indices, for which futures contracts are traded, was higher than .99, indicating a very strong tendency for the indices to move together.

From the graphs of the four indices and the information given in the preceding paragraphs concerning the correlations among the indices and their performance over the decade of the 1970, it should be possible to adduce some rules-of-thumb concerning the relative movements of the indices.

1. Other things being equal, the more small stocks included in the index, the more volatile the index should be.
2. Other things being equal, the more stocks represented in an index the less volatile the index should be, due to the portfolio effect of more complete diversification.
3. Other things being equal, the more small stocks included in the index, the greater the growth in the index should be.
4. Other things being equal, an arithmetic index should grow more rapidly than a geometric index.

These are to be taken only as rules of thumb and not as ironclad laws, but they do have some justification. For example, the Dow Jones Industrial Average includes only the most stodgy blue chip firms, so it should not be very volatile, relative to a broader index such as the S and P 500 or the NYSE indices. As more and more small firms are included, the volatility of the index should increase, although the inclusion of more diverse stocks makes the index representative of a more fully diversified portfolio. As more small stocks are included in the index, the greater is the representation of stocks with good growth potential, so such an index might be expected to grow more rapidly. The method of calculation is also very important. Since the Value Line Index is the broadest index, it is the most diversified, so one might expect its variability to be the lowest and its growth to be the highest. But since it is computed as a geometric average, rather than on an arithmetic basis, it tends to have a lower growth and a lower variability. Obviously, some of the factors mentioned in the preceding list count in different ways for different indices, and it is not simple to say which factors predominate. More can be said about the relative volatility of the indices by looking at the information concerning the different futures contracts.

THE STOCK INDEX FUTURES CONTRACTS

All three futures contracts share certain basic similarities in terms of the calculation of their value and the method by which they are settled. These features are summarized in Table 7.7. Each futures contract has its respective index's current value times $500 as the contract amount. On Friday April 22, 1983 the Dow Jones Industrial Average closed at 1196.30, an all time record. The S and P Index finished trading at 160.42; the NYSE Index was at 92.15; the Value Line Average reached 187.33. In terms of the dollar amounts on each contract, the S and P Index was at $80,210, the NYSE Index was at $46,075, and the Value Line Average futures contract stood at $93,665. All these dollar figures are for the value of the index underlying each futures contract, and it must be remembered that each of these indices were near their all time highs. For the S and P and NYFE futures contract, the minimal price increment, or one tick, was .05, or $25.00. The Value Line contract, traded by the Kansas City Board of Trade, has a daily price limit of 5 full points, or $2500 in either direction from the preceding day's close and a minimal price movement of $5.00. By contrast the S and P 500 contract, which is traded by the Chicago Mercantile Exchange and the NYSE Index contract, traded by the New York Futures Exchange, have no price limits currently in effect.

All three contracts share the feature of *cash settlement*. There is no delivery in the stock index futures market. For the Value Line contract, the final settlement price depends upon the closing value of the Value Line Index on the last trading day of the delivery month, with the delivery months being March, June, September, and December. Similarly, for the S and P 500 contract, the delivery months are March, June, September, and December, with final settlement of open contracts taking place on the third Thursday of the delivery month. For the NYSE Index contract, the final settlement value depends on the difference between the daily settlement price on the last day of trading and the final value of the Index itself on the last business day of the month. Again, contract maturities fall in March, June, September, and December.

TABLE 7.7
Features of Stock Index Futures Contracts.

Feature	(KCBT) Kansas City Board of Trade	(CME) Chicago Mercantile Exchange	(NYFE) New York Futures Exchange
(1) Location	Kansas City	Chicago	New York
(2) Underlying market index	Value Line Composite Average (VLA). This is an equally weighted index of approximately 1700 stocks. Geometric average is used.	Standard and Poor's 500 index (S&P 500). This is a value-weighted index of 500 stocks. Arithmetic average is used.	NYSE Composite Index. It is a value-weighted average of *all* common stocks listed on the NYSE. Arithmetic average is used.
(3) Contract size (value of contract)	Five hundred times the Value Line average (about $65,000).	Five hundred times the S&P index (about $60,000).	Five hundred times the NYSE composite index (about $35,000).
(4) Minimum price change	Tick size is 0.01 points. The minimum change would cause the value of the contract to change by $5.	Tick size is 0.05 points. This represents a change of $25 per tick.	Tick size is 0.05 points. This represents a change of $25 per tick.
(5) Daily price change limits	Five points daily price limit is in effect. Each point represents $500.	No limits currently in effect.	No limits currently in effect.
(6) Margins (minimum customer margin set by the exchange)	Initial margin / Maintenance margin / Trader $6500 / $2000 / Speculator $2500 / $1500 / Hedger $ 400 / $ 200 / Spreaders	Initial margin / Maintenance margin / Trader $6000 / $2500 / Speculator $2500 / $1500 / Hedger $ 400 / $ 200 / Spreaders	Initial margin / Maintenance margin / Trader $3500 / $1500 / Speculator $1500 / $ 750 / Hedger $ 200 / $ 100 / Spreaders
(7) Delivery concept	Cash settlement. Actual value of VLA determines the payment. Final settlement is the last trading day of the expiring month. Delivery months are March, June, September, and December.	Cash settlement. Actual value of S&P 500 index determines the payment. Final settlement of open contracts occurs on the third Thursday of the delivery month. Delivery months are March, June, September, and December.	Cash settlement. Actual value of NYSE composite determines the payment. Settlement is based on the difference between the settlement price on the next to the last day of trading in the month and the value of NYSE composite index at the close of trading. Delivery months are March, June, September, and December.
(8) Volume of trading and approximate dollar value (September 13, 1982)	4077 $275 million	13,708 $845 million	4356 $156 million

SOURCE: Modest and Sundaresan, "The Relationship Between Spot and Futures Prices in Stock Index Futures Markets: Some Preliminary Evidence," 18–19.

Figure 7.7 shows the quotations for stock index futures as they were reported in *Barron's* for the trading day of April 22, 1983. The organization of the quotations is similar to those of other commodities. Particularly interesting is the relative success of each of the contracts. In spite of the fact that it was the first to begin trading, the Value Line contract lags behind the other two contracts by a large amount, with an open interest barely exceeding three thousand contracts. The clearly dominating contract is the S and P 500, with volume in excess of 150,000 contracts and open interest of more than 25,000. The NYSE Index contract occupies a middle ground. In view of the difficulties experienced by the New York Futures Exchange, with very low volume on its CD contract, the success of the index contract is critical to the survival of the NYFE.

In all of the discussion of the various contracts on the different indices, one index is clearly missing from the ranks—the Dow Jones Industrials. This index, without doubt the most closely watched index of all, surprisingly has no futures contract based on it. The Chicago Board of Trade attempted to trade a contract based on the Dow, but Dow Jones, Inc. sued to block this trading practice. Currently, the Chicago Board of Trade has still been unable to enter the stock index futures derby. If the Chicago Board of Trade is successful in the litigation, it is likely that the Dow Jones contract could succeed. If so, we might reasonably expect some "shaking out" of the market, with the potential for the Value Line contract to fail. This seems likely if we notice the extreme lack of liquidity in all contract maturities except for the nearby contract.

ALTERNATIVE MODELS OF STOCK INDEX FUTURES PRICES

Throughout the discussion of futures prices, constant recourse has been made to two models that purport to explain the rational behavior of futures prices, the *cost-of-carry* model and the view that futures prices equal expected future spot prices. When the conditions of the cost-of-carry model are violated, arbitrage opportunities arise, and when the futures prices do not equal expected future spot prices, there can be attractive speculative opportunities. Generally, one might hope that the two models are consistent, yet in some cases, such as stock index futures, the consistency between the two models is not always clear. This section shows how the two models of rational futures pricing lead to apparently different conclusions, and suggests some ways in which the apparent conflicts might be resolved.

With the newness of the market for stock index futures, the principles governing their pricing are just starting to be worked out. As a result, much of what is presented here must be regarded as provisional. As a starting point, the analysis employs the following assumptions:

FIGURE 7.7
Stock Index Futures Quotations.

STOCK-INDEX FUTURES
Kansas City Board of Trade
(Value Line)

	Open	High	Low	Close	Change	Open Interest	Volume
June '83	184.90	186.95	183.00	185.85	+ .70	2,433	9,406
Sept '83	186.05	187.55	184.20	186.85	+ .60	513	288
Dec '83	187.05	188.50	186.00	187.75	+ .75	176	26
Mar '84	189.00	189.00	189.00	188.65	+ .60	35	8
Index	184.59	187.50	184.59	187.33	+ 2.75		

Volume: 9,728.   Open Interest: 3,157.

Chicago Mercantile Exchange
(S&P 500)

	Open	High	Low	Close	Change	Open Interest	Volume
June '83	158.00	160.70	157.00	159.80	+ 1.60	23,497	146,517
Sept '83	158.95	161.60	157.85	160.65	+ 1.50	1,711	3,588
Dec '83	160.40	162.70b	159.35	161.90	+ 1.50	163	68
Mar '84	160.80	163.80b	160.50a	163.10	+ 1.60	8	13
S&P500	158.88	161.08	158.41	160.42	+ 1.67		

Volume: 150,184.   Open Interest: 25,379.

New York Futures Exchange
(NYSE Composite)

	Open	High	Low	Close	Change	Open Interest	Volume
June '83	90.90	92.45	90.30	˙91.95	+ .95	7,534	62,705
Sept '83	91.60	93.00	90.80	92.55	+ .95	718	1,315
Dec '83	92.25	93.40	91.55	93.10	+ .95	498	133
Mar '84	92.80	93.90	92.50	93.65	+ .95	210	25
Index	91.17	92.50	91.01	92.15	+ 97		

Volume: 84,178.   Open Interest: 9.017, + 266.

SOURCE: *Barron's*, April 25, 1983.

1. There are no transactions costs, so that a trader can costlessly rebalance a portfolio at any time. This also implies that the cost of carry equals the financing rate.
2. There is actual delivery of the stock index futures contract.
3. Only one time period is under consideration, which extends from the present at $t=0$ to $t=1$.
4. Dividends for the period are known with certainty at the outset and are paid at the end of the period.
5. The stock index, on which the futures contract is traded, is a true representation of the market, and is constructed arithmetically, like the S and P 500 or NYSE Indices.

These assumptions will be relaxed in the later discussion, but for now they are useful to make the discussion clearer.

In addition to these assumptions, we can use some simple mathematical notation. $F(t)$ is the futures price at time t for the futures contract that matures at time $t+1$. $D(m)$ is the dividend yield on the index, $R(m)$ is the return on the market for the period, and it is also the return on the Index, since it has been assumed that the index offers a true representation of the market. Finally, $I(t)$ is the value of the index at time t. The central claim of the view that futures prices equal expected future spot prices can be represented in this notation as:

$$F(0) = E[\tilde{I}(1)] \tag{7.4}$$

Since the index truly depicts the market, it must also be the case that:

$$R(m) = \frac{I(1) - I(0)}{I(0)} + D(m) \tag{7.5}$$

In other words, the return on the market equals the sum of the capital appreciation rate on the stock plus the dividend yield. The dividend yield is treated separately here, since stock indices are typically the computed net of dividends.

Computing the expected value of the uncertain return on the market and the uncertain level of the index one period later gives:

$$E[\tilde{R}(m)] = \frac{E[\tilde{I}(1)] - I(0)}{I(0)} + D(m) \tag{7.6}$$

Substituting $F(0)$ from equation (7.4) into equation (7.6) gives:

$$E[\tilde{R}(m)] = \frac{F(0) - I(0)}{I(0)} + D(m) \tag{7.7}$$

Solving for $F(0)$ and rearranging terms yields:

$$F(0) = I(0)\{1 + E[\tilde{R}(m)] - D(m)\} \tag{7.8}$$

Equation (7.8) simply says that the futures price at time 0 should equal the value of the index at $t=0$ plus the expected appreciation on the index between the present and the time of delivery. The expected rate of appreciation on the index is the expected return on the market minus the dividend yield. This is reasonable since the index is a true representation of the market and the stock index does not include the dividends that are paid on the stocks. Equation (7.8) represents an important result, and one that will be used later.

Turning now to the cost-of-carry model yields a somewhat different conclusion. Equation (7.9) presents the basic *no arbitrage* condition that defines the cost-of-carry line of reasoning.

$$F(0) = [1 + R(c)] I(0) - D(m) I(0) \tag{7.9}$$

where $R(c)$ is the percentage cost-of-carry for one period, and is equal to the financing rate by assumption. Equation (7.9) simply states that the futures price must be equal to the current spot cost of the deliverable good plus the cost of carrying that good forward to delivery. In this case, the cost of carry is simply the financing cost, $R(c)$. Additionally, however, it must be noted that the dividends are lost from the original value of the index, and that fact is reflected by the final term of equation (7.9). Factoring out the $I(0)$ term gives:

$$F(0) = I(0)[1 + R(c) - D(m)] \qquad (7.10)$$

Substituting the value of $F(0)$ from equation (7.8) into (7.10) gives the following expression:

$$I(0)\{1 + E[\tilde{R}(m)] - D(m)\} = I(0)[1 + R(c) - D(m)]$$

Simplifying expression (7.11) yields the following startling conclusion:

$$E[R(\tilde{m})] \overset{?}{=} R(c) \qquad (7.12)$$

If the analysis to this point is correct, the two models of futures prices imply that the expected return on the market must be equal to the financing cost. Yet, as has been noted above, the financing cost seems to be roughly equal to a very low money market interest rate, such as the repo rate. Surely, the expected return on the market is not as low, or lower than, the repo rate.

If the result in expression (7.12) is unappealing, there are only a limited number of ways to reject that conclusion rationally. We may reject one of the pricing models and thereby avoid the conclusion of (7.12). Alternatively, we might find some step in the analysis that is inadmissible, particularly some of the assumptions that were made to secure this result might be inappropriate.

Many of the early studies to appear on the pricing of stock index futures used the cost-of-carry model and its no arbitrage conditions to stipulate permissible bounds for stock index futures prices. These studies have not always been fully realistic in their treatment of actual market conditions. The no arbitrage conditions of the cost-of-carry model can be very useful and should never be violated. However, the no arbitrage conditions emerge from the assumption that traders would take advantage of any momentarily available profits that would arise when the no arbitrage conditions were violated. In order for traders' profit motives to be used as an effective device, they must actually be able to trade in the ways indicated by the no arbitrage argument. This means that a trader must be very careful when making a no arbitrage kind of argument to take into account the actual costs associated with trading in the market, as well as the actual terms of the contract.

In the brief mathematical analysis that was used to derive the apparent anomaly of expression (7.12), several assumptions were used, and it is important to scrutinize them more carefully to see if they are all realistic. The two most critical assumptions concerned the actual delivery of stocks against the stock index futures contract and the assumption that there are no transaction costs. The market mechanism that insures the price relationship of equation (7.9) is the actual chance that one would acquire the spot commodity, sell the futures contract, and carry the commodity forward to delivery against the futures contract, or engage in the *reverse arbitrage* strategy. This is clear from earlier chapters, particularly chapters 3 and 4. With stock index futures, however, there is no actual delivery against the futures contract, so no arbitrageur could really implement the strategy of delivering against the over-priced futures contract.

Even though a trader cannot actually deliver against the futures contract, might there be some other market mechanism to insure that the price relationship of equation (7.9) will be maintained? Many participants in the market appear to have actual holdings of stocks that closely match the indices that are being traded. The so-called *index funds* often arrange their portfolios to track the performance of the S and P 500. If the futures price were too high, relative to its value in equation (7.9), a trader could buy the stock index at time 0 and hold it over the next period while simultaneously selling the stock index futures contract and creating a (nearly) perfect hedge. This strategy is depicted in Table 7.8, in which a trader confronts an overpriced futures contract. The proper response is to sell the futures contract, buy the index, and realize the arbitrage profit at the maturity of the futures contract. The Table shows no change in the futures price over time, but since the spot index and futures contract must converge at maturity, there is no loss of generality. If the strategy shown in Table 7.8 is workable, it appears that there is a sufficient mechanism in the marketplace to enforce the no arbitrage condition of equation (7.9).

Table 7.8 obviously neglects transactions costs in acquiring and selling the stocks, however. For most traders, these costs to trade all of the stocks in the index would be very high. There are, however, low cost traders, such as stock index mutual funds, who would have low marginal transactions costs. Furthermore, one can create a small portfolio that is highly correlated with the major indices, thereby avoiding much of the transaction costs. These considerations imply that transactions costs are important, but there will be traders for whom they are less dramatic than for others. For true arbitrage, however, a trader must actually acquire the index at time 0 and sell it at time 1. Whether one has very high or very low transactions costs, such trading will be expensive, and the transaction costs make the strategy of Table 7.8 difficult to implement. Although this is by no means a satisfactory resolution of the problem, it may be that transaction costs are sufficiently large to frustrate the actual market transactions that would insure the no arbitrage condition.

Before leaving the apparent conflict between the no arbitrage condition and the expected price model, another implication of Table 7.8 needs attention. In a framework, such as this, the four values, $F(0)$, $I(0)$, $R(c)$, and $D(m)$ must all be mutually consistent to avoid the presence of arbitrage opportunities. The rule of consistency may be stated as:

TABLE 7.8
Arbitrage in Stock Index Futures.

$$
\begin{aligned}
\text{Assume:}\quad F(O) &= \$110 \\
I(O) &= \$100 \\
R(c) &= 12\% \\
D(m) &= 5\%
\end{aligned}
$$

	Stock Market	Futures Market
T = 0	Borrow $100 at 12%.	Sell the futures at $110.
	Buy the stocks in the index at $100.	
T = 1	Receive dividends of $5.	Buy the futures at $110.
	Sell stocks for $110.	
	Pay debt of $112.	
	Profit = $3	Profit/Loss $0

Total Profit: $3

The percentage difference between $F(0)$ and $I(0)$ must be equal to or less than the difference in rates between $R(c)$ and $D(m)$ in order to avoid arbitrage opportunities.

In the Table, the percentage difference between $F(0)$ and $I(0)$ is 10%. If $R(c)$ is 12%, then $D(m)$ must be only 2%. Any higher dividend rate will yield an arbitrage opportunity. This conclusion also follows directly from equation (7.12). If the dividend yield is high, exceeding the carrying charge rate, $R(c)$, then the futures price could lie below the current spot price of the index. This result will have important implications in the next section on the price performance of the stock index futures contracts.

THE PRICE PERFORMANCE OF STOCK INDEX FUTURES

In the early trading of stock index futures, it was not unusual to see that the futures prices for the indices were lower than the current prices. This implies that expected future levels of the indices were lower than the present levels. Such a conclusion would also imply that the expected return on holding the market portfolio, as represented by the stock index, would have negative expected returns. Such a conclusion would not be consistent with the most basic pricing models of finance. Such a conclusion is premature, however; it neglects the important role of dividend flows and their effects on the valuation of stock index futures.

Figure 7.8 shows the projected daily payments for dividends on the stocks underlying the S and P 500 over the period from November 1982 to September 1983, with the futures maturity dates also indicated. It is

FIGURE 7.8

Projected Dividend Payments by Time of the Year.

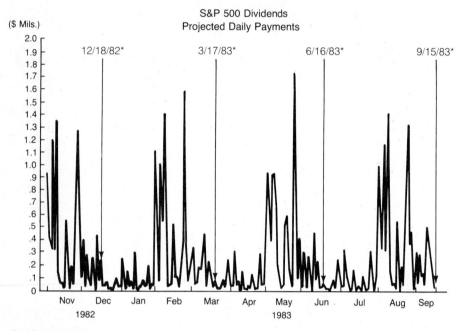

S&P 500 Dividends
Projected Daily Payments

*Contract expiration.
Source: Merrill Lynch, "Special Analysis: Valuation of Stock Index Futures," p. 11.

well established that the payment of dividends results in a drop in the stock price of almost exactly the same amount. From equation (7.9) it is clear that a higher dividend rate means that the permissible maximum value of the futures price is decreased, other things being equal. Consider a situation in which the dividend payout between the present moment and the maturity of the futures contract is quite high. In such a situation, it is easy to imagine a futures price lower than the spot price. While there have not yet been any comprehensive studies of stock index futures prices, the fact that the futures price may be less than the spot price cannot be taken as evidence of irrational pricing.

Another interesting feature of futures price behavior in the stock index futures market concerns the greater volatility of futures prices, as opposed to spot prices. Table 7.9 presents the volatility measures for the different indices. Where the volatility is measured as the standard deviation of the daily percentage price changes in the values of the index. There is a definite tendency for the futures to be more volatile than the index itself. Likewise, there is a tendency for the more distant contracts to have a higher volatility than the nearby contracts. This impression is

TABLE 7.9
Standard Deviation of Daily Percentage Price Changes, June–December, 1982.

	Index	*Nearby*	*Dec 82*	*Mar 83*	*Jun 83*
S and P 500	1.34	1.79	1.82	1.83	1.83
NYSE	1.25	1.96	2.02	2.05	2.05
Value Line	1.00	1.70	1.74	1.73	1.72

SOURCE: "Commodities Magazine," February 1983, 50.

confirmed by Table 7.10, which shows the relationship between the index prices and the different futures prices over the same period. When the daily percentage changes in the futures are regressed on the daily percentage change in the index itself, the beta coefficient may be interpreted as a measure of the volatility of the futures relative to the index itself. If the beta coefficient is equal to 1, the same level of volatility is indicated. If the beta coefficient exceeds 1, then there is greater volatility in the futures price changes. In Table 7.10, all of the estimated beta coefficients exceed 1, although the results are not statistically significant in general. The estimated values, however, do confirm the greater volatility of the futures relative to the spot values of the index itself.

This result is not too surprising whether we believe in the expected price model or the carrying charges model of futures prices. According to equation (7.8), a change in the value of the index, $I(0)$, should have a greater effect on $F(0)$ if the bracketed term exceeds 1. The term in brackets will generally be greater than 1, since the expected return on the market index normally exceeds the dividend yield. From the perspective of the carrying charges model, as represented by equation (7.10), the same result is obtained. If the carrying charge, $R(c)$, exceeds the dividend yield, $D(m)$, the futures price should change more radically than the index price. By the same token, in both equations (7.8) and (7.10), the higher the dividend yield on the index is, the less should be the difference in volatility between the futures price and the index price.

In spite of the fact that the market is too new to allow a complete analysis of pricing rationality, some preliminary studies have been completed with interesting results. Modest and Sundaresan apply the carrying charges model to form permissible bounds for futures prices and try to take into account the actual transaction costs that would be incurred in trading the futures and the stocks in the indices.[2] The bounds depend critically on the assumptions of a $25 round trip transaction cost for the futures contract and $.10 per share transaction costs in the stock itself. We must also assume that the T-bill rate is the appropriate interest rate for all calculations of carrying charges. One additional, and very important point, concerns the assumption that we make regarding the use of proceeds from short selling stocks. If a trader does not have full use of

TABLE 7.10
Beta Coefficients from the Regression of Futures on Spot Prices.

	Constant	Beta	Std. Error
S&P 500			
Nearby	− 0.03	1.17	0.85%
Dec. '82	− 0.03	1.18	0.88
March '83	− 0.03	1.18	0.89
June '83	− 0.04	1.17	0.88
NYSE			
Nearby	− 0.05	1.34	1.00
Dec. '82	− 0.06	1.37	1.05
March '83	− 0.07	1.39	1.06
June '83	− 0.06	1.40	1.06
VLA			
Nearby	− 0.03	1.26	1.14
Dec. '82	− 0.04	1.29	1.17
March '83	− 0.05	1.29	1.15
June '83	− 0.05	1.30	1.13

Note: The constant and beta are derived from regression analysis of daily percent changes.

SOURCE: "Commodities Magazine," February 1983, 52.

the proceeds from short sales, due to margin requirements, then the interest on the proceeds that cannot be used has a marked impact on the analysis.

Figure 7.9 shows Modest and Sundaresan's calculated no arbitrage boundaries and the actual futures prices for the December 1982 futures contract. The graphs track the futures prices from April 21 through September 15, 1982. The dotted lines on the top graph show the bounds, which are adjusted for dividends and which assume that half the proceeds from short sales are available. The actual futures price is represented by the solid line. Clearly, the future's price lies within the bounds except for near misses on two occasions. On the whole, these results are fully consistent with the rationality of futures pricing. In another part of their study, the bounds were also adjusted for dividends, but with the assumption that one has use of 100% of the proceeds from short sales. In this situation, there were consistently available arbitrage opportunities.

The resolution of the question hinges on determining the correct transaction costs, including the availability of proceeds from short sales. The situation is highly reminiscent of the distinction between "pure" and "quasi" arbitrage made by Rendleman and Carabini. For a new entrant

FIGURE 7.9

No Arbitrage Bounds and Futures Prices.

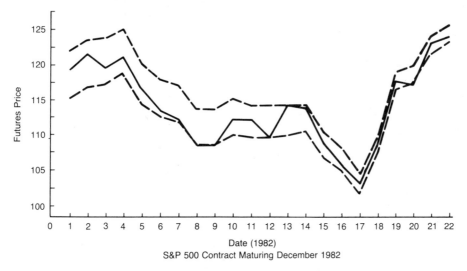

Date (1982)
S&P 500 Contract Maturing December 1982

Source: Modest and Sundaresan, "The Relationship Between Spot and Futures Prices in Stock Index Futures Markets: Some Preliminary Evidence."

to the market, the relevant use of proceeds is only 50%, due to margin requirements imposed by the Federal Reserve Board. In the jargon of Rendleman and Carabini, the evidence seems to be that there are no available pure arbitrage opportunities, since the loss of the use of half the proceeds wipes out any opportunity. For a trader holding an existing stock portfolio, the situation may be different. Instead of literally selling short, such a trader might merely divest part of his or her portfolio and not confront the margin requirement. If that is correct, Modest and Sundaresan's results point to an arbitrage opportunity. In the early period covered by their graph, it appears that the opportunity may have been sufficiently large to stimulate real trading interest. Later in the period, the results are nearly consistent with the no arbitrage condition. Whether these results can be explained by inaccurate transaction costs assumptions, the presence of genuine arbitrage opportunities, or a market seasoning process is not fully clear.

One point that Modest and Sundaresan do not fully consider is the difference in the tax implications of holding futures versus the holding of stocks themselves. Cornell and French find pricing discrepancies between the values of stock index futures implied by the carrying charges model and the actually observed prices when taxes are ignored. These results are basically consistent with those of Modest and Sundaresan. However, Cornell and French argue that holding the stock itself carries with it an option regarding taxes.[3] The holder of a stock has the option to realize a loss and take it in the short term. Gains, by contrast, can be deferred for more favorable capital gains treatment. The trader in the futures market has no such option. The option clearly has a value that needs to be considered in comparing futures versus spot positions in stock indices.

Cornell and French compute the value of the tax option as the difference between the observed market price and the price implied by the carrying charges model. While the tax option clearly has a value, the technique adopted by Cornell and French assumes that the stock index futures is priced rationally, and they compute the value of the option in accordance with that fundamental belief. For the purpose of trying to evaluate the price performance characteristics of the stock index futures contract, note that the tax timing option would have a value, but that a trader cannot immediately assume that its value is equal to the discrepancy between the observed market price and the theoretically justified price assuming no tax timing option.

The question of the price performance of stock index futures remains an issue that is not fully resolved.[4] Open questions remain concerning the theoretically correct price, the correct assumptions regarding the use of proceeds from short sales, the proper transaction costs, the appropriate way to estimate transaction costs on the sale or purchase of stock in the index, and the treatment of the dividends paid on the stocks comprising the index. Resolution of these questions must await further research, which, in turn, will depend on the accumulation of a greater amount of data.

These uncertainties notwithstanding, the limited empirical evidence that is available does show that the futures prices tend to *approximate* rationality. This is particularly true for the period following the initial introduction and seasoning of the market. Given the more complete evidence on the other types of futures contracts, we might expect a similar level of efficiency from stock index futures, especially after their initial seasoning, which has already occurred. In the absence of complete empirical evidence, we cannot assert dogmatically that the stock index futures market is efficient. On the other hand, given the mass of evidence on other futures contracts and the initial evidence on stock index futures, we should not expect to make fantastic profits from finding inefficiencies in stock index futures prices.

SPECULATING WITH STOCK INDEX FUTURES

Speculation with stock index futures is an exciting affair. Futures contracts allow the speculator to make the most straightforward speculation on the direction of the market or to make very sophisticated spread transactions to tailor the futures position to more precise opinions about the direction of stock prices. Further, the low transactions costs in the

FIGURE 7.10

Relative Volatilities of Value Line and NYSE Indices.

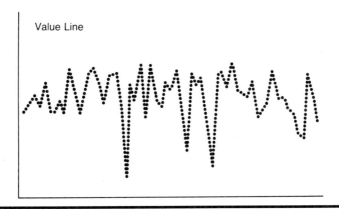

futures market make the speculation much easier to undertake. With three different broad market indices, the speculative opportunities are virtually endless.

One of the simplest speculative positions arises from a belief about impending market movements. If a trader anticipates a major market rally, he or she could simply buy a futures contract and hope for a price rise on the futures contract when the rally actually occurs. While this course of action is very simple, it does not do full justice to the complexity of the speculative opportunity. The trader might also consider which contract maturity is desirable as a trading vehicle and which of the three contracts to trade.

In major market moves, stocks of small firms tend to move more dramatically than the stocks of large well-capitalized firms. If the trader believes that a major advance is impending, then he or she has a definite reason to prefer either the NYSE Index or the Value Line Index to the S and P 500 Index. Since the S and P 500 Index is dominated by large firms, it can be expected to react more sluggishly to major market moves. Other things being equal, we would expect the Value Line Index to be the most responsive to market surges, since it has the greatest weighting of small firms.

With these differential response factors in mind, one conservative speculative position strategy could use a spread between two indices. If the trader anticipates a major market increase, but wishes to closely control her risk exposure, she might use a spread between the Value Line and the NYSE indices. As Figure 7.10 shows, the Value Line Index does, in fact, seem to be more responsive to market moves than does the NYSE Index, and this is in spite of the inherently conservative geometric average used in the computation of the Value Line Index. If the expectation of a major market rally is fulfilled, then the Value Line Index can be

TABLE 7.11
A Conservative Inter-Commodity Spread.

Stock Market	Futures Market
April 22	Buy 1 September Value Line contract at 186.85
	Sell 1 September NYSE contract at 92.55
May 6	Sell 1 September Value Line contract at 197.80
	Buy 1 September NYSE contract at 97.05

	Value Line	NYSE
Sell	197.80	92.55
Buy	186.85	97.05
Gain/(Loss)	10.95	(4.50)
× 500	$5475	($2250)
	Total: + $3225	

expected to have a greater percentage move than the NYSE Index, as it has in the past. This fact, coupled with the greater absolute value of the Value Line Index, should mean a greater price movement in the Value Line Index.

Consistent with this outlook, the transactions of Table 7.11 show how to initiate a spread to speculate on an anticipated market rally. The prescient speculator buys 1 September 1983 Value Line futures contract at 186.85 on April 22, 1983 and sells 1 September 1983 NYSE Index contract at 92.55. Her wisdom in doing so is soon validated by one of the greatest market rallies in history. Not wishing to be greedy, she elects to close her position on May 6, 1983. She sells the Value Line contract at 197.80 and buys the NYSE Index contract at 97.05. Her spread has worked perfectly. The Value Line futures has gained 5.86% while the NYSE Index contract gained only 4.86%. This percentage difference is magnified by the absolute values of the indices, so the gain on the Value Line position of $5475 more than offsets the loss on the NYSE contract of $2250, for a total gain of $3225.

Earlier we noted that the more distant contracts tend to respond to a given market move more than the nearby contracts and more than the index itself. The speculator could have initiated an intra-commodity spread to take advantage of the anticipated market rally. One possible set of transactions is shown in Table 7.12 using the S and P Index contract and the same dates. The speculator believes that the more distant contracts will be more responsive to a market move than the nearby contracts. Believing that the market will rise, she buys the more distant December 1983 contract at 161.90 on April 22, while simultaneously selling the

TABLE 7.12
A Conservative Intra-Commodity Spread.

Stock Market	Futures Market
April 22, 1983	Buy 1 December 83 S and P 500 contract at 161.90
	Sell 1 June 83 S and P 500 contrat at 159.80
May 6, 1983	Buy 1 June 83 S and P 500 contract at 167.50
	Sell 1 December 83 S and P 500 contract at 169.75

	JUN 83	DEC 83
Sell	159.80	169.75
Buy	167.50	161.90
Gain/(Loss)	(7.70)	7.85
× 500	($3850)	$3925
	Total: + $75.	

more nearby June 1983 contract at 159.80. By May 6, 1983, the rally has occurred, so she reverses her position by buying the June contract at 167.50 and selling the December contract at 169.75. As the table in the bottom shows, the June contract has moved 7.70 points and the more sensitive December contract has moved 7.85 points. The strategy has worked, in a certain sense, because the more distant contract was more sensitive, but the difference in the price changes was not very large. In fact, the gross profit on the spread was only $75, hardly enough to cover the transaction costs.

In an important sense, both spreads were too conservative. In this example, the trader correctly anticipated the market move. An outright long position in any contract would have worked well, but the conservative trader managed to protect herself completely out of the benefits that could have been obtained, given the major character of the market advance. For the speculator committed to spread trading, the stock index futures market presents a problem, because the different contracts tend to be so highly correlated. One way to still maintain the risk control advantages of the spread technique, but to be somewhat more aggressive than either of these strategies, would have been to go long on the most sensitive contract and to short the least sensitive contract. Consistent with this outlook, a trader could have bought the distant Value Line contract and sold the nearby NYSE Index contract.

As Table 7.13 shows, this gives a somewhat more aggressive position. Still, when spreading even the most volatile contract against the least volatile, the price action is still not overwhelmingly powerful. For many speculators, it will be necessary to trade different numbers of con-

TABLE 7.13
A More Aggressive Spread.

Stock Market	Futures Market
April 22, 1983	Buy 1 March 84 Value Line contract at 188.65
	Sell 1 June 83 NYSE Index contract at 91.95
May 6, 1983	Sell 1 March 84 Value Line contract at 199.75
	Buy 1 June 83 NYSE Index contract at 96.40

	Value Line	NYSE
Sell	199.75	91.95
Buy	188.65	96.40
Gain/(Loss)	11.10	(4.45)
× 500	$5550	($2225)
	Total: $3325	

tracts on the two sides of the spread. If the speculator had bought three Value Line contracts and sold only the one NYSE Index contracts at the prices shown in Table 7.13, the total profit would have been $14,425. By choosing different weights for the two sides of the spread, one can achieve whatever degree of risk is desired.

PORTFOLIO MANAGEMENT WITH STOCK INDEX FUTURES

The hedging use of stock index futures applies directly to the management of stock portfolios.[5] As will become clear, the usefulness of stock index futures in portfolio management stems from the fact that they so directly represent the market portfolio. Before the advent of stock index futures, there was no comparable way of trading an instrument that gave the price performance so directly tied to a broad market index. Further, it must be acknowledged that the stock index futures have great potential in portfolio management due also to their very low transaction costs, relative to other media.

A Short Hedge and Hedge Ratio Calculation

As a first case, consider the manager of a well diversified stock portfolio having a value of $20,000,000 and assume that the portfolio has a BETA of 1.22 when measured relative to the S and P 500. This implies that a movement of 1% in the S and P 500 index would be expected to induce a change of 1.22% in the value of the stock portfolio. The portfolio manager fears that a bear market is imminent and wishes to hedge his portfolio's value against that possibility. One strategy would be to liquidate the portfolio and place the proceeds into short term debt instruments and then, after the bear market, return the funds to the stock market. Such a plan is radically infeasible. First, the transaction costs from such a strategy are likely to be quite high and second, if the fund is large, the liquidation of the portfolio might possibly affect the prices that could be obtained for the individual securities comprising the portfolio.

An obvious alternative to the extreme policy of liquidation would be to use the S and P 500 stock index futures contract. By selling the appropriate number of futures contracts, it should be possible to offset the effect of the bear market on the portfolio by generating gains in the futures market. One kind of naive strategy might involve trading one dollar of the value underlying the index futures contract for each dollar of the portfolio's value. Assuming that the S and P Index futures contract stands at 112.00, the advocated number of futures contracts would be given by:

$$\frac{\$ \textbf{Value of Portfolio}}{\$ \textbf{Value of Contract}} = \frac{\$20,000,000}{\$112 \times 500} = 357 \textbf{ contracts} \quad (7.13)$$

One problem with this approach is that it ignores the higher volatility of the stock portfolio relative to that of the S and P 500 Index. As noted above, the BETA of the stock portfolio, as measured against the index, was 1.22. Table 7.14 shows the potential results of a hedge consistent with these facts. The portfolio manager lays down the hedge on March 14, selling 357 December futures contracts against the $20,000,000 stock portfolio. By August 16, his fears have been realized and the market has fallen. The S and P index, and the futures, have both fallen by 4.46% to 107. The stock portfolio, with its greater volatility, has fallen exactly 1.22 times as much, generating a loss of $1,089,286. This leaves a net loss on the hedge of $196,786. The failure to consider the differential volatility between the stock portfolio and the index futures contract leads to sub-optimal hedging results.

The International Monetary Market recommends a strategy for avoiding this problem—weighting the hedge ratio by the BETA of the stock portfolio. According to this scenario, equation (7.13) should read:

$$\frac{\$ \textbf{Value of Portfolio}}{\$ \textbf{Value of Contract}} \times \textbf{Portfolio BETA} = \textbf{\# of contracts} (7.14)$$

In this example, it would imply that the correct number of contracts to trade would be:

$$\frac{\$20,000,000}{\$112 \times 500} \times 1.22 = 436 \textbf{ contracts}$$

If this many contracts had been traded, then the futures gain reported in Table 7.14 would have been $1,090,000, almost exactly offsetting the loss

TABLE 7.14
A Short Hedge.

Stock Market	Futures Market
March 14	
Hold $20,000,000 in a stock portfolio	Sell 357 S and P 500 December futures contracts at 112.00.
August 16	
Stock portfolio falls by 5.45% to $18,910,714.	S and P futures contract falls by 4.46% to 107.00
Loss $1,089,286	Gain $892,500

Net Loss: $196,786

on the spot position of $1,089,286. Note, however, that these excellent results depend on two crucial assumptions. First, such results could be achieved only if the movement of the stock portfolio during the hedge period exactly corresponded to the volatility implied by its BETA. Second, the technique of the International Monetary Market uses the BETA of the stock portfolio as measured against the S and P Index itself. This assumes that the futures contracts moves exactly in tandem with the spot index. This assumption is clearly violated by recent market experience. As noted in Table 7.10, the futures contracts for all of the indices are more volatile than the indices themselves. This is reflected by the fact that the futures contracts have BETAS in excess of 1 when they are measured relative to the stock index itself. The methodology advocated by the IMM does not take this into account, since it implicitly assumes the index and the futures contracts to have the same price movements, which would imply equal BETAS.

To take this added complication into account is not difficult, and the derivation of the appropriate hedge ratio is presented in the Appendix to this chapter. The hedge ratio in the Appendix is the hedge ratio to give a zero projected wealth change at the end of the hedging horizon. For this kind of hedge, one should merely use a hedge ratio equal to the negative of the ratio of the BETA of the stock portfolio to the underlying spot index times the ratio of the value of the stock portfolio to the value of the index underlying the futures contract.

A Long Hedge

As with all other futures contracts, both long and short hedges are possible. Imagine a pension fund manager convinced that she stands at the beginning of an extended bull market, but the contributions to the pension fund, which will be $3,000,000, are not now available and will not be available for three months. Waiting three months for the funds to in-

TABLE 7.15

A Long Hedge With Stock Index Futures.

Stock Market	Futures Market
May 19 A pension fund manager anticipates having $3,000,000 to invest in three months.	Buys 64 September NYSE Index futures at 94.40.
August 15 $3,000,000 becomes available for investment.	The market has risen and the S and P futures stands at 98.50.
Stock prices have risen, so the $3,000,000 will not buy the same shares that it would have on May 19.	Futures profit: $131,200

vest in the stock market could mean that the bull market would be missed altogether. An alternative to missing the market move would be to use the stock index futures market. The pension manager could simply buy an amount of a stock index futures contract that would be equivalent in dollar commitments to the anticipated inflow of investable funds. On May 19, with the September NYSE Index futures contract standing at 94.40, the futures contract represents an underlying cash value of $47,200. The pension manager can secure her position in the market by committing to $3,000,000 worth of futures. Since she expects the funds in three months, the September contract is a natural to use, so she buys 64 September contracts, as shown in Table 7.15. By August 15, the market has risen, so the $3,000,000 could not buy the same shares that would have been possible on May 19. To offset this fact, the pension manager has earned a futures profit of $131,200. This gain in the futures market helps offset the new higher prices that would be incurred in the stock purchases.

CONCLUSION

A More Sophisticated Application of Stock Index Futures

The applications of stock index futures to portfolio management are still being explored, and future research can be expected to yield a rich variety of applications. This example explores the use of futures contracts to create a combined position between futures and a stock portfolio that will have minimum risk. Figlewski and Kon have shown that the hedge position that minimizes risk equals the stock portfolio's BETA.[6] In Figure 7.11, the minimum risk position is shown where the hedge ratio

FIGURE 7.11

Risk and Return Possibilities with Stock Index Futures.

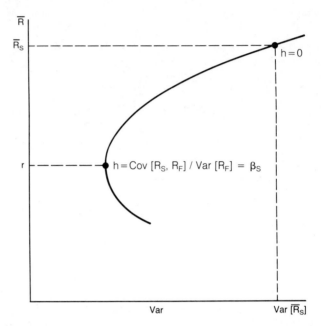

Source: Figlewski and Kon, "Portfolio Management with Stock Index Futures," p. 54.

(h) equals the BETA of the stock portfolio. In such a case, only residual risk remains in the combined stock/futures position. Note also that a trader can achieve varying degrees of risk reduction and expected returns by choosing other hedge ratios. At the point where $h = 0$, the trader has no hedge, and this point simply represents the unhedged portfolio. By varying h he can achieve any position on the envelope curve shown in Figure 7.ll, but he would only consider points between $h = 0$ and the minimum risk hedge ratio, since all others are dominated in a mean-variance sense.

Consider the same case, except assume that the stock portfolio being hedged is fully diversified. This implies that there will be no residual or undiversifiable risk in the stock portfolio itself. The application of the minimum variance hedge ratio to a fully diversified portfolio implies that all systematic risk can be eliminated as well. For such a case, the diagram drawn by Figlewski and Kon would actually touch the vertical axis. There would be no risk remaining, neither systematic nor unsystematic. For a riskless position, only the risk-free rate of return can be earned; otherwise, arbitrage opportunities would be available. With a fully hedged position, a trader avoids any return due to capital appreciation and receives only the dividend stream. As was argued earlier, the presence of a fully functioning stock index futures market implies that the equilibrium rate of dividends on the market portfolio must be equal to the risk-free rate.

Return to a Former Theme

As argued earlier in this chapter, the advent of the stock index futures market presents some special challenges to the attempt to reconcile the carrying charges model of futures prices and the view that futures prices equal expected future spot prices. In a market as new as the stock index futures market, it is not surprising that new problems will present themselves. When markets are new and not fully understood, they provide various opportunities—those for research to discover the economic realities that should govern prices in the market and, perhaps more importantly, opportunities for profit.

NOTES

1. See Arnold Bernhard & Co., Inc., "The Value Line Stock Market Averages."
2. D. Modest and M. Sundaresan. "The Relationship Between Spot and Futures Prices in Stock Index Futures Markets: Some Preliminary Evidence," *Journal of Futures Markets, 3,* 1983, 15–41.
3. B. Cornell and K. French. "Taxes and the Pricing of Stock Index Futures," *Journal of Finance,* June 1983, 675–694.
4. At least one author, in a preliminary study, tentatively concludes that the stock index futures market is inefficient. See S. Figlewski. "Why Are Prices for Stock Index Futures So Low?" Finance Working Paper No. 138, University of California at Berkeley. It should be kept in mind that Figlewski regards this conclusion as subject to revision.
5. The hedging potential of stock index futures has been widely recognized even in the early stage of trading. See: N. Weiner. "The Hedging Rationale for a Stock Index Futures Contract," *Journal of Futures Markets, 1,* 59–76; S. Figlewski. "Hedging with Stock Index Futures: Theory and Application in a New Market," Finance Working Paper No. 139, University of California at Berkeley; S. Figlewski and S. Kon. "Portfolio Management with Stock Index Futures," *Financial Analysts Journal,* January–February 1982, 52–60; D. Grant. "How to Optimize with Stock Index Futures," *Journal of Portfolio Management,* Spring 1982, 32–36; and D. Grant. "A Market Index Futures Contract and Portfolio Selection," *Journal of Economics and Business, 34,* 1982, 387–390.
6. See S. Figlewski and S. Kon. "Portfolio Management with Stock Index Futures," *Financial Analysts Journal,* January –February 1982, 52–60.

Chapter 7 Appendix

One way of stating the goal of hedging in stock index futures is to specify that a fluctuation in the level of the market should not cause any wealth change. Arithmetically, the net change in wealth can be expressed as:

$$P_i R_i + P_j N R_j \qquad \text{(A.1)}$$

where

P_i = **value in dollars of the stock portfolio**

P_j = **value of the stock index underlying the futures contract**

R_i = **return on the stock portfolio**

R_j = **"return" on the futures position, defined as the percentage change in the futures quotation.**

N = **the number of futures contracts to trade**

To find the correct N, in this case the value of N that makes the combined stock/futures position invariant to changes in the market as measured by the return on a given index, one can differentiate expression (A.1) with respect to the expected return on the index, R_x, set the result equal to zero, and solve for N:

$$\frac{d\{P_i \, \overline{R}_i + P_j \, N \, \overline{R}_j\}}{d \, \overline{R}_x} = 0 \qquad \text{(A.2)}$$

$$\frac{d\overline{R}_i}{d\overline{R}_x} \, P_i + \frac{d\overline{R}_j}{d\overline{R}_x} \, P_j N = 0 \qquad \text{(A.3)}$$

According to the capital asset pricing model, the expected return on a stock portfolio, R_i, is given by:

$$\overline{R}_i = R_f + \beta_i \, [\overline{R}_m - R_f] \qquad \text{(A.4)}$$

where β_i is the coefficient from regressing R_i on R_m.

In (A.4) R_m has two components, the capital appreciation and dividend yield. Assuming that the index on which the futures contract is written is a perfect proxy for the market, it must be the case that:

$$\overline{R}_m = \overline{R}_x + \overline{D}_m \qquad \text{(A.5)}$$

where D_m = the expected dividend yield on the market.

Substituting (A.4) and (A.5), as well as parallel equations for the futures position, into (A.3), gives:

$$\frac{d[R_f + \beta_j \, \overline{R}_x + \beta_i \overline{D}_m - \beta_i R_f]P_i}{d\overline{R}_x} + \frac{d[R_f + \beta_j \overline{R}_x + \beta_j \overline{D}_m - \beta_j R_f]P_j N}{d\overline{R}_x} = 0$$

(A.6)

Carrying out the differentiation on (A.6) gives:

$$\beta_i P_i + \beta_j P_j N = 0 \tag{A.7}$$

Solving (A.7) for N gives:

$$N = - \frac{\beta_i \, P_i}{\beta_j \, P_j} \tag{A.8}$$

Equation (A.8) says that the number of futures contracts to trade to avoid any anticipated wealth change depends on the size of the spot position (P_i) relative to the value of the index underlying the futures contract (P_j) and the volatility of the stock portfolio (β_i) relative to the volatility of the futures contract (β_j). The negative sign in (A.8) indicates that one must sell futures to hedge a long position in the stock portfolio.

8 Options on Futures and Commodity Funds

INTRODUCTION

The introduction of financial futures contracts documented in Chapters 5–7 constitutes one of the most dramatic changes in the financial markets in the United States during the last decade. The advent of futures on foreign currencies, on debt instruments, and now on stock indices, represents a significant widening of the trading opportunities open to speculators and hedgers. During this period, market professionals have struggled to stay abreast of the tide of innovation. Their struggle is not yet over.

The participant in the financial markets must learn to deal with yet another fundamentally different kind of instrument—an option written on a futures contract. Certainly the beginning of an organized stock options exchange in 1973 rivals the development of the futures market for its impact on the financial system. Now, just one decade after the beginning of the options market and financial futures, the market must absorb the new options on futures. To further complicate matters, for many instruments there are options on the instruments themselves as well as options on the futures on the same instruments.

The pricing principles for options contracts are quite complex and a number of books have been devoted just to options.[1] Because of the complexity of the options market, a thorough discussion of option pricing is beyond the scope of this book. As a consequence, this chapter presents only an institutional approach to these new instruments and an analysis of option pricing at the time of expiration.

In addition to considering options on futures, this chapter also explores another major phenomenon associated with the futures market—the origination of commodity funds. Somewhat like mutual funds for stocks, commodity funds provide a way to speculate in a wide variety of commodities. The main advantage of commodity funds is that they provide a way to achieve a substantial degree of diversification acoss commodities while limiting transaction costs. In this brief exploration of commodity funds, we will explore for a final time some of the key ideas developed throughout this book.

FEATURES OF OPTION TRADING

Options come in two varieties—*call options* and *put options.* The owner of a call option has the right to buy a given good at a pre-determined price for a specified period of time. The owner of a call receives this right from another trader in the option market by paying a fee called the *premium.* So, in exchange for the premium, the writer or seller of a call option grants to the buyer a specific right. The owner of the call may pay to the writer of the call a pre-determined price, the *exercise price* or *striking price,* and the writer of the call will deliver the specific good in exchange for that payment. Most options, and all options traded on exchanges, have an expiration date, after which time the option cannot be exercised and becomes worthless.[2]

Option contracts are written to stipulate that exercise can take place any time before expiration (an American option), or only at the time of expiration (a European option). All exchange traded options in the United States are American options. (Interestingly, most options traded in Europe are also American options.) In spite of these differences in construction, an American option on an asset or instrument that has no cash flows should never be exercised prior to its expiration, so the technical difference between American and European options is of limited practical importance.[3]

In constrast to call options, the owner of a put option has the right to sell a given good to another party at a pre-determined price, with the right to do so lasting until the expiration of the option. To buy a put option, one must pay another trader a premium, and for this premium the writer of the put option agrees to buy a given good at the pre-determined price, the exercise price or striking price. The transaction can occur at the discretion of the owner of the put option.

Options are not a recent invention. There was an active market for commodity options in the 1880s, which was subsequently outlawed by Congress. More familiar today are the exchange-traded stock options that began in 1973. In the United States, stock options are traded on the Chicago Board Options Exchange, the Philadelphia Exchange, and the American Exchange. Since the market for stock options is more familiar to the investing public, a brief survey of some rudimentary features of stock option pricing will serve as a useful introduction to the discussion of options on futures.

Consider a call option with an exercise price of $100 on a particular stock, and assume that the initial premium paid for this option was $5. The left hand panel of Figure 8.1. shows the profit and loss position for both the writer and buyer of this option at the time of expiration. The profit and loss depends on the value of the stock price at the time of expiration.[4] For the owner of the call option, there will be no exercise of the option at any price up to $100. To exercise the option when the stock price is less than $100 would merely mean that one would be paying the

$100 exercise price for a stock that was worth less than $100. As a result, for any stock price less than $100, the option will not be exercised, and it will be allowed to expire worthless. In such a case, the owner of the call option will suffer a total loss of $5, the amount that was paid for the option at the outset. By the same token, the writer of the call option will already have received $5 as his premium. Since the option will not be exercised at prices less than $100, the writer of the option will have $5 to keep as his profit.

As the stock price exceeds $100, the owner of the call will have an incentive to exercise the option. As shown in the Figure, the owner of the call option will have a zero profit if the stock price is at $105. This is the case, since he will exercise his option, pay $100 for a stock worth $105, and this $5 profit will exactly offset what he paid for the option initially. Similarly, the writer of the call option will have a zero profit if the stock is selling for $105 since he will be forced to give up a stock worth $105 and receive only $100 for it. However, the $5 premium initially paid to the writer will offset that loss, and his total profit will be zero. When the stock price is above $105 at expiration, the owner of the call will have a positive profit. As the ray in the owner's graph shows, the profit is theoretically unlimited for the owner of a call. At expiration, the owner's profit will be equal to the stock price (S), minus the exercise price (E) minus the initial premium for the call (C). By the same token, the seller of a call option has potentially unlimited losses. For every dollar the stock price lies above $105, the writer of the call will suffer a dollar net loss. Since stock prices have no upper limit, the seller of a call has no upper limit on his loss. From the seller's point of view, his profit position is given by the premium on the call (C) plus the exercise price (E) minus the value of the stock (S).

Several further points regarding the relative positions of the buyer and writer of a call option require comment. Using the notation of the preceding paragraph, it is possible to see the combined position of both the buyer and seller:

Buyer's Profit:	$S - E - C$
Seller's Profit:	$C + E - S$
Net Position	0

When we combine the profits of the buyer and seller, it is apparent that they cancel each other out. Since there are always even numbers of buyers and sellers, the net profit in the options market will always be zero, in the absence of transaction costs. This means that the options market is a *zero sum game,* since one trader's gain must be another's loss.

Another interesting fact in the options market concerns the conditions under which options will be exercised at expiration. It has already been noted that the buyer of the option in the Figure will suffer a loss if

FIGURE 8.1

Option Profits at Expiration.

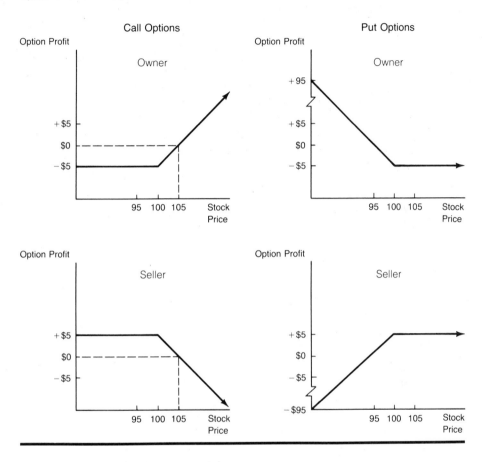

Call Options

Put Options

Owner

Owner

Seller

Seller

the stock price is less than $105 at expiration. This fact notwithstanding, the buyer of the option will exercise the option at its maturity if the stock price exceeds the exercise price. In terms of the present example, this means that the option will be excercised at maturity if the stock price exceeds $100. The value of the call option at the option's maturity is its value if it is exercised immediately, and this quantity is known as the *intrinsic value* of the option. So the intrinsic value of the option is always equal to the stock price minus the exercise price, or $S - E$, if S exceeds E. Otherwise, the intrinsic value of the option is zero. Even if the owner of the call option will lose money on the entire position, he will still want to capture the intrinsic value of the option at expiration in order to reduce his loss. To see this clearly, consider a stock price of $103. In this case, the owner of the call option will suffer a loss of $2 ($103 − $100

− $5). But the only way to keep the loss at only $2 is by exercising the option. If the option is not exercised, it will expire worthless, and the owner of the call will lose the entire $5 paid as the premium.

The value of a call option can never be less than the greater of its intrinsic value or zero. At expiration the option's value must be exactly equal to the intrinsic value or to zero. Prior to expiration, however, the value of the option may exceed its intrinsic value, even when the intrinsic value is positive. Owning an American call option always gives the owner the right to immediately capture the intrinsic value of the option simply by exercising the option. But the trader also has the option to wait for exercise. In the normal event, this means that the value of an option with time remaining until its expiration will exceed even a positive intrinsic value. In a landmark contribution to finance, Black and Scholes devised a theoretical formula for the value of a call option with time to expiration. Their theoretical value depends on only five values: the exercise price, the current stock price, the risk-free rate of interest, the time to expiration, and the volatility or riskiness of the stock on which the option is written.

In spite of the complexity of the mathematics of the Black and Scholes model, the formula is fairly intuitive, particularly in considering the ways in which the five factors mentioned above affect the value of the option. It is natural that, the longer the option has to expiration, the greater value the option has, other things being equal. It is always better to have an option with a longer, rather than a shorter, time to expiration. Other factors held constant, the greater the value of the stock on which the option is held, the greater is the value of the option. If all other factors are the same, one would prefer to hold an option on a stock worth $100 rather than on a stock worth $1. The value of an option varies inversely with the exercise price. Since one must pay the exercise price to acquire the underlying stock, an option with a lower exercise price is worth more than one with a higher exercise price. One of the advantages of owning an option is that one has the right to defer paying for the stock until the expiration of the option. The higher the interest rate, the greater the value of being able to defer that payment. So, other things being equal, the higher the interest rate, the greater the value of the option. Similarly, owning an option fixes the amount that one must pay to acquire the underlying asset. Having a fixed amount to pay reduces risk, so the more risky the underlying stock, the greater the value of having the option to purchase the underlying stock at a fixed exercise price. This means that the value of the option will be greater the riskier the underlying stock, other things being equal. In sum, then, the price of an option will be higher the greater the interest rate, the riskiness of the underlying stock, the stock price, and the time to expiration. By contrast, the higher the exercise price, the lower will be the value of the option.

Put options can also be analyzed in a manner similar to that applied to call options. The profit of the owner of a put, when the put option is at expiration, depends on the same factors that pertained to the call. If one exercises a put option, one has paid the premium for the option (P), surrenders the stock (S), and receives the exercise price (E). By contrast, the writer of the put has received the premium (P), receives the stock (S) and must pay the exercise price (E). As was the case with call options, the net profit for buyer and seller considered together is zero:

Buyer's Profit:	$E - S - P$
Seller's Profit:	$P + S - E$
Net Profit:	**0**

The value of a put option depends on the same factors that operated in the case of a call option. Since call options tend to be much more heavily traded, and since the mathematics of call option pricing is more fully developed, the rest of the discussion of options in this chapter focuses on call options.

OPTIONS OR OPTIONS ON FUTURES?

With the development of options on futures and the wider availability of options on different underlying goods, there are many more opportunities for trading to take a particular risk position in the pursuit of profits or to avoid certain kinds of risk. As an indication of the choices available, there are a number of goods, besides stocks, for which options are traded. For many of these goods there are also futures contracts and options on the futures contracts. In its left-hand panel, Figure 8.2 presents the quotations for four of the major options on futures, those on Treasury-Bonds, Gold, the S and P 500 Index, and the NYSE Index. Options on the Value Line Futures contract also exist, but they seem to have little trading interest. In the Figure, the option quotations are divided into put and calls and then further divided into the different contract maturities and striking prices.

For illustrative purposes, consider the options on the Treasury Bond futures. For the futures contract expiring in December, a trader may buy a call option for 2-45 (two and 45/64ths) that will entitle the holder to acquire the December Treasury Bond futures contract by paying the additional striking price of 74, where 74 is equivalent to 74-00 in the regular Treasury-Bond futures quotation. The Treasury-Bond futures contract itself, for the December delivery, had a settlement price on the same day of 75-12, as is shown in the right-hand panel of futures quotations. As another example, a trader could buy an option on the September NYSE Index futures at a striking price of 98 by paying the option premium of 3.20. Anytime before expiration in September, the holder of that option could acquire the September futures contract for 98.00 instead of its cur-

FIGURE 8.2

Quotation for Options on Futures.

Futures Options

Thursday, March 1, 1984

Chicago Board of Trade

TREASURY BONDS—$100,000; points and 64ths of 100%

Strike Price	Calls—Last			Puts—Last		
	Jun	Sep	Dec	Jun	Sep	Dec
62	....	....	....	0-01	0-12	0-21
64	....	....	....	0-06	0-28	0-48
66	2-31	2-36	2-32	0-24	0-63	1-31
68	1-13	1-33	1-37	1-05	1-59	2-16
70	0-29	0-52	1-06	2-21	3-07	....
72	0-11	0-24	0-34	3-62	4-38	....
74	0-02	0-10	0-20	5-59	6-34	
76	0-01	0-04	0-10	....	....	....
78	....	0-01	....	....	....	....
80	....	0-01	....	....	....	....

Est. total vol. 15,000
Calls: Wed vol. 11,839; open int. 72,169
Puts: Wed vol. 5,700; open int. 33,519

Comex, New York

GOLD—100 troy ounces; dollars per troy ounce.

Strike Price	Calls—Last			Puts—Last		
	Apr	June	Aug	Apr	June	Aug
340	57.80	64.50	....	.10	.80	1.20
360	37.80	44.50	52.00	.10	1.70	3.10
380	18.00	28.00	35.50	.50	4.30	6.20
400	3.70	14.30	22.50	6.00	9.60	12.00
420	.40	6.20	12.20	23.00	22.00	21.50
440	.10	2.90	7.00	42.50	....	34.50
460	.10	1.30	4.30	....	....	51.00
480	.10	....	2.50	....	....	68.50
500	.10	....	1.70	....	....	88.50
530	.10	....	.90	....	....	....

Est. total vol. 3,000
Calls: Wed vol. 1,861; open int. 37,263
Puts: Wed vol. 1,270; open int. 23,439

Chicago Mercantile Exchange

S&P 500 STOCK INDEX—Price = $500 times premium.

Strike Price	Calls—Settle			Puts—Settle		
	Mar	Jun	Sep	Mar	Jun	Sep
135	....	....	....	....	....	....
140	....	....	....	....	....	....
145	13.70	....	....	.002	.45	....
150	8.70	11.70	....	.05	1.10	....
155	4.20	7.80	....	.50	2.10	....
160	.90	4.55	....	2.25	3.90	5.05
165	.10	2.40	4.85	6.35	6.70	7.45
170	.002	1.20	3.20	11.25	10.50	....
175	.002	.70	1.95	16.25	14.85	....
180	.002	.35	1.10	....	....	....
185	.002	.15	....	....	....	....

Estimated total vol. 2,278.
Calls: Wed. vol. 2,136; open int. 19,518
Puts: Wed. vol. 2,062; open int. 18,713

W. GERMAN MARK

W. GERMAN MARK—125,000 marks, cents per mark

Strike Price	Calls—Settle		Puts—Settle	
	Mar	Jun	Mar	Jun
34	....	....	....	....
35	3.56	4.00	0.01	0.04
36	2.56	3.00	0.01	0.08
37	1.56	2.11	0.01	0.18
38	0.62	1.42	0.09	0.47
39	0.10	0.86	0.51	0.84
40	0.03	0.50	....	....
41	....	0.34	....	....
Futures	.3837	.3901		

Estimated total vol. 1,648.
Calls: Wed vol. 1,773; open int. 7,113.
Puts: Wed vol. 529; open int. 5,092.

N.Y. Futures Exchange

NYSE Composite Index—Price = $500 times premium.

Strike Price	Calls—Settle			Puts—Settle		
	Mar	Jun	Sep	Mar	Jun	Sep
88	3.85	5.65	7.25	.35	1.05	1.55
90	2.25	4.25	5.90	.75	1.65	2.20
92	1.10	3.10	4.70	1.60	2.50	3.00
94	.40	2.15	3.65	2.90	3.55	3.95
96	.15	1.45	2.85	4.65	4.85	5.15
98	.05	.95	2.15	6.50	6.35	6.45
100	.05	.60	1.60	8.50	8.00	7.90
102	.05	.35	1.20	10.50	9.75	9.50
104	.05	.20	.80	12.50	11.60	11.10

Estimated total vol. 1,153
Calls: Wed. vol. 946; open int. 7,094
Puts: Wed. vol. 392; open int. 3,545

rent market price. As the right-hand panel shows, the September futures itself was trading for 96.90.

It should also be observed that there are options on the *actuals* themselves, in addition to the options on the futures. Figure 8.3 presents quotations for interest rate and foreign currency options traded by the American Exchange, the Chicago Board Options Exchange, and the Philadelphia Exchange. Notice that these options are on specific debt in-

FIGURE 8.3
Interest Rate and Foreign Currency Options.

Interest Rate Options

Thursday, March 1, 1984
For Notes and Bonds, decimals in closing prices represent 32nds; 1.1 means 1 1/32. For Bills, decimals in closing prices represent basis points; $25 per .01

American Exchange

U.S. TREASURY NOTE—$100,000 principal value

Underlying Issue	Strike Price	Calls—Last			Puts—Last		
		Mar	Apr	May	Mar	Apr	May
11¾ note due 11/15/93	96	....	....	2.05	....	....	....

13-WEEK U.S. TREASURY BILL $1 million principal value

	Strike Price	Calls—Last			Puts—Last		
		Mar	Jun	Sep	Mar	Jun	Sep
91		....	0.08	....	....	....	....

Total call vol. 45   Call open int. 1019
Total put vol. 20   Put open int. 911

Chicago Board Options Exchange

U.S. TREASURY BOND—$100,000 principal value

Underlying Issue	Strike Price	Calls—Last			Puts—Last		
		Mar	Jun	Sept	Mar	Jun	Sept
14% bond due 11/11	126	....	....	....	0.23	....	....
		Mar	Jun	Sept	Mar	Jun	Sept
12% bond due 8/13	98	0.23	1.12	....	0.12	1.24	....
	100	0.05	....	....	....	....	....
	102	....	....	....	0.14	....	....
		Mar	Jun	Sept	Mar	Jun	Sept
10¾% bond due 11/12	86	....	....	....	0.16	....	....
	88	0.01	0.23	....	2.03	3.05	....
	90	....	....	....	4.04	....	....

U.S. TREASURY BOND—$20,000 principal value

Underlying Issue	Strike Price	Calls—Last			Puts—Last		
		Mar	Jun	Sept	Mar	Jun	Sept
14% bond due 11/11		(NO TRADES)					
		Mar	Jun	Sept	Mar	Jun	Sept
12% bond due 8/13		(NO TRADES)					
		Mar	Jun	Sept	Mar	Jun	Sept
10¾% bond due 11/12	90	0.01	....	....	....	....	....

Total call vol. 199   Call open int. 7728
Total put vol. 447   Put open int. 5510

Foreign Currency Options

Thursday, March 1, 1984

Philadelphia Exchange

Option & Underlying	Strike Price	Calls—Last			Puts—Last		
		Mar	Jun	Sep	Mar	Jun	Sep
12,500 British Pounds-cents per unit.							
BPound	135	r	r	14.20	r	r	r
148.30	.140	8.50	8.85	9.90	r	0.60	1.25
148.30	.145	3.25	4.85	6.80	0.15	1.40	r
148.30	.150	0.30	2.50	3.85	2.50	3.80	r
148.30	.155	r	1.10	s	r	7.25	s
50,000 Canadian Dollars-cents per unit.							
CDollar	..80	r	0.34	0.55	0.19	0.35	r
79.93	...81	r	0.09	0.27	r	r	r
62,500 West German Marks-cents per unit.							
DMark	.. 36	2.36	2.95	r	r	0.12	0.25
38.50	...37	1.55	2.04	r	r	0.27	r
38.50	...38	0.65	1.32	1.87	0.18	0.50	r
38.50	...39	0.20	0.82	1.45	r	0.92	r
38.50	...40	0.02	0.52	s	r	r	s
6,250,000 Japanese Yen-100ths of a cent per unit.							
JYen	... 42	0.88	r	2.09	r	0.17	r
42.85	...43	0.19	0.91	r	r	0.47	r
42.85	...44	0.02	0.50	0.99	r	r	r
62,500 Swiss Francs-cents per unit.							
SFranc	..45	1.25	r	r	0.05	r	r
46.11	...46	0.45	1.40	r	0.23	0.55	0.68
46.11	...47	0.07	0.94	r	1.00	r	r
46.11	...48	0.01	0.56	r	r	r	r

Total call vol.   2,924   Call open int.   42,365
Total put vol.   3,087   Put open int.   30,755
r—Not traded. s—No option offered. o—Old.
Last is premium (purchase price).

struments in the case of the interest rate options and on given amounts of foreign currency in the case of the options on foreign exchange. Additionally, and not reflected in the Figure, there are options on stock indices as well with both the Chicago Board Options Exchange and the American Exchange trading options on stock market indices of their own design. These two markets are quite distinct, with the interest rate options and foreign currency options being regulated by the Securities and Exchange Commision, while the options on futures are regulated by the Commodity Futures Trading Commission.

OPTIONS ON TREASURY-BOND FUTURES AND NYSE INDEX FUTURES

To explore the potential uses of options on futures, this section focuses on two of the major options contracts that exist on futures, those on Treasury Bonds and those on the NYSE Index. Both of these have met with considerable success. Figure 8.4 shows the growth in the open interest of options on Treasury-Bond futures during the early months of trading. Notice also from this graph that the heaviest interest by far is focused on the nearby futures contract.

In the case of the option on the Treasury-Bond futures contract, the striking prices are set by the exchange at two point intervals. Each two points represents $2000, since the contracts are all based on the $100,000 face value of the Treasury-Bond futures contract. The daily price limit on the option contract is $2000, the same as the daily price limit on the futures contract itself. Like the price limit on the futures contract, the price limit on the options contract can be expanded during particularly volatile trading periods. Trading in the options on T-Bond futures ceases at least five business days before the first notice day for delivery on the futures contract. In practice, this means that options will stop trading near the end of the month preceding the futures delivery month, and unexercised futures options will expire on the first Saturday after the end of trading.

For options on the NYSE Index futures contract, each option is written for one futures contract, with each point of the premium being worth $500. In the example given above, then, the option premium of 3.20 would translate into $1600. The striking prices are also set at full two point intervals, and trading continues until the very end of trading in the underlying futures contract. As is the case with the futures contract itself, there are no price limits on the futures option.

WHY OPTIONS ON FUTURES?

In order for a market to emerge for options on futures, as it certainly seems to have done, there must be some perceived benefit or economic purpose for its existence. From one point of view, it seems unlikely that there would be any need for a market for options on futures contracts, but a number of potential benefits have been cited to explain why. Some people believe that options on futures are more attractive than options on the actual underlying goods.

Without doubt, the prime rationale for the existence of options on futures is a function of its different price performance characteristics, as opposed to the futures contract. Taking a position in the futures market means that one is immediately exposed to a theoretically unlimited risk of gain or loss. This is not the case for the buyer of an option. As Figure

FIGURE 8.4

Growth of Options on T-Bond Futures.

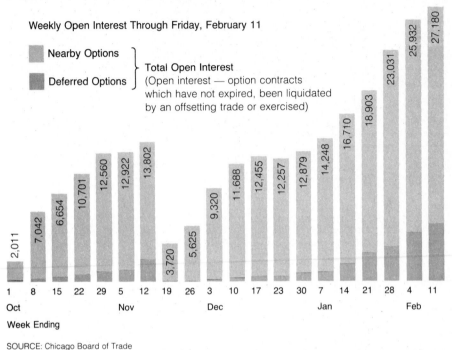

Weekly Open Interest Through Friday, February 11

Nearby Options ⎫
Deferred Options ⎬ Total Open Interest
(Open interest — option contracts which have not expired, been liquidated by an offsetting trade or exercised)

Week Ending

SOURCE: Chicago Board of Trade

8.5 shows, futures and options on futures have quite different payoff results in the same set of circumstances. In the top panel, the position of the purchaser of a T-Bond futures contract is shown, under the assumption that he bought the futures contract at a price of 70.00 and that he is holding it to expiration. For every point the futures price exceeds 70.00 at expiration, the buyer has a $1000 gain and a $1000 loss for every point the futures price falls below 70.00. For the purchaser of a T-Bond futures call option, where the striking price was 70.00 and the original premium was 3.00, the profit and loss picture is quite different. The most the purchaser of the futures option can lose is the entire 3.00 amount of the premium, or $3,000. At any final futures price of 73.00 or less, the purchaser of the futures option has no profit. For futures prices greater than 73.00, the profit of the futures option buyer increases point for point with the futures price. These graphs show that the positions being assumed by the two traders are radically different. The purchase of a call option limits the potential loss to the amount of the premium. For the purchaser of the futures contract, there is no such limitation. On the other hand, the purchaser of the futures contract will make more, $3,000 more in this example, than the purchaser of the option contract at any price above 70.00.

FIGURE 8.5
Characteristics of Futures and Options on Futures.

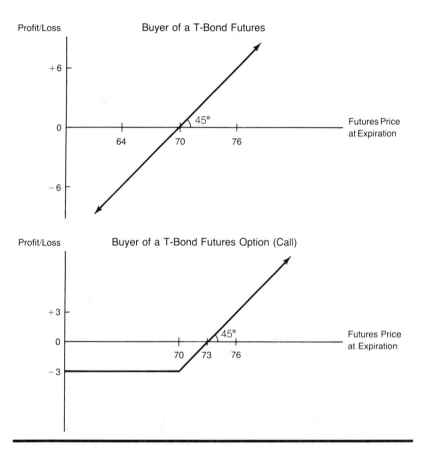

In the case of the sale of the futures contract, there is also unlimited potential for gain and loss. For the writer of the futures call option, there is also potential for unlimited losses. Since the buyer's gains are the seller's loss, and vice versa, in both these markets, it is easy to see graphically what both profit and loss results could be. The writer of a call option has limited potential gains (limited to the amount of the premiums he receives) and unlimited potential losses (equal to the unlimited potential gains of the purchaser of the call option.

While these different profit and loss characteristics for futures and futures options are extremely important, other reasons have been advanced for the existence of options on futures. One argument stresses the greater liquidity afforded by the futures market as a reason for favoring options on futures as opposed to options on the actual commodity itself.[5] For example, the supply of a particular Treasury Bond issue is fixed. There simply will be no more 14s of 2011 issued. This means that there is

an upper bound on the deliverable supply of the good against which a straight interest rate option is written. By contrast, traders can create additional supplies of futures contracts, which suggests that liquidity problems might not be so severe if options are written on futures contracts as opposed to the underlying good itself.

Another reason for preferring options on futures to options on the physical good itself is the economy and ease of exercise. To exercise an option on the good itself, one must have the entire cash value of the striking price. To exercise an option of a futures contract, the amount of money necessary, in addition to the original option premium, is only the incremental futures margin to cover any gain or loss between the current futures price at the time of exercise and the striking price. For traders with capital constraints, this difference can be important in extending the possibilities for leverage.

SPECULATING WITH OPTIONS ON FUTURES

Uses of options on futures can be designed for speculation or for hedging. One who believes that the futures price is too low could simply buy the futures or, alternatively, buy a call option on the futures contract. The choice would depend on what one preferred regarding the risk exposure. Figure 8.5 shows the outcomes for the two positions as the futures price varies from the original price at expiration. Another way of profiting from an anticipated increase in the futures would be to sell a put at a striking price near the current price. If the futures price goes up, then the put option would not be exercised and the writer of the put would keep the premium. These strategies of buying or writing single options are very straightforward, but more interesting possibilities arise from positions using more than one option, or from combining options with futures. Given the possible combinations of options and futures, one can contract for virtually any desired outcome as a function of the futures price at the time of expiration. The following examples illustrate some of these strategies in order to show the possible outcomes.

As a first example, consider a speculator who believes the there is a good chance of an increase in the price of the T-Bond futures contract. One way of profiting from such a position is to buy both a call option on the futures and the futures contract itself. Assume that this speculator faces the same option and futures prices shown in Figure 8.5, and that he or she elects to buy the call and to buy the futures contract. In the upper panel of Figure 8.6, the profit and loss graphs for the two instruments are imposed on the same set of axes. The bottom panel shows the profits and losses for the combined positions. For futures prices in excess of 71.50, there is a profit. As the slope of the line indicates, the profits grow twice as rapidly, due to the combined influence of the futures and the call. On the loss side, for futures prices less than 71.50, the rate of loss is

FIGURE 8.6

Profit/Loss Graph at Expiration for Buying a Call and Buying a Futures Contract.

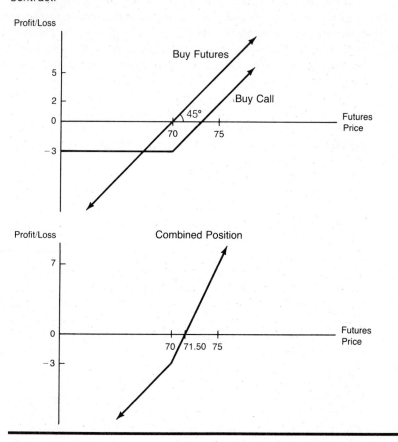

quite severe. For prices between 70.00 and 71.50, the rate of loss is the same as the rate of gain. For prices less than 70.00, no additional loss is incurred for the futures contract, and the slope of the loss line is the same as for the futures contract alone. This means that there is a considerable down-side risk remaining.

Perhaps the down-side risk could be eliminated, or at least reduced, by using the futures contract in combination with a different type of option. The upper panel of Figure 8.7 shows the profit and loss graphs at expiration for buying the futures contract and buying a put option with a striking price of 70 and a premium of 8.00. The bottom panel shows the combined position results. For all futures prices less than 78.00 at expiration, there is a loss, but the loss is limited to the amount of the put premium, or 8.00. The purchase of the put eliminates the chance of any greater loss on the futures position. As the futures price lies below 70.00, the put gains in value so that each dollar lost on the futures contract is exactly offset by the gain on the value of the put. The graph of this combined position should appear familiar; it is really the graph of a call option on the futures, with a striking price of 70.00 and a premium of 8.00. By combining the futures and the put option, we have a call option.

As a different kind of example, using the same instruments, consider a speculator who believes that the price of the T-Bond futures is much more volatile than is appreciated by other traders. By trading a combined position of options the trader can take advantage of higher than anticipated volatility in the price of the underlying futures. In its upper panel, Figure 8.8 shows the profit and loss graph at expiration from buying a put and a call option on the same underlying T-Bond future, where the futures, put, and call are as described above. Such a position is known as a *straddle*. The upper panel reflects the 3.00 premium paid for the call option and the 8.00 premium paid for the put option. The combined position, or straddle, shown in the bottom panel, is the result of adding the two profit and loss graphs for the individual option contracts. If the expiration price of the futures contract is at 70.00, both the call and put options will expire worthless, generating a total loss on the straddle of 11.00 (the amount of the two premia). If there is a major price move in either direction, however, the purchaser of the straddle stands to make a profit. With a futures price at expiration in excess of 81.00, the straddle becomes profitable, as it does at any futures price at expiration less than 59.00. Essentially, the purchaser of a straddle is betting that there will be a large price movement in the underlying good in one direction or the other, without really taking any position on whether the price change will be an increase or a decrease. The position of the seller of a straddle is not shown in the Figure but it is clear that it would be simply the mirror image of the purchase of a straddle reflected around the zero profit line. The seller of a straddle, accordingly, is betting that there will not be a major move in the value of the underlying futures contract.

RISK CONTROL WITH OPTIONS ON FUTURES

As noted in the preceding chapter on stock index futures, the existence of the futures market gives many investors a range of instruments that they could never achieve before. For all but very large institutional investors, it has been very difficult to duplicate the price movement of the major equity indices. With futures that has certainly changed, and with options on futures the kinds of techniques available for controlling the returns distribution of a stock position and a futures position have also been expanded. Consider an investor in a broad market portfolio of equities who has a substantial paper gain. Without a futures market or futures options, it is very difficult to protect that gain without realizing it and incurring large transaction costs. By using options on futures, it is possible to "buy insurance" to protect the gains that have already been achieved.

To illustrate this use of the options on the futures contract, consider

Figure 8.7
Profit/Loss Graph at Expiration for Buying a Put and Buying a Futures Contract.

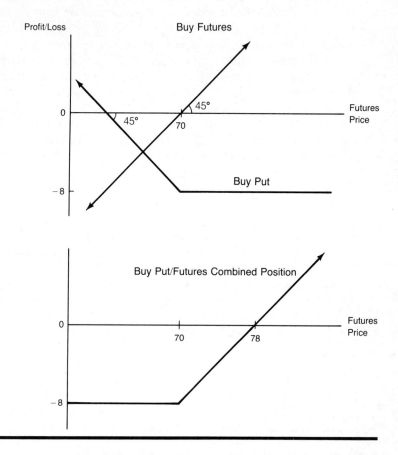

a trader in the NYSE Index futures contract who originally bought the futures contract at 72.00 and has enjoyed its rise to 80.00. This gain of 8 full points represents a paper gain of $4000, since each full point is worth $500. Hoping that the market advance will continue, and bring further profits, the trader is reluctant to abandon her futures position. However, she would like to secure some protection against a drop in the market and the ensuing loss of her gains. One strategy would be to buy a put option with a striking price below the current level of the futures price. If the futures price is now 80.00, there will be a put option with a striking price of 78.00, since the options are opened at two point intervals. The trader could buy a put option with a 78.00 striking price for, perhaps, .80 points. Doing so would protect against a dramatic drop in the market and help secure the majority of her paper profit. Figure 8.9 shows, in the

FIGURE 8.8

Profit/Loss Graph for Buying a Straddle at Expiration.

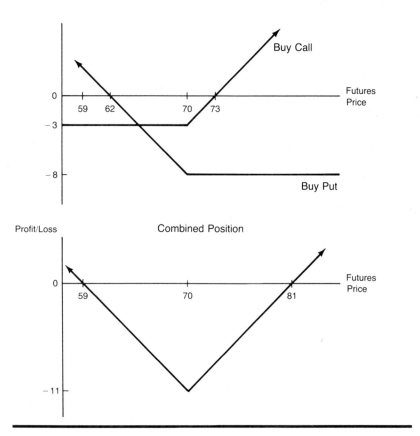

upper panel, the profit and loss position for the individual instruments in this situation. When we consider the futures contract alone, it is clear that the paper profit of 8.00 is quite vulnerable to any changes in the market. Since the graph depicts the situation at the expiration of the futures contract, it is clear that the futures profit will vary dollar for dollar with any change in the futures price.

By combining the futures contract with a put option on the futures contract, an important measure of protection can be achieved. Buying a put option with a striking price of 78.00 means that there will be no loss on the futures contract, beyond that which would result from a drop in the futures price from 80.00 to 78.00. As the futures price falls below 78.00, each dollar of loss on the futures contract at expiration is exactly offset by a gain on the put option. In order to achieve this insurance, the trader must pay the premium for the put option. In this case, the premium is .80. Paying this premium reduces the profit by the amount of

FIGURE 8.9
Protecting a Profit in a Long Stock Index Futures Position.

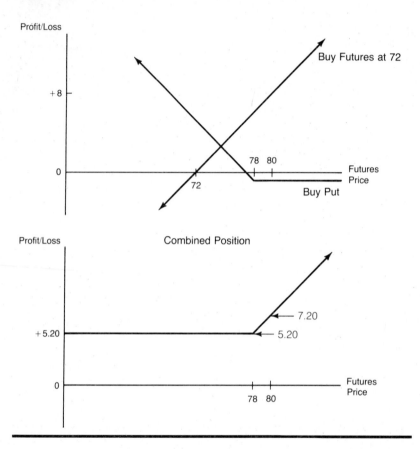

the premium for all futures prices in excess of 78.00. In an important sense, the trader has a hedge against any serious erosion of the futures profit, and this hedge has the explicit cost of the put's premium.

Just as a trader could buy a put in the preceding case to protect a paper gain in a long futures position, there is a technique for protecting a gain in a short futures position. This strategy can be illustrated in a similar situation. Assume that the trader transacted with the NYSE Index futures at the price of 72.00, but instead of buying the futures contract, he sold the futures. As the price of the futures deviates from 72.00, the trader makes a gain for each drop in the futures price. Notice in the upper panel of Figure 8.10 that the ordinary way of putting the futures price on the horizontal axis has been changed, so that the farther to the right one goes, the smaller the futures price. This is necessary with a short position so that gains still appear above the horizontal axis. With a drop in futures prices to 66.00, the short seller has a paper profit of 6.00.

FIGURE 8.10

Protecting a Profit in a Short Stock Index Futures Position.

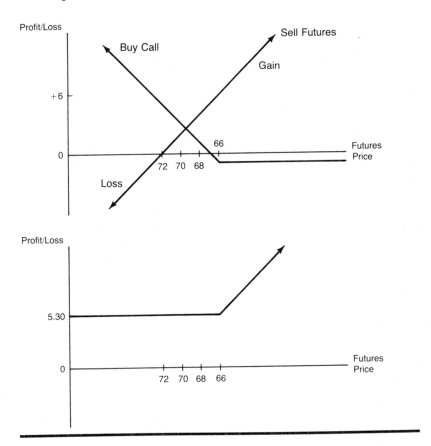

Wishing to secure this profit, the trader buys a call option at 66.00, with the same maturity as that of the futures contract, and pays a premium of 00.70. For each increase in the price of the futures contract at expiration, the trader loses a dollar on the futures contract, but gains a dollar on the call option. The bottom panel of the Figure shows the outcome of the total position as the futures price varies. No matter what the futures price does, after the call is purchased, the profit cannot be less than 5.30, (the 6.00 original profit minus the .70 paid for the call option). As the futures price falls below 66.00, the trader's profits will increase dollar for dollar. The important feature of the transaction is the assurance that the final realized profit will not be less than 5.30, and the fact that this assurance was achieved by paying the .70 premium for the call option.

In these two cases, if options on the futures contracts available had not been, it would have been impossible to secure the same return characteristics with the use of futures alone. Options on the futures contracts provide a way of altering the return characteristics of futures positions that will sometimes be useful. It must also be acknowledged, however, that the options on futures are fairly new. This implies that their performance characteristics and the full range of their potential uses is probably not fully understood.

COMMODITY FUNDS

As an outgrowth of the explosion in futures markets, *commodity funds* have developed in recent years. A commodity fund is roughly analogous to a stock mutual fund. Both offer the investor the chance to participate in a widely diversified holding, with presumably greater benefit from diversification than could be achieved by the individual investor alone. They also reduce the transaction costs that would otherwise be faced. This reduction arises because the manager of the mutual fund or commodity fund can achieve economies of scale in information and in transacting.

In other respects, however, commodity funds and mutual funds are radically different. When a trader invests in a stock mutual fund, he or she is acquiring fractional ownership of the entire portfolio that constitutes the mutual fund's holdings. Commodity funds are quite different. Trading a futures contract does not confer any ownership right to the good underlying the futures contract. A futures contract does not represent an ownership claim; it is not an asset. Further, trading a futures contract does not require any investment, but only the margin as a security deposit. These differences between mutual funds and commodity funds indicate the special kind of opportunity that commodity funds present.

Most commodity funds are *closed-end funds*. They seek to raise a pre-determined amount of funds, and once that level of funding has been reached, no new money is accepted. The fund managers and advisors then begin trading futures contracts. The pool of money that was acquired from the investors is used to meet margin calls and to provide a liquidity pool against possible losses. Most of the contributed money is kept in liquid money market instruments where it will be readily available for margin calls.

The fund managers earn money for their performance based on a combination of sales charges and fees expressed as a percentage of the assets in the fund. Some funds, however, charge no initial sales fee. The offering of a fund is conducted by a general partner, with the assistance of an underwriter. Also, most funds use the services of a trading advisor. In stipulating the terms of the offering, the fund must state the maximum size that is to be offered. This may range from less than $1 million to more than $50 million, with most being in the range of $5 to $15 million. To begin an investment in a fund, one buys units of the fund, which are typically set to have a value of approximately $1000. If the total cost of the unit is different from the starting value of the unit, then the difference is a sales charge. Table 8.1 shows the funds in the process of being registered or offered to the public, along with their respective sizes. One can see that the minimum investment falls generally in the range of $2000 to $5000, and that many are approved for IRAs.

Commodity Fund Performance

When we consider that the futures market is a zero sum game, in the absence of transaction costs, it is surprising to note the extent to which commodity funds tend to have highly correlated results. We might initially expect that there would not be such a strong correlation, since winners and losers have to even out. Nonetheless, in March 1983, 48 of the 57 commodity funds followed by *Commodities Magazine* had losses, while October 1982 showed losses for 41 of 51, while January 1983 witnessed gains by 46 of the 52 funds then on the market. In the stock market, such tendencies for fund results could be explained by the influence of major market movements on all of the funds together. In the futures market, however, with one fund's gains being the potential losses of another, there is not such a reason for highly correlated fund performance. The main reason for the highly correlated performance across funds stems from the similarity of techniques employed for directing their trading strategies. Most of the funds direct their trading by following technical trading rules. With the majority of funds following similar trading strategies, it is only to be expected that their results would be highly correlated.

Since technical trading rules focus on following trends in prices, one might expect funds to experience periods of dramatic gains, as well as dramatic losses. For the first ten months of 1982, Table 8.2 shows the ten funds with the best and worst performances. Gains and losses of assets up to 50% of the original value are not unprecedented. As with any position in futures, dramatic price movements can easily happen. Ideally, however, holding positions in a number of futures contracts might help reduce such extreme variability.

In spite of the fact that the commodity funds can be likened to a mutual fund of commodity futures positions, their results do indicate extremely high variability, as is reflected in Table 8.3. This Table shows the performance for each of the funds for the years 1981–1982, and for early 1983. Since some of the funds started in mid-year, the percentage performance for some funds and some years is not based on a whole year. The performance figures do, however, reflect any cash distributions that might have been made by the funds. Clearly, the different funds reflect extremely diverse performances. Notice, also, that performances are generally very inconsistent across time periods.

TABLE 8.1
Commodity Funds in Registration or Being Offered, May 1983.

Name of fund	General partner	Name of fund	General partner
Challenger Fund I	Challenger Mgmt.	Palo Alto Futures Fund	Paine Webber Futures Mgmt.
Columbia Futures Fund	Tapman	Paragon Fund	Spinnaker Trading Co.
Commodity Venture II	Hayden Cm.	Security Pacific Financial Futures	BEHR Futures Mang.
Dearborn Street Fund	LaSalle St. Mgmt.	Sunshine Futures	Don Charles
EuroAmerica Futures	Offshore Corp.	Thomson Commodity Partners III	Thomson McKinnon Fut.
Gemini Commodity Fund	Ceres Investment	Wright Financial Futures Fund	Marshall Wright Mgmt.
North American Commodity Fund II	N. American Invest. Kopko; William Hall		

Underwriter(s)	Trading advisor(s)	Max. size registered	Est. starting unit value	Total cost of unit	Minimum investment	Features
Mutual Service	Thomte	$800,000	90	100	2,500	Approved for IRA
Balfour, Maclaine; Dean Witter	Tapman	15 mill.	1,000	1,050	5,250	Approved for IRA
Shearson	Atlantic Assoc.	15 mill.	960	1,000	5,000	2,000 for IRA
A. G. Becker	A. O. Management	15 mill.	920	1,000	5,000	2,000 for IRA
Heinold	Miliburn Partners	51.5 mill.	1,000	1,030	5,150	2,060 for IRA
A. G. Edwards	Futures Mgmt. (Iowa); Buell Commodity	10 mill.	1,000	1,000	5,000	
North American Invest. Corp.	Trendview	1.5 mill.	920	1,000	3,000	2,000 for IRA
Paine Webber Jackson Curtis	Desai	10 mill.	1,000	1,000	5,000	Approved for IRA
Consolidated Invest.	Spinnaker Trading Co.	5 mill.	900	1,000	2,000	
Bateman, Eichler; Drexel Burnham	Security Pacific Financial Futures	5 mill.	1,000	1,000	5,000	
Don Charles Invest.	Don Charles Cm.	5 mill.	900	1,000	5,000	Open-ended; IRAs
Thomson McKinnon Securities	Cibola; Paul Dean	15 mill.	1,000	1,060	3,000	Approved for IRA
Financial Futures Securities	Marshall Wright Mgmt.	5 mill.	920	1,000	5,000	

SOURCE: *Managed Account Reports*, 200 Joseph Square, Columbia, Md. 21044, 301-730-5365

TABLE 8.2
Best and Worst Performance Among Commodity Funds—1982.
Through October 31, 1982.

The Ten Best	1982 Gain*
1 Chancellor Financial Futures Fund	51.4%
2 Admiral Fund*	47.4
3 Aires Commodity Fund	38.5
4 Thomson Fin. Fur. Partners I	37.9
5 The Galileo Futures Fund	36.6
6 Horizon Futures	33.2
7 The Resource Fund	27.6
8 Commodity Venture	27.4
9 The Future Fund	27.3
10 Lake Forest Fund	26.9

The Ten Worst	1982 Loss*
1 Western Capital Fund I	(52.7)%
2 S.E.K. Commodity Fund I	(37.1)
3 Princeton Futures Fund	(36.7)
4 Boston Futures Fund III	(30.6)
5 Princeton Futures Fund II	(23.3)
6 Midwest Commodity Fund I	(20.1)
7 Global Futures Fund	(19.3)
8 McCormick Commodity Fund I	(11.1)
9 Heinold Recovery Fund II	(4.8)
10 Commodity Strategy Partners	(4.1)

*Through Oct. 31, including cash distributions.

Financial World, December 1–15, 1982, 33.

What Should Be Expected From Commodity Funds?

It is interesting to speculate about the likely results that might be experienced if all of the funds were taken together. From the ideas presented in this book, we can anticipate the performance of the funds as a whole; the many funds participating in the futures market represent a microcosm of the market as a whole. If the funds were only participating in the futures market, without holding any debt instruments and without incurring any transaction costs or management expenses, then we would expect the average return across the funds to be approximately zero. Even with highly correlated performances, the futures trading of a large number of funds should net out to zero profit over a sufficiently long period of time.

TABLE 8.3
Commodity Fund Performance.

Fund	Start-up Date	Offering Unit Value	Unit Value 12-31-81	1981* Perfor-mance	Unit Value 12-31-82	1982* Perfor-mance	Unit Value 1-31-83	1983* Perfor-mance	Perf. Since Start-up
Admiral Fund	12-81	$1,000	$ 955	(4.5)%	$1,076	33.6%	$1,239	15.1%	43.9
Aries Commodity Fund	2-80	1,000	920	(19.0)	1,177	27.9	1,233	4.7	23.3
Boston Futures Fund I	1-80	957	1,065	18.9	682	(34.5)	832	22.0	(9.7)
Boston Futures Fund II	8-80	957	1,025	14.7	622	(38.3)	771	23.6	(12.1)
Boston Futures Fund III	6-82	930	—	—	640	(31.2)	822	28.4	(11.6)
Boston Futures Fund IV	11-82	851	—	—	741	(12.9)	868	17.1	2.0
Chancellor Financial Fut. Fund	3-81	1,000	751	(4.9)	958	27.8	984	2.7	18.4
Chancellor Financial Fut. Fund II	10-81	1,000	893	(10.7)	918	2.8	1,115	21.4	11.5
Chancellor Financial Fut. Fund III	3-82	872	—	—	772	(11.5)	795	3.0	(9.2)
Chancellor Futures Fund	2-80	942	1,277	22.0	1,236	4.6	1,342	8.6	53.1
Clark Street Futures Fund	11-82	871	—	—	879	0.9	937	6.6	7.6
Commodity Strategy Partners	8-82	963	—	—	803	(16.6)	860	7.1	(10.7)
Commodity Trend Timing Fund	1-80	963	1.467	28.0	1,440	(1.8)	1,549	7.6	76.4
Commodity Trend Timing Fund II	12-82	955	—	—	957	0.2	1,016	6.2	6.4
Commodity Venture Fund	11-80	950	1,374	49.8	1,568	25.0	1,696	8.2	110.1
Enterprise Futures	11-81	1,000	997	(0.3)	1,086	8.9	1,182	8.8	18.2
Futures Fund	7-79	1,000	3,127	34.5	4,209	34.6	4,393	4.4	339.9
Futures Fund II	4-82	1,000	—	—	1,041	4.1	1,089	4.6	8.9
Galileo Futures	3-79	1,000	891	(19.5)	914	2.6	1,020	11.6	17.0
Global Futures	9-81	1,000	1,033	3.3	739	(28.5)	937	26.8	(6.3)
Harvest Futures Fund I	6-78	1,000	2,987	(2.2)	3,784	33.4	5,114	35.1	456.4
Harvest Futures Fund II	2-80	970	491	(2.7)	661	34.6	928	40.4	(4.3)
Heinold III. Comm. Fund	1-78	1,000	2,854	75.6	2,878	0.8	2,759	(4.1)	175.9
Heinold Recovery Fund I	3-78	465	771	(32.7)	767	(0.5)	726	(5.3)	77.6
Heinold Recovery Fund II	3-78	189	269	(41.1)	238	(11.5)	241	1.3	27.5

Fund	Date								
Horizons Futures Fund	10-80	1,000	1,095	(5.3)	1,503	37.3	1,592	5.9	59.2
Hutton Commodity Part.	2-80	1,000	1,055	(0.1)	1,013	5.5	1,162	14.7	16.2
E. F. Hutton Commodity Ltd.	12-80	1,000	1,103	21.5	1,013	0.9	1,377	36.0	37.7
Hutton Com. Reserve Fund	10-82	987	—	—	950	(3.8)	983	3.5	(0.4)
Lake Forest Fund	1-81	1,000	599	(40.1)	602	0.5	662	10.0	(33.8)
LaSalle Street Fut. Fund	9-81	937	975	4.0	1,133	20.2	1,197	5.6	27.7
Matterhorn Comm. Partners	6-81	950	954	0.4	1,090	14.2	1,195	18.8	25.8
McCormick Comm. Fund I	2-82	916	—	—	972	6.1	1,158	19.1	26.4
McCormick Comm. Fund II	10-82	920	—	—	627	(31.8)	906	44.5	1.5
Midwest Comm. Fund I	6-81	1,000	866	(13.4)	784	(9.5)	923	17.7	(7.7)
Monetary Futures Fund	11-82	976	—	—	851	(12.8)	863	1.4	(11.6)
Peavey Com. Fut. Fund I	10-80	876	894	21.8	571	(36.1)	710	24.3	(0.1)
Peavey Com. Fut. Fund II	4-81	847	892	25.3	575	(35.5)	707	23.0	(16.5)
Peavey Com. Fut. Fund III	8-82	909	—	—	895	(1.4)	1,032	15.2	13.2
Princeton Futures Fund	3-81	989	1,068	7.9	613	(43.0)	708	15.5	(28.4)
Princeton Futures Fund II	11-81	986	973	(1.3)	767	(21.0)	856	11.6	(13.2)
Saturn Commodity	2-81	1,000	781	(21.9)	847	8.4	941	11.1	(5.9)
S.E.K. Commodity Fund I	7-82	1,000	—	—	593	(40.7)	785	32.4	(21.5)
Sycamore Futures	10-82	1,000	—	—	877	(12.3)	865	(1.4)	(13.5)
Resource Fund	8-78	1,000	3,411	38.8	4,248	24.5	4,613	8.6	361.3
Thomson Comm. Ptnrs. I	8-81	1,000	1,124	12.4	1,113	(1.0)	1,105	(0.7)	10.5
Thomson Comm. Ptnrs. II	12-82	940	—	—	954	1.5	1,064	11.5	13.2
Thomson Fin. Fut. Ptnrs. I	3-82	1,000	—	—	1,345	34.5	1,228	(8.7)	22.8
Thomson McKinnon Fut. Fund	11-78	942	1,685	36.6	1,676	(0.5)	1,742	2.8	111.5
Vista Futures	4-81	932	1,034	10.9	970	(6.2)	1,162	19.8	24.7
Western Capital Fund I	11-81	1,000	922	(7.8)	423	(54.1)	415	(1.9)	(58.5)
Dean Witter Reynolds Comm. Ptnrs.	3-81	1,000	967	(3.3)	1,085	12.2	1,196	10.2	19.6

*Includes cash distributions   SOURCE: *Financial World*, March 31, 1983

But the funds hold over 50% of their assets in money market instruments for the purpose of meeting margin calls. These monies, and presumably most of the remainder, earn interest. Since the funds hold debt instruments, they should earn a positive return in an efficient market. From these expected gains in the money market instruments, however, transaction costs, management fees, and any other expenses must be subtracted. As a result, we can expect the entire group of funds to earn something less than the money market interest rate.

Table 8.4 summarizes the performance of the funds presented in Table 8.3. For 1981 the 36 funds had an average increase in wealth of 5.43%, with a standard deviation of 24.49%. In 1982, the average wealth change was −1.72%, with a standard deviation of 22.98%. (It should be noted that these figures may be biased slightly high, since some funds may have failed during these two years and would not be reported here for that reason.) These results, although shown for only two years, are consistent with expectations. If anything, the commodity funds seem to have under-performed expectations or reflect very high transaction and management costs. Also, two years is not a very long period over which to judge the performance of the funds. As a group, the commodity funds have not performed spectacularly well over their brief period of popularity.

CONCLUSION

One of the most important points about the discussion of commodity funds is the opportunity it affords to see how the principles articulated in this book come into play. Given the emergence of a new industry, such as commodity funds, the potential investor should be able to appraise the suitability of the funds for his or her investment strategy. This book has tried to develop tools suitable for that purpose. By explaining the operation of futures markets, the different kinds of contracts available, the alternative uses of the futures markets, and a way of thinking about the profits one should expect, the reader should be equipped to independently appraise new opportunities, such as those presented by commodity funds.

With specific reference, once again, to commodity funds, potential investors should realize that they are accepting a low expected return, lower than the money market level of interest rates, and are accepting a very high level of risk. This conclusion is based on the assumption that investors pick a fund at random, or choose a fund that is based on average investment expertise. As is always the case with speculation, if investors can choose the futures contracts that will enjoy superior perfor-

TABLE 8.4
Group Characteristics of Commodity Fund Performance, 1981–1982.

	1981	1982
Number of Funds in Sample	36	52
Mean % Return	5.43	–1.72
Standard Deviation of Return	24.49	22.98

mance, they can make a fortune. In the case of commodity funds, they need not choose the best futures contracts. Instead, they need to choose the fund whose managers can choose the best futures contracts. For a well-developed financial market, like the futures market, there is little reason to believe that a given individual possesses the superior insight necessary for a high probability of success. As a result, it appears that the futures market confers the greatest benefit to those who wish to use them to hedge risk or to gather information about the market's expectation of future prices.

NOTES

1. Two comprehensive books covering options are: R. Bookstaber. *Option Pricing and Strategies in Investing,* Reading, MA: Addision–Wesley, 1981 and R. Jarrow and A. Rudd. *Option Pricing,* Homewood, IL: Richard D. Irwin, Inc., 1983. Of the two, the Bookstaber volume is much less mathematical. Another book, more oriented toward traders, is W. Welch, *Strategies for Put and Call Option Trading.*

2. Many different kinds of options arise in both business connections and the ordinary conduct of life. As an example, the option pricing model has been used to value corporate equities. The stockholders have the option to become complete owners of a firm simply by paying the exercise price of redeeming all outstanding debt. In this case, the option has no exercise date, as long as there is non-maturing debt outstanding. For this kind of analysis, see the classic paper, F. Black and M. Scholes. "The Pricing of Options and Corporate Liabilities," *Journal of Political Economy,* May 1973, 637–659.

3. For a proof that one should not exercise options on non-dividend paying stocks, see R. Merton. "Theory of Rational Option Pricing," *Bell Journal of Economics and Management Science,* Spring 1973, 141–183. The argument asserts that an option embodies a claim on the asset for a given period of time. If the option is exercised, the chance to wait is discarded. But the chance to wait for exercise can never have a value less than zero, so the market value of the option can never be less than the greater of its intrinsic value or zero. Sometimes, however, the market will place a positive value on the chance to wait, so the market price of the option will exceed its positive intrinsic value.

4. The great contribution of the Black and Scholes paper was to provide a closed-form solution to the value of an option prior to expiration. Doing so involves an extended analysis and a set of complicated assumptions that are beyond the scope of this book. For that reason, this discussion of options focuses on the value of options at the time of expiration. For a presentation of the mathematics of options on futures, and a discussion of some of their potential uses, see A. Wolf. "Fundamentals of Commodity Options on Futures," *Journal of Futures Markets, 2,* 1982, 391–408.

5. See J. Sinquefield. "Understanding Options on Futures," *Mortgage Banking,* July 1982, 35–40.

ACKNOWLEDGMENTS (cont.)

permission. **Table 8.3.** From "Commodity Funds: Nice While It Lasted," *Financial World,* March 31, 1983, p. 55. Copyright © 1983 by Financial World Partners. Reprinted by permission. **Figure 2.10.** From *Futures Guide to Technical Analysis,* p. 39. Copyright © 1982 Merrill Lynch Futures Inc. Reprinted by permission. **Figure 4.1.** From *1984 Commodity Year Book.* Copyright © 1984 by Commodity Research Bureau, Inc., 75 Montgomery St., Jersey City, NJ 07302. Reprinted by permission. **Figure 4.5.** From "Gold: How long will tight money pressure prices?" by John G. Powers, *Commodities,* March 1982, p. 45. Copyright © 1982 by Commodities Magazine, Inc. Reprinted by permission. **Figure 4.6.** From *1983 Commodity Year Book.* Copyright © 1983 by Commodity Research Bureau, Inc., 75 Montgomery St., Jersey City, NJ 07302. Reprinted by permission. **Figure 4.15.** From "Grain bulls' worst fears become reality" by Susan Abbott, *Commodities,* November 1982, p. 45. Copyright © 1982 by Commodities Magazine, Inc. Reprinted by permission. **Figure 5.8.** From "The Efficiency of the Treasury Bill Futures Market" by Richard J. Rendleman, Jr. and Christopher E. Carabini, *The Journal of Finance,* Vol. 34, No. 4, September 1979, p. 907. Copyright © 1979 by the American Finance Association. Reprinted by permission. **Figure 5.9.** From "Are There Arbitrage Opportunities in the Treasury-Bond Futures Market?" by R. Kolb, G. Gay, and J. Jordan. *Journal of Futures Markets,* Vol. 2, No. 3, Fall 1982, pp. 217–230. Copyright © 1982 by John Wiley & Sons, Inc. Reprinted by permission. **Figure 6.5.** From *Economic Perspectives,* Winter 1982, Volume VI, Issue 3. Published by the Federal Reserve Bank of Chicago. **Figure 7.1.** "S&P 500 Stock Index" from S&P 500 *Stock Market Encyclopedia,* Vol. 5, No. 1, p. vi. Copyright © 1983 Standard & Poor's Corporation. Reprinted by permission. **Figures 7.2, 7.5, 7.6.** From *"The Market Will Fluctuate . . ." Introducing New York Stock Exchange Index Futures.* Reprinted by permission of the New York Futures Exchange. **Figure 7.4.** From *The Value Line Investment Survey,* August 10, 1984, p. 40. Copyright © 1984 Value Line, Inc. Reprinted by permission of the publisher. **Figure 7.11.** From "Portfolio Management with Stock Index Futures" by Stephen Figlewski and Stanley J. Kon, *Financial Analysts Journal,* January–February 1982, p. 54. Reprinted by permission. **Figure 7.8** From *Special Analysis: Valuation of Stock Index Futures,* published by Merrill Lynch. Reprinted by permission. **Figures 4.7, 4.8, and 4.9.** From "Gold holds explosive potential" by Pamela Aden-Ayales and Mary Anne Aden-Harter, *Commodities,* April 1982. Copyright © 1982 by Commodities Magazine, Inc. Reprinted by permission of Commodities Magazine, Inc. and Pamela Aden-Ayales. **Figure 7.7.** Table reprinted by permission from *Barron's,* April 25, 1983. Copyright © Dow Jones & Company, Inc., 1983. All Rights Reserved. **Table 6.7.** From "The Sad Results of the 1980/81 Forecasts" by William Ollard, *Euromoney,* August 1981, p. 45. Copyright © Euromoney Publications Ltd., 1981. Reprinted by permission. **Table 7.7, Figure 7.9.** From "The Relationship Between Spot and Futures Prices in Stock Index Futures Markets: Some Preliminary Evidence" by D. Modest and M. Sundaresan, *Journal of Futures Markets,* Vol. 3, 1983, pp. 18–19, 29. Copyright © 1983 John Wiley & Sons, Inc. Reprinted by permission. **Table 5.5.** Robert W. Kolb, *Interest Rate Futures: A Comprehensive Introduction,* 1983. Reprinted by permission of Reston Publishing Company, a Prentice-Hall Company, 11480 Sunset Hills Road, Reston VA 22090.

Index